RELIGIOUS STUDIES

Religious Studies: The Key Concepts is an accessible, A–Z resource, defining and explaining key terms and ideas central to the study of religion. Exploring broad and recurring themes which are applicable in both Eastern and Western religions, cross-cultural examples are provided for each term to give a comprehensive overview of the subject.
Subjects covered include:

- Afterlife
- Comparative religion
- Festivals
- Ethics
- Gender
- Monotheism

- World religions
- Modernity
- Pilgrimage
- Sacred
- Theism
- Secularization

With cross-referencing and further reading provided throughout, this book provides an inclusive map of the discipline, and is an essential reference for all students, academics and researchers.

Carl Olson is Professor of Religious Studies at Allegheny College where he has held the National Endowment for the Humanities Chair and the Teacher-Scholar Professorship of the Humanities. He is currently a permanent fellow of Clare Hall, University of Cambridge.

Also available from Routledge

Islam: The Key Concepts
Kecia Ali and Oliver Leaman
978–0–415–39629–4

Fifty Key Jewish Thinkers (Second Edition)
Dan Cohn-Sherbok
978–0–415–77141–2

Fifty Key Figures in Islam
Roy Jackson
978–0–415–35468–4

Fifty Major Cities of the Bible
John Laughlin
978–0–415–22315–7

Fifty Key Christian Thinkers
Peter McEnhill and George Newlands
978–0–415–17050–5

RELIGIOUS STUDIES

The Key Concepts

Carl Olson

Routledge
Taylor & Francis Group
LONDON AND NEW YORK

First published 2011
by Routledge
2 Park Square, Milton Park, Abingdon, Oxon OX14 4RN

Simultaneously published in the USA and Canada
by Routledge
711 Third Avenue, New York, NY 10017

Routledge is an imprint of the Taylor & Francis Group, an informa business

Typeset in Times New Roman by
Book Now Ltd, London

British Library Cataloguing in Publication Data
A catalogue record for this book is available from the British Library

Library of Congress Cataloging in Publication Data
Olson, Carl.
Religious studies: the key concepts / Carl Olson.
p. cm.
Includes bibliographical references.
1. Religion—Dictionaries. I. Title.
BL31.O47 2011
200.3—dc22
2010013586

ISBN10: 0–415–48721–8 (hbk)
ISBN10: 0–415–48722–6 (pbk)
ISBN10: 0–203–84191–3 (ebk)

ISBN13: 978–0–415–48721–4 (hbk)
ISBN13: 978–0–415–48722–1 (pbk)
ISBN13: 978–0–203–84191–4 (ebk)

This book is dedicated to three long-time friends with profound gratitude for helping me find the right path for me, although we all went our own separate ways.

Richard Ernie Oehrlein

Mike Bailin

Edward Deuce Doherty

CONTENTS

PREFACE

The primary purpose of this book is to provide a resource for readers seeking a definition of key concepts in the field of Religious Studies. Each entry is defined, with cross-cultural examples of each concept provided to illustrate a particular notion. Suggestions for further reading are provided at the conclusion of almost every definition and these are tied to a bibliography at the end of the book.

The inclusion of a particular concept in this book depends upon its cross-cultural importance. Therefore, concepts with only a Christian relevance, for example, are for the most part not included in the book, with purgatory serving as an exception because it complements the entries for heaven and hell in the Christian context and even non-Christian religions, although it is absent in other religions. The structure of the book includes a cross-cultural emphasis because this reflects my personal comparative approach to the study of religion. The entries are arranged alphabetically. This approach and structure affords readers a simple and accessible reference work for use in introductory courses in Religious Studies as supplemental reading.

Not only is each concept defined and examples of it given from, ideally, both Eastern and Western religious cultures, but some examples of indigenous religions (African and Native American Indian) are also used to illustrate certain concepts. The fundamental criterion used in deciding whether or not to include a particular concept is its ability to elucidate the field of Religious Studies and the complex nature of religion. The book begins with an introduction to the nature of religion by reviewing the ways in which it has been defined, its origins in ancient culture, and the limitations of its applicability to non-Western cultures. The introduction also includes a brief overview of the field of Religious Studies. The book then goes on to consider and define particular concepts.

By necessity, the entries are short in this book because I have attempted to balance breadth with depth of coverage because of the nature and richness of the particular subjects; many of these concepts could have been discussed in book-length works. The suggested readings are intended to point interested readers in the direction of more complete books on a particular concept. There are numerous entries that I wanted to include, but because of limitations imposed on the length of this book difficult decisions had to be made for the sake of brevity.

I what to thank Gary Kessler of California State University for recommending me to the press for this book, and I am grateful to the staff at Routledge for nurturing this project, especially Leslie Riddle, Amanda Lucas, David Avital, Katherine Ong, and Sophie Thomson. Thanks to my colleagues in Religious Studies at Allegheny College: Glenn, Eric, Rabbi Ron, Vika, Bill, and Eric the Elder. Their commitment to teaching, scholarship, and good cheer contribute to a productive academic environment. When other colleges were retrenching during a recession Allegheny boldly ventured forth under the leadership of our own Batman and Robin dynamic duo, President Jim Mullen and Dean Linda DeMerritt. I am also grateful for the moral support from Peggy, grandmother extraordinary. I sincerely appreciate the hard work of Sarah Roncolato, a winsome and vivacious lady of many talents, who checked the manuscript for this book. Finally, it is terrific to be reunited with Mike and Ernie, who functioned as role models for me many years ago, after decades apart.

LIST OF KEY CONCEPTS

Afterlife
Agency
Agnosticism
Ancestors
Animism
Antinomianism
Apocalypse
Architecture
Art
Asceticism
Atheism
Belief
Blood
Body
Celibacy
Chaos
Church
Clothing
Comic
Community
Comparative religion
Conversion
Cosmology
Covenant
Cult
Culture
Cursing
Dance
Death
Demons
Doctrine

Dreams
Drugs
Earth
Ecology
Economy
Emotion
Eroticism
Ethics
Evil
Experience
Faith
Festivals
Fire
Food
Gender
Gifts
Goddesses
Gods
Grace
Harmony
Healing
Heaven
Henotheism
Heresy
Heterodoxy
Holiness
Holy persons
Homosexuality
Images
Incarnation
Interpretation/hermeneutics

Judgment
Kingship
Knowledge
Language
Last things
Law
Liberation
Liminality
Love
Madness
Magic
Martyrdom
Material dimension
Meditation
Memory
Metaphors
Millenarianism
Modernity
Monasticism
Monism
Monotheism
Music
Mysticism
Myth
Narrative
Nature
Oral tradition
Orthodoxy
Other
Pacifism
Pain
Pantheism
Perception
Performance
Pilgrimage
Play
Pluralism
Politics
Pollution
Polytheism
Possession

Postmodernism
Power
Prayer
Priest
Prophet
Psychology
Purgatory
Purification
Rationality
Reality
Reductionism
Relics
Revelation
Rites of Passage
Ritual
Sacraments
Sacred
Sacrifice
Saint
Salvation
Sanctification
Scripture
Sects
Secularization
Self
Sexuality
Shamanism
Sin
Society
Soul
Space: sacred and profane
Speech acts
Spirits
Suffering
Sun
Symbols
Taboo
Theatrical performances
Theism
Theology
Time

Totemism
Truth
Violence/non-violence
Visions

Women
World religions
Worldview
Worship

RELIGION AND RELIGIOUS STUDIES

An introduction

Religion is a subject that nearly everyone feels comfortable identifying without much trouble because it seems so apparent. When people attempt to define its nature, however, they find that it is difficult to execute this task in a way that everyone can recognize the subject of the definition. Moreover, the difficulty of defining the nature of religion is even more evident when a person attempts to apply the term and its definition to cultures outside of one's own religious milieu. An excellent example of such a problem is shared by Robert Ellwood. While on his way to Japan during a sabbatical leave, a person asks him why he is traveling to Japan. Ellwood responds that he is going to Japan to study its religion, to which the other person replies that Japan does not have any religion. What this casual encounter exemplifies is that the term "religion" does not have cross-cultural applicability in many cases. But until something better arrives, it is this inadequate term from a cross-cultural perspective that we have at the present time.

ORIGINS OF THE CONCEPT OF RELIGION

The term religion is derived from the Latin *religio* that originally refers to the human fear of God or other divine beings. It incorporates an intimate association with formal ceremonies and rites, such as sacrifice, during the course of its development. Its precise Latin etymology is unclear; Cicero traces it to *relegere*, which refers to gathering together, repeatedly passing over, or to read over again. Others look to the Latin term *religare* which means binding together. Both derivations suggest the social aspects of *religio*. It is confirmed by Saint Augustine, a church bishop in North Africa, in the early fifth century that *religio* expresses human social bonds and relationships, and to use the term to refer to worship of God creates confusion. Subsequent Western scholars have labored to find an acceptable definition that captures the nature of religion.

There are not only many definitions of religion, but there are also different approaches to the subject that reflect occurrences in intellectual history at the time of particular scholars. These approaches include the following: theological, anthropological, sociological, historical, phenomenological, psychological, economical, hermeneutical, feminist, economical, racial, cognitive science, and postmodern. Each different methodological approach to the subject of religion or some aspect of it shapes the scholar's definition of religion.

THE EVOLUTIONARY APPROACH

With the exception of the liberal theologian Friedrich Schleiermacher's (1766–1834) emphasis on examining the nature of religion from the perspective of an individual's experience identified with a feeling of absolute dependence in an encounter with something representing a greater power than oneself, the early nineteenth-century quest to find the nature of religion was influenced by the Darwinian–Spencerian theory of evolution, which was connected to a perceived need to be scientific when examining religion. It is possible to witness the influence of the theory of evolution in the work of Edward B. Tylor (1832–1917), a pioneer in the field of anthropology, and in that of James George Frazer (1854–1941), whose famous multi-volume *The Golden Bough*, originally published in 1890 in two volumes, grew eventually to twelve volumes. Even though Tylor's evidence from missionaries is suspect, he defined religion in a minimum way as a belief in spiritual beings. Using various dimensions of religion, Tylor examined the evolution of humans from primitive forms of society to more advanced modern versions in the West, which he used as his measuring stick, and theorized the following scheme of evolutionary development: hunter-gather or "savage" stage; domestication of animals and plants in the "barbaric" stage; finally, art and writing ushered into existence the civilized stage. This evolutionary scheme was reflected in his ambitious goal of outlining a "science of culture" based on objective observations and not speculation. Tylor also sought to isolate survivals in modern culture from previous primitive (his prejudicial term for an

AN INTRODUCTION

indigenous people) forms of culture by comparing higher forms of civilization in the West with simple, inferior religious cultures. Using what he claimed was objective observation and a comparative approach to his subject, Tylor discovered animism, a belief in the existence of deceased souls, as the foundation of religion for indigenous peoples.

In a similar way, Frazer, the acknowledged father of anthropology, envisioned the evolutionary scheme as moving from magic, to religion, and finally to science. With respect to magic, it operated by two laws: similarity and contact, which Frazer contended was an erroneous system of natural law, a fallacious guide of conduct, and therefore a false science. As an example of propitiation and conciliation of presupposed supernatural powers in comparison to human beings, religion was basically opposed to magic, which he defined as a false discipline and erroneous association of ideas that can never become a science, but was more akin to a form of art. Although there were other theorists at this moment of Western intellectual history making contributions to the study of religion, Frazer and Tylor were typical of those replacing the theological depiction of human nature as fallen and sinful with the more scientific theory of evolution, and the observation that human institutions were human products and not of divine origin.

Another nineteenth-century figure of significance was Friedrich Max Müller (1823–1900), a scholar trained in comparative philology before turning to comparative religion and mythology. Believing all knowledge was based on comparison, Müller adopted a comparative approach seeking to devise a new science that would adhere to the laws of cause and effect, being both inductive and comparative. He argued, for instance, for the importance of solar mythology because its gods and heroes originated in solar metaphors, and he speculated that India was the location for the origin of all religion. Within the context of his science of religion, Müller held a grand vision that included a revitalization of Christianity, altering one's views of others, finding common ground between different cultures, teaching cross-cultural lessons, and becoming aware of the inevitable decay of religion for which he found evidence in language. Encompassing this scenario, there would be an evolution toward the reconstruction of the City of God on earth that would include both East and West. According to Müller, religion reflected the human ability to perceive the infinite or eternal truth. In fact, all religions were able to some degree to perceive and manifest the following elements: belief in God or gods, immortality of the soul, and the possibility of future salvation.

In contrast to those seeking to discern the evolution of religion, there was a dissenter in Andrew Lang (1844–1912), an isolated voice among the evolutionary theorists. Lang's work would eventually mark a turn

3

away from the quest for the origins of religion. Lang was critical of the evolutionary religion theorists, believing they lacked reliable evidence and historical testimony, promoting a more critical and skeptical approach to religion. Lang's scholarship did not deter theorists such as Lucien Lévy-Bruhl (1857–1939), who compared primitive mentality unfavorably to scientific thinking, and Herbert Spencer (1820–1903), who traced the origins of religion from ancestor worship to higher forms of religion, in part to indicate primitive notions in Christianity with its belief in the Holy Ghost and funeral customs. Although the application of the evolutionary scheme to religion would wane, the emphasis on the scientific approach to the study of religion would continue to be a goal for later scholars.

THE QUEST FOR A SCIENCE OF RELIGION

The call for a science of religion was answered by two Dutch scholars: Cornelis P. Tiele (1830–1902) and Pierre D. Chantepie de la Saussaye (1848–1920). Tiele wanted to break out of the hermeneutical circle by developing a science of religion that included the deductive method to analyze all the data. He then applied a two-stage morphological description, as used by botanists and biologists, with the aim of identifying the essence or source of religion and the ontological study of the permanent elements in religion. Tiele's science of religion investigated a plethora of facts that invited classification, inference, comparison, and understanding. From the context of an objective position, the mind of a scientific scholar was able to unite the religious facts and distinguish the forms of religion from religion itself. Tiele's universal approach to the study of religion was shaped by the philosophy of the German thinker G. W. F. Hegel (1770–1831) and his phenomenology.

Manifesting a different type of universalism from Tiele, Chantepie de la Saussaye presupposed that in all religions there was a fundamental unity. This unity could be discerned by the method of phenomenology, which consisted in describing, sorting, classifying, and comparing the perceptually manifest components of religion that he thought negated the need to find the origin or essence of religion. The phenomenological method was associated with a philosophy of religion and a historical perspective. The former enabled a scholar to find the manifestations of religion, whereas the latter determined the essence of religion with the assistance of ethnography.

4

Sociologists and anthropologists of the twentieth century also made contributions to the quest for a science of religion. Émile Durkheim (1858–1917), often called the father of sociology, argued that what was distinctive about religion was the distinction between the sacred and the profane. The former was taboo and must not be touched by the profane, suggesting that the sacred was isolated, forbidden, and in need of protection from the profane. Within society, the source of the sacred was identified with totemism, an elementary form of religion. Durkheim used the methods of classification and comparison as part of his sociological or social scientific type of approach to religion that he eventually equated to society. Similar to many who preceded him, Durkheim relied on secondary testimony of travelers and missionaries for his evidence, which was often filtered through Christian presuppositions and biases about the nature of religion. Nonetheless, Durkheim insisted that religion represented the ultimate goals and ideals of a society while also serving as a cohesive social force.

When the field of anthropology was emerging Bronislaw K. Malinowski (1884–1942), a Polish scholar, introduced the participant observer method that led to more accurate accounts of the religious culture studied and a description about how the particular religion functioned within the society. Malinowski, founding father of anthropological fieldwork with his study of people in the Trobriand Islands off Papua New Guinea, found the theory of evolution unnecessary for explaining religion. He distinguished between magic and religion, although both of them functioned to alleviate anxiety associated with the difficulties and uncertainties of human existence. From his functionalist perspective, Malinowski stressed that religion originated as a response to emotional stress and functioned as a catharsis for humans. By equating function with the purpose of something, Malinowski argued that religion and magic shared their genesis in human emotional states, but they differed in the sense that magic was utilitarian and instrumental, whereas religion possessed no utility and embodied an end in itself.

From within the discipline of anthropology later in its history, an influential definition of religion was offered by Clifford Geertz, an American anthropologist, as a symbolic system that established emotions and motivations, ordered human existence, provided a convincing factuality, and the emotions and motivations of the system gave the impression of being realistic. In critical response to Geertz's definition of religion, Talal Asad found it too abstract and estranged from the social, historical, and political influences that normally shaped a symbol. Nonetheless, Roy Rappaport, another social scientist, argued that religion emerged with language, which means that it was as equally old as language and humanity. Rappaport

5

admitted that the concept of religion was vague, but this did not mean that it was vacuous. Enough was known about what people inferred by the term to proceed with the study of it.

PSYCHOLOGICAL APPROACHES TO RELIGION

Before the theoretical advent of psychology, the experiential and subjective aspects of religion attracted the attention of the liberal German theologian Friedrich Schleiermacher (1766–1834), who identified religion with a feeling of absolute dependence when encountering something greater than oneself. If Schleiermacher identified the essence of religion as the feeling of absolute dependence, it was another German scholar Rudolf Otto (1869–1937) who discovered the essence of religion in a subjective experience of the numinous, a unique, irreducible or *sui generis* (unique of its kind) phenomenon, and an a priori category. This meant that religion was set apart as something special and internal to the experience of the subject. Schleiermacher and Otto used evidence from the Bible to construct their theories.

The subjective experience of religion was explored by those within the field of psychology, another social science, which also offered its own definitions. William James (1842–1910), an early pioneer of the field, was interested in religious experience that he thought was not abnormal, in contrast to other opinions. If one took a person in solitude, considered that person's feelings, actions, and experiences, and understood that the person stood in relation to what was considered divine, one got an idea of James's understanding of religion. From James's perspective elements such as dogma and theology were secondary features of religion in contrast to conscious states of experience. James drew a distinction between healthy-minded ("once-born") and sick souls ("twice-born") for the purpose of indicating that the latter type of person experienced a second birth by dying to their former way of life.

Viewing himself as a scientist and advocating scientific knowledge as the cure for the ills of civilization, Sigmund Freud (1856–1939) discovered the origins of religion in the Oedipus complex, connecting it to a projection of infantile dependencies onto external reality and making religion a manifestation of mental illness. Driven by this complex, the son killed his father in order to gain access to the women of the society, a violent deed followed by remorse and guilt, which motivated a son to substitute and worship a totem animal to replace the slain father. Religion was thus a projection of infantile forms of dependency onto external reality. In his classic book *Future of an Illusion*, Freud argued that religious beliefs could neither be proven nor refuted, but people wanted them to be true. Unfortunately, they were mere illusions, which made the acceptance of the truths of reason and science difficult to embrace. While reworking Freud's theory of religion, René Girard, a French theorist, equated the sacred (religion) with violence.

Rejecting the Freudian theory of the Oedipus complex, the inevitable struggle between father and son over access to the women, incestuous feeling by a son toward his mother, and the conclusion that religion represented a neurosis, Carl Jung (1875–1961), a Swiss psychologist, traced the origins of religion to the collective unconscious where universal archetypes were to be discovered. These archetypes were associated with such experiences as birth, death, desires, and danger, and they appeared in dreams, myths, and symbols of religion. These psychologists of religion – James, Freud, Girard, and Jung – perceived their work as scientific and themselves as scientists of the mind.

PHENOMENOLOGY AND THE HISTORY
OF RELIGIONS

Due to the influence of Edmund Husserl's notion of phenomenology, an attempt to develop philosophy as a rigorous science by returning to the things themselves, with its two stages of eidetic reduction and phenomenological reduction proper, the phenomenological method came into vogue in the twentieth century as a scientific method for studying religion distinct from the social science approaches of sociology, anthropology, and psychology. The first stage of Husserl's method enabled a scholar to focus perceptual attention on the essence (*eidos*), meaning pure generalities or structure for Husserl. From this stage, one moved from particular phenomena on to general essences via the *epoché* (bracketing) of one's natural beliefs about objects of experience, a procedure that stripped away questions about objective truth. Based in the intentionality of consciousness that asserted that an awaken person is conscious of something. Husserl wanted to take the raw data of sensations and create a synthetic unity that would shape the essence of things. According to Husserl, intentionality gave genuine identity to the data and even provided a continuous identity regardless of the changing modifications of the data within the stream of consciousness.

An acknowledged phenomenologist of religion was Geradus van der Leeuw (1890–1930), a Dutch scholar, who identified the nature of religion with power and aimed to understand religion rather than explaining it by means of *epoché* and empathy. Van der Leeuw divided religion into five parts: the object of religion; the subject of religion; the object and subject in their reciprocal relationship (inward and outward action); the world; and forms (religions). This structure focused on what appeared without neglecting the subject that perceived the phenomena. By considering these parts as they related to religion, it was possible to discover that power belonged to both the subjective and objective aspects. Becoming familiar with the life stream in which phenomena appeared, the scholar contemplated its essence before intuitively analyzing it. The experience of similar phenomena was connected to ideal types, which he conceived as structured connections and instruments of understanding that lacked spatiotemporal reality, though they manifested another kind of reality connected to meaning.

Another self-acknowledged phenomenologist was Ninian Smart (1927–2001), who was also influenced by the philosopher of language, Ludwig Wittgenstein (1889–1951) and his notion of family resemblance. By seeking family resemblances of religious phenomena, Smart avoided the search for the essence of phenomena. In his scholarship, Smart identified six dimensions of religion: doctrine; mythology; ethics; ritual; social institutions; and religious experience. Smart intended to call attention to the dynamic nature of religion.

John Hicks was also influenced by Wittgenstein's theory of family resemblance within the context of his philosophy of language, which prompted Hick to conclude that religion could not be defined, even though it can be described. Although the plurality of religions made it impossible to find their essence, they did share family resemblances that helped to account for the many similarities and differences among them. Within a cross-cultural context, religions shared a concern for the real, a neutral concept that affirmed different forms of transcendent belief.

Around the mid-twentieth century, the history of religion school emerged with the scholarship of Mircea Eliade (1907–1986), who defined religion as the sacred as distinct from the profane. Besides being set apart from everything else and being surrounded by the profane, the sacred was dialectic in the sense of possessing the power to transform a natural object, equivalent to a power, saturated with being, and identified with reality. Jonathan Z. Smith also used an historical approach, and criticized Eliade for his emphasis on sameness and for missing the fact that religion was a creation and abstraction of a scholar's mind, suggesting that religion was not an empirical category. Smith asserted that religion, a human creation for which humans must take responsibility, was a quest for power that enabled humans to manipulate and negotiate their situation in order to have space in which to meaningfully dwell.

Along similar lines of scholarship, Sam Gill, a scholar of Native American Indian religion, denied that religion could be equated with the sacred, an ultimate concern, with belief in a God or gods, or *sui generis*. Similar to Smith, Gill argued that religion was an academic creation and those studying it had to be aware of its multi-cultural nature. Following similar lines of argument, John Hinnels asserted that religion per se did not exist, but it was possible to agree that the plural "religions" possessed adherents. He concluded that, although religion was a misleading term, it possessed usefulness, if the scholar used it acknowledging that all labels or categories had their limitations. The positions of Smith and Gill probably gave too much agency to scholars who were more accurately applying a label to something that people were practicing.

A wider version of the positions of Smith and Gill with political implications was offered by Daniel Dubuisson, who began with the observation that cultures were human creations. Dubuisson argued that religion was a Western creation and reference point used to conceive others from the East. The West used its creation to measure and interreact with other cultures from an assumed superior and prestigious position. This example of Western ethnocentrism was a part of the West's dominant cosmographical formation that represented an unassailable norm that was devoid of scientific status. In response to Dubuisson, it was probably too simplistic to view religion as an invention of the West imposed on foreign cultures. Martin Riesebrodt argued that evidence of interreligious polemics, the process of syncretism, and royal proclamations of ancient India and China demonstrated that non-Western cultures had recognized diverse religious traditions, even if not classifying certain features as religion. This suggested that religion was not a universal concept; but rather a local concept used by scholars beyond the limits of its origins. Scholars have used the term "religion" to comprehend unfamiliar and strange thoughts, actions, and behavior encountered in their scholarship.

POSTMODERN AND COGNITIVE VIEWS OF RELIGION

Although postmodernism is difficult to define because its meaning differs from one thinker to another, it does share some features among its adherents, such as a reaction to Enlightenment philosophy and the development of certain trends in modernism. Postmodernists stress difference, becoming, contingency, relativity, and chance. They are generally opposed to metaphysics and ontological foundations for things of the world. They are convinced that there are no timeless or universal truths, although some accept a multiplicity of truths. Knowledge is always incomplete, fragmented, and victim to historical and cultural forces beyond the control of anyone. The individual person is a decentered, fragmented, unstable, erring, wandering, decadent, and liminal being living on the fringes of society. The iconoclastic spirit of postmodernism is political and revolutionary, and leads to discontinuity, rupture, irregularity, plurality, and experimental adventures within a realm of the simulacrum, a hyper-reality that simulates life.

From the postmodern perspective of Jacques Derrida, religion is a response to the other before the presence of the other and oneself. In this encounter, God serves as a witness in the sense that God is already there, as prior to being itself. Derrida summarizes this stating: "Everything begins with the presence of that absence." (Derrida 1998: 27) This presence/absence is God, an unnamable witness. Looking at the origin of the Latin term for religion, one can find that it is applied to foreign things. As a response, religion is both ambiguous and ambivalent. It is preferable to understand religion as an ellipsis (a mark of absence), suggesting that religion is elusive and difficult to grasp with any precision or certainty.

Along these lines of observation, another postmodern thinker, Mark C. Taylor, points to the elusive nature of religion because its subject matter is constantly slipping from one's grasp. What makes religion so difficult to grasp is that it is continually withdrawing from the seeker. Religion disappears in its coming to be, but it yet allows appearances to emerge in its continual withdrawal. Thus religion is neither really here nor some place else. Because of its slippery nature, it is difficult to know precisely where to look for religion with any certainty; it could even appear in its withdrawal in strange places. In a later book, Taylor makes an effort to define the elusive nature of religion:

> Religion is an emergent, adaptive network of symbols, myths, and rituals that, on the one hand, figure schemata of feeling, thinking, and acting in ways that lend life meaning and purpose and, on the other hand, disrupt, dislocate, and disfigure every stabilizing structure.
>
> (M. Taylor 2007: 12)

Religion is akin to a double-edged sacrificial knife that gives people meaning and a sense of purpose, while undermining the stability of human existence with its destructive aspect.

In addition to postmodern discussions of religion, the latest approach is applying the findings from cognitive science to the study of religion, which also necessarily revives the theory of evolution for understanding the development of religion. Within the context of their evolutionary and mentalist approach to religion, cognitive theorists of religion think that it is possible to derive causal explanations for human behavior and ideas within the human mind. The anthropologist Pascal Boyer thinks, for instance, that religion is a natural consequence of the evolution of the mind because religious behavior and ideas survive, are passed down to younger generations, and naturally fit into intuitive, psychological mental processes. In what he calls the by-product hypothesis, Boyer states that certain thoughts and actions survive because they coincide with selected evolutionary features.

From another cognitive scientific perspective, Justin Barrett, another anthropologist, argues that the brain is a complex organ with specialized subsystems that all humans have in common regardless of their culture. These mental subsystems shape internal and external stimuli by constraining and informing religious and non-religious thought and behavior. By focusing on the fundamental and recurrent dynamics of the system of the mind, a scholar is able to offer predictions and explanations. Along similar lines of argument, the archaeologist Steven Mithen and anthropologist Robert McCauley think that the structure of the mind accounts for religious thought and behavior, natural by-products of the mind, whereas Harvey Whitehouse, a British anthropologist, thinks that only certain aspects of religion can be called natural because much of religion is still variable and mysterious.

Whitehouse identifies two different clusters of variables that have a tendency to be selected in the process of religious transmission. These two modes of religiosity are imagistic and doctrinal, each are depended on and constrained by different selective systems of memory. Through the convergence of analogical precepts and practices, the imagistic mode is transmitted by means of ritual. It becomes impressed on one's memory through heightened emotion, whereas the doctrinal mode of religiosity represents a codification of knowledge, and becomes a coherent collection of beliefs, which is transmitted by repetitive instruction and customary ritual performance.

TYPES OF DEFINITIONS OF RELIGION

In summary, definitions of religion manifest five general types: experiential, substantive, functionalist, family resemblance, and postmodern. The experiential definition attempts to isolate a primary religious experience and construct a theory around it (Otto's idea of the holy and cognitive

11

science are good examples). The substantive definition seeks to identify a central belief, such as a belief in spiritual beings, as the basis of a defini- tion. A functionalist position seeks to discern how religion operates in the life of a society, whereas the family resemblance position looks for over- lapping similarities, such as theoretical (beliefs, myths, and doctrines), practical (rites and moral codes), social (institutions, social behavior, and sacred personages), and experiential (emotions, visions, or trances) aspects. The postmodern position stresses the unstable and ambiguous nature of religion.

Another way to classify these various definitions is through the dis- tinction between polythetic and monothetical approaches. The former views no particular aspect of religion as necessary and considers several features as sufficient for the inclusion of a particular aspect to become a member of what is called religion. A good example of the polythetic definition is the family resemblance approach. The monothetical repre- sents a traditional approach to the subject that insists that all characteris- tics are necessary for a particular aspect to be included as part of religion by insisting on its substantive nature. By describing what religions do, this type reflects a functionalist position.

Regardless of the type of definition, the inability of scholars to agree on a definition of religion and its problematic nature motivated Wilfred Cantwell Smith to argue that scholars should abandon the term religion and replace it with faith. Smith's suggestion unfortunately gives rise to other problems when attempting to apply a term like faith to aspects of Hinduism, Buddhism, and Daoism where it is not germane. The substitu- tion of the term "culture" for religion is equally problematic. The adop- tion of indigenous categories presents a reverse set of problems from a cross-cultural perspective. The term "religion" is a problematic concept that embodies many cross-cultural deficiencies, but is widely recognized, if vaguely, in the West and its habitual usage would be difficult to break without causing further confusion.

RELIGIOUS STUDIES

Following in the footsteps of the German philosophers Hegel and Nietzsche, some theologians in the 1960s declared that God is dead, lead- ing to a *Time Magazine* cover announcing the news in bold, red letters against a black background. More recent postmodern thinkers have fol- lowed the chorus about the demise of a supernatural being, although dif- ferent thinkers mean a variety of things with respect to the demise of

God. If God is in fact dead (whatever one might mean by such a statement), Religious Studies is alive and thriving. According to a "White Paper" published by the American Academy of Religion, Religious Studies majors have increased twenty-two percent in the past decade with similar percentage increases in the number of total courses offered, course enrollments, and faculty positions in the field at the national level in America. The number of majors is even greater in public institutions with a forty percent increase. According to the study, courses in Islam and Hinduism almost doubled from 2000 to 2005, while courses in Christian theology, Hebrew scripture, and New Testament were flat or down. This result points to a shift in the field "away from the study of Christianity in isolation." This impetus has led to a rethinking of the "Seminary Model" for the Religious Studies department, a reconsideration that began decades ago as some colleges and universities moved toward a more cross-cultural and multi-methodological approach to the subject.

Although theology was called the "queen of the sciences' during the Middle Ages, it does not tell us much about modern Religious Studies, a recent academic discipline taught in earlier times by faculty with seminary backgrounds. In the present-day academy, there is a movement to expunge theology from the undergraduate curriculum, an extreme position with which many academics do not concur because theology is part of the intellectual heritage of various religious traditions and not simply the Christian tradition. Thus theology forms part of the history of ideas as does philosophy, psychology, and many other disciplines.

As an academic discipline, Religious Studies was the product of Enlightenment thought. Enlightenment thinkers, such as Immanuel Kant, sought to know all kinds of things within an optimistic context that believed human reason and understanding could grasp anything within limits of these intellectual tools. This optimism was combined with an intellectual curiosity, individual freedom, tolerance, and confidence in the inevitable nature of progress related to scientific discoveries and rationality. Enlightenment thinkers were convinced they could learn the secrets of nature and the physical laws that governed the universe with the ultimate goal of gaining control of nature in order to improve human life. At the center of the Enlightenment vision there stood the rational, self-determined, autonomous human being, possessing epistemological optimism and a self-confident sense of anthropocentrism. This optimistic vision extended to the study of religions and their concepts.

The discipline of Religious Studies can be traced back to an academic German distinction between *Religionswissenschaft* (science of religions) in contrast to *Naturwissenschaft* (natural science).The former field is part of what German scholars call *Geistwissenschaften* (sciences of the human spirit) in contrast to *Naturwissenschaft*. Without being modeled necessarily on the natural sciences, the German term *Wissenschaft* (science) includes humanistic and social studies that are regarded as rigorous scholarly sciences, whereas the English usage tends to refer to the natural scientific model. Thus the German term *Wissenschaft* is much wider in meaning and scope than the English term. In contrast to natural science, the study of religion is concerned with data connected to persons. During the term's formative period of usage, *Religionswissenschaften* served as a synonym for comparative religion and a historical/philological science.

In eighteenth-century America, Benjamin Franklin and Thomas Jefferson conceived of colleges that would be essentially secular and practical, resulting in the founding respectively of the University of Pennsylvania and the College of William and Mary. Unlike Franklin and Jefferson, other American educators thought that American colleges and universities should be nurtured by Christian values in the nineteenth century. The late nineteenth century witnessed a movement away from the Christian-centric type of education with the rise of the modern university, toward more specialization and the subsequent diversification of subjects into academic fields. After World War II, there was a rapid expansion of higher education during which the academic study of religion began to prosper on a broader scale; its nature and mission altered in a way that helped it break free of the seminary curriculum model. The reduction or total elimination of required religion courses and/or chapel attendance as requirements for graduation at many church-related institutions gave impetus to more imaginative approaches to the study of religion and the development of more pluralistic course offerings. Although economic prosperity and general higher education growth in the 1960s and 70s in America contributed to the expansion of religion programs, the study of religion was also aided by the American federal courts drawing an important distinction between religious indoctrination and teaching "about" religion. The courts ruled, culminating with the 1963 United State Supreme Court decision in *Abington* v. *Schempp*, that it was constitutionally permissible to teach about religion in a state setting, a ruling that included teaching the Bible objectively as a part of a secular program of education. This ruling came at a time of rapid expansion in American higher education, giving impetus to the development and expansion of departments of Religious Studies, with course offerings in Eastern religious traditions proving to be very popular with undergraduate students. This prompted graduate programs to turn out well trained teachers to meet the demand. Even church-related colleges and universities broadened their course offerings beyond biblical study and theology. Besides courses in Eastern religious traditions and the standard types of offerings in the Western tradition, it is not unusual to find offerings on subjects such as ritual, myth, feminist approaches to religion, gay issues and religion, black religion, ecology and religion, theory and method, special topics such as death or the nature of the self treated in a cross-culturally manner, and the sociology and psychology of religion. Many contemporary Religious Studies departments are multi-cultural and multi-disciplinary, and they thus can offer courses that are typically cross-listed with other departments within the curriculum.

The history of Religious Studies in Great Britain tends to be a relatively recent phenomenon, with its real birth located in the 1960s when the expansion of English universities make it possible for the new discipline to develop, even though its emergence is controversial in England. The Manchester Department of Comparative Religion is the first theological faculty in Europe to require each student to take at least one course in the subject. The Faculty of Divinity at Cambridge University includes members that teach non-Western religions, whereas the School of Oriental Studies at Oxford University gives students an opportunity to study foreign religious traditions. The first genuine department of Religious Studies was established at the University of Lancaster, offering courses in the major religious traditions and various methodological approaches to the study of religion.

The situation in Scotland has been depicted as initially an export industry with renowned scholars such as James Legge, a sinologist of the nineteenth century and John Nicol Farquhar, a historian of Indian religion (1861–1929), leaving to teach in other countries. There have been, however, notable exceptions to the Scottish diaspora, such as John and William Muir, known respectively for the study of Sanskrit and a book on Muhammad, Richard Bell who worked on the Qur'an, W. Montgomery Watt who was a scholar of Islam, James Hastings, editor of the *Encyclopedia of Religion and Ethics*, and the Scottish judge Adam Gifford who established the annual Gifford Lectures at the University of Edinburgh providing a platform for the ideas of many leading scholars. The 1960s marked a period of social and educational change and expansion that gave an impetus to Religious Studies, though the 1980s provided evidence of setbacks due to political and social changes. In 1991, Religious Studies was supported by the Millar Report by stressing the educational value of Religious Studies.

If Religious Studies is multi-cultural and multi-disciplinary, can it be stated that it is truly a discipline? According to Walter Capps, it is a discipline because it manifests a second-order tradition, which is "a coordinated account of the primary schools of interpretation, methods of approach, traditions of scholarship, and, most significantly, a shared

15

living memory of the ways in which all of these constitutive factors are related to each other" (Capps 1995: xvi). This shared memory informs students that Religious Studies is a descriptive, comparative, and inter-disciplinary discipline that seeks to make data concerning religion encountered in research intelligible by interpreting, systematizing, and synthesizing material. Religious Studies is composed of many intellec-tual interests that draws on other disciplines, such as psychology, sociol-ogy, anthropology, ecology, gender studies, and cognitive science, and the methods that accompany these disciplines. These various methods are instrumental because they form a function that can be logical, conceptual, and logistical by bringing a particular subject into focus. Overall, Religious Studies uses multiple methods and investigates many subjects associated with the subject of religion.

Jean-Luc Marion, a postmodern religious thinker, characterizes reli-gion as a "saturated phenomenon." By characterizing religion as satu-rated, Marion points to its excessive nature in the sense that it renders itself nearly invisible in its excessiveness. The concepts that follow in this book are part of the excessive and rich nature of religion. But there is no single concept that captures its essence. Each concept adds to an understanding of its nature because each concept is part of the whole without any single concept able to dominate its nature. Each concept helps a reader grasp how abundantly complex religion is and how diffi-cult it is to define precisely. Hence, the concepts to follow contribute to our understanding of the saturated nature of religion.

As the following concepts are defined, they are usually followed by examples taken from ancient and modern religions manifested throughout the course of history and from religious traditions that span the globe. These illustrations from various religious traditions spanning the vast sweep of time and space are intended to be part of the definition of the concepts. It is presupposed that straightforward definitions of concepts are not only dull, which would be akin to reading a dictionary, but that they are inadequate in helping readers understand the concepts. If the concepts in this book are, moreover, abstractions to some degree, the various illus-trations are intended to make the concept come to life in a concrete way for a reader and to demonstrate that the concepts are or have been mean-ingful and alive in the everyday modes of life of practitioners.

Because of the plethora of concepts in Religious Studies, any author of a book of this type is forced to be selective and acknowledge that one cannot be exhaustive, which would be more appropriate for a multi-volume encyclopedia. Some selections are rather obvious such as doc-trine, ritual, gods, myth, rites of passage, or salvation, whereas other possibly less obvious entries are selected with the intention of stimulating the imagination of a student novice to the field with concepts such as the comic, dance, drugs, eroticism, madness, or harmony.

Based on the previous condensed overview of the concept of religion and the field of Religious Studies, it can be affirmed that they are contested concepts, but they also apparently embody contradictory elements. The selections for this book reflect their contradictory nature, which helps us to witness them as representing a conjunction of opposites at times as evident by concepts such as doctrine and the comic, orthodoxy and heterodoxy, purity and pollution, and violence and non-violence. Other selections appear because they broaden the horizons of grasping religion instead of understanding it as something sober and static, which is my rationale for including the comic, festivals, and play. Such selections are made with the explicit intention to demonstrate to students that religion and Religious Studies are not static entities, but are rather subject to historical vicissitudes and continue to dynamically change. In addition, some concepts differ according to the religious culture in which they are discovered. This point possesses two important implications: no single definition of a concept is totally adequate, and the illustrative examples taken from variety of religions from East and West, ancient and modern, and simple and complex religious cultures are part of the definition of a concept. Therefore, a concept is further defined by the various examples, and they should be grasped as part of the definition and not merely illustrations of a concept, which necessarily means that definitions of a concept unfold further by means of the examples provided. Embodied within the individual definitions of concepts the reader will notice terms in bold letters. This practice is intended to refer the reader to a more complete definition in another location.

Further reading: Barrett (2000); Boyer (1994); Capps (1995); A. Cunningham (1990); Derrida (1998); Dubuisson(2003); Gill (1994); McCauley (2000); Marion (1991); Mithen (1996); Olson (2003); Rappaport (1999); Riesebrodt (2004); J. Z. Smith (1978, 1982, 1987, 1998, 2004); W. C. Smith (1963, 1981); M. Taylor (2007); Walls (1990); Whitehouse (2000); C. Williams (1990)

RELIGIOUS STUDIES

The Key Concepts

AFTERLIFE

Although there is a wide variety of belief about the afterlife from a cross-cultural perspective, this richness possesses a common thread that concerns the destiny of the individual after death. Within many cultures, it is the soul that survives in contrast to the perishable body, although the soul is not always considered immortal. Among the Native American Ojibwa, there is a belief in two souls: body- or ego-soul and free-soul. The latter soul possesses a separate existence from the body, being able to travel during sleep. After death, the free-soul becomes a ghost that is eventually reunited in the afterlife with the body-soul.

Afterlife beliefs are often reflected by a culture's conception of **heaven** and hell. These beliefs frequently have social consequences reflected by notions of good and bad behavior and rewards promised for positive actions. These types of conviction are evidence that earthly existence helps to determine one's destiny in the afterlife. In many religious cultures, some form of **judgment** determines whether or not one's deeds merit a pleasant or painful destiny. These destinies are conceptualized as a paradise akin to a heaven or a painful place like hell, although such a clear distinction is not always the case, however, because some religious cultures believe in a more ambiguous or shadowy place, such as the ancient Jewish notion of Sheol, a dark place where the dead are inert. For the ancient Egyptians, the dead go to the underworld of Osiris where the deceased confesses to sins that he/she did not commit, tries to establish his/her righteousness, is judged by a panel of gods, appears before Osiris, and his/her heart (location of emotions and intellect) is weighted against a feather, a symbol of cosmic harmony and justice (*Ma'at*). Those with heavy hearts are thrown to a hideous monster made of many different animals.

Further reading: Obayashi (1992); Taylor (2001); Vecsey (1983)

AGENCY

This is a relatively new concept in the field, borrowed from the philosophical writings of Donald Davidson and Charles Taylor. Donaldson is interested in agency and interpretation that he claims includes the pattern of interaction between speakers and their environments. The irrational is internal, for instance, to an agent, and is a matter of not adhering to rational norms. Thus, irrational behavior is a failure to conform fully to the rational pattern of the remaining agent's attitudes and behaviors.

Within a cultural context, agency refers to the way that individuals behave despite their social and religious context. A person might have been raised in a strict religious home, but decides not to participate in religion in adult life. This type of person is acting upon their own personal agency and contrary to their life history and social conditioning. In spite of cultural conditioning, a person is free to choose another option unexpected by other members of one's family or **society**. This scenario indicates that individuals have a role in shaping their personal lives, are not mere products of the prevailing **culture**, and that there are limits upon a culture to get members to conform.

Due to the influence of the poststructural thinker Michel Foucault, agency is interpreted as a form of resistance against the ideologies of a culture. In this case, agency is a **power** exercised, for instance, by an oppressed person or group against cultural forces. Beyond mere free will or resistance, agency is a capability to make something happen, as in **rites of passage** that transform adolescents into adults, ordinary men into kings, unmarried to married, and the dead into ancestors.

The transformative potential of agency does not mean that a person must exercise it. It is possible to let it remain simply potential. The efficacy of an individual's agency can be measured by the success or failure of a rite. The exercise of agency through rites suggests that agency is not simply an individual capability, but is also distributed through a cultural network that includes social and religious institutions, political leaders, community, family, local groups, and councils.

In his discussion of agency, Charles Taylor makes a case for it as an individual mental process by distinguishing between disengaged and engaged agency. With the former type, the agent fully distinguishes oneself from the rational and social worlds. Therefore, the subject's identity is no longer defined by what lies external to the subject in the world. The engaged agent is an embodied subject who is engaged in and open to the world. In other words, the engaged agent acts in the world and on the world. Embodiment is the subject's form of agency, and it represents a context for one's experience as a context conferring meaning.

Further reading: Davidson (1980); Foucault (1994); Taylor (1985)

AGNOSTICISM

This is a conceptual position related to the negation of the Greek term *gnōstos* (meaning to know), implying not to know, for instance, whether

God exists or not. To be certain or to have *faith* that *God* exists represents a *theistic* position, whereas to deny the existence of God is *atheism*. Being agnostic does not necessarily mean that a person is not deeply religious, although it is commonly used to describe someone who is detached from religious commitments or is unwilling to speculate about something that cannot be empirically validated.

In the nineteenth century, agnosticism becomes associated with the scientific perspective by T. H. Huxley (1825–1895), who claims that Christian **doctrine** represents unverifiable speculation that cannot withstand the scrutiny of the scientific method. During this historical period, agnosticism finds favor with other scientifically inclined intellectuals such as Charles Darwin, John Stuart Mill, Herbert Spencer, and others. Within twentieth-century philosophy, agnosticism is adopted by many logical positivists and postmodernists in the latter half of the century. Some agnostics claim that the existence of God, for instance, cannot be proven or disproved. It is thus preferable to be detached from such metaphysical speculation.

ANCESTORS

In many religious cultures throughout history, ancestors are deceased family members that are intimately related to the living and are regarded as family leaders and members of the *community*, even though no longer alive. Ancestors are imagined to be spiritual superintendents of family affairs, continuing to hold titles, such as mother or father, after *death* that they held when alive. These features are evident in the traditional Chinese family *cult* where every home possesses an ancestral altar that hold a number of wooden spirit tablets with each of them representing a deceased ancestor. The presence of these spirit tablets indicates that the dead continue to occupy a place in family activities.

The ancestral cult and reverence presuppose the commemoration of the departed by name, which suggests **worship** directed specifically to him or her. Using an ancestor's name during **ritual** action, suggests that the departed is invested with distinctive attributes similar to any person. This also means that ancestors are to be distinguished from the high gods. In traditional Chinese religion, the ancestor cult is composed of two parts: mortuary rites immediately following **death** and sacrificial rites that maintain a long-term relationship between the living and the dead. The mortuary rites are performed for the benefit and **salvation** of the **soul** in China, whereas the sacrificial rites are performed to stabilize the relationship between the dead and the living at two locations: home and ancestral temple. The family sacrifices of a more elaborate variety are observed on the death day anniversary, **festival** days, and the first and fifteenth of each month. And these sacrifices feature kowtowing before the ancestral spirit tablets, burning of incense, candles, and paper money, offering of food and drink, and concluding with wishes that the ancestors enjoy the offerings. The offerings are a means of communicating with the dead and providing them with sustenance in their next life.

Ancestor reverence is directly rooted in the social structure of a **society** and embedded into the kinship, domestic and descent relations and institutions. Ancestor worship (a disputed notion) in China is a lineage cult with the major responsibility to perform the necessary rites resting on the oldest living son, who accepts the role as a right and a duty. This is because he replaces his father in the social structure. Among the Ashanti of Africa, each lineage owns a blackened stool that serves as a shrine of its ancestors. Offerings of food and drink are made on the stool.

Ancestors play an important role in many religions because they are believed to act as guardians of the social and moral order. They rise above the transitory human level by virtue of constituting fundamental categories of moral and legal thought. This invests them with sacred significance, their sanctioned rights and duties unchallenged by the living. Thus ancestors make social members conform to expected norms of behavior, whereas any deviation from the norms incurs ancestral disapproval. The ancestral cult reflects the need of a society to maintain itself. If a society depends on its ancestors, the departed also depend on the living, forming a mutually beneficial system that helps to enhance the continuity of the social structure. This is apparent among the Tonga, a Bantu people of northern South Africa, whose ancestors validate the pattern of life, bind together potentially divergent kin groups, and reinforce primary status changes among adults.

When an older person dies a break in the social fabric is experienced by survivors. This type of social rift calls for a reinstatement of the deceased into the family and its lineage by means of ritual. The deceased often do not receive rites until they manifest themselves in the life of their descendents.

In many religions, the dead are considered impure. Among the Dogon of Africa, death disperses a person's vital force, which constitutes the impurity of death. By being impure, the dead create disorder, which functions as a warning to the living. This is interpreted by the living as the dead appealing to them to regularize their position. In the Dogon society, order is established by a cult in which millet beer plays a central role as it is believed that the ancestor impregnates the beer giving it intoxicating powers. Thus, ancestors introduce disorder into the beer, which excites the drinker and motivates him to establish the ancestor in the **cult**.

Although ancestors possess authority over the living, they may behave capriciously or ambivalently in the sense they can behave punitively or benevolently. Because the deceased is a kind and generous person while alive, this does not necessarily mean that they will act the same way when they become ancestors. As a general rule, ancestors can only intervene where they have authority. For those who break the social norms, the ancestors dispense punishment. Among the Apache of the American southwest, ancestral punishment is called ghost sickness, owl sickness, or darkness sickness. It is called owl sickness, for instance, because a ghost returns in the form of an owl. Symptoms of the disease include irregular beating of the heart, choking sensations, and faintness. Other accompanying symptoms are trembling, weeping, and headache, which are all symptomatic of fright.

If we consider the relationship between an ancestor and the living, the latter owe obedience, economic service, and respect to the ancestor. Among the Lo Dagaa of Africa, a person is obligated to return to the ancestor any wealth acquired by inheritance. This can mean, for instance, that an heir must periodically sacrifice a portion of livestock to the ancestor. Not only do ancestors intervene in human affairs, and punish the living, they also have the **power** to ward off evil and misfortune. A witch among the Lovedu, a Bantu people of Africa, cannot kill a person without the consent of an ancestor, and medicines are ineffective without the cooperation of ancestors. Finally, it is common to find the living appealing to ancestors for good crops, fertility, good fortune, and success.

Although ancestors have an intimate relationship with the living, they also have an independent existence in the **afterlife**. Among the Ashanti of Africa, there is a world of spirits where all ancestors live a life similar to that on earth. In the culture of the Mende of Sierra Leone, the life of ancestors is also similar to that of people on earth.

Further reading: Colson (1962); Jordan (1969); Opler (1965); Rattray (1969); Ray (1976); Turner (1968); Xu (1948)

ANIMISM

This concept is derived from the Latin term *anima* (spirit), which is a **belief** that things within **nature** – animate and sometimes inanimate – are energized by **spirits**. Animism is most often a feature of some indigenous religions and, as a result of being discovered by Christian missionaries, is negatively associated with the history of Western colonialism, being considered something strange and inferior when compared to Christianity. In 1708, Georg Stahl, a German physician and chemist, theorizes that a physical element, which he identifies as *anima*, vitalizes living bodies. In his *A Natural History of Religion* published in 1757, philosopher David Hume observes that humans attribute to the world around them signs of human likeness, which he thinks is absurd, vulgar, and ignorant. After these thinkers pass from the scene, animism plays an important theoretical role in the quest for the origin of religion.

Under the influence of Darwinian thought and the search for the origins of religion, James Frazer (1854–1914), an earlier theorist of religion, calls attention to a tendency among indigenous people to claim that their plants possess souls, which he views as evidence of religious evolution that develops into **polytheism**. In 1871, Edward Tylor, an early anthropologist, adopts Stahl's term animism to characterize the essence of religion. Tylor argues that animism is not only an identifying feature of primitive religions, but also a ubiquitous religious concept. Tylor thinks that animism forms the foundation for the **belief** in higher spiritual beings. By attributing souls to inanimate objects of nature, indigenous people are making an erroneous attribution. Tylor is convinced that aspects of animism survive in contemporary religion, such as the belief in human **souls** or ghosts.

With the rejection of evolutionary schemes for the development of religion, the search for the origin of religion, and the aftermath of colonialism, the concept of animism falls out of favor as a hermeneutical concept for indigenous religions. The revival of the concept is associated with the lack of an adequate term to replace it. During his fieldwork with the Native American Ojibwa in Manitoba, Canada, Hallowell discovers that the natives believe that rocks are animate to the extent that some rocks and weather systems are conceived to be persons. It is believed by the Ojibwa that stones can speak, and weather phenomenon, such as thunder, is imagined to be birds that can demonstrate either affection or hostility. Hallowell also discovers that animism among the Ojibwa is restrictive in the sense that not everything is experienced as living.

Animism is closely related to **totemism**, although they should be distinguished. The latter uses natural images, whereas the former uses sociological representations to construct order in **nature**. Therefore, totemic belief systems model **society** after nature, whereas animism constructs nature after society.

Further reading: Hallowell (1975); Harvey (2006); Stringer (1999); Tylor (1871)

ANTINOMIANISM

A concept derived from the Greek terms *anti* (against) and *nomos* (law). It refers to those within a religious tradition who think that laws do not apply to them because they have spiritually transcended secular or religious law, and thus need not obey common laws or social regulations. It can also designate those who view laws as confining, restrictive, and obstructive of spiritual attainment and thus justly violated in order to attain their religious goal. Aghori *ascetics* of the Hindu Śaiva tradition, for instance, act contrary to prevailing social norms since the Middle Ages in India by eating the flesh of corpses, carrying a skull bowl with which to beg their food, drinking intoxicants, living in cremation grounds, and covering their bodies with ashes from cremated corpses. Left-handed Tantric schools partake of five items that are forbidden to orthodox members of Hindu *society*: wine, meat, fish, parched grain (probably an intoxicant), and illicit sex. Since the Sanskrit terms begin with the letter M, these five forbidden items and practices are called the five Ms. The behavior of the Aghori ascetics and Tantric adepts is contrary to and violates social and religious norms from the perspective of established patterns of action. By violating these norms, the ascetics think that they can stimulate their inner spiritual energy and accelerate their path to *liberation*.

Further reading: White (1996, 2005)

APOCALYPSE

A concept derived from a Greek term *apokalypsis* meaning to uncover, unveil, or reveal. This is often a **revelation** about the end of **time** in Jewish and Christian writings that is expressed by bizarre **visions**, strange **symbolism**, and supernatural happenings. An apocalypse represents a secret knowledge about the heavenly world or destiny of the current world. In Hebrew **Scriptures**, the book of Isaiah (24–27) is often called, for instance, the little apocalypse in which the writer portrays the final **judgment** of **God** upon all nations as a cosmic catastrophe. This type of literature tends to be composed during times of persecution, making secrecy paramount in order to keep teachings from the persecuting political powers. Therefore, it is composed in a spiritual code language that makes it a sealed book against others external to the inner circle of the faithful. An excellent example is the Hebrew book of Daniel, which is composed shortly after the outbreak of the Maccabean wars around 165 BCE by a Hasidim (loyal, pious one), whose religious faith demands total loyalty to the Torah (law) regardless of the consequences. The writer of Daniel believes that he is living during the last days, and he relates a series of **visions** during which he sees four beasts, regarded as antithetical to God's creation, arising from a watery chaos, until the last and worst beast with ten horns appears to him. The book of Daniel also manifests a trial for the righteous and the wicked along with a mention of the resurrection of the dead (12.2).

Jewish apocalyptic speculation influences the Christian book of Revelation, which depicts the coming of a new **heaven** and **earth** at the end of **time**. This book is attributed to the apostle John and is composed approximately sixty years after the **death** of Jesus, during a period when Christians are being persecuted for not worshiping the Roman emperor. The book opens with a declaration by Jesus that establishes his **power** over **death**. The book of Revelation is organized according to the number seven in terms of messages, seals, trumpets, bowls, and visions because it is a number with cosmic significance and represented **reality**. The text also refers to a millennium, a reference to the thousand year rule of Christ on earth during which Satan is bound. At the beginning of the millennium, there is a resurrection of the righteous or martyrs, according to the book. At the end of this period of peace, Satan is released and a final battle between good and evil takes place. Once Satan is defeated, a second resurrection of all the dead occurs before the final **judgment** is rendered by **God**.

Further reading: Cohn (1993); Himmelfarb (1993); McGinn (1979, 1994)

ARCHITECTURE

Religious edifices are human creations symbolic of the spirituality of religious traditions. When a religious structure is constructed it transforms the space it occupies, altering the lives of those living within its environment and sphere of influence. Architectural structures are equally expressions and sources of religious **experiences**. These buildings also interweave disclosure and hiddenness of their spiritual messages by using stones and mortar in a symbolic way in which the material gives birth to the spiritual. In addition to being material symbols of a culture's religion, architectural structures stand autonomous in the sense of possessing an inherent freedom, while simultaneously supporting the social web of interrelationships within a **society**.

From a cross-cultural perspective, there are many different examples of artistic structures: Jewish synagogues, Buddhist *stupas* (memorial structures), Muslim mosques, Christian churches, and Hindu temples. Each of these examples possesses it own style, purpose, and symbolism that embodies information about the religious tradition. The Gothic-style Christian church in Europe stresses, for instance, the transcendence of **God** with its soaring spires pointing upward toward **heaven**. The interior height of the building makes a worshiper feel insignificant. The ground plan is modeled on the cross, its stained glass windows depict biblical scenes, and these windows invoke light symbolism associated with the beauty of heaven.

In contrast, the base of the Muslim mosque (*masjid* in Arabic that means a place of prostration) is modeled on the symbolically square **earth** and its dome signifies heaven based on Muslim cosmology. An externally important physical feature of a mosque is the minaret, a tower used to call the faithful to **prayer**. An internal feature of the mosque is the *mihrāb*, a niche indicating the direction of Mecca for prayer and a place where an *imān* (prayer leader) stands during daily prayer. Another significant feature is the *minbar* (seat or chair) that dates to the time of the **prophet** Muhammad. Placed at a right angle to the *mihrāb*, it is a raised place from which sermons are delivered, such as a pulpit in a Christian **church**.

Similar to the ground plan of an Islamic mosque, a Hindu temple consists of squares in a different way because they depict heavenly space on earth and each square is inhabited by a deity. The temple ground plan functions as a sacred geometric diagram (*maṇḍala*), which reflects the essential structure of the universe and a miniature version of a divine world. Hindu temples are constructed according to a system of precise mathematical measurements, which enables them to exist harmoniously with the mathematical foundation of the cosmos. Some temple ground plans are thought to represent the **body** of a cosmic man, which suggests that humans are a microcosm of the wider cosmos. Sometimes temples suggest bodily sheaths or layers, with the outer layers representing the physical body and the interior sanctum of the temple symbolizing the immortal **self**.

North Indian temples are frequently modeled on mountains with their ascending towers that stand at the center of the world and symbolically connect heaven, earth, and the underworld. In contrast, South Indian temples consist of seven rectangular walls arranged concentrically. At the four entrance points, there are soaring pyramidal structures (*gopurams*) often adorned with divine images. Many southern temples also have tanks full of water used on ceremonial occasions.

29

Temples are a later addition to Buddhism in Asia, which manifest its early architectural focus on *stūpas* (memorial mounds) for the remains (relics) of holy persons. Buddhists believe that the relics of the Buddha, for instance, are infused with morality, concentration, wisdom, or other such qualities. Because the relics are believed to possess life, it is accepted that the Buddha is present and alive wherever the relics are located. Much like mosques, churches, and temples, *stūpas* are places of **pilgrimage** and locations for the acquisition of merit.

In the Chinese Daoist tradition, a distinction is made between two models of temple architecture: metaphorical and cosmological. The metaphorical model imitates the architecture of administrative residences and becomes the residence of an official. The metaphorical structure is characterized by a curved roof, ending, for instance, in a swallow-tailed point, possesses red pillars and doors, has statues of lions at the entrance, and a bell and drum suspended on either side of the door. In the cosmological model, temples are paradigms of the world in which the principal door opens toward the south and contains images of a Green Dragon and White Tiger on either side of the door, representing, respectively, the eastern direction and the western direction. A celestial vault is represented by a dome located inside the roof, indicative of a **sacred** mountain, which stands for the paradise of the Immortals (legendary figures and heroes of sacred myths). On the top of the roof, two earthenware dragons confront each other over a flaming pearl, representing the radiant energy that emanates from the incense burner located in the center of the temple. The incense burner manifests the essential element of **worship** and social unity. The architectural edifices mentioned serve social, economic, educational, and political functions in their religions. Because many of these cross-cultural structures are built with donations from wealthy nobles or religious organizations, they are also symbols of temporal power, manifesting the socio-economic status, cultural power, and superiority of the donors.

Further reading: Humphrey and Vitebsky (1997); Kramrisch (1946); Leidy (2008); Petruccioli and Priani (2002)

ART

Representing the **material dimension** of religion, art is a human creation that enables one to give expression to one's **faith**, imagination, beauty, emotions, religious history, and **worldview**. Religious art not only expresses spiritual messages, but also serves as a potential source of inspiration for new sources of religious **experience**. Because religious art embodies both disclosure and hiddenness, it is open to endless reinterpretation and revalorization.

Within the Islamic world, art and **faith** are, for instance, traditionally linked, with the former considered another sign (*āyāt*) of **God** and a reflection of divine unity amidst earthly multiplicity. With its bases in wisdom (*hikmah*), Muslim art can be used to praise and serve God, and supports the remembrance of the one true God, which comes from a supra-individual inspiration and wisdom that comes from God. Islamic art avoids naturalism. It prefers abstract and geometric design because this is believed to free the human spirit. This attitude results in only minor importance being accorded to paintings and portraitures, with the exception being illustrated manuscripts. Anthropomorphic artistic representation is rejected as idolatry (*shirk*), a possible veneration or invocation of anything except God, who alone is the proper focus of worship and prayer.

There are three basic elements to Islamic art: line and angle are used in buildings and in fixed geometric designs resembling crystals associated with ice and coolness, with the intention of relieving the senses from the heat and aridity of the Middle East; this is also enhanced by the use of all shades of blue and green colors. A third element is the motif of flowers and other vegetation usually combined with geometric patterns, intending to suggest refreshment, order, and growth. This style of art is called Arabesque.

The noblest form of art in the Muslim world is calligraphy because it renders visible the word of God and emulates a divine revelatory act. In addition to enhancing recollection of God, calligraphy serves as a sign for the cultured human, a disciplined mind, and the **soul**. The Arabic term for pen (*nūn*) resembles an ink-pot with which the archetypes of all beings are written. Each letter possesses its own personality, and serves as a visual symbol of a particular divine quality. Arabic script is written from right to left, signifying moving from the field of action toward the human heart. The script contains two dimensions: vertical that confers hieratic dignity, which corresponds to the essence of things and the unalterable character of each letter, and horizontal that links letters together into a continuous flow and expresses the process of becoming or matter that links one thing to another.

The Native American Navaho are famous for the geometric designs of their pottery and sand paintings, an impermanent form of art that is used to cure the ill. Depicting Navaho deities or mythological events, the artist uses pinches of colored sand to create his work. A patient sits on the painting with the aim of identifying the patient with the sacred figures depicted in it. As the figures in the painting are obliterated by the patient sitting on them, it is believed that they are transformed into the patient, which suggests that at the conclusion of the ceremony the sick person becomes the painting. At that point, the patient enters the sphere of the Holy People, which provides the ill person with **healing** and **harmony**.

In contrast to Muslim and Navaho art, Hindus view the aim of art as embellishment. Therefore, Hindu art is not intended to imitate or to accurately depict **nature**, because its purpose is to portray nature as it should be ideally. The task of the Hindu artist is to render a subject in its paradigmatic or its idealized form. In other words, the artist creates concrete or metal models of divine archetypes. Thus Hindu art is an attempt to present **heaven** on **earth**. In order to accomplish this task, the artist must mentally identify with the idealized object or deity being created, fashioning an object from the image in his mind. If the artist is successful, a work of art can enable a viewer to experience *rasa* (aesthetic mood) that can culminate in a transcendental bliss. The function of the deities depicted on the *gopurams* (pyramidal structures at the entrance to temples located at the four cardinal directions) is to teach ordinary people stories and give theological messages from the epic and purāṇic literature.

From these diverse examples, it is possible to understand the many roles played by art within religious traditions. Art can stimulate a viewer's emotions and aesthetic sensibilities. Since paintings and images tell stories, art possesses a didactic or teaching purpose. For the Catholic tradition, Michelangelo's paintings in the Sistine Chapel in Rome, for instance, teach viewers biblical stories. Books can be transformed into works of art by an artist creating an illustrated manuscript. Native American Iroquois use masks during rituals and dance performances that transform the wearer into a powerful spirit. The artistic creation of religious symbols on large vehicles, such as trucks and buses, in Pakistan not only adopt these vehicles into the culture, but, more importantly, they function to protect the driver and passengers. This is especially true when a vehicle contains on its side a large eye that is intended to protect passengers from the evil eye. The prophylactic role of religious objects is evident on the divine image or cards with divine images attached to the car dashboards of Hindu and Sikh vehicles in India.

Further reading: Blair and Bloom (1995); Cort (1996); Cragg and Speight (1980); Davis (1997)

ASCETICISM

This concept is related etymologically to the Greek term *askēsis* (to exercise). Thus an ascetic is analogous to a spiritual athlete in Greek parlance. More specifically, an ascetic exercises behavior that is intended to control his **body** and mind. This regimen assumes a variety of practices: self-denial of **food** and sleep, vows of **celibacy** and silence, and renunciation of the world; it also includes various forms of bodily mortification, such as self-flagellation, offering of pieces of one's flesh, and other forms of self-inflicted **pain**.

These arduous types of behavior are not embraced by the mainline traditions of Judaism and Islam, although ascetic practices can be identified in these traditions. The book of Numbers in the Hebrew Scriptures mentions the Nazirite, who are required to refrain from wine, vinegar, grapes, and raisins, and from cutting their hair or beard. In addition, biblical **prophets** live ascetic lifestyles, and communities such as the Essences, who live in the area of the Dead Sea, take a vow of **celibacy** and follow a strict vegetarian diet. Because ascetic practices are contrary to the inherent goodness of God's creation, Islam is suspicious of it, but it still embraces elements of asceticism in such practices as almsgiving, which can be construed as a form of asceticism. Along with fasting during the holy month of Ramadan, the annual **pilgrimage** to Mecca adopts ascetic forms of denial because pilgrims have to enter into a condition of **purity** (*ihram*) while on pilgrimage. Islam also manifests a tradition during its history of wandering mendicants leading an ascetic lifestyle.

Asceticism can be an end in itself as evident in some forms of Hinduism, which motivates the Buddha to criticize it based on his own personal experience with asceticism. The Buddha is opposed to extreme forms of asceticism. Contrary to the moderate path to liberation taught by the Buddha, many practice asceticism to gain discipline, to cultivate virtue, to attain supernatural powers, and to become god-like.

These types of motivations are evident in the long history of asceticism in Hinduism among its world-renouncers (*saṃnyāsins*), sanctioned by the legal texts as a legitimate and final two stages of life (*āśrama*): forest dweller and renouncer. The final stage is considered to be beyond mere retirement from the world suggested by the forest dweller because it involves a dedication to achieve the goal of liberation. This tradition of asceticism continues for centuries, reaching a plateau with Śaivism and its ascetic deity who serve as a paradigm to inspire human behavior. A group of ascetics called the Pāśupatas, who **worship** Śiva as the Lord of Beasts, live in or around cremation grounds in order to have access to the ashes of cremated bodies that they use to cover their bodies, which is considered an act of **purification** and a necessity for obtaining a superhuman **body** devoid of negative karma. Many of these ascetics wander naked or wear a single cloth. An advanced stage of their ascetic practice includes acting mad in order to incur the censor of others, which is part of their attempt to rid themselves of bad karma.

The emphasis on asceticism among Śaiva practitioners is also stressed by Jainism for its monks, as part of a regimen to purify the soul of karmic residues. It is essential for a monk to restrain himself and create a body heat (*tapas*) that consumes negative karma by means of asceticism. The pervasiveness of the spirit of asceticism within Jainism is embodied in its five basic vows: non-violence, speaking the truth, not stealing, celibacy, and detachment from the world. These five vows are obligatory for all monks and nuns, whereas lay people strive to adhere to them to the best of their ability.

Beginning with the call of Jesus to consider choosing a life of poverty (Matt. 19.21) and the use of the verb *askeō* in Acts (24.16), there is a long history of ascetic practice in Christian history that dates to St. Anthony and the so-called "desert fathers," men who lead a life of isolation and eat only Eucharist wafers. The desert, a desolate and remote location, is a place where **God** can be found, as demonstrated by Moses, and simultaneously a place where demons dwell, making it a location associated with danger. Later **monastic** affiliated nuns and monks also lead lives of ascetic discipline because Christian asceticism is a sign of sanctity. From the fourth century, voluntary abstinence for ascetic reasons is completely legitimate from the perspective of the **church**, whereas it is considered heretical to abstain because one hated the material creation of God. It is perfectly permissible for a Christian to transform their **body** and thereby make it an instrument of the **spirit** just as God originally intends for it.

Early and medieval Christian asceticism is practiced within the context of the expectation of the imminent end of the world for which those practicing asceticism are preparing themselves. Along with the eschatological expectations, there is an anticipation and even embrace of **martyrdom**. It is common for stories of martyrs to be read to crowds on the feast days for martyrs, shaping the minds of potential ascetics who wish to become heroic like a martyr. A number of medieval nuns, according to hagiographical **narratives**, subsist on the Eucharist alone or fast for extended periods, a pattern of practice that suggests *anorexia nervosa* to some scholars, whereas some monks wear a spiked chain around their thighs or some other type of devise to cause them **pain** as part of a regimen of self-mortification. Female ascetics drastically renounce their identity as women

34

with its child-bearing and household chores by rejecting marriage. Ascetic women also reject their social status by wearing coarse **clothing** and refusing all power of sexual attraction by means of their clothing, downcast gaze, and eating habits that make their bodies less feminine in appearance. These types of extreme behavior are practiced by some in all Christian denominations, but the larger Roman Catholic Church also builds ascetic practices into its faith for everyone, with the observation of fasting during Lent and refraining from eating meat on Friday.

Asceticism possesses a close relationship to **culture**. According to Harpham, asceticism forms the ground of culture, which allows for communication within culture. Because self-denial is necessary for a person to live in a culture, asceticism assists social integration and functioning. Asceticism still remains ambivalent because it creates polarities between culture and what is anti-culture or asceticism. By means of self-denial, a person integrates into a cultural system that makes communication possible, empowers a person, and equips a person for productive living. Thus asceticism possesses wider implications beyond religion.

Within the religious sphere, an essential feature of asceticism is its repetitive nature. By means of performing asceticism, the ascetic becomes a different person living in a different religious culture. Moreover, the ascetic creates an alternative culture, which becomes true for its creators, by means of his/her learned and repeated behavior. In addition to creating something new, asceticism enables a person to function within this new culture, gives the ascetic a method of translating theoretical and strategic concepts into patterns of behavior, transforms perception of the world, and provides the means for newly discovered knowledge and understanding to be re-incorporated into a new world.

Further reading: Brown (1988); Bynum (1987); Clark (1986); Cort (2001); Eliade (1969); Fischer (1979); Harpham (1987); Wimbush and Valantasis (1995)

ATHEISM

A conviction that there is no **God** or that the existence of an absolute divine being cannot be proven. Atheism is distinguished from agnosticism, a profession of uncertainty or suspension of **belief** about the existence of God. Atheism is often assumed to be a modern notion, but there is evidence of it in ancient Jewish religion (Ps. 14.1) and Indian Vedic

BELIEF

religion in the Rig Veda (2.12; 8.89). According to the historical Buddha, gods are part of the world of appearance, are not all-powerful, are impermanent, and are reborn just like humans, which leads some scholars to characterize the Buddha as an atheist. The Buddha teaches that no god can save a person from the world of **suffering** because **liberation** must be achieved by a person's own efforts.

Modern atheism is given impetus by the German philosopher Ludwig Feuerbach (1804–1872) who influences Karl Marx (1818–1883), German social and political theorist and father of Communism. Using the dialectic of his philosophical mentor Hegel, Feuerbach argues that God is a projection of humanity's own self-alienation. By **worshiping** God, humans are actually worshiping themselves. The best example is Jesus, a man worshiped as a God.

Some postmodern thinkers embrace the atheist position with their proclamation that God is dead. Mark C. Taylor is an excellent example because he thinks that the **death** of God results in the self-devaluation of the highest values. Criticizing what he calls humanistic atheists for lacking intellectual courage, Taylor asserts that the death of God also signals demise of the **self**. In other words, if God is dead the self must also be dead because the self needs something with which to relate in order to find its identity and meaning. Taylor's radical sense of the death of God involves death becoming the absolute master because God is experienced as death itself.

Further reading: Feuerbach (1967); Taylor (1984)

BELIEF

From indigenous to international religions, beliefs are convictions, assertions, and habitually accepted unquestioning viewpoints that define a religious culture's **worldview**, its way of life, its social structure, the nature of human existence and its problems, the solution to the problems of life, and an often concise statement of the fundamental agreed upon religious claims. Statements of belief unite a people and differentiate them from outsiders. From a cross-cultural perspective, beliefs can prove to be very durable over a long period of time. This does not imply that beliefs are static once they are established because they continue to be altered and refined according to historical circumstances by religious thinkers.

Beliefs can be accepted within an oral culture and transmitted verbally from generation to another, or beliefs can be transmitted by written documents. Sometimes, beliefs are partially embodied in **myths** and **rituals** of a people. The Four Noble Truths and Eightfold Path of the Buddha are examples of the belief system of formative Buddhism. The Four Noble Truths summarize the fundamental problem of life and its solution: (1) all life is **suffering**; (2) suffering is due to ignorant craving; (3) the solution is the attainment of nirvāṇa; (4) there is a the path to achieve **liberation**. The Eightfold Path combines wisdom (right view and thought), moral action (right speech, behavior, and livelihood), and **meditation** (right effort, mindfulness, and concentration). In comparison to the basic message of the Buddha, the Hindu religious tradition does not have anything comparable because Hindus tend to be tolerant about beliefs, whereas they are traditionally not as lenient when it comes to behavior, which suggests that Hinduism is not as much an **orthodoxy** as it is an orthopraxis.

Muslims make a basic distinction between things to be believed (*īmān*) and things to be done in rites (*dīn*). Beliefs are summarized by the Five Pillars of Islam: (1) confession of **faith**; (2) **prayer** five times a day; (3) almsgiving; (4) fasting during the holy month of Ramadan from sunrise to sunset; and (5) **pilgrimage** (*hajj*) to Mecca at least once during a lifetime for a believer. These fundamental tenets of the Islamic faith are not only the basic requirements for all Muslims, but they also tend to bind together the **community**, reinforce the collective sense of being a Muslim, impose a pattern of discipline, and symbolically express unity.

Similar to Buddhism and Islam, Christianity summarizes its basic beliefs in creeds, a word that is derived from the Latin term *credo*, "I believe." The Apostles' Creed is used in the West as a fundamental statement of faith that recognizes a creator God, an only son of **God** named Jesus Christ, born to a virgin, the **suffering**, crucifixion, **death**, burial, and resurrection on the third day after death. Jesus ascends to **heaven** where he sits at the right hand of God. At the end time, Jesus will return to **earth** to **judge** the living and dead. The creed concludes with a statement of other beliefs in the Holy Spirit, the holy Catholic Church, the communion of **saints**, forgiveness of sins, resurrection of the **body**, and everlasting life. An expansion of this basic confession of beliefs is provided by the Nicene Creed, a creed accepted by the eastern branch of Christianity around the fifth century and the western Roman Catholic tradition in 1014.

Further reading: Pelikan (1971, 2003)

BLOOD

In biological terms, blood carries nutrients and oxygen to the cells of the bodies of animals, but it also carries symbolic significance within the context of religion. Within Christianity, the blood of Christ, a sacrificial lamb, saves sinners from eternal damnation. In the Jewish context, shed or menstrual blood is considered defiling and drinking blood is **taboo**. Blood is central to the Jewish **covenant** with **God** in the form of sacrifice and circumcision (Exod. 24.8). In addition to its communal bonding effect in Judaism, blood operates as a protective power as in the narrative of protecting homes from the coming plague by marking them with blood (Exod. 13.7–13), as a purifying agent for a house infected with mold, or as an application to those suffering from leprosy, likened to a mold growing on a person (Lev. 14). Among the ancient Hittites, blood is also used as a **purifying** agent to purify a temple or a divine **image**. Similar restrictions and ambiguous attitudes related to blood are evident in Islam and Hinduism.

Although blood is considered **polluting** in Hinduism, it is also recognized as the sap of life, and plays an important role in **worship** of the **goddess** Kālī, who delights in bloody sacrifices to her. Kālī is constantly described as drinking blood flowing from decapitated heads of humans, demons, or animal victims, whose blood turns into an immortal nectar. Her close association with blood suggests that she is related to strength, vigor, and life. Not only does she give life, but the goddess demands a continuous flow of fresh blood as sustenance to sustain her creative efforts.

In classical Chinese religion, blood is considered dirty, polluting, and powerful. Menstrual blood is considered unclean and a fluid that the female body does not need. By coming into contact with such blood, a person is barred from worshiping the gods. From another perspective, menstrual blood is considered powerful because it creates babies. Another power possessed by blood is its ability to exorcise **evil spirits**. Moreover, flowing blood is associated with **power**, as evident in a report by De Groot describing blood spurting from the bodies of decapitated criminals near Amoy, China, which is collected and used for life-strengthening medicines.

Along with **death**, blood is a source of **pollution** in the Shinto religion, an indigenous religion of Japan. A contaminated person must undergo **ritual** isolation for a stated period of time and even longer when intending to approach a shrine. Any violation incurs the danger of a sudden punishment from the offended deity in the form of sickness, **madness**, accident, or **fire**.

These various examples enable one to understand that the significance and meaning of blood changes, depending on the context within a particular religion and can appear to be contradictory. Blood is associated with both life and death, **sacred** and profane, **pure** and impure distinctions. Blood is a dangerous fluid associated with **pain**, procreation, and life. It also plays significant roles in **rites of passage** and **sacrifice**.

Further reading: Bettelheim (1962); De Groot (1969); Eliade (1958); Roux (1988)

BODY

The human body is conceived in a multitude of ways by diverse religious traditions. Hindus view it as a vehicle for the soul, as illusory, and as something that must be controlled in order to make spiritual progress, whereas Buddhists depict it as a trap or a heap of rubbish. The Zen master Dōgen refers, however, to the human body as a means of attaining **liberation**. Hindu and Buddhist forms of Tantra have envisioned the human body as a microcosm of a larger macrocosmic **reality**. Christians view the body in a variety of ways, from that made in the image of **God** to serving as a prison for the **soul**.

In many religious traditions, the body is an entity always changing within the flux of **time** from that of infant, toddler, adolescent, adult, to old person. This process comes to an end with the **death** of the body. The human body also performs certain necessary tasks such as working, running, walking, eating, sleeping, and performing **ritual** tasks. Humans encounter other beings within the world as embodied entities. The human body is, moreover, associated with polluting activities such as urinating, defecating, spitting, crying, sexual intercourse, or menstruation, which in many religions are considered sources of impurity. At its margins, the body discharges secretions such as urine, feces, semen, menses, saliva, phlegm, tears, skin, and sweat. These types of impurities involve necessary social precautions to avoid **polluting** others or of being polluted oneself. Therefore, the integrity of the human body is constantly under threat by the continual inflow and outflow of impurities. The human body is both resilient and fragile because, although it enables us to do creative physical acts, such as jumping, running, or throwing, it is easily injured, maimed, or destroyed. In order to protect the body, we clothe it, wash it, feed it, and give it medicine when ill.

The body is an entity created by a biological process of sex, genetic heritance, and nurturing. The human body is rather malleable because it can be trained to execute a wide variety of tasks from athletic to religious. Although the body is something given to us, it is not unusual to modify it for specific purposes, such as guarding the royal harem with eunuchs in religious cultures such as Indian, Chinese, and Islamic. It is also common for the body to be modified by religious practices, such as tonsure, circumcision, tattooing, scarring, fasting, or flagellation. The religious motivation behind these forms of bodily modification differs depending on the religious cultural context, with some of these bodily modifications accompanying **rites of passage**, atonement for transgressions, or attempts to tame and control the body.

As embodied beings within the world, humans experience **sexual** drives that a person can follow, feel guilty about, or attempt to control by means of **ascetic** practices such as **celibacy** and/or **meditation**. These sexual drives within an embodied condition suggest that the body is a sensitive substance with the ability to produce both **pain** and pleasure. Other than being a sensitive substance, the human body is a visible, tangible object in **space** and **time**. A person can touch their body, touch other bodies, or be touched by other bodies. The same is true of the senses of smell, taste, hearing, and **perception**.

The human body can transform itself into a sign that functions in a self-referential manner and as a referent for **others** by means of its ability to give itself meaning. When the human body becomes a **symbol** it can serve as a bridge connecting **nature** and **culture**. Functioning as a sign or symbol, the body can become an ambivalent entity from a cross-cultural perspective. Nonetheless, the body possesses the potential to embody and reveal cultural values and attitudes. In the Middle East and India, the body is hierarchically ordered, which makes a person's feet the lowest part of the body. To kick another person or strike them with a shoe or sandal is considered an insult and means of polluting another person. In Muslim **prayer**, a believer's forehead, which is considered the noblest part of a person, comes into contact with the ground in a powerful symbolic action of submission to **God**.

In addition to functioning as a sign or symbol, the body is simply flesh, which expresses its lustful nature, making the body threatening and dangerous unless it is controlled and regulated by social processes. Although the body is biologically given, it is still the result of numerous social and cultural practices, behaviors, and discourses that operate in concert to construct the body as a social artifact. This scenario suggests that the body is both a biological **gift** and socially constructed. **Society** and **culture** informs a people what they can and cannot do with their bodies by setting boundaries and giving a proper cultural image of the body.

Thinkers from diverse fields have offered their insights into the human body. The French philosopher Maurice Merleau-Ponty, for instance, discusses human bodies as organisms capable of **perception**. According to Merleau-Ponty, the human body and the perceived world form a single system of intentional relations that form correlations, implying that to experience the body is to perceive the world and vice versa, rendering the body and the world into an inseparable, internal relation. Mary Douglas, a British anthropologist, views the body as a **metaphor** for **reality** and a symbolic system depicting **society**. Michel Foucault, a French poststructural thinker, concentrates his focus on the body as a product of a relationship between **power** and **knowledge**. The philosophers George Lakoff and Mark Johnson point out the role that the body plays within mental conceptualization, which is only possible through the body.

Postmodern thinkers present a different slant on the body. Jacques Derrida claims that the body is not one's own because one's relationship to one's body does not mean that a person is the body or that he/she possess it in any true sense. A person's body is more akin to a deprivation because their body is not merely something that they do not have, but it is actually something that has been stolen from that person by the **other**. In contrast to Derrida, Emmanuel Levinas conceives of the lived body as a crossroad of physical forces.

Likewise, the postmodern philosophical team of Deleuze and Guattari view the body as a complex interplay of social and symbolic forces, which excludes its being a substance, an essence, a medium, or a thing, suggesting that the body is involved in a multiplicity of elements within a number of sign systems. Moreover, all bodies are causes in the sense of being causes in relation to each other and for each other, although the relationship between them is not be construed as a cause and effect relation. Invoking French artist Antonin Artaud's concept of a body without organs, Deleuze and Guattari want to demonstrate its relationship with the constant flows or particles of foreign bodies. The body without organs lacks depth or internal organization, and is more akin to a flow of forces on a surface of intensities. The egg-like appearance and smooth surface of the body without organs represents its exterior prior to being stratified, organized, regulated, and hierarchized by being inscribed by such items as race, **culture**, and deities. Standing against organization, regulation, and the tendency to hierarchize it, the body without organs forms a boundary or limit that resists such negative tendencies.

Prior to these Western thinkers, the Indian religious thinker Rāmānuja defines the body as a mode of the **self**, implying that it is dependent on the self and cannot exist apart from that which supports it. Although subordinate to the self, the body sustains the self and provides it with the means for its release, whereas the self animates, guides, and supports the body. The basic difference between the self and body is that the former is eternal and the latter is perishable. Moreover, the body and self, for Rāmānuja, are modes of God and constitute the body of God, who animates and sustains the body and self.

In spite of the tendency during the formative development of Buddhism to view the body as impermanent, impure, and foul, another positive view of the body is offered within the Buddhist tradition in medieval Japan by the Zen master Dōgen, who views the body in a non-dualistic way, enabling him to equate the body with items of nature, such as trees, grass, wind, rain, water, and **fire**. Humans are separated from the world by their bodies. In fact, no one can be absolutely certain where one's body ends and where precisely the world begins, and vice versa. Dōgen does not reject the body, but rather he says that we quest with our bodies, and we attain **liberation** with our bodies. Moreover, consciousness and the body penetrate each other and are inextricably interwoven, with the body forming the ground for the evolving of consciousness. The body is also identical to time and the Buddha-nature.

Further reading: Deleuze and Guattari (1983, 1988); Derrida (1978); Dōgon (2007); Douglas (1966); Foucault (1978); Lakoff and Johnson (1999); Levinas (1998); Merleau-Ponty (1962); Rāmānuja (1971); Shilling (2005)

CELIBACY

As a practice of refraining from **sexual** relations, celibacy can be found cross-culturally in religious traditions. From a Western context, celibacy originates from the Latin term *caelebs*, which means "alone or single." The Latin meaning is a bit misleading because it is possible to be celibate and live in a **community** with other celibates, although uniformly of the same **gender**. In Hinduism, celibacy is called *brahmacarya*, which is practiced by ascetics and students (*brahmacārin*) studying the sacred literature. Since the terms celibacy and student come from the same Sanskrit root, this suggests that celibacy is practically synonymous with being a student. A vow of celibacy is essential for a Buddhist monk or nun because its practice is part of a regimen to control and conquer sensual desire by refraining from heterosexual, homosexual, or lesbian relationships, whereas engaging in sexual relations increases a person's desires, which Buddhists recognize as self-defeating. Other religious traditions, such as Judaism, Islam, Chinese religions with the exception of Buddhism, and indigenous traditions, tend to reject celibacy, although it is possible to find celibacy practiced at specific times and under certain circumstances within these traditions.

On the surface, celibacy seems to be a rather simple notion in the sense that a person takes a vow or merely personally intends to practice it outside of an institutional context. It is actually complex because of its interconnection with the **worldview**, divine models, social values, **gender** relations, ethical implications, religious roles or offices, understanding of the physical **body**, and its practitioner's connection to spiritual and political **power**. In ancient Greece and Rome, citizens are expected to reproduce, while those choosing to remain unmarried are penalized by the government. By virtue of their religious office, the Vestal Virgins are granted an exemption. The emphasis on reproducing in classical culture hides a conviction that sexual pleasure is potentially dangerous and antisocial. Sexual orgasm is compared to a minor seizure of epilepsy and the loss of a person's vital spirit. Greek and Roman thinkers advocate self-control and reason along with reproduction. Judaism also emphasizes marriage and reproduction because they are normal and a divine ordinance, although exceptions can be discovered, with celibacy forced by the menstrual cycle of a wife, and the celibacy of **prophets**, and groups such as the Essences, a communal Jewish sect active during the war of 66–70 CE when the Second Temple is destroyed by the Romans.

Celibacy can contribute to the creation of an exalted status and play a role in the construction of a person's identity. Jesus and the Buddha are two historical religious figures who are celibate during their teaching careers, and both of them become models for others to imitate. Based on textual evidence, Jesus and the Buddha are charismatic figures. It is possible to grasp their charisma as grounded in their celibacy, which points to their other-worldly focus, although their messages are very different.

Celibacy can also represent a negotiation regarding social values and cultural attitudes. The Protestant reformer Martin Luther denounces celibacy because it lacks scriptural grounds, sets clergy apart from the laity, and can become a substitute for **faith** itself. Within the context of Islam, the prophet Muhammad serves as a model for married life. In fact, the Qur'an (57.27) denounces celibacy as a human invention and not a practice sanctioned by **God**. The **mystical** Sufi movement debates the merits of celibacy and some Sufis adopt celibacy as a form of social protest. In sharp contrast to Protestant Christianity and Islam, celibacy fits neatly into the social and cultural values of the Jain community, where there is a conviction that celibacy protects the **soul** from the harm associated with **sexual** activity. Jains believe that the act of sexual intercourse destroys numerous single-sense creatures believed to dwell in the generative organs of humans. Therefore, the Jains also believe that there is a direct connection between celibacy and **non-violence** (*ahiṃsā*), a paramount virtue among the adherents. Indigenous cultures such as Native American Indians reject celibacy in favor of stressing sexuality because of its role in the survival and perpetuation of these societies. It is, however, possible to discern episodic instances of its practice, such as the game called *anetsā* among the Cherokee and certain ritual occasions such as a vision quest among the Plains Indians.

In some religious traditions, it is possible to renounce sexual relations and gain sacred status and economic support from **society**. Buddhist monks and nuns take vows of celibacy that enable them to become members of a fraternity of fellow monks and nuns. This entitles them to support by the local community in terms of shelter, food, clothing, and medicine. In turn, these celibates share the teachings of the Buddha and participate in particular ceremonies, such as funerals, for the benefit of the people. A Catholic priest or monk takes a vow of celibacy, and receives economic support by the laity and the institution for which they perform religious services.

Celibacy represents an invisible mark on the human **body**, an inscription that is often accompanied by distinctive types of **clothing** to differentiate the celibate from ordinary people. The robes of Buddhist monks and nuns, the attire of Catholic priests, monks, and nuns, the rags and natural material worn by some Hindu ascetics, the nakedness of Jain renouncers and Hindu ascetics are indicative of a special status that is also often associated with celibacy.

In many religious traditions, celibacy reflects a concern for maintaining purity and thus holiness, which represents order, unity, and perfection with respect to a person. Thus celibacy can be grasped as part of a process of becoming holy, complete, perfect, and clean. In classical Hinduism, sexual relations are considered polluting, and any kind of **pollution** is considered dangerous.

The practice of celibacy is frequently associated with the acquisition of **power** in such religious traditions as Hinduism and Buddhism, whereas the loss of **power** is connected to the resumption of sexual relations. The *Jātaka* tales, or stories of the former lives of the historical Buddha, contain a narrative about the Buddha as a powerful ascetic with the ability to fly because of his assiduous practice of arduous **asceticism**. Spying the queen sunbathing naked in a courtyard, he submits to his lust and engages in sexual congress with the queen, and he then discovers after his tryst that he has lost all of his powers. Besides the ability to fly, ascetics, monks, and yogis are known to acquire other powers: the ability to read other minds, to see into the future, to witness past lives, to lift heavy objects, to endure extreme pain, and other forms.

Further reading: Olson (2008)

CHAOS

In various religious traditions, chaos is described in negative terms: as an immaterial mass, unlike anything within the world, or as something indefinable that cannot be explained by anyone. It is akin to the negation of the present, existing world. Among the ancient Egyptians, chaos exists before the sky and **earth** and prior to humans and **death**. The Egyptians envision original creation as a shaping of a formless material – chaos – into an ordered world. Prior to creation, there is a boundless ocean called Nun, a dark, watery abyss, which represents the primordial substance out of which the world would be formed by a demiurge, who is submerged within the chaos and preceded any **gods**. If the original chaos is an undifferentiated, unitary state, it is the demiurge that embodies the process of differentiation. In later Egyptian history, the demiurge is identified with Ra, the sun god, or Ptah, the earth god.

Among the ancient Mesopotamians and Indians, it is possible to find accounts of an original creation returning to chaos and being restored by a heroic deity. In Mesopotamia, this figure is identified as Ninurta, and he defeats Anzu to restore the world. In the ancient Vedic myth of India, it is the heroic deity Indra who is recruited by the gods to defeat Vritra, a cosmic serpent who envelopes the entire world. Drinking three vats of *soma,* a powerful hallucinogen liquid, for strength, Indra split open the serpents head releasing the cosmic waters. Thereafter, Indra assumes leadership of the divine pantheon as a reward, which is agreed to prior to his exploits with the other gods, for his heroic deed.

Further reading: Anderson (1967); Eliade (1965)

CHURCH

This concept is of Christian origin and use, originally meaning "assembling together." The church is a type of religious society that evolves

45

from a charismatic leader and a circle of disciples forming a brotherhood. At the end of the period of brotherhood, there is a reorganization and the introduction of discipline and development of a new type of organization – an ecclesiastical body – called the church. The church refers historically to the believers and followers of Jesus Christ. This **community** is composed of believers representing a separate group. A church is usually an open, inclusive, and eventually a bureaucratic organization that holds and often promotes the values of the larger society in which it exists.

The early Christian tradition utilizes enduring **metaphors** to express the meaning of the church for them by imaging the church as a Mater Ecclesia, as the apostle Paul does in Galatians (4.21–31) by discussing the universal mother nourishing her children. And Jesus (Matt. 23.37) refers to the holy city of Jerusalem in maternal terms. The church is called the bride of Christ (Rev. 19.7; Rom. 7.4; Eph. 5.23; 2 Cor. 11.2–4), and in Galatians (4.21–31) Paul refers to the church as a second Eve. With respect to this nuptial symbolism, the Christian church father Irenaeus (c. 140–c. 200) describes Christ as the divine bridegroom standing in a marital relationship with his bride the church, whereas Tertullian (c. 160–c. 225) emphasizes the virginity of the church without blemishes, calls her a virgin free from the stain of fornication, and the Second Eve – mother of the living. Another early Christian thinker, Clement of Alexandria (150–220), agrees that the church is both virgin and mother, but he adds that her baptized converts become her children and she nurses them with holy milk. The bridal **metaphor** can also be found in the work of Origen (185–253) when he states that the church is constituted by those who are mystically united with the Logos (Word) in a spiritual marriage. In the bridal chamber, the **soul** is joined, according to Origen, to the Logos, and it experiences spiritual intercourse. Augustine (354–430), bishop of Hippo in North Africa, continues the bride metaphorical **language** in which the bride is joined to the bridegroom in the flesh, making the nuptial union that of word and flesh. Whatever the metaphors used to describe the church, it is believed to prefigure and prepare members for a complete transformation of the entire social and historical order into one inclusive **society** under **God**.

The fully developed church defines **doctrine**, forms rules of **faith** or creed, standardizes forms of **worship**, and establishes a constitution to govern it. With the establishment of the mature church, the prior oral tradition is written down to preserve it and traditions of the religion are accepted. Membership in a church is the result of an individual's birth. The authority of the church is hierarchically constructed and centralized, and its clergy is distinguished from the laity. The church evolves by compromising with the secular world by, for instance, accepting the prevailing social and political structure through supporting the existing **socio-political** powers during peace and war.

Three types of churches can be identified: universal, ecclesia, and class church or denomination. The universal church combines both church and **sect** tendencies by its inclusive nature and its ability to integrate members of society and to satisfy the needs of individuals. The Roman Catholic Church of the thirteenth century is a good example of this type. The ecclesia is also inclusive, but it is less successful in incorporating the **sect** tendencies in comparison to the universal church. It is, however, more successful in reinforcing the existing pattern of social integration than in fulfilling personal function of religion. It can be grasped as the universal church in a state of rigidification, much as established national churches. The class church or denomination is less successful in achieving universality than the ecclesia because it tends to minimize the sectarian tendency to criticize or withdraw from the social order, and it is limited by class, race, and sometimes regional boundaries.

Further reading: Wilson (1982); Yinger (1970)

CLOTHING

The wearing of garments functions to cover the body, to provide protection from the weather, to make a socio-economic statement (by donning expensive gowns or suits), to indicate type of employment, acceptance or non-acceptance of social norms, and for participation in types of sport. Special clothing is worn to mark special occasions such as graduations, or it is used to distinguish a lay person from someone holding a religious position. Besides these practical uses, clothing also operates to signify certain responsibilities, duties, or **power** possessed when wearing particular garments. This function of clothing implies that it must be at least partially visible to convey its intended message. Wearing something as simple as a clerical collar or a nun's habit conveys a spiritual commitment and status by the wearer to others. Even within a particular religious organization, clothing distinguishes upper level office holders from others. In China and Japan, distinguished Buddhist monks are given purple robes as a visible symbol of their exalted status within the monastic **community**. Certain kinds of vestments in Roman Catholicism, for instance, are donned for the performance of rituals and thus could be called ritual clothing that is only worn for the performance of specific rites of the church.

Special religious clothing is not always visible. The Hebrew Bible refers to an injunction to wear fringed garments (Num. 15.37–40). God and Moses instruct Aaron and his sons to wear "holy garments" or "linen breeches" (Exod. 28.1, 42). Jewish men don a four-cornered cloth (*tallit*) with fringes around their shoulders when praying. The fringes are intended to help a Jew remember the commandments of God, whereas Assyrians and Babylonians believe that wearing garments with fringes possess talismanic **power**. Mormons wear a garment of the holy priesthood that must touch the body throughout their lives and not simply for ritual occasions. This garment is worn beneath a person's underwear and is thus not visible to others, whereas the aprons worn by Freemasons are visible and often elaborately decorated, recalling for them the protective garb of builders and the leaves and skins worn by Adam and Eve after leaving paradise, symbolizing innocence, **truth**, integrity, and **purity**.

In India throughout its history, ascetic groups wear garments made of grass, tree bark, owl feathers, deerskins, and hair. Some Śaiva ascetics go completely naked as do Jain monks, especially those of the Digambara (wind clad) sect. The nakedness of these ascetics is indicative of their detachment from and renunciation of the world. In contrast, the Buddha does not advocate nakedness, and texts refer to yellow or ochre colored robes. During the initial two decades of the movement, Buddhists wear discarded rags that they sew together. When robes are donated to monks they are cut up and sown together probably to reduce their value. The robes of Buddhist monks are not considered a form of penance, as are the coarse garments of some Christian monks that irritate their skin. The wardrobe of a Buddhist monk consists of three robes: an outer cloak, an inner robber worn as a toga, and a final robe used as underclothing. Although the robes can be made of a number of fabrics, Buddhist monks are forbidden to decorate the robes with gold or silver trim or to dye the robes with a distinctive color. Monks also use a strip of cloth that functions as a belt intended to keep their undergarment from falling. Besides the robes, Buddhist monks are allowed to wear sandals made from a single strand of rope in public but not in the monastery. Buddhist attire results in a common appearance for all monks and stresses equality among members.

Clothing need not simply distinguish between the laity and religious professionals. There are instances when members of a religious movement don distinctive clothing in order to call attention to their religious convictions. For instance, in India, the members of the Rāmnāmi Samāj, which consists mostly of Untouchables, wear unconventional clothing. While other Untouchables attempt to blend into the Indian social fabric, this group wears long caps and shawls, tall peacock feather hats, and sometimes a set of ankle bells. Some sect members don a ritual shawl that consists of thick white cotton cloth covered with the name of their deity Rāma. The shawl is usually worn when chanting the name of their **god**.

Clothing just as unusual is worn by **shamans** in central Asia. The shaman's costume includes a cap, a caftan hung with iron disks and figures signifying mythical animals, a mask, a kerchief with which to cover his eyes in order to enter the spirit world by his own inner light, and an iron or copper pectoral. A drum is also often an essential part of the costume. The shaman communicates with spirits of the other world, and aspects of his clothing testify to it.

Further reading: Lamb (2002); Storm (1987); Tarlo (1996)

COMIC

The foundation of the comic is seriousness, a precondition, without which the comic would be reduced to cynical contempt. The comic lies on the boundary between the **sacred** and profane, the rational and irrational, **faith** and despair, and cosmos and chaos. The comic keeps faith from leading to despair and dogmatism. Hence faith needs the comic to avoid falling into something superficial, empty, or helpless.

The comic and the sacred mutually benefit from their relationship because without each other they are prey to distortion. The comic apart from the sacred can, for instance, become irresponsible, while the sacred apart from the comic may become inhuman. The comic and its accompanying humor enable a person to transcend the tension inherent between the sacred and the profane, and to capture a state in which categories, tools of order and irrationality, do not exist. The comic moves within the freedom of irrationality, of suspended order, and nonsense. Therefore, the comic represents a **chaos** of infinite potentiality and creative possibility.

The comic is both playful and innocent, and without it human beings become inhuman. A human being's awkwardness within the world is comical as well as serious and tragic. The comic suggests that to be truly human one must be able to laugh at oneself and one's situation. The comic and laughter are not simply gaiety, but they rather manifest a person's struggle against hopelessness and despair. The comic celebrates life by mocking its absurdities. Thus, when the comic and humor exist there is still hope.

The comic possesses the ability to collapse cultural categories. By confounding and confusing social distinctions, the comic suggests that the socially lowly are valuable, advocating that the comic is also more equalitarian, inclusive, and empathetic. The comic perspective is socially necessary in order for humans to avoid tragedy, to become free, and magnanimous.

Among Native American Indians of North America, the clown and trickster personify figures who are embodiments of the comic. The clown is a figure of self-contradiction, manifests contempt for all status, functions as an imposter, breaks taboos, receives punishment for his transgressions, and assumes the role of a disorderly figure. These general characteristics of a clown are manifested by the clown's undignified, unreasonable, grotesque and even idiotic behavior, such as the Pueblo clowns that burlesque sacred dancers and lampoon holy figures, Hopi clowns that dress like women and perform obscene stunts in public, Zuni clowns that eat refuse, or Hopi clowns that drink gallons of urine.

In addition to these major characteristics of the clown, there is a close relationship between them and **healing** because they are believed to possess magical medicine among Native Americans. The clowns acquire their healing **powers** by violating a **taboo**. Within Native American Indian religions, clowns grant success in hunting and war, and give luck in gambling, love, happiness, and prosperity. From another perspective, clowns are feared because they can inflict disease and cause **suffering**, but they also make people laugh and enable them to escape everyday problems for a time.

In contrast to the clown, the trickster is often depicted in the folklore of indigenous religions as a wandering vagabond, who can assume human or animal forms. The animal form suggests the trickster's clever and wily traits. Whatever forms he assumes, the trickster is an individualist who survives by means of his personal cunning and prowess, although he can also be ignorant and foolish. Thus it is not unusual to find him outwitting others and himself at the same time, scenarios that unfold within the context of a world of games.

The basic metaphor for the life of the trickster is the trick, which means that tricking and being tricked are inevitable features of the struggle to survive. Since the world is full of tricks and life plays tricks on us, it is necessary for the trickster to rely on his own abilities to endure in the trickiness of life. Due in part to the nature of the world and his own nature, the trickster does not have a clearly defined social status and wanders from one misadventure to another, which are episodes devoid of logic or dramatic connection. By grabbing the necessities of life and meeting the challenges of existence by making them into a game, these misadventures are about survival and defending what one gains by trickery.

Ananse, a spider, is an example of an African trickster among the Ashanti. This ambiguous figure is someone who fools others and is a fool himself, as when he steals some beans, hides them under his hat, burns his head, and is rendered bald. In other tales, he is depicted as subtle and gross, wily and stupid, a schemer and thief, and a lecher and an ingrate. And yet, the Ashanti think that he is wonderful because without him life would be boring. Even though Ananse spreads cultural forces, agriculture, and human **society**, he also is responsible for jealously, an anti-social force. In a risqué **narrative**, Ananse tricks Akwasi (the jealous one), an anti-social, sterile husband of Aso, with whom Ananse successfully schemes to have sexual relations.

The trickster is also a popular religious figure among Native American Indians, such as the Tricky One of the Winnebago, the spider Inktomi of the Sioux, and the Old Man (Napi) of the Blackfoot. The Winnebago figure serves as a mediator between human beings and the gods, gives culture to humans, creates **language**, communicates with animals, is responsible for forms and colors, and plays tricks. The Winnebago trickster can transform himself into any shape, as in the narrative when he becomes a woman, marries the chief's son, and gives birth to three children. He strangely treats his own body as something foreign, as when he causes his hands to fight each other, juggles his eyes and goes blind when he throws them too high into a tree, and he is described as carrying his penis in a box that he carries on his back.

The narrative pattern of the trickster combines order and disorder, foolishness and wisdom, history and timelessness, which are indicative of his ambiguous nature. The trickster is a riddle, who heals the **memory** of people and liberates their imagination. His comedic actions are life-affirming, and he points to the sacredness and worth of life. The trickster's comedic actions suggest that humans are rooted in the world, but he also indicates that it is possible to win **liberation**. To read the often humorous trickster narratives is to witness an oxymoronic imagination at **play** and to see that life is conceived to be a challenge, which the trickster transforms into a game.

Further reading: Berger (1997); Handelman (1981); Hyers (1969, 1981); Hynes and Doty (1993); Mandel (1970); Markarius (1970); Morreall (1983); Opler (1965); Parsons and Beads (1934); Radin (1956); Ricketts (1966); Titiev (1972); Zucker (1967)

COMMUNITY

Within the larger **society**, a community is a group of people united in their **beliefs**, practices, and **experiences** that motivates them to cooperate and work together for the attainment of social and religious goals. A particular community is not only a gathering of individuals, but it is also an ideal constructed in the minds of its members. Communities operate to socialize their members by encouraging certain types of behavior. When members become socialized they help to foster stability and a sense of well-being. By differentiating themselves from others, a community can create tensions with outsiders that could theoretically lead to conflict. Not only do communities possess a social dimension, they also have a historical aspect that extends through time and across generations of members. In contrast to other kinds of social groups, communities are distinct because of the spiritual quality of their beliefs, practices, and experiences. By implementing social agendas and shaping the behavior of its members, communities can exert **power** in the larger social world for change, stability, or conflict.

The community in Islam is called the *umma* (Arabic for people), which historically begins in Medina after the migration (*hijra*) from Mecca with the so-called believers. During this formative period of Islam, immigrants and their Medinan Muslim hosts called helpers (*Ansar*) form a unique brotherhood under the leadership of Muhammad. Even the worldwide community of Islam is called *umma* and an individual can enter by reciting the confession of faith (*shahada*). This community shares beliefs, ceremonies, and laws, and accepts the Qur'an as a revelation from **God**. In contrast to the pre-Arabian tribal and polytheistic **cultures** against which they react and define themselves, Muslim practices, such as **prayer**, almsgiving, fasting, and **pilgrimage**, unite them into a religious community.

In contrast to formative Islam, Buddhism promotes two communities: a lay community and the Saṃgha (assembly or gathering) of monks and nuns. It is the duty of the lay community to provide for the welfare of the monks and nuns, whereas monks and nuns dispense teachings and ceremonial services for the laity. Although the Saṃgha originally includes the laity, the two communities are bound together ideally by mutual giving. Two essential features of the Buddhist monastic community are prominent: no religious leader is theoretically necessary and the rules of the monastic community are intended to guide it. The rules also form the bond between monks creating a brotherhood. The monastic community is one of the three jewels (*triratna*) of the Buddha with which everyone is encouraged to seek refuge. The irony of the Buddhist monastic community is that a monk must renounce society before becoming a monk, and he then becomes dependent upon it for his necessities. During the formative period of Christianity, the evangelist Luke defines the early Christian community in Acts (2.42) as a fellowship (*koinōnia*) grounded in the members' relationship to Jesus Christ, acceptance of the apostle's message, sharing communal meals (eucharist), and common prayer. Similar notions of a Christian community are evident in the letters of Paul and Johannine literature. Later Christianity witnesses the development of various monastic orders – Benedictines, Franciscans, Dominicans, Jesuits and others – representing new kinds of religious communities within the overarching structure of the Roman Catholic Church.

In India, Hinduism is a collection of diverse communities that are differentiated by caste affiliation, religious sect, temple association, village identity, or ethnic identity. Often community identities coalesce around a religious figure or teaching, and they form *sampradāyas* (**sects**). An excellent example is the Bengali saint Caitanya and his inspired Gaudiya Vaishnava Sampradāya, who worship the deity Krishna. More historically recent examples of Hindu communities are the so-called *samāj* (**society**, tradition); for instance, the reform movements of the Brahmo Samāj and Ārya Samāj in the nineteenth century.

Further reading: Olson (2005, 2008); Porterfield (1998); Wach (1944)

COMPARATIVE RELIGION

Comparative religion is a subfield of Religious Studies concerned with comparing one religious tradition with another with respect to **belief** systems, **myths**, **rituals**, practices, artistic activities, social aspects, and **theologies**. The discipline of comparative religion originates in the West during a period of colonialism and its accompanying convictions about cultural superiority, adherence to the fundamental presupposition about the superiority of Christianity, and embrace of the theory of evolution, which induces scholars to look for patterns of religious evolution. This threefold context falls into disfavor in more recent times because it obstructs genuine understanding of a religious tradition other than the one in which the scholar operates. With their faith in science, some scholars also want to expose the magical and superstitious aspects of Christianity that should be replaced by empirical and rational science.

Even though it is possible to find some antecedents of comparative religion in the West, it basically erupts during the nineteenth century within the field of anthropology, with figures such as Edward B. Tylor (1832–1917) and Sir James George Frazer (1854–1941). Tylor devises a preconceived plan of human evolution: savage or hunter-gatherer; barbaric stage, characterized by domestication of animals and plants; and civilized stage, which begins with the art of writing. According to Tylor, **animism** is the foundation of religion among lower tribes, and this originates from a belief in the existence of the deceased person's **soul**. Tylor is especially interested in what he calls "survivals," **beliefs** or customs that are perpetuated from the past by force of habit to the present time, which he refers to as superstitions. Frazer's evolutionary sequence is somewhat different: magic, religion, and science. Religion, a propitiation and conciliation of powers, is believed to be superior to humans and stands in fundamental opposition to **magic** and science, with magic being necessarily false because it represents the mistaken application of the association of ideas. Frazer envisions a day when magic and religion would be replaced by science. This day can be hastened by a comparative study of the beliefs and institutions of humankind, which can expose weak points of modern **society**.

Like Tylor and Frazer, Lucien Lévy-Bruhl (1857–1939), a French anthropologist, uses the comparative method to contrast archaic mentality with modern Western modes of scientific thinking. Finding the former lacking in rigor and **rationality**, Lévy-Bruhl labels archaic mentality "prelogical reasoning," **mystical**, and affectional participation, because some archaic people conceive of themselves as animals or birds without thinking metaphorically or symbolically about this type of identity. Prelogical thinking thus does not avoid contradictions because of its indifference to logical laws of contradiction.

Another important figure in the development of comparative religion is Max Müller (1823–1900), an Oxford University professor and editor of the famous *Sacred Books of the East* collection, who is called by many the father of comparative religion. Within the visionary context of united humankind, Müller calls for a science of religion that must be comparative because all knowledge is comparative as well as inductive, adhering to the laws of cause and effect. Not only can the comparative method give a scholar a broader perspective, but it can also lead to a fuller understanding of the nature of religion. Comparative religion, moreover, enables a scholar to test their own religion against others.

While Müller and others are developing their use of comparative religion, two Dutch scholars are making important contributions: Cornelis

Petrus Tiele (1830–1902) and Pierre D. Chantepie de la Saussaye (1848–1920). Tiele's approach to the study of religion includes using empirical, historical, and comparative elements to classify religious phenomena, and a study of the permanent elements in religion within the context of change. Chantepie de la Saussaye wants to develop a science of religion, which can have a comparative component along with phenomenological and psychological aspects.

A comparative religion approach to the study of religion is combined with the methods of phenomenology and history by such scholars as Rudolf Otto (1869–1937), Gerardus van der Leeuw (1890–1950), Mircea Eliade (1907–1986), Ninian Smart (1927–2001), Jonathan Z. Smith, and others. According to Eliade, a scholar must take an encyclopedic approach to one's subject in order to grasp the structure of a religious phenomenon, and one must use comparison along with morphological classification. Smith criticizes Eliade's comparative approach for being too impressionistic, for being unhistorical and ignoring linear development, and blind to differences because Eliade concentrates on sameness. Scholars continue to debate the merits and wisdom of comparative religion to the present time. Nonetheless, comparative religion can be viewed from an historical perspective as a precursor to the establishment of the discipline of Religious Studies.

Further reading: Capps (1995); Martin (1996); Paden (1988); Patton and Ray (2000); Saler (1993); Sharpe (1986); Smith (1978, 1990)

CONVERSION

In the West, conversion can be traced back to the Latin term *conversio*, which represents a translation of the Greek *metanoia*, literally meaning "going the other way." It involves the adoption of a new religious commitment and identity different from one's former status or membership either in another religion or none at all. Conversion can occur from outside a religious tradition or within it, from, for instance, one denomination to another; it can also occur suddenly or gradually depending on the religious context and person. Conversion to another religion can occur for a variety of reasons, such as personal conviction, marital conversion to the religion of a spouse, deathbed conversion, or forced conversion done within a context of persecution. Most religions of the world do not seek to convert others, with Christianity and Islam being the two major exceptions. Even though many religions do not attempt to convert others, it is generally possible to become a Jew, a Hindu, or a Buddhist.

During the early history of America, the Puritan **faith** manifests two movements with respect to conversion: downward and upward. The first movement involves an internationalization of the Calvinist conception of **God** as judge and humans as sinful and depraved beings. Humans need **salvation**, but they are unable to achieve it by their own means. This downward movement is accompanied by fears of damnation and feelings of despair and terror at the prospect of condemnation to hell. When followers give up attempting to save themselves, rely on God, and wait for His grace they end the first movement. The upward movement depends on the acceptance of God as gracious and loving, which is often accompanied by feelings of joy, hope of salvation, and communion with God. There are also effects on a person's body, such as swooning, falling to the ground, lying speechless and inert, trembling convulsions, raptures, ecstasies, visions, and trances. Many people having a conversion experience also respond with external signs, such as laughter, joyfully clapping hands, and jumping up and down. These types of traits suggest that conversion is a complex notion.

Besides these experiential features, conversions to Christianity by non-Christians usually involve confession, repentance of sins, acceptance of Christ, a commitment to live a life from this moment forward that is acceptable to God, and baptism into the **faith**. Most Christian groups believe that baptism is essential to **salvation**. In other religions, some form of **purification** is considered necessary for admittance.

Further readings: Buckser and Glazier (2003); Gelpi 1998); Rambo (1993); Taves (1999)

COSMOLOGY

This concept originates with the Greek terms *kosmos* (world, universe) and *logos* (word, doctrine) and represents a reflection on the world as a structured and meaningful whole. There are two related notions: cosmogony and cosmography. The former relates how the world originated and the latter term refers to the extent of the world. Accounts of cosmologies are preserved in **myths** that may recount the activity of divine beings or describe the world as being an independent entity. Two very different examples of cosmology are offered by the ancient Buddhists and Dogon of Africa.

Within an infinite sea of **time** and **space**, ancient Buddhists teach that there are innumerable world systems just like the place that they inhabit on **earth**. It is impossible to precisely determine how the world originated, but it is possible to know that it is governed by natural laws; it is subject to a cyclic flow of time that is divided into eons (*kalpas*), which represent the duration of time between the origin of the world and its destruction, after which the cycle begins again in a never-ending sequence. The formative Buddhist cosmos consists of three tiers consisting of thirty-one planes of existence. These numerous planes descend from the base of Mt. Meru, which is the center of the cosmos, surrounded by four continents with India (Jambudipā) located in the south. The **earth** is established on water that rests on wind which in turn rests on **space**. This cosmic scenario strongly suggests that there is no stability because the cosmos does not rest on a solid basis.

The three tiers of the Buddhist cosmos consists of the following: nonform (*arupa-loka*); the world of form (*rūpa-loka*); and the world of desire (*kāma-loka*). Each world is subject to the law of cause and effect (*karma*) and thus to the cycle of rebirth. This overall structure is arranged hierarchically from the finest and most spiritual to the grossest at the bottom. At the highest level, there is a threefold division of the heavens and assorted divine beings, whereas human beings reside in the realm of desire on the fifth level. The world of desire includes a fourfold realm of punishment, which houses **demons**, hungry ghosts, animals, and various hells.

In contrast to the Buddhist cosmology, the Dogon of Africa cosmogony exhibit three phases: creation, revolt, and restoration. Existing alone and depended upon nothing but himself, Amma, supreme **god**, is shaped like an egg made of his four collar bones joined together. Amma's bones divide the egg into four quarters, which contain the four elements: **fire**, air, **earth**, and water. The joints between the bones represent the four cardinal directions of space. Therefore, the cosmic egg contains both the substance and structure of the universe. Into the egg, Amma places two hundred and sixty-six signs, which represent his creative thought, and he traces within himself the design of the cosmos and its future development. The initial attempt at creation is a failure, but the second attempt is more successful, with the world organized around the image of a human being. Within the seventh sheath, a part breaks through, and it produces a separate segment that represents a principle of incompleteness, imperfection, singularity, and disorder. Thus the Dogon cosmology includes order and disorder.

The cosmic revolt is initiated by Ogo, an impatient male twin, who breaks forth from his placenta with the intention of seizing his twin sister for himself, although Amma foresees Ogo's revolt and removes the other female twin. Breaking all cosmic rules, Ogo imposes his own disorder upon the creative process, but Amma transforms the placenta into the earth that assumes the shape of a human figure. Since the placenta is Ogo's, it is technically also his mother, the **earth**, with whom he then copulates, thereby defiling the earth through this act of incest, resulting in a sterile and dry earth bereft of its creative potential and creating the first race of deformed, monstrous beings, who reproduce through incestuous unions.

The restoration of the cosmos begins with Amma sacrificing Nommo Semu, the other male twin. In another version of the **narrative**, Amma commands castration that results with slitting placenta and penis, which separates the victim from his placenta and his penis. By returning to the sky and stealing the four sexual souls of his castrated twin, Ogo continues his revolt by placing the **souls** on his own foreskin, but Ogo is circumcised by the teeth of his brother, which dooms Ogo to **celibacy** and sterility. Ogo is later transformed into Pale Fox who wanders the surface of the earth searching for his female soul. Beforehand, Amma sacrifices Nommo and scatters his dismembered body in the four directions, which function to restore cosmic order. After Nommo is restored to life, he is made ruler of the universe, and from his four spirits, which are created by Amma, and their offspring come the ancestors of the Dogon, who are sent to earth in a great ark that possesses everything necessary for life and for the restoration of the earth. As a final sacrifice, Amma offers Lebe, an offspring of Nommo, but the god restores Lebe to life in the form of a snake, whose bones remain in the earth where they continue to enrich it. This final restoration of the cosmos mediates the opposition between order and disorder, and it restores the original order that is disrupted by the principles of disorder: **emotion**, irrationality, sterility, and singularity.

The Dogon and Buddhist cosmologies enable one to witness two very different versions of the origin and structure of the world that embody within them religious values and its effect on human existence. The Dogon and Buddhist examples reflect the complexity of cosmology, and they help humans find their place in the world and provide an explanation of their current situation. The cosmologies reflect philosophical issues, such as the cyclic, precarious, and impermanent nature of the cosmos for the Buddhist, whereas the Dogon cosmology manifests cultural values such as **community**, the necessity to avoid incest, and the **ritual** importance of circumcision.

Further reading: Eliade (1959); Griaule (1965); Long (1963); Olson (2005)

COVENANT

A covenant consists of an agreement between two parties to abide by its terms. In the ancient Near East, it represents a treaty between a dominant nation and a subservient one. The ancient Hebrews extend the concept beyond its political context. There are basically two types of covenants: parity and suzerainty. The parity covenant is a reciprocal agreement in which both parties bind themselves to each other by bilateral obligation. A suzerainty covenant is unilateral and made between, for instance, a king – its author – and his vassals, which is a pact between unequal parties. Within the covenant, the vassal finds protection and security, but, as the inferior party, the vassal is obligated to obey the commands issued by the king, although great attention is given to the king's deeds of generosity. In the context of ancient Israelite religion, Yahweh freely initiates the covenant and is free to terminate it at His discretion.

The ancient Hebrews extend the concept of covenant (*brit*) beyond its political context. They conceive of a covenant as an invitation (Gen. 19.15) made by **God** to His chosen people. God is the superior and the people are the weaker party in an agreement between unequals. Even though the covenant is an invitation, the people enter into it by means of their own free will. Each party pledges to adhere to an agreement, and each is accountable to the other within the context of legal obligations. When the covenant is broken it is emotionally renewed (Jer. 33.31–33) because of the love of God for Israel.

The Hebrew Pentateuch represents a series of covenants: Mosaic, Abrahamic, and Mosaic and Israel. With respect to Abraham's covenant with God, it is God who informed Abraham that he would become the father of a multitude of nations and would be given the land of Canaan. The primary mark of this covenant is circumcision for all males. Those not circumcised would not be included among Abraham's people, and they would be guilty of breaking the covenant (Gen. 17.14).

The covenant at Sinai is inseparable from the deliverance from Egypt and God's guidance of His people through the wilderness. The Sinai covenant includes an important condition: obey and keep the covenant. This places the people in a situation where they have to make a decision; it also calls them to participate in the divine purpose. In the end, the people would be Yahweh's personal possession. The covenant is sealed by a **sacrifice** and communal meal.

The concept of the covenant is so powerful in ancient Israel that it is also used as a **metaphor** to express other types of relationships. The covenant brings together people of equal status (Gen. 21.32). It is characteristic of a relationship between a king and a council of elders (1 Chron. 11.30). It is also used as an expression of love (Num. 25.12) and a marriage vow (Prov. 2.17). The covenant also expresses the relationship between God, Noah, and the animal kingdom (Gen. 9). Within the natural sphere, it also is a metaphor for night and day (Jer. 33.20).

Further reading: Eichrodt (1961); Mendenhall (1953); Peters (2003)

CULT

This is a notion with acquired negative connotations in the contemporary world because it is associated with that which is suspicious, bizarre, and exploitive. If one looks beyond these types of negative accretions to the notion, a cult is usually a small group of people who gravitate around a leader who may be charismatic. A good example is the early Jesus movement with its charismatic teacher and his body of followers. A cult group is distinguished from a **church**, denomination, or **sect**. A cult stands in tension with the prevailing culture, and it is marginal to that culture. Some scholars have defined cults as ephemeral, tending to fragment after the leader's death. They tend to be more focused on individual problems than the broader issues of **society**. Before the birth of Jesus, there are important cults in ancient Greece that are called mystery cults because of the necessity for a vow of secrecy.

The Greek mystery cults are known to function as voluntary religious options and supplements to the prevailing civic religion instead of a viable alternative. **Myths** are associated with the cults that relate tales of the supernatural beings. The cults promise a means of enhancing a person's life and **afterlife**. During the secret initiations, aspirants are able to construct a unique relationship with the cult's deity. The Eleusinian mysteries have initiates drink a concoction called *kykeōn* in imitation of the **goddess** Demeter. On the fifth day of this mystery, initiates don white garments and carry torches on a **pilgrimage** from Athens to Eleusis. During the pilgrimage, initiates have yellow ribbons tied on their right hands and left legs. This event culminates on the third day with the initiation within the confines of a walled area.

A couple of the Greek mystery cults are centered on male divine figures. Attracting soldiers and others by stressing brotherhood, the cult of Mithras embraces seven grades of initiation with the central role played by the sacrifice of a bull. The Bacchic mysteries focus on Dionysus (or Bacchus), which embraces **madness, sexuality,** and ecstatic trance states. The Greek historian Herodotus discusses a group of initiates wandering aimlessly at night overcome with madness and ecstatic states. The phallus is often used to stress iconographical depictions of male generative power and sexuality by members.

Ecstatic trance states also play a role in the cult of Meter (mother **goddess**). Cult members endure **pain** while engaged in ecstatic trance states. Some ecstatic dancers castrate themselves while in such a state, which signifies an offering of their male virility to the goddess, and they thereafter serve the goddess as her eunuch **priests.** The cult includes the *taurobolium* or bull sacrifice, which features castrating a bull and sprinkling the blood from its testicles on the initiates crouching in a pit underneath the platform where the sacrifice occurs. The various Greek cults stress secrecy, personal choice, and the promise of a direct experience of the holy.

Further reading: Burkert (1987); Detienne (1989); Johnston (2004); Lewis (1971); Stark and Bainbridge (1985)

CULTURE

The concept begins with the Latin term *colere*, an etymological root of the terms cultus and colonize. The notion originally refers to cultivating crops and animals. Then, it changes to mean human development, suggesting the cultivation of people. From this meaning, it evolves to indicate an abstract state of achieved development grounded on products of educated or creative people that come to form a collection or body of artistic works. In a general sense, culture is the totality of a social, historical, and creative heritage of human beings who represent a particular social group. A particular culture includes the human products of a **society** with a shared history and location. These human products include **language, art** and **architecture,** style of dress, distinct **foods,** social behavior, **music,** intellectual heritage, **ethics,** a legal system, government, religion, and a **worldview.** Although there may be periods when it appears to be stationary, a particular culture is never completely static. In many cultures devoid of secularism and/or advanced technology, the religion and culture are so intertwined that it is difficult to differentiate them. Thus, in some cases, religion and culture are nearly synonymous with each other.

The conception of the nature of culture develops from Roman times where it signifies cultivating the land to cultivating the human mind by means of philosophy, according to the Roman writer Cicero. This notion is rediscovered in nineteenth-century Europe by the German thinkers Wilhelm von Humbolt (1767–1835) and Friedrich Schleiermacher (1768–1834), who use it to convey a sense of self-cultivation associated with art, learning, and music. The first German thinker to call attention to the plurality of cultures is arguably Johann Gottfried von Herder (1744–1803), who sets the stage for further development of the concept.

From a historical context, the usage of the concept of culture is a recent event. Raymond Williams in *Culture and Society* traces it to the English literary tradition that reacted in part to an emergent middle class whose interests are shaped by a developing industrial economy and a new evolving social order. By the nineteenth century, culture refers to human products and natural growth, which transforms culture into a thing in itself. Consequently, culture becomes habit of mind, intellectual development, body of arts, and the material, intellectual, and spiritual dimensions of an entire way of life. Besides Williams's contribution to the subject, Ringer (1969) distinguishes two concepts of culture in Germany: *Kultur* and *Bildung*, or spiritual formation. These concepts are inseparable from the notion of education (*Erziehung*). More than the narrow sense of instruction, education refers to something more spiritual and humanistic, implying internal **self**-development and integration of the self within a process of self-cultivation.

The concept of culture is important to anthropologists who have conceived of it in different ways. Edward B. Tylor in his *Primitive Culture* (1871) defines culture as a complex whole that includes custom, belief, knowledge, art, morals, law, and other human creations. Contrary to Tylor, Ruth Benedict, Franz Boas, and Margaret Mead emphasize cultural traits not wholes, by stressing culture from a more contextualist approach. For Clifford Geertz (1973), culture is a set of symbolic meanings shared by groups. These webs of meaning and value constitute ways of life that are historically transmitted from one generation to the next. Culture, a system of meaning, is interchangeable with religion, whose meanings are embodied in **symbols**.

Reacting against such theories of culture, the historian Masuzawa calls attention to its indiscriminate usage, its excessive intellectual baggage, its semantically vague and confused nature, and connects it to the power of the ideology of modernity. Beyond more than a concept, culture is an argument, moral persuasion, and an epistemological position that identifies us. Masuzawa reminds us that culture and religion are both historically specific and recent formations and culture should not be used as an ideology of modernity. Culture is less a neutral category than a theoretical argument centered in a particular method and viewpoint.

Further reading: Bourdieu (1990); Geertz (1973); Masuzawa (2005); Ringer (1969); Smith (1978, 2004); Sperber (1996); Tylor (1871); Williams (1963)

CURSING

From one perspective, cursing is a negative **speech act** that attempts to harm another party. Its opposite is a blessing, a positive act, which is usually given by an authoritative person, such as a priest or parent. Cursing and blessing are both forms of communication with the divine in the form of oaths and operate magically without additional **ritual** actions, although the former tends to bring the name of **God** into disrepute. This is the rationale for Jesus (Matt. 5.33–37) and Muhammad instructing followers to abstain from swearing oaths. Aware of the power of cursing, Jewish rabbis only permit it when religiously motivated.

In ancient Greece and Rome, curses (*katadesmoi, defixioiones*) are written back to front or as nonsense script on lead, wax, or papyrus and buried in wells, other subterranean areas, or tombs because the curser is attempting to elicit the assistance of underworld powers. Two important forms of Greco-Roman curses are direct formulas that use a first-person verb to curse another person, a **performative** utterance that is expected to make the curse work automatically. The second type of formula uses an imperative verb that directs divine actions, demons, or the dead to harm a victim. These types of formulas are believed to have an automatic effect, which is the reason they have to be destroyed immediately by an intended victim. Generally, there are three types of curses: revenge, binding, and conditional. Having been harmed in the past, a person utters a revenge curse in order to punish the offending party. Without reference to right or wrong, the binding curse is intended to restrain another person in any action that that rival might take in the future with regards to athletics, legal issues, economics, or love. It is a common belief that curses empower the politically disenfranchised. The conditional curse implies that if an event occurs then the cause will come to fruition.

In the Hebrew Bible, God curses the serpent (Gen. 3.14) and Adam and Eve (3.17) for their transgression. In addition, Cain is cursed from the earth (Gen. 4.11) for his misdeed. According to the Book of Proverbs (26.2), an undeserved curse is not effective, and it may revert back upon the person who utters it. The Christian apostle Paul associates curses with Jesus' crucifixion in Galatians (3.13). As in ancient Greco-Roman culture, a curse is a weapon of the powerless, the wronged, the oppressed, and of the righteous.

In Islamic Morocco, a curse is an intentional form of injury among ordinary people. It is common to curse the mother or father of the object of one's anger. In Moroccan society, social rank gives potency to a curse, which means, for instance, that a husband's curse upon his wife is as potent as that of his father, and the efficacy of a curse is influenced by the guilt or innocence of the person on whom it is pronounced. There are generally two types of Moroccan curses: categorical and conditional. The former type means that a person calls down upon himself some evil in the event of what he says is not true. In the conditional case, the curse is directed against another person, which is called *ar* (shame). This implies that if a person does not do what is asked of one some misfortune will befall that person. Moroccans might also say, "I am in your *ar*," which implies that one is cursed if one does not assist the person pronouncing the curse.

Further reading: Beard (2004); Combs-Schilling (1989); Eickelman (1976)

DANCE

A complex concept that often assumes the form of **art**, social interactions, entertainment, **worship**, and **play**. In many cultures, dance expresses a vital energy or life force with an ability to celebrate joy and sorrow and to bring people together to observe some event. In some forms of Christian service and Hindu **worship**, dance is an integral part of the service. In a South Indian temple in the city of Puri, for instance, temple dancers (*devadasis*) entertain the deity like courtesans performing before an earthly king. The female temple dancers are believed to secrete a holy fluid onto the temple floor over which devotees roll their bodies. Dance also possesses the ability to produce power or empower the dancer. Classical Indian dancers and actors in the Japanese Nō theater not only tell stories by their dancing, but they represent high *culture* in their countries. In some cultural contexts, dance is conceived as a form of *play*. Among the Samburu people of northern Kenya, who live as pastoral nomads, the term play is used as a *metaphor* for dancing and singing, and communal dancing is also a form of play among the Venda of southern Africa.

Within the context of many cultures, dance, a form of **body language**, is a metaphor of sexual relations. Among the Lugbara tribe of Uganda, it is possible to find courtship dances among the younger people. The dance performances of the Temiar, a tribe located on the Malayan peninsula, provide an opportunity for young people to flirt with each other, whereas the African Azande beer dance functions to channel the forces of sex into socially harmless patterns. Among the Melpa of the highlands of Papua, New Guinea, the tribe's *morli* dances are boisterous affairs that manifest high sexual tensions along with sexually explicit performances. These types of societies manifest non-verbal, **sexual** messages, operating to release underlying social tensions and aggressive feelings. These dances also synthesize **body**, thought, and feelings as they convey their non-verbal messages. Moreover, dance is a way of arranging and categorizing human **experience**; intends some purpose while revealing movements, something aesthetic, a process, or a means of conceptualization.

Dance possesses the ability to transform a person from an inferior social status to a higher one. This is especially evident in initiation rites among some religions. Within the context of some indigenous religions, male and female adolescents dance their initiations. For instance, the Venda of southern Africa require young girls to dance in a circle, creating an enclosed space symbolizing a womb. A young woman becomes a womb in which a fetus, which is symbolized by the bass drum, is nourished by the strenuous dancing that signifies sexual intercourse, with the semen represented by the ashes of the fire. Among the Samburu of northern Kenya, boys dance into adulthood by means of its circumcision dance.

In some contexts, dance is associated with **violence**, which tends to make it frequently marginal and anomalous. The Swahili of east Africa have a dance called *beningoma* that is a caricature of a military parade, promoting masculine display and competition between rival dance groups which sometimes overflows into outbreaks of violence. The energy and violence associated with dance stands in contrast to everyday life, transporting participants out of their structured environment and into a timeless realm. By means of the ecstatic nature of dance, the dancers literally stand outside of normal **society** and its social interaction.

Some religious groups, such as the Puritans of the Christian tradition, prohibit dancing because they think that it represents the Devil's handiwork. Islam also forbids dancing, with the exception of the Sufi movement and their whirling dances that transport dancers into ecstatic trance states during which they can commune with God.

Further reading: Adams and Apostolus-Cappadona (1990); Hanna (1987); Spencer (1985)

DEATH

As a biological, social, and historical occurrence, death represents the end of life and is a certain fact of living. As the German phenomenologist Martin Heidegger elucidates in his classic work *Sein und Zeit* (*Being and Time*) published in 1927, death is the only thing in life that is certain, non-relative, irreversible and imminent. Heidegger states that death makes an individual whole by completing the totality of a person's life. The individual is a being-unto-death, which implies a way of life that looks at the possibility of death as an intimate part of life, while it also isolates a person and throws the person back upon himself. According to Heidegger, death is not simply an event that puts an end to one's life because it is a part of life itself. This suggests that death is always present in a person's life; it is here and now. Death is always mine, which means that one must die one's own death because no one can take one's place in death. Heidegger observes also that death represents the possibility of all possibilities, implying that it stands ahead of us, and forms the ultimate possibility for us because we are always moving towards it. The final thing that we can be is dead. Moreover, death is an unsurpassable possibility, and cannot be avoided. It is a non-relational possibility because death dissolves all social relations.

The certainty and unavoidability of death that Heidegger mentions is shared by religious traditions around the globe. Various religious have been fascinated about the origin of death, and have shared **narratives** about its beginnings over the course of generations. The Judeo-Christian tradition mythically explains that death is the result of a transgression of a divine decree. In other traditions, death is attributed to a cruel and arbitrary act of a demonic being, a frequent adversary of the creator god. Sometimes, death is attributed to an accident, such as the message that fails among some African cultures. In one version, a deity sends a chameleon with a message that humans will be immortal. A little later, a lizard is sent by the god with an exact opposite message. Because the chameleon stops along the way, the lizard arrives first with its message that humans must die a tragic accident that results in human mortality. In a more absurd **narrative** of Melanesian origin, the narrative relates that originally humans could rejuvenate themselves when they grow old by sloughing off their skin. Having sloughed off her skin, a woman is unrecognized by her child when she returns home. In order to pacify the child, she put on her old skin, and her act stops the effectiveness of the process. A Micronesian myth relates a tale of a wrong choice made by cultural ancestors in the story of the stone and the banana. According to this narrative, the sky is very near to the earth at the beginning of time, and the creator being can let down his gate to humans by sending down a rope, a form of communication between the earth and the sky. On a given day, the creator sends down a stone tied to the rope. The ancestors do not want the stone because they do not know what to do with it, so they call upon the creator to send something else, who complies with their request by sending a banana tied to the end of the rope, which the ancestors joyfully accept. Then, they hear a voice from the sky: "Because you have chosen the banana, so shall your life be. When the tree gives birth to offspring, when the parent's stem dies and its place is taken by the young stems. So shall you die! If you had chosen the stone, your life would have been like the stone—changeless and immortal."

In ancient Jewish religion, **God** gives life and takes it (1 Sam. 2.6; Deut. 32.39) with death the punishment for **sin**. Death is an inevitable human destiny, and it is called the king of terrors in Job (18.18). In addition, the dead are considered unclean and thus cause **pollution** to the living (Num. 19.11; Lev. 11.35). Ancient Jews dispose of the dead by burial without embalming, which is an Egyptian treatment of the dead. The grave is called the habitation of the dead (Isa. 22.16), and there is importance attached to being buried alongside family members. Ancient Jews do not have a concept of the **soul**, and after death a person becomes a shadowy double of the living person and returns to dust – inanimate matter – from which the person originated (Job 34.14; Gen. 3.19). At the end of time, the dead experience bodily resurrection (Isa. 26.19; Dan. 12.2). In response to death, the survivors mourn by tearing clothing, eating a funeral bread, fasting, breast beating, sprinkling ashes over their heads, sitting in ashes, covering the upper lip, going barefoot and bareheaded, shaving off hair, and even mutilating themselves. Besides the grief experienced by survivors, these mourning practices can possibly be related to making oneself unrecognizable to the deceased, thus avoiding initiating their envy or malice.

Early Christians adopt many Jewish observances surrounding death, although Christians also conceive of death as a sleep and the grave as a resting place (John 11.13; 1 Thess. 4.13). A former Jew such as the apostle Paul accepts that death is the punishment for sin (Rom. 6.7, 23). The death of Jesus is, however, a unique historical event because it is united with his resurrection, which holds forth the promise of eternal life (1 Cor. 15.21–22). Therefore, the death and resurrection of Jesus form a unity of a single **salvation** event (2 Cor. 5.15). The death of Christ is interpreted as a propitiatory **sacrifice**, which functions as a means for the forgiveness of sins and cancels the guilt associated with sin. Along with this notion of a propitiatory sacrifice, there is the concept of a vicarious sacrifice, suggesting that Jesus dies for us, and these are both merged by Paul in his letters (2 Cor. 5.14). From the punishment imposed by sin, the death of Christ redeems or ransoms all beings and gives them freedom from punishment, freedom from the guilt of sin, and freedom from sin and death. Within the context of classical Hinduism, it is possible to find two responses to death: ritual and renunciation of the world. The ritual response to death involves a funeral procession led by the chief mourner (e.g. eldest son). With the exception of burying young children, women dying during child birth, or **holy persons**, the normal mode of disposal of a cadaver is cremation. Prior to the cremation, the plot is **purified**, and **sacred** mantras (repetitive utterances) are recited to scare away **demons** and ghosts. The corpse is filled with ghee, (a product of the cow) to purify it, the hair and nails are cut, and it is washed with water. The widow lies down on the left, or inauspicious, side of the corpse, but she is asked to leave by the younger brother of the deceased, a disciple, or servant. Cremation is conceived as a **sacrifice**, a means of conducting the corpse to heaven as a sacrificial **gift**. The **fire** is considered the means of conveying the **body** to the gods. It is believed that the cremation releases the **soul** from the body. Survivors are **polluted** by the death and need to purify themselves after an appropriate time period. After the cremation, the bones of the deceased are collected, washed, and deposited in an urn or tied together in a black antelope skin, which can be burned again or buried. Finally, a last rite – twelve days after cremation – unites the spirit of the deceased with its **ancestors**. Cooked white rice is formed into a ball, representing the spirit of the deceased, for ten days, with each day representing the symbolic creation of a new body.

A second Hindu response to death is renunciation of the world, a means for transcending the world by a symbolic death. The rationale is the following: if one is already dead, one cannot die again. The renouncer (*saṃnyāsin*) wanders about homeless, without comforts or possessions, begging for his subsistence, and devoid of social connections. The symbolic death of the renouncer is accomplished by **ascetic** practices associated with *tapas* (literally heat), which serves as an inner funeral pyre that symbolically consumes a renouncer's body.

Within the teachings of the Buddha, death is directly connection with his First Noble Truth: all life is suffering. Death is inevitable and affects everyone without exception. The universality of death and its effects on survivors is evident in the parable of the mustard seed, a tale which relates the story of a grieving mother whose son suddenly died. Approaching the Buddha because of his renowned miraculous powers to heal, the distraught mother is instructed by the Buddha to go from house to house in the city in search of a few grains of mustard seed which will provide the proper antidote to the child's condition, although the mother can only accept a mustard seed from a household in which no one has ever died. After searching many houses, she discovers that not a single household can be found that has never experienced the death of a family member. This lesson enables her to recognize the truth that death is inevitable. Within Buddhist lore, the demonic Māra (derived from the verb to die) functions as a **symbol** of death and the impermanency of everything in the world. Over the centuries, Buddhist monks have meditated on death by proceeding to a cremation ground or burial area to mediate on the decaying bodies, bones, and ashes of corpses, and thus have learnt about the brevity of life, its uncertainty, and its impermanence and the certainty of death.

According to the Daoist text, the *Zhuangzi*, life and death are two aspects of the same reality, which implies that the change from one to another is as natural as the succession of day and night. Since death is natural, humans should not fear or desire it, but they should accept it as one's destiny. Overall, death is merely an integral part of a vast cosmic process of change.

In virtually all cultures, death is handled by **ritual** procedures manifested as **rites of passage**: separation, transition, and incorporation. Rites of separation entail the separation of the living from the death. Physical items of separation include the grave, coffin, or cemetery, while **purification** procedures render the deceased ready for burial or cremation. Among the African Dinka, a dead male is stripped of his decorations and ornaments, his head is shaved and his body washed and anointed with oil. The body is then placed on its side in the grave with its head facing west, and buried by people facing away from the grave and pushing dirt backwards into the grave. The mourners are purified by the burning smoke of straw taken from the home of the deceased blowing over them. The mourners are then sprinkled by the remains of a sacrificed ram.

The rites of transition involve the transition of the living, such as a wife to widow; and it entails the transition of the death to the other world. Within the Ngaju religion, the transition is symbolized by a coffin shaped like a boat for the journey to the village of the dead. The dead go either to the upper world where they change into mythical hawks or to the underworld where they change into mythical water snakes.

The rites of incorporation are twofold: incorporation of the living with **society** and incorporation of the deceased into the other world. The first type of incorporation involves rites that lift all regulations and prohibitions associated with mourning. A common feature is a meal shared with others after the funeral or at a commemorative celebration. In the Tibetan culture, for instance, the soul of the deceased is given instruction by a Buddhist priest, which is based on the teachings contained in the *Bardo Thödol* (*Tibetan Book of the Dead*), in order for it to find the other world.

Further reading: Ariès (1981); Bloch and Parry (1982); Obayashi (1992); Parry (1994); Reynolds and Waugh (1977)

DEMONS

These are malevolent spiritual figures, found in many religions, that afflict people with illness and insanity, especially when they possess them. In some religious traditions, they remain ambiguous evil figures, while in other traditions they are personified; for instance, as the Devil in Christianity, Iblīs in Islam, or Māra in Buddhism. Demons often function as counter forces to creator deities by attempting to undo or disrupt what has been created, attempting to corrupt, punish, and afflict humans.

In ancient Hindu religious history, a broad category of demons are called *asuras*. These demons are continuously at odds with the **gods** of the Hindu pantheon. An ancient identifiable *asura* is Vritra, who encompasses the cosmos and returns it to **chaos**. Vritra is eventually defeated by Indra, a deity chosen by the gods for this task. In later sectarian Hinduism, Krishna is recorded defeating many demons in the spirit of **play**. Vishnu becomes incarnate to defeat various demonic beings, often by tricking them as when he appears as a dwarf and defeats the demon Bali by taking three strides, with the last step crushing the demon. The goddess Durgā is renowned for defeating the buffalo demon while Kālī expands her mouth to drink the blood of Raktabīja, a demon who could replicate himself when a drop of his blood fell to the earth.

Demonic figures also play an important role in Chinese culture where it is believed that the *kuei* **soul** of a person can become an evil demon after a person's **death** and torment the living. An infamous Chinese demon is Chiyou, an antagonist of the Yellow Emperor, who is described as a monster with teeth two inches long, the body of a man, hooves of a bull, four eyes, and six hands. He could eat iron and stones without breaking his teeth. He is associated in Chinese culture with the forge in which weapons are created. Another bizarre figure is Gonggong who is described as a serpent with a human head and red hair. A vassal of Gonggong is Xiangliu who is described as having nine heads and the body of a serpent.

Further reading: Ogden (2002); Russell (1977, 1981, 1984, 1986)

DOCTRINE

Derived from the Latin *doctrina*, the concept refers to the body of teachings of a **church** or religion. In the Christian context, doctrine is what a church believes, teaches, and confesses, based on the word of **God**, giving the church an opportunity to define itself and its structure. What is believed is doctrine present in devotion, spirituality, and **worship**, whereas the church teaches worship based on the word of God and communicated to practitioners by proclamation, instruction, and **theology**. What is confessed refers to the testimony of the church against false teaching from within the church and attacks from outside of it, using polemics, apologetics, creeds, and dogma. In short, Christian doctrine is the saving **knowledge** derived from the word of God. The definition of the nature of the Trinity, virgin birth, transubstantiation, Immaculate Conception, Calvinist predestination, and **grace** are all examples of Christian doctrine, whereas the doctrine of the Buddha is summarized by the Four Noble Truths that define the root problem of human existence and the means of overcoming it.

Overall, doctrine operates to form a person's attitude towards the world and the divine. Doctrines describe the way things are in fact, explain things and why things are the way they are, and they reconcile apparent contradictions. By defining what is orthodox, doctrines contribute to defining the boundaries of **community**, and thus avoid motivating **heresy** or dissent. Doctrines support apologetic functions. Finally, doctrine can respond to external contradictions possibly caused by new developments in the sciences.

Further reading: Pelikan (1971); Smart (1996)

DREAMS

Occurring during sleep, dreams are often bizarre images of physical distortions, strange environments, character metamorphoses, unrealistic juxtapositioning of people's actions, sudden alterations of locations, supernatural achievements, impossible happenings, and odd behavior. Humans encounter themselves, other people from daily life, deceased people, and total strangers and creatures in an inexplicable realm of fantasy that dreams enable people to reach. Dreaming is a universal human phenomenon that reflects something about a person's identity and what a person cares about most in their life, although specific dreams are not necessarily universal.

Dreams are a source for religious concepts, **experience**, and guidance. Native American Indians take dreams seriously as indicators and messengers about what a person should do with their life or other mundane events by bringing individuals into contact with supernatural beings. Dreams contribute to **healing**, acquiring of **powers**, and wisdom among Native American Indians. Among such religions, dreams overlap with **visions**, trance states, **possession**, and hallucination. Even though they happen in a private realm, Native American Indians often make their dreams public by means of **myth**, public narrative, confession, or by drawing depictions on shields or tents. Due to the images that they produce, dreams manifest a content that is a form of seeing. **Emotions**, imagination, and delusion based on waking experience can generate dreams during sleep. Moreover, dreams possess a **liminal** nature because they occur between waking consciousness and being unconscious, and some religions believe that the **soul** wanders during sleep.

In India, dreams are believed to give a sleeper a glimpse of **god** amidst an ability to see the real and the unreal. In this sense, dreams not only reflect **reality**, but they can bring it about. Hindus have traditionally believed that having a series of dreams and not being able to recall them is a wasteful exercise. Having an auspicious dream and suddenly awakening is believed to bring good luck. Hindus also believed that it is possible to dream the dreams of other people.

In general, dreams have two directions: backward and forward. The former is directed to a beginning point, whereas the latter leads to a destructive ending. Dreams also function like **memory**, a lost and restored memory. By recalling and restoring lost memory, dreams can expand our identity by helping to unbind a dreamer from the present, open and expand boundaries, help to recall former experiences, and disclose prior ruptures in a dreamer's life.

Further reading: Bulkeley (2008); Shulman and Stroumsa (1999)

DRUGS

Within the context of ordinary life, drugs can cure illness by destroying germs, or they can destroy the patient if they are misused. In a religious context, drugs have been used to alter states of consciousness in ancient religious cultures and more contemporary **cults** surrounding drugs such as

LSD. Ancient Indian society develops a sacrificial cult around the hallucinogenic *soma* – deified drink of immortality – that enables priests to directly communicate with divine beings and give each party strength and long life. This elixir of immortality that consists of **fire** and water is guarded by **demonic** beings. Carried by an eagle, it is the **god** Indra who steals the liquid for humans and gods. Being the king of plants, a person drinking *soma* partakes of immortality or divinity, which is often expressed by light imagery. *Soma* is able to help its drinker achieve **power**, execute deeds, and discover mysterious worlds far beyond his/her normal capabilities. It is historically interesting that the Buddha forbids monks and nuns from using mind-altering substances because their use distorts the mind and makes it difficult to concentrate the mind for the purposes of **meditation**, although it is perfectly permissible to use drugs to cure illness.

Green buttons found growing around the roots of the peyote cactus in the American southwest are chewed by members of a movement called the Native American Church to induce alternated states of consciousness. It is possible to trace the origin of what is called the peyote **cult**, to John Wilson, an adopted Indian. Changing his name to Big Moon, Wilson promotes the cult because it causes **visions** that are so important in Native American Indian culture. The peyote also causes nausea, headaches, and vomiting, which are interpreted as forms of **purification**, but the visions provide assurance of being in contact with supernatural beings. The peyote cult takes many variations that include all-night meetings in a tipi around a crescent-shaped earthen mound that symbolizes the moon. As a special drum, gourd rattle, and carved staff are passed around, participants performed ritual singing, **prayer** and consumption of peyote. It is believed that the Holy Spirit resides in the peyote, that Jesus is identical to it, and that it possesses spiritual and medicinal **powers**. The **visions** produced by ingesting peyote serve to develop a socially conscious form of religion and helps one to learn the road of peyote, which is defined as leading to material well-being, health, long life, and tranquility in this life and bliss in the next life.

Drugs used in a religious context possess an experiential foundation. Drugs are directly associated with **visions, knowledge**, and wisdom. Drugs can also operate as a socially cohesive element among members, functioning to reveal to a person a new sense of identity. Drug cults often stand in opposition to the established social order, and represent a creative religion of renewal in response to certain existential needs. Drug cults are also revolutionary movements intended to renew and reform social, cultural, and political life.

Further reading: Aberle (1991); Kripal (2001); Lewis (1971); Slotkin (1975)

EARTH

Conceived from a religious perspective, the earth is a symbolic web of significance that includes its life-giving **powers**, ability to sustain life, and tendency to accept the bodies of the dead. In some religious cultures, the earth is personified as a mother **goddess**, although this tendency is not universal because there are counter examples such as the Egyptian **god** Geb. Moreover, the earth is not universally **sacred** because some religions conceive of the earth as sacred only in some locations, as is evident among Native American Indians.

In Native American religions, such as those of the Navaho and Zuni, the earth is believed to give life to humans, whereas Gaia of ancient Greek **culture** gives birth to the sky, and is replaced herself by other deities associated with the earth. In indigenous cultures of Oceania, Africa, ancient India, Japan, and Egypt, the earth enters into a creative partnership with the sky, whose rains fertilizes the earth and stimulates its bounty. This scenario suggests that the earth plays an often passive role, or in the case of ancient Chinese cosmogony, the earth and **heaven** are products of *qi* (the basic stuff of the universe), and they produce *yin* (female principle equated with the earth) and *yang* (male principle associated with heaven) in turn. In contrast to ancient China, other cultures view the earth as the untiring womb that bestows life directly, such as the mother Aditi of ancient India, or the figure of Lajja lying on her back with her legs spread apart, suggesting both sexual availability and giving birth. The fertile womb of the earth produces fruit trees and grass for consumption by different domestic and wild animals. The life-giving **powers** of the earth are interconnected with notions of fecundity, inexhaustible creativity, and life. Serving as the foundation for all life, the earth is symbolically a divine potency and energy.

Besides giving life, the earth sustains life by feeding and nurturing its creatures in both literal and symbolic ways. The earth preserves its creatures, who are dependent upon it emotionally and psychologically, by giving them a sense of safety and security – those standing on the earth assume that it is permanent and firm due to its solidity and immense size. This type of feeling is challenged, of course, during natural disasters such as a flood or earthquake. Nonetheless, there is generally a sense that the earth surrounds and encompasses humans in a broad network of relations with other humans, animals, plant life, forests, water, deserts, and mountains. The practice of placing newborn infants upon the earth or placing the infirm and dying upon the earth are examples of witnessing to the life-sustaining, nurturing, protecting and curing symbolic powers of the earth.

If **food** is a visual sign of the creative and sustaining powers of the earth, the life-giving and nurturing features of the earth are often connected to and given expression in mystery **cults** such as the Eleusinian and Avestan mysteries, respectively of ancient Greece and Iran. Embodied within the mysterious nature of the life-bestowing and sustaining aspects of the earth, there are also dangerous and life-threatening features of the earth in its poisonous plants, reptiles, and rapacious animals. Thus, the physical beauty of the earth hides its dangers because **death** is not far from the surface of the earth, and is often symbolically present upon its surface in the form of natural disasters of numerous kinds.

Eventually, all creatures return to the earth at their **death**. In most religious cultures, the earth accepts the dead without discrimination and functions as a repository of the dead. The close symbolic connection between the earth and the underworld is evident in the ancient Egyptian myth of Osiris and his becoming ruler of the underworld. Due in part to the residence of the dead, its mention of mineral riches, and hidden treasures, the interior of the earth is symbolically mysterious and the location of secret **knowledge**. The secret knowledge contained within the earth is often connected to fate and oracles as, for example, with the ancient Babylonian oracle Ea, a deity consulted to discern future events and discover the divine will. Likewise, the Egyptian goddess Ma-a-t is connected to the mysteries of the earth with its underworld and realm of the dead.

Caves, mines, and grottoes represent underground labyrinths that are commonly associated with the rebirth symbolism connected to initiation rites, and also equated with the vagina of the earth. These various wombs of the earth contain fertile riches in the form of mineral wealth and life-giving waters. The womb of the earth is the perpetual giver of life, wisdom, and riches, as well the regenerator of new life. In general, the religious significance of the earth is connected to its symbolism of producing life, sustaining it, and being a repository of the dead.

Further reading: Berthong and Tucker (1998); Chapple and Tucker (2000); Girardot *et al.* (2001); Gottlieb (1996)

ECOLOGY

This term is first coined by Ernst Haeckel, a German disciple of the evolutionary theorist Charles Darwin, in 1866 to indicate a pattern of interaction between organisms and their environment. The application of the notion of ecology to religion is a more recent construction. Grounded in the work of American researchers in the field of cultural ecology, an investigation into the ways that the natural environment is affected by culture, this newly constructed field is also concerned about the interrelationship between an ecosystem and culture and how the environment is mediated by culture. Whereas cultural ecology wants to stress the investigation of the interaction between **nature** and **culture**, the so-called ecology of religion is more concerned with a group's adaptation to a particular kind of natural environment and the kind of religion that is produced by certain kinds of environment, such as a jungle forest, desert, mountainous region, or open plains. Therefore, ecology of religion tends to be a comparative and cross-cultural discipline in a search for the ways that different cultures in diverse locations adapt to their environment and how it affects the religion.

The ecology of religion should not be confused with a historically earlier notion called Naturism associated with the work of German scholars Max Müller and Wilhelm Schmidt. Müller focuses on the powerful feelings and emotions of people evoked by natural phenomena, such as thunder, lightning, rain, flood, scorching sun, and excessive heat. Schmidt argues that the terror and wonder induced by natural forces causes some people to personify nature by means of a misuse of language and to attribute these powers to spiritual beings. Ecologists of religion should be distinguished from these types of reflections on nature.

Ecologists of religion begin with human beings in their natural environment, in order to examine how people relate to other animal species and plant life with respect to responsibilities and to what extent human destiny is intertwined with other species. The ecology of religion is concerned with issues about either accepting or conforming to the natural environment, or whether it is best to attempt to improve it by taking a more active approach by altering, shaping, and developing it with the long-term hope of perfecting it.

According to some theorists, some religions invite an ecological approach because such themes are already present in the religion. The Buddhist's emphasis on non-violence toward all living creatures, for example, possesses ecological implications. The Buddhist and Hindu notion of rebirth into possible lower or higher forms of life also raises important ecological issues. Within Japanese Shinto, nature is generally conceived as **sacred** and a source of spiritual fulfillment. Chinese Daoism advocates living harmoniously within the flux of *yin* and *yang*, which are respectively conceived as female and male principles that alternate, and allows nature to manifest itself in the harmonious interplay of the two polar principles that are considered complementary.

Different ecological issues are raised by Native American peoples such as the Mitassini Cree, a hunting, trapping, and gathering culture located around James Bay in northern Canada. For the Cree, animals live social lives similar to humans. It is important to establish a rapport with the animals and their spirit masters; otherwise the animals will not give themselves to the hunter. A similar type of respect for animals is evident among the Northern Saulteaux people, who respect the bears that they hunt by addressing the animal using specific names, apologizing to the animal for killing it, giving reasons for the killing, dressing the animal after its death, hanging its parts on a pole, and making offerings to it. Alaskan Eskimos express a similar spirit towards animals in their bladder festivals, at which the bladders of game animals, which symbolize their **souls**, are inflated, painted, and hung in the men's **society** house to honor the animals. These kinds of attitudes and behaviors invite an ecological investigation of such religions.

Within the context of an environmental crisis and as a response to the harmful behavior of humans toward nature, a new emphasis called "deep ecology" represents an ethical and religious attitude toward nature as valuable and spiritually vital. Although "deep ecology" is defined differently by authors, there is a general agreement that ethics is important, nature is valuable for its own sake, and different philosophies of nature are permissible in an attempt to create a platform of basic values to spur new kinds of environmental activism. In addition, deep ecology concentrates on wholeness, views humans as interrelated with nature, stresses an intuitive and sensual communion with nature, and promotes humility toward nature and a spirit of letting nature be without superimposing human designs upon it. Finally, there is encouragement for people to view nature as sacred and to be open to learning lessons from other religious cultures.

Further reading: Barnhill and Gottlieb (2001); Callicot and Ames (1989); Kinsley (1995)

ECONOMY

This concept is rooted in Greek **culture** where it refers to members of a domestic household. At the present time, economy refers to a broader concept that includes production of goods and services, exchange, distribution, consumption, profit making, price setting, and market forces.

The ancient Babylonians develop forms of economics with laws governing transactions and courts to adjudicate disputes. The subsistence farming nature of ancient economies is evident in the use of the Shekel, an ancient unit of weight and currency related, for instance, to a mass of barley. Gold and silver coins are introduced by the Lydians, according to the Greek historian Herodotus. Even into the Middle Ages in the West, exchange of goods occurs within social groups. The first banks are founded by Jakob Fugger (1459–1525) and Giovanni di Bicci de'Medici (1360–1428), who are former merchants. Global discoveries beyond Europe open the world to a global economy characterized by trading in goods. The first stock exchange is founded in Antwerp in 1513. Within the context of colonialism and the rise of nation states, mercantilism attempts to bridge the gap between private wealth and national economies. During the Industrial Revolution, Adam Smith (1723–1790), a Scotsman, states that the basis for free trade is self-interest and the prices of products are due to the law of supply and demand along with the division of labor. This notion of supply and demand relates to the problem of overpopulation by Thomas Malthus (1766–1834). By the end of the eighteenth century, the concept of "economy" becomes an autonomous aspect of human life, and is perceived to accompany the **secularization** and subsequent decline of religion, according to some theorists, and to operate according to its own natural laws. Recognizing the fundamental nature of economy to society, Karl Marx perceives that religion, a definitive form of alienation, is being driven from human life by capitalistic materialism, but other scholars take a different perspective about the potential of economy to undermine religion.

In his *The Protestant Ethic and the Spirit of Capitalism* (1904–1905), Max Weber argues that the origins of capitalism can be found in the intrinsic character of Christian religious beliefs, especially Protestant convictions. The notion of a religious calling in Lutheranism gives a dignity to all work and reinforces a belief that the religious life can be pursued within the world and that worldly success confirms that one is an instrument of God's will. Calvinism gives a person, according to Weber, an opportunity to prove oneself within the context of a belief in predestination, a doctrine that motivates people to look for signs of being chosen and saved. Salvational status is associated with worldly success as a sign that one is favored by **God**. Not only does Protestantism encourage dedication to industrial labor, but it also contributes to the development of the entrepreneurial spirit so necessary for taking risks.

Besides the Marxist reactions to capitalism, there arises in America the Social Gospel Movement and in Britain the Christian socialist movements, as a response to problems surrounding issues of poverty and exploitation inherent in capitalism, and from which emerges the modern welfare state. This suggests that religious **beliefs** not only help to foster economics, but these beliefs also paradoxically challenge economic excess. During the 1980s, governments are forced to intervene because of the tremendous growth of multi-national corporations and their monopolistic tendencies. This intervention follows the advice of John Maynard Keynes, an English economist, for just such actions in capitalist economies. Consumerism, a hedonist aspect of economy, with value placed on the accumulation of goods, becomes significant along with the rapid economic growth of countries such as Japan, Taiwan, South Korea, Singapore, China, and India. Now citizens of the world are part of a global economy, forcing diverse religious traditions to confront economic realities such as consumerism and materialism.

As the sociologist Talbott Parsons asserts, economic activity is essential to human life but economics does not fully determine events or lives, and it is not completely determined itself. There is a tension between religious beliefs and economic activity, a universal impulse. It is not unusual to find economic and religious matters becoming conflated with, for instance, **myth** and **ritual** and then being directed toward economic functions within the control of religious personnel.

Further reading: Dean and Waterman (1999); Graber (2001); Parsons (1967); Weber (1930)

EMOTION

Characterized as a personal feeling that gives rise to pleasure or **pain**, emotion can also give rise to desire or fear. Even though they presuppose concepts of social relationships and institutions, emotions tend to be temporary, fleeting, and repetitive during the normal course of life, although it is possible to become consumed by a particular emotion, such as greed, and allow it to dominate one's life. Some emotions like hate are generally considered negative because they potentially lead to interpersonal and social tension, whereas other emotions such as love, benevolence, friendliness, admiration, or gratitude are able to accomplish interpersonal and social bonding.

As a general rule, devotional types of religion tend to encourage positive emotions, while **ascetic** types of religious movements call for the control or eradication of emotions. Judaism, Christianity, Islam, and Sikhism, and devotional Hindu and Buddhist movements condone or even encourage emotions, especially **love**, within their confines. **Monastic**, ascetic, or mystic types of religiosity tend to control the emotions because they generally obstruct progress towards more ecstatic types of **experience**, although there are many exceptions when it comes to an emotion such as love.

Emotions are socially constructed appraisals of given situations grounded in cultural beliefs and values. Laughter is, for instance, a metonym whereby emotional physiological effects represent the emotion. Emotional judgments involve the **self** more deeply in relationship to other persons, things, or events. Emotions are culturally relative in large part because they are learned, acquired, or nurtured within a particular religious culture rather than acquired naturally, and different emotions become identified by others within a religion. If different situations within a religion trigger emotional responses, such as humor or fear, there is no cross-cultural, universal, objective situation that explains all innate responses. Emotions involve moral **judgments** pertaining to social situations. By expressing pity for a person suffering from old age, illness, or mental incapacity, emotions elicit a prescribed or expected response that is culturally ingrained in a person. Moreover, emotions possess moral consequences for the way persons relate to others and the social system.

Further reading: Lakoff and Kovecses (1983); Lynch (1990)

EROTICISM

This concept is derived from the Greek term *eros* (desire, **love**), although eroticism is not simply about desire and love. Eroticism is excessive in its nature; it also tends to be marginal with respect to the prevailing social structure, its marginal characteristic marking the limits of human experience. Eroticism is potentially subversive because it is marked by insatiability and ceaseless desire; it is not the act of sex itself because it possesses more in common with anticipation than fulfillment. Eroticism is more like the sexual tease that does not end and is never fully satisfied. There is a close association between eroticism and religion in that they both render visible the bodily nature of religious **experience**. Christian, Hindu, and Muslim **mystics** write about their experiences in erotic terms.

In the Hebrew Scriptures, the Song of Songs expresses an individual's love of God in very erotic terms in a manner similar to Christian, Islamic and Hindu mysticism. In the Hindu tradition, the poet Jayadeva in his *Gītāgovinda* expresses the love relationship between the **goddess** Rādhā and Krishna as an intense, passionate, violent, and erotic encounter that occurs within a context of divine **play** in a world of joy and bliss. The erotic nature of their relationship is heightened by its dangerous and illicit quality. Within Krishna devotional religion, there is also a close interconnection between eroticism, **madness**, and ecstasy. Rādhā is a paradigm for the human **soul** searching for God and the highest **ecstatic** state in a condition accompanied by incoherent speech, irrational behavior, and painful **emotions**.

In his theory of religion, George Bataille focuses on the relationship between eroticism and **mysticism**. According to Bataille, eroticism is the conscious search for sensual pleasure in which a person does not gain anything or become enriched like engaging in work. Eroticism is a realm of pure **play**, whose essence is to obey the pull of seduction in response to passion. Striking one at the center of one's being, eroticism gives one a foretaste of continuity, which presupposes a partial dissolution of the person as that person exists in the realm of discontinuity. By participating in erotic activity, individual beings have their fundamental continuity revealed to them, which stands in contrast to normal discontinuous existence.

By exposing one's flesh for others to see, the individual becomes dispossessed by its nudity. This nakedness and dispossession of the **self** are partially indicative of radical and anti-social aspects of eroticism that tend to break down established social patterns. Eroticism is also anti-social by its very nature because it is a solitary activity done in secret outside the confines of everyday life.

Eroticism must not be confused with an ordinary sexual act or desire. Eroticism, an aspect of an individual's inner life, represents a disequilibrium that stimulates a person to call their own being into question. With respect to desire and its object, eroticism is transgressive in the sense that it is a desire that overcomes **taboo**. Desire and transgression, a violent principle that causes **chaos**, helps to create the apparent insane world of eroticism. The final sense of eroticism is **death**, which is opened by the former. By means of eroticism, death returns a person from their discontinuous way of life to continuity. Some of Bataille's novels explore the union of the erotic and death.

Further reading: Bataille (1962, 1991); Hollywood (2002); Kripal (2001); Miller (1977)

ETHICS

This concept reflects proper rules of conduct recognized as valid by a particular religious tradition. Ethics also suggests the values and moral principles related to human conduct and the analysis of such actions.

Rules about what constitutes correct behavior can vary according to a person's status in life, such as whether one is an adult or child. Ethics is often used interchangeably with morals in the West because morality is a Latin cognate of a Greek root for ethics that covers such notions as custom, habit, character, and personal disposition.

Buddhism draws a distinction between rules of discipline (*vinaya*) and virtues (*sīla*). Since rules are the correct path of action, they should necessarily be followed, whereas virtues are the foundation of the moral/ ethical life, which allows a virtuous person to develop wisdom. In order for a person to lead an ethical life, the Buddha established a guideline summarized by the five precepts: (1) non-violence (*ahimsā*); (2) non-stealing; (3) chastity; (4) abstaining from false speech; (5) not using intoxicants. In order to practice non-violence, the development of loving kindness (*mettā*) and compassion (*karuṇā*) are necessary.

If the foundation of Buddhist ethics originated from the wise guidance of the Buddha, Islamic ethics are constructed on a threefold belief: Allah, His **judgment**, and the necessity of virtuous deeds. Therefore, Islamic ethics are based on eschatology or the coming Day of **Judgment**. Until that day arrives, a Muslim is guided by some general ethical principles: duty to **God** who enjoins a person to do what is good and just, moderation, forgiveness, repelling **evil** with what is better, limited liability – which means that no one should be obligated beyond one's capacity – and awareness that God rewards good and punishes evil. These principles suggest that there is an ethical relationship between God and humans that begins with God's guidance that humans are obliged to accept. In fact, belief is accepting guidance and choosing the right path. Whether a person chooses the Islamic path or the Buddhist path that being can be confident that they have selected correctly because the choices reside with divine guidance or that of an enlightened being. In other words, a person's ethical choices originate with an authoritative figure.

Further reading: Harvey (2000); Izutsu (1966)

EVIL

Evil refers to transgressions of religious injunctions and/or being in a wrongful condition due to an innate flaw, corrupted nature, or original sin. According to some religious traditions, humans are living in an evil and degenerate age, or are moving toward an evil age. The *kali yuga* is the present degenerate age in which humans live in Hinduism, whereas the notion of *mappo* in Japanese Pure Land Buddhism calls attention to the decline of the Buddhist law or doctrine. *Mappo* refers to three phases of the law whereby it becomes more difficult to practice the law and attain enlightenment until the third and final stage when it is impossible to accomplish either correct practice or **liberation**. The final phase of *mappo* occurs at a moment when humans are moving toward the imminent end of the world and are within the grasp of evil and governed by neurotic cravings and desires. The notions of *mappo* and the *kali yuga* are examples of doctrines arising from within religions that view **time** as cyclical, whereas the Judeo-Christian-Islamic tradition looks forward in a linear way to a final defeat of evil at the conclusion of history. Besides these types of dire scenarios, evil is personified in many religious traditions into an identifiable figure, such as Māra in Buddhism, the Devil in Christianity, or Iblīs in Islam.

Unlike Gnosticism and Manichaeism with their teaching that evil is due to the basic evil nature of matter, Christianity traces it to the **myth** of Adam and Eve and the choice of evil over good by the primordial parents of humanity. Augustine, a seminal Christian thinker of the fifth century, argues that evil comes from the direct misuse of human freedom connected with original sin. If human nature is fundamentally corrupted from birth in Christianity, this is not the case in Eastern religions, which view human beings as good by nature but needing nurturing and education as in Chinese Confucian thought, or being aware of the problems of consciousness as in Buddhist philosophy.

Evil (*pāpa*) is located in states of mind in Buddhism that cause a person to stray from the path to **liberation**. Evil arises from conscious and unconscious intentions that have been shaped by greed, hatred, and delusion, which account for the triple roots of evil. Since the individual is a free agent responsible for his/her actions and everything is ultimately impermanent, all deeds lead to karmic consequences and rebirth. Positive deeds lead to a favorable rebirth, whereas negative deeds lead to sorrowful modes of rebirth.

Further reading: Ling (1962); Mathews (2001); Morrow (2003); O'Flaherty (1976): Ricoeur (1967)

EXPERIENCE

This is a vague concept difficult to define because it is subjective, ineffable, and unique to a person having the experience, inaccessible to others, and contextual in the sense of happening within particular religious communities. As the religious scholar Wayne Proudfoot demonstrates, the term is of relatively recent origin. A good example is its use by Friedrich Schleiermacher (1768–1834), a liberal German religious thinker, and his discussion of religion as consciousness of absolute dependence. It is impossible for a researcher to have direct access to a religious experience of another person as it is being experienced, although a researcher can have secondary access by means of first or second-hand accounts of a religious experience as it might appear in an autobiographical or a biographical account. Another feature of experience that makes it difficult to define is its wide variety; an experience can be **mystical** or ecstatic, and can take the form of a trance, **visions**, **dreams**, feelings, moods, dispositions, **faith**, or enlightenment. Within some religious traditions, it is presupposed that an individual must have some type of experience in order to be saved or liberated. Sometimes a religious experience alters an individual's life and turns that individual to a religious path, such as the Christian apostle Paul while walking along the road to Damascus.

When a religious experience happens to an individual it modifies the individual's consciousness, which can be either intentional or non-intentional. The intentional type of modification involves awareness by a subject of something objective that is external to his/her consciousness, which originates from interpreting or misinterpreting objective data. When an individual interprets such external data he/she utilizes concepts. By becoming aware of an object, one becomes conscious of something (this is called intentionality), whereas the non-intentional type of modification of consciousness does not depend on something external, and thus represents a mode of consciousness that involves feelings.

A religious experience can manifest itself in a variety of forms that include: feeling absolutely united with the world, called panenhenic feeling; or a person can have a more numinous type of experience, when one experiences something as wholly other than oneself – a mysterious **power** that both repels and attracts a person at the same time; or a person may have a more contemplative type of experience that does not postulate an external other, but does give a feeling that the normal subject–object distinction disappears. Different types of feelings and attitudes are generated by the numinous and contemplative kinds of experiences, such as fear, trembling, respect, abjection, and humility in the former, whereas the contemplative type of experience is more apt to produce serenity, confidence, certainty, calm, bliss, and happiness. Since neither type is restrictive, there is some overlap of both types. The numinous tends to be associated with a devotional type of religiosity, while the contemplative tends to be mystical and creates self-awareness, a sense of wisdom, and equanimity.

Whether stimulated by group practices or triggered by internal subjective incidents, religious experience often transforms the individual, changing their prior thought and behavioral patterns. Sometimes an individual chooses a life of isolation, while in other cases the individual gathers together a small **community** or returns to the original community and transforms, revitalizes, redirects, or reshapes it.

Over the last couple of centuries, various people have argued for a residue in conscious experience that cannot be reduced to something else; this is called pure consciousness or subjectivity, ur-consciousness, or pre-reflective consciousness. This type of non-reducible consciousness is free from the individual ego. Numerous scholars are critical of this type of perennial thought that claims that there is a common ground to all religious experience. According to these scholars, even "pure experience" is an experience of something because humans are able to experience things at different levels of consciousness: a primary consciousness shared with animals lacking an awareness of awareness and a secondary level of consciousness when humans experience things without thinking about it. Below the levels of primary and secondary experience, there is also a variety of mental activity that occurs. Due to the subjective nature of conscious experience, neither side can verify their claims, although it is important to acknowledge that religious experiences are often shaped and even determined by the history, **doctrine**, communal, or cultural context in which a particular experience happens. Religious experiences neither occur in a vacuum nor are they static.

Among the Native American Indians of the northern plains, young men go on a **vision** quest, which can result in hallucinations, **dreams**, and unusual auditory or visual stimulus. These various phenomena are interpreted by Indians as a communication with supernatural beings. The primary motivations for going on a vision quest include the following: seeking visions during times of disease and death in order to receive help; to become brave before war expeditions; at childbirth to discern the proper name of a child; as an act of thanksgiving; or to realize an individual's oneness with all things. Once motivated to seek a vision, an individual passes through two phases: quest and action. The second phase is a process by which an individual's vision is legitimized. As a result of having a vision, an individual may acquire power, advice, or certain ritual privileges. This solicited type of vision comes after a period of fasting and self-mortification; or the visions can come suddenly, spontaneously, and totally unexpected in the form of dreams.

The solicited type of vision follows a pattern of purifying baths, sacred smoking, nightly vigils, isolation in a remote place, **meditation**, and visit by a **spirit**. The process includes self-mortification, which can include offering pieces of one's flesh, a form of self-torture, and fasting and going thirsty. These forms of self-mortification are believed to make a supplicant weak and pitiable before the spirits, who are overcome by pity and grant visions. An Indian might have a vision of terrible Thunder beings, animals, an old man, or the sun. Any of these figures communicate important messages that are revealing and useful to the person eager for them.

Religious experiences in other traditions are somewhat more abstract, such as the Buddhist notion of nirvāṇa, which metaphorically means the blowing out of a flame. The experience or attainment of nirvāṇa represents the end of suffering, desire, causation, and rebirth. The early Buddhist tradition distinguishes two kinds of nirvāṇa: with a basis remaining and without a basis remaining. The former refers to an embodied experience and the latter represents final nirvāṇa, which represents a complete cessation of the psycho-physical aspects of a person, whereas the embodied experience includes the cessation of defiled outflows. The experience is described positively as equanimity and blissful.

The highest experience in Hindu, Advaita Vedānta, is expressed as the realization of being, pure consciousness, and bliss. For the tantric thinker Abhinavagupta, there are several levels of bliss. Different devotional traditions in India describe love of God as a blissful experience. Within Krishna devotion, the bliss of love is also associated with passion and **eroticism** that overwhelms a devotee.

Further reading: Katz (1983); Olson (2005, 2007); Otto (1928); Powers (1982); Proudfoot (1985); Taves (2009)

FAITH

A concept that reflects a personal act of adherence associated with an inclination, commitment, and acceptance of claims made by a religion. In some contexts, it is to believe in **God**, an unperceived being of imagined great **power**. Faith has been defined differently by thinkers even within the same religious tradition, and it plays a central role in the path of **salvation** in many religions from a cross-cultural perspective.

In the early Christian tradition, the apostle Paul urges his listeners to walk in the path of faith (2 Cor. 5.7). Not only did Paul include faith among the primary Christian virtues along with hope and **love** (1 Cor. 13.13), he also preached about justification by faith alone, by which he implies that faith is a **gift** of grace from God. Moreover, it becomes the foundation of Christian **belief**. The Protestant reformer Martin Luther (1483–1546) argues against stressing good works that can be used to coerce God, and he instead preaches about the necessity of justification by faith in order to be saved. Over the course of Christian history, other religious thinkers offer reflections on, and definitions of, faith; this is particularly true of more contemporary thinkers.

Søren Kierkegaard (1813–1855) defines faith as uncertainty held fast with passionate inwardness. For Kierkegaard, objective certainty with respect to faith is its most dangerous enemy because faith is a venture and a risk. Faith throws one into despair and out of this comes consolation that means greater suffering. Faith is also beyond reason and against it. In his work *Fear and Trembling*, Kierkegaard writes about the example of Abraham's **sacrifice** of Isaac, his favorite son, in response to a command by God, an order contrary to the ethical demand not to kill. Kierkegaard uses the example of Abraham's faith to serve as a representation of Christian faith that is opaque and irrational. Since Christ is the absolute paradox, the object of Christian faith is the absurd, the paradoxical, and the incomprehensible. The absurd is a technical expression for the conviction that with God all things are possible. To adopt this absurd and paradoxical faith, a Christian must be mad and take a leap of despair.

Within the Abrahamic traditions of **monotheistic** religions, faith also plays a central role in Islam where it is counted as one of the five pillars of the religion. In fact, the confession of faith (*shahādah*) represents the first pillar of Islam, and it affirms that "There is no God but Allah and Muhammad is His prophet." When a Muslim recites this formula sincere intention (*niyyah*) is essential. This implies that religious acts, such as the confession of faith, must not be done in a perfunctory or mechanical way. Proper intention is also a defense against inattentive and external performance.

The Hindu *Bhagavad Gītā*, a section of the much larger epic *Mahābhārata*, attempts to synthesize three paths to **salvation: knowledge**, good deeds, and devotion, with the author favoring the final means. Devotion is both a means to a goal and the goal itself. A self-forgetting love, seeing the world as a manifestation of God, and surrendering to the deity are all requirements of the path of devotion, but the basic requirement is faith (*śraddhā*). The religious insights of this text are developed further by the Hindu thinker Rāmānuja (1050–1137), whose philosophical position represents a qualified non-dualism because the ultimate **reality** is not devoid of characteristics and is qualified by the self and the world. According to Rāmānuja, the path of knowledge leads to devotion, at which time the self is completely subservient to God, and one takes refuge at the feet of God, provoking the grace of God and gift of faith.

Faith plays a major role in the later development of Buddhism, and contributes to it becoming a worldwide religion. Pure Land Buddhism is the best example of this trend. The Pure Land is a paradise, governed by the bodhisattva Amitābha, into which a person strives to be reborn by means of a combination of performing good deeds and faith, although a shorter version of the basic text—*Pure Land Sūtra*—claims that only faith and **prayer** are necessary. When Pure Land Buddhism enters Japan during the Kamakura era (1185–1333), the fundamental tension between works and faith continues to be discussed by thinkers such as Hōnen, founder of the Jōdo (Pure Land) school, and his disciple Shinran (1173–1262), who establishes the Jōdo Shinshu (True Pure Land) sect. Both men agree that they are living during a dark period of history when the **doctrine** of Buddhism finds itself in a state of decline, but they disagree about the effort that a person can make to be saved, although they also agree that faith is essential for salvation by means of the grace of Amitābha.

Further reading: Kierkegaard (1954); Olson (2005, 2007); Otto (1928); Smith (1979)

FESTIVALS

These are special times during the course of a year when ordinary work is suspended while people celebrate some event. Often, social distinctions are obliterated during festivals. During the Western medieval Feast of Fools, the town fool becomes a monarch for a day, thereby overturning the social order. Festivals can work to re-establish a relational bond between a devotee and a deity. The festival's ability to overturn pre-established social structures and to reunite parties suggests that the festival forms a basis for change and stability. Festivals represent a time that is repetitive in two fundamental senses: it repeats actions of the divine beings and often re-enacts the birth of the cosmos, and thereby represents renewal. The Hindu Sastri festival celebrates, for instance, the victory of Skanda, a son of the high god Śiva, over demonic beings, which saves cultural order and ushers in a new age.

An essential feature of festivity is excess, a combination of destruction and waste, accompanied by dancing, singing, eating, and drinking. This joyous time is pure revelry, during which participants excessively overindulge with respect to festival activities. A wonderful example of such a situation is the Holi festival in India celebrating devotion to Krishna, during which devotees act as the deity's cowherd companions by dousing others with brightly colored dyes and water, and women beat men with sticks and wet rags This represents a return to a primordial chaos that is newly created and rediscovered and which functions as an annual renewal of society.

Within cross-cultural contexts, festivals often involve public processions of **sacred** objects, such as a cross or image of the Virgin Mary in Christianity, a relic like the tooth of the Buddha in Sri Lanka, or an icon of a Hindu deity. In Hinduism, the procession of an icon of a deity allows the divine being an opportunity to manifest itself to its devotees and represents a new theophany (manifestation of the God). Moreover, festive celebrations affirm life despite failure, illness, **suffering**, and **death**. Festivals affirm life even though things are done in reverse during festivals, but they are never an end in themselves because they always express joy about something, while also embodying a time of intense **emotion** and change. The celebrative and affirmative aspects of festivals are a form of **play** that embodies personal and cultural **memory** and opens the future to participants with a sense of hope.

Many festivals are connected to mythical or historical events or the agricultural cycle, and consist of different lengths of **time**. Among devotees of the Hindu god Vishnu, the Swing festival marks the beginning of spring and during this time an image of the deity is suspended on a plank under a specially built pavilion. A twelve-day festival is represented by the Vaikuntha Ekādasī for Vishnu, which commemorates the victory of the goddess Ekādasī over demonic beings; whereas the Dīpāvali is a complex annual four-day event that incorporates five different festivals: worship of wealth, celebration of Vishnu's victory over a **demon**, Lakshmī **worship**, celebration of Vishnu's victory over the demon Bali, and a celebration of the sibling affection between Yama (Lord of Death) and his sister, Yamunā.

Festivals of rural Thailand, a predominately Buddhist country, are closely interwoven with the cycle of the village agricultural calendar, such as the four-day-long Songkrān festival that forms a New Year celebration marked by the final day of the festival. Villagers give gifts of food to monks, clean their homes, burn trash, and clean themselves. The festival also includes bathing an **image** of the Buddha, offerings to departed **ancestors**, and a transfer of merit to the departed. A large *stūpa* (memorial mound) is built and adorned with three flags, signifying the three refuges: the Buddha, dhamma (doctrine), and Sangha (monastic community). Young people engage in water sports, which can become a rowdy activity. In Thailand, a festival connected to soliciting rain is the Rocket festival (Bunbangfai; literally "merit of firing rockets"), which also includes some mischievous behavior.

Further reading: Caillois (1961); Coomaraswamy (1941); Cox (1969); Hawley (1981); Huizinga (1955); Östor (1980); Tambiah (1970)

FIRE

The discovery of this element in prehistoric time, which is probably acci-
dental, enabled pre-historic humans to make a transition from a raw to a
cooked diet, which is associated with more developed forms of culture.
In his study of South Indian cultures, the anthropologist Lévi-Strauss
relates a variety of **myths** about the origin of fire in his work *The Raw
and the Cooked*. In many versions, Indians lack fire, but they learn about
it and appropriate it for their own uses from the jaguar, thus enabling
them to cook **food**, warm themselves, and light the village at night. If
cooked food is equivalent to being civilized, it is the element of fire that
makes this possible for humans. During his research, Lévi-Strauss finds
that the Indians identify two kinds of fire: celestial and destructive and
terrestrial and creative. The former type of fire takes life and the latter
type makes life possible.

Fire is a primary element in many cultures. Along with wood, metal,
earth, and water, fire is a basic element within ancient Chinese culture.
In the Hindu *Bhagavad Gītā* (13.1–6), the self is composed of five great
elements (earth, water, air, space, and fire). In Pali Buddhism, form (matter) consists of air, water, earth, and fire, according to the great scholar
Buddhaghosa. In his work *Ratnāvali*, the Buddhist philosopher Nāgārjuna
claims that a human is a set of six elements that includes fire. Buddhism
also depicts fire as involved in the future destruction of the world,
whereas the major **monotheistic faiths** associate fire directly with hell in
the Hebrew Scriptures (Isa. 66.24) and the Qur'an (22.20). Moreover, in
Islam the **spirits** (*jinn*) are made of fire.

The importance of fire is evident in ancient Greek and Iranian cultures.
In ancient Greece, the cultural hero Prometheus steals fire and knowledge
of arts and crafts from Hephaestus and Athena, and he gives these items
to humans. Along with the **blood** of a pig, fire purifies a person guilty of
homicide. In Zoroastrianism, fire is sacred and central to the cultic activity. Zoroastrians believe that fire is a living symbol of righteousness, and
it is represented by three grades: *Atash Bahram*, which is always kept
burning even during the night; *Atash Adaran*, which is served by priests;
and *Dadgah*, which can be served by a priest or layperson.

Similar to the centrality of fire in Zoroastrianism is the fire cult of the
ancient Indian Vedic religion where it is used to send food to the gods in
return for rain. Fire is called the messenger of the gods, and is personified
as the deity Agni. Fire possesses the ability to **purify** people, to transform
profane areas into holy places for sacrificial purposes, necessary for the
cremation of the dead, and to drive away **evil spirits**. The household fire

is instructive because it defines the unity of a family, although fire is also an ambivalent, dangerous, and unpredictable **power** that can destroy a family. Nonetheless, a family is encouraged to **worship** it for protection. Three sacrificial fires are the norm for major public sacrifices, with each sitting on an altar representing different parts of the triple-structured Vedic universe with Agni, god of fire, functioning as the connecting link between the fires. In later Vedic culture, the image of the ritual fire is akin to an internal fire for the digestion of food, and is adopted by yogis, who equated it with their internal fire created by ascetic practices that consumes the seeds of actions by the fire of **knowledge**.

Cross-cultural evidence suggests that fire is both creative and destructive, associated with civilization in the form of cooked food, central to some religious **cults**, possesses the **power** to purify people and things, and can transform people and things. Fire is also used to transport food to the gods. In many cultures, it is considered a basic element of life. When it is used metaphorically it is connected to the fire of passion, procreation, and life.

Further reading: Boyce (1979); Knipe (1975); Lévi-Strauss (1970)

FOOD

If what humans eat sustains their existence and helps them to thrive, food is synonymous with life itself because it contains nutritious elements that cause physical well-being, shapes personal temperament, influences emotional changes, and bestows longevity. By the proper food intake, one can regulate one's mental condition, aesthetic feelings, and spiritual attainments. Food also plays a role as a commodity within a mutual transactional exchange between humans or between individuals and **god**, a situation that manifests a connection between god, food, and life in a cosmological triangle. Moreover, these food transactions between a god and humans help to determine the existence of the universe.

In Hinduism food plays an essential role in ancient **sacrifice**, religious speculation, devotional **worship**, and purity and **pollution** regulations. Within the context of the ancient Vedic animal sacrifice, the sacrificer unites with the world of the gods, a unity often expressed as the sacrificer becoming food. Since the gods only accept cooked food, the sacrificer is reminded of his inferior status by waiting to consume his portion of the sacrificed animal. In the ancient Upanishads, food is a manifestation of, and a part of, the highest **reality** or Brahman. In addition, food forms one of the five sheaths of the **self**. In ancient India, food is associated with life-cycle speculation, as when consumed food, for instance, creates semen and from that semen a person arises.

Within the context of devotional Hinduism, humans make food offerings to a deity, and these are returned as gracious food leftovers (*prasāda*) for human consumption. Food also plays an important role during **pilgrimage** and **festival** occasions. Leaders of devotional religion often use food as a **metaphor** to express, for instance, a devotee's longing for the nectar of devotion. Or the profuse **love** between a god and devotee is expressed by an outpouring of milk, which signifies *rasa* (literally juice, sap, liquid) that includes the connotation of flavor or taste. *Rasa* is not something added to food to enhance its flavor, but it is rather an essential ingredient within the food.

Because of the saliva naturally produced by eating, food is intimately associated with purity regulations, especially for higher caste individuals in Hinduism. In order to maintain **ritual purity**, only vegetarian food is permissible for members of the Brahmin caste. Onions and garlic are considered strong foods and thus inappropriate for Brahmins; foods that resemble meat in color like pumpkins, tomatoes, radishes, and carrots are also forbidden. Distinctions are traditionally made with food between imperfect (*kaccā*) and perfect food (*pakkā*). What makes a food perfect is whether or not it is cooked with cow products such as butter or milk. Another distinction is made for Brahmin caste members between meals whose basis is boiled rice and others consisting of fruits, fried foods, sweets, and dishes cooked in water. Depending on the context, food in Hinduism can also be distinguished into subtle/gross, pure/impure, hot/cold, boiled/fried, human/divine, good/bad, temple/home, and feasting/fasting.

In northern India, it is possible to encounter the notion of *mast* (happy, carefree) as an ideal of personhood, which is associated with food. Besides drinking marijuana, *mast* helps a person feel *mast* (happy) because food is consumed to nourish both the physical and the emotional self. Vegetarian food produces, for instance, the moral characteristics of peacefulness, truthfulness, compassion, kindness, and sympathy, making food a moral and a material substance that imbues people with its own moral and material qualities.

It is believed in many religious traditions that an improper diet can place a person at risk of ill health. An unhealthy person can be restored to good health by a proper diet that creates the right type of inner balance. Therefore, it is important to maintain a controlled level of nourishment in order to promote a healthy **body**. Gluttony is immoral and upsets a proper bodily balance, which can, however, be corrected by fasting; in many religious contexts fasting makes the **soul** dominant over the body, whereas with gluttony the opposite is true. As part of their regimen, **ascetics** control their intake of food in order to achieve their spiritual goal.

From a cross-cultural perspective, the concept of food manifests cosmic and social dimensions. In addition to being equated with reality in some instances, food transaction within a society includes a wide variety of recipients that includes gods, **ancestors**, **demons**, family, guests, and beggars. These food transactions constitute a social code that defines and reinforces hierarchical social structures.

Further reading: Harper (1964); Khare (1992a,b); Lynch (1990); Srinavas (1952); Toomey (1992)

GENDER

Among feminist writers and others, it is common to distinguish sex from gender because the former represents a biologically inherited attribute, whereas gender refers to cultural expectations of what it means to be one sex or another, with particular cultural perceptions that differ from one **culture** to another. Among cultural elements, religion plays a central role in constructing gendered social roles by promoting a patriarchical perspective as the social norm. Thus gender is a social, historical, and artificial construct. Even though feminist scholars agree that gender is socially constructed and possesses general importance for the study of religion, they express wide, multidimensional, and complex views about the issues of sex and gender and about the role of women in diverse religious traditions.

Feminist scholars approach the concept of gender within the cultural context of patriarchy and sexism. Patriarchy is often defined as a historical, social, cultural, and political institutionalization of male **power** that results in the domination, subordination, and marginalization of women. The all-embracing specter of patriarchy is supported by sexism, which can be defined as the ideology of male supremacy. The feminist struggle against sexism and patriarchical domination is radically pushed to a point where it even calls into question prior feminist agreement about the definitions of sex and gender.

The feminist Christine Delphy argues, for instance, that sex, male, and female are equally social constructs. This implies that sex is a social and historical notion and not a biological one. In fact, humans have a

93

pre-understanding of sex that they interpret through their grasp of gender. Judith Butler argues that gender precedes sex. But as a concept gender is established on sexual roles, although both are socially constructed notions. Moreover, gender is productive in the sense that it produces sex and establishes it as something prior to culture.

Judith Butler, a poststructural feminist, argues that gender supports the category of sex by means of cultural imperatives such as heterosexuality. It is naturalized and institutionalized heterosexuality that regulates gender as a binary relation through differentiating male from female by means of practices associated with heterosexual desire. Within **culture**, the gender/sex distinction is performed in a way that embodies a political imperative that identifies a person. If one looks behind expressions of gender, there is, however, no genuine gender identity; it is just people performing their expected social roles.

Further reading: Butler (1990); Delphy (1993); King (1987, 1995)

GIFTS

Within a web of social relations, unique items or services are given to **others** who may reciprocate the gesture. The social significance of gifts can give personal information about the people doing the giving and receiving, the objects given and received, and what this practice tells us about social relations within a particular context. The bestowing of gifts is an important cross-cultural feature of various religious traditions. Islam builds giving gifts, for instance, into the five pillars of the **faith** with the injunction of *zakāt* (almsgiving), a term related to **purity**. The Qur'an (9.103) refers to the offering of one's wealth that purifies a person and their remaining wealth. *Zakāt* is an obligatory contribution of one-fortieth of one's annual income. It is distinguished from *sadaqāt*, which is a free-will offering (58.13–14). The act of giving is best understood in the Muslim context as a loan made to **God** that will be repaid manifold and will help a person repent and atone for sins. Jews and Christians are also encouraged to be generous with their gifts, as are Buddhists and Hindus.

The Buddhist term for giving, generosity, or charity is *dāna*, an important virtue that must be executed selflessly and without expectation of reward. Within Therāvada Buddhism, it refers to the laity giving alms to the monastic community and monks giving teachings to the laity, creating a mutual giving society. Lay followers receive merit, a balance of good karma produced by positive deeds, for their generosity that can benefit them in a future life. They received greater merit if the **monk** or nun to whom they give is a virtuous paragon, a practice that places pressure on monks and nuns to conform to the highest standards for the monastic life. Within Mahāyāna Buddhism, giving is a perfection that a bodhisattva must cultivate and is closely associated with compassion (*karuṇā*) and loving kindness (*maitri*). In all branches of Buddhism, it is not unusual to find a tension between merit that is based on Buddhist teachings and merit that is socially based and associated with social prestige grounded in a person's family lineage, wealth, and political power.

The Hindu religious tradition makes a distinction between a gift called *daksinā*, an exchange for ritual services rendered by Brahmin **priests**, and another type termed *dan*, a giving vital to village life because the donor gets rid of danger, various kinds of afflictions, and **evil** or **sin**. The merit associated with a *daksinā* type of gift is tied to the mental attitude of the giver, the manner in which the gift is acquired, the worthiness of the giver and recipient, and the humble way in which it is given to another. In comparison to *daksinā*, the *dan* type of gift involves more of an obligation to accept than any right to claim a gift. From the perspective of Brahmins, there is a poison in the gift because it embodies the sin and evil of the donor and therefore is associated with inauspiciousness. By giving, the donor has an opportunity to transfer inauspiciousness to the donee and create a successful outcome for him/herself.

There is a long history in India of gifts having political consequences because generous kings could assert their control over others by means of their patronage, using gifts as a political tool to achieve their ends. The generosity of kings creates a dilemma for Brahmin priests because accepting any royal gift involves accepting social superiority by a monarch and political inferiority compared to the king.

Several theories have been advanced to grasp the concept of the gift. In 1924 Marcel Mauss, a French anthropologist, publishes his major work on the subject in the *L'Année sociologique* (republished by the Presses Universitaires de France in 1950 as simply *The Gift*). Mauss's theory of the gift concentrates more on circulation and consumption rather than on productive consumption and consumptive production as with Marxian theory. According to Mauss, the giving of something to another person is not a voluntary action because any gift involves obligation and economic self-interest. A person gives to another person because one is obligated to act in this way. The person receiving a gift is then involuntarily obligated to reciprocate with another gift, a scenario that is imposed upon both parties or social groups. Mauss identifies a threefold sequence of obligation: to give, to receive, and to reciprocate. The obligatory nature of the gift does not mean for Mauss that a gift is never free; it does, however, suggest that, by fulfilling the obligation to give, it is recreated by the reaffirmation of the social relationships of which the obligation is a part from the commencement of the exchange. Mauss conceives of the process of exchange in a rather broad way because the exchange goes beyond mere economic goods; it includes social acts of politeness conceived in a liberal way that encompass such activities as rituals, dances, festivals, banquets, military service and can even involve the exchange of women and children.

When a person gives a gift to someone that person is not merely giving some inert or neutral object, but is rather giving an active part of him/herself. This suggests that a gift is inalienably connected to the giver. Mauss is further suggesting that a gift is something personal and alive with a special **power** that not only generates itself, but also possesses the power to renew the relationship between the giving and receiving parties. Thus, a gift possesses a vitality, which often includes individuality for Mauss. By giving part of him/herself in the gift, a person participates in it, but this also creates a lasting spiritual bond between persons.

The dynamic nature of the gift is evident in the phenomenon of the potlatch, a kind of orgy of generosity in some indigenous societies that can become violent, exaggerated, and antagonistic. The potlatch is an all-encompassing competition that revolves around honor and prestige for the participants in a reciprocal pattern that creates obligations among the parties. The competitive nature of the potlatch is similar to a game that a participant risks losing, which means for the loser a loss of social rank and status. It is the obligation to reciprocate that Mauss identifies as the essence of the potlatch.

It is precisely the excessive, destructive, disruptive, and irrational nature of the potlatch that captures the attention of the **postmodern** thinker George Bataille, who sees it as an acquisition of **power**. Bataille envisions a relationship between power, a surpassing virtue of gift-giving, and renunciation. The power that the giver gains over the recipient manifests the absurdity of gifts. The intertwining of power, obligation, and absurdity allows Bataille to show that the gift is not some homogenous pattern of exchange, but rather more akin to a heterogeneous and irrational phenomenon.

Jacques Derrida, another postmodern thinker, treats the concept of the gift in an even more radical way than Bataille by placing it within the flux of **time**, which renders the gift impossible due to the predominance of time. The gift is only possible at a paradoxical moment when time is torn apart because the present is related to temporal synthesis, which makes it impossible to think the present moment of the gift. The gift is also impossible in another sense related to its three conditions of donor, gift, and donee. These three conditions of the gift produce its destruction. In other words, the reciprocity of the gift, its return or exchange, annuls the gift. Derrida attempts to imagine the nature of the gift devoid of reciprocity, return, exchange, or debt. For a gift to be truly what it is, or a pure gift, there must be absolutely no returning of the gift and the donor must not expect any restitution. Thus, if we push the gift to its limits, Derrida argues that it will not appear as a gift to either the donor or donee. It is important to grasp the gift as an event, which is prior to any relationship of donor and donee that taints the gift of its **purity**. The event of the gift adheres to principles of disorder and is thus devoid of rules or concepts. Within the flux of time, the moment of giving and receiving are two events that cannot exist simultaneously in time because they are separated in the flow of time. To look for the gift, is to seek the impossible, which is a form of **madness**.

Further reading: Bataille (1991); Berking (1999); Derrida (1992); Godelier (1999); Mauss (1990)

GODDESSES

A goddess is a powerful divine being, defined in large part by her sexual identity along with her creative and destructive powers. Within the context of **polytheistic** religions, the goddess is depicted with ordinary human features. Among the Yoruba of Nigeria, Oshun is described as river born; she is identified with cool waters that help to explain her vivacious character. Described as beautiful and sweet tempered, Oshun's hips sway like a slow rolling river, her sensuousness embodies the divine spark in human sexual life. She reveals pleasure and loves rich gifts of silk, perfume, sweet food, and jewelry. She is famous as a great coquette, flirting with men and taking delight in their seduction. In the past, Oshun is the wife of many gods but none of them could keep her for any length of time. After being transported to Cuba, she becomes Puta Santa, or the whore **saint**, who possesses the **power** to bestow children especially to barren women.

Among Native American Indians, many goddesses are associated with various aspects of **nature**. The Sioux Buffalo Calf Woman is an **earth** goddess, a mistress of buffalo, and a **cultural** heroine for establishing social institutions and introducing the sacred pipe that is used in the seven rites of the tribe. Among the Iroquois, there are three goddesses, identified with corn, beans, and squash, that clothe them and which they protect. The corn goddess functions, for instance, in three ways: she is the corn itself, she is its spiritual protector, and she is the patroness of humans who cultivate it. The Huichol Indians of Mexico worship a number of goddesses called Our Mothers, who are associated with motherhood, growth, fertility and water. The Eskimo worship Sedna, Sea Woman, who lives at the bottom of the ocean in a big domed house that is guarded by seals who bite intruders. Sedna is described as frightening with one eye, a body covered with dirt, tangled hair, and no fingers. She is both the mistress and creator of sea animals. Instead of a home in the bottom of the ocean, Our Grandmother of the Shawnee lives in a house (wigwam) in the sky from which she spies on her children. She possesses great mental **powers** as shown by the fact, for instance, that she can answer questions before they are even asked. Besides her role as a cultural heroine by teaching people about the necessities of life, she rules over the abode of the **dead**, and is associated with the end of **time** when she will gather virtuous people into a basket that she weaves all night once her little dog stops unraveling the basket of the previous day.

A **polytheistic** religion such as Hinduism manifests many goddess figures such as Aditi, Śrī Laksmi, Rādhā, Sītā, Durgā, Kālī, and many village goddesses associated with a disease such as smallpox. Naked and immodest, Kālī is called the Black One because of the dark color of her **body**. She is depicted with four arms in which she holds, respectively, a sword, a noose, a freshly severed human head, and a cup made from half a human skull that is filled with blood. She is attired with a necklace of human heads, newly cut human hands dangle from her waistband, and two dead infants serve as her earrings. She appears with a sunken belly, sagging breasts, and disheveled hair, a mouth with large fangs, a lolling tongue, **blood** trickling out of her corners of her mouth, and sunken reddish eyes. She sustains herself on the blood of humans and demons. Her dancing represents the pulsating of the universe, although her dancing can become destructive when it becomes uncontrolled. She threatens the world with her **madness** and perverse desire to bring about the destruction of the world. Finally, she is closely identified with **time** as its mistress, symbolized by her lolling tongue that consumes everything, and **death**, which is symbolized by her raised and bloody sword. Kālī's nature and appearance manifests the goddess as frightening, awesome, and terrible.

Generally, goddesses are creative figures with strong, powerful, and dynamic characters. In many patriarchical **cultures**, **women** are expected to be passive, submissive, and inferior. But goddesses within these male-dominated cultures are life-giving, powerful, aggressive, and transformative, and can also be destructive. There is no connection between male dominance within a culture and the acknowledgement of the powers of goddesses that influences male attitudes towards women. Nonetheless, there are some feminist writers who welcome the advent of the goddess into Western culture to counterbalance male-dominated concepts of divine beings.

Further reading: Hultkrantz (1983); Kinsley (1975); Murphy (1983); Olson (1983)

GODS

A masculine divine being who can be either transcendent and thus beyond human **perception** or immanent within the world as an incarnation who is visible to sight. A God is often defined as all-powerful, omniscient, eternal, creative, wrathful, moral, and an active judge. Gods can be active in the daily lives of people, or distant and inactive. Greek gods act as immoral humans, the ancient Hebrew God chooses a people and enters into a **covenant** with them, the Christian God is declared Trinitarian, the Muslim God is singular, the Hindu god Śiva is androgynous, Krishna is playful and erotic, and other Hindu gods, such as Agni, Indra, and Varuna, are historically eclipsed by more recent figures. Gods are distinguished by their religious context in three fundamental ways: **monotheism** (a single deity): **polytheism** (many deities); and **pantheism** (equates god with forces and laws of the universe).

Although possibly active originally creating the world, some deities become distant, inactive creators, who tend to disappear from the **ritual cult**. Being basically distant and inactive, they are replaced by other supernatural figures such as **ancestors'** fertility **spirits**, or a great **goddess**. An excellent example of a distant, inactive, and silent god is Olorum of the Yoruba of Africa. Forever aloof from the course of history, creation is executed by his intermediates as he reigns as a secluded and impersonal monarch. Olorum's nature excludes any possibility of a personal relationship with humans.

A more prominent historical figure is Nhialic of the Dinka of Africa, who creates humans from clay. He continues to act as the sole creator of human beings by shaping them in the womb and by giving them life. Nhialic, a personal and fatherly figure, helps to alleviate major misfortunes.

A more complex divine being is found among the Native American Sioux with Wakantanka, a name derived from *wakan* (sacred) and *tanka* (great, large, big), who is called the Great Spirit or Great Mystery.

Although he is often called Grandfather or Father, Wakantanka is usually not personified, although aspects of it are embodied in the sense of the embodiment of all supernatural beings and **powers**. Wakantanka possesses a collective meaning because it is hierarchically ranked in groups of fours: (1) superior *wakan* (sun, sky, earth, and rock); (2) associates of the superior *wakan* (moon, wind, falling star, and thunder-being) – a linking of the superior and their associates (e.g. **sun** and moon, sky and wind, **earth** and falling star, and rock and thunder-being), which is called *wakan kin* (the sacred), is without beginning, and is responsible for creating the universe and humans; (3) lower *wakan* (buffalo, two-legged bear and human, four winds, and whirlwind); (4) and those similar to *wakan* (shades, life or breath, potency), which are part of *wakan kin*. The Sioux Wankantanka suggests that not only is the sky impregnated with **sacred** force, but the earth and its inhabitants are also forms of a theophany (manifestation of a divine being).

In general, transcendent gods are omniscience, a trait usually associated with their acute ability to hear and see everything that happens on earth. The ancient Hindu deity Varuna is, for instance, assisted by spies. This suggests that it is impossible to keep secrets from him, and he holds a noose by which he can bind humans. When divine laws or **covenants** are broken transcendent gods exercise sanctions against the transgressors by punishing them according to their deeds, often with the vengeful use of weather or physical illness. Those who adhere to divine standards are often rewarded in this life and the next. Although a transcendent deity, Yahweh operates within history for his chosen people and punishes them when they transgress the divine **covenant**.

The Muslim Allah is a transcendent deity called al-Wāhid (the One) and al-Rahmān, al-Rahīm (the compassionate and the merciful). Allah possesses ninety-nine beautiful names that are grasped as realities and not simply as attributes. Allah is the creator, sustainer, and judge. Allah does not create for sport, but His creative acts are purposeful and meaningful (21.16–17), which suggests that the universe is not a product of chance. Allah's **power** is expressed as His ability to measure things out, which implies that He creates the laws by which nature works and bestows on everything their range of potentialities. The wisdom and power of Allah are visible in **nature** and in the course of history.

Divine beings such as Śiva, Krishna, Aphrodite, Hermaphrodite, Heracles, and Dionysus are all defined in some contexts as androgynous gods because they embody masculine and feminine principles. The Hindu deity Śiva is combined with Śakti, with the former representing the unchanging aspect of the godhead while the latter feminine aspect stands for the changing and dynamic feature of the divine being. Just as the **sun** does not exist without its light, Śiva cannot exist without Śakti, a form of divine consciousness and creative power of the deity. From an iconographical perspective, the androgynous nature of Śiva is expressed in his pillar or phallic form that rises from the *yoni* (vagina) of Śakti. Similar points can be made about Krishna and the goddess Rādhā in Hinduism. The Greek goddess Aphrodite, worshipped by the people of Cyprus as a bearded figure, is further described as possessing a woman's **body** and **clothing** but the beard and sexual organ of a male. Due to the sexual union of Eros, a son of Aphrodite and Hermes, and the nymph Salmakis, the androgynous Hermaphrodite is born. According to another tradition, he is the offspring of Hermes and Aphrodite. In a Greek myth of Heracles, he exchanges clothing with Omphale. On the island of Cos, the **priests** of Heracles don feminine clothing in imitation of the deity. Roman worshippers of Hercules also wear women's garments, whereas worshippers of Dionysus, who evolves from a virulent male figure to a later very effeminate deity, assume the saffron-colored veil of women in imitation of their god.

In theistic religious traditions, theologians readily admit that God cannot be genuinely known because of God's transcendence, the limits of human **knowledge**, and the inadequate nature of **language** to express the nature of God. Beyond the categories of **time** and **space**, God is not an object among other objects, which places God beyond human language and knowledge. Thus, theistic theologians resort to apophatic **theology**, a kind of negative path characterized by affirming what God is not. Other theologians use another approach called the analogy of being (*analogia entis*) that draws lessons between God's nature as a Creator, for instance, and what He produces. And still other thinkers argue that God is a projection of human wishes, whereas some postmodern thinkers claim that the theistic God is indeed dead.

Further reading: Olson (2007); Peters (2003); Powers (1977); Ray (1976)

GRACE

A concept that is germane in devotional types of religion. In the West, grace is derived from the Latin *gratia*, and is connected to the notion of gift. During the fourth century, Augustine, a bishop in North Africa, states that **salvation** is a **gift** from **God**, rather than a reward for good deeds, which leads to a protracted discussion within the Latin **church** about merit and grace. For Augustine, grace is a liberating force affecting a person's free will and freeing it from its bondage to **sin**; it also possesses the ability to heal people. Augustine distinguishes three types of grace: prevenient grace prepares humans for conversion; operative grace stresses how God works on the sinner without any assistance; cooperative grace refers to God's collaboration with the sinner to achieve regeneration and growth in holiness. During the Middle Ages, Augustine's insights into grace are developed more systematically by Thomas Aquinas, who distinguishes between actual grace, a freely given grace, and habitual grace that means a created habit of grace within the **soul**. Habitual grace refers to something that happens in the soul that makes it acceptable to God. During the Reformation period, Martin Luther stresses "justification by faith alone." By this he means the justification of the sinner is based on the grace of God and is received by the sinner through faith; God does what is necessary to save a sinner, and that faith is a gift of God.

The distinctive Catholic and Protestant views of grace are re-enacted in southern India by the Śrī Vaishnavism sect, which split into two major schools over the issue of grace during the fourteenth century. The so-called Cat-hold School defines surrender to God as receptivity or lack of opposition to divine grace, similar to a mother cat carrying her kittens, which entails no effort on their part. This suggests that God takes the initiative, saving a person without that individual expending any effort. In contrast to this school, the so-called Monkey-hold School argues that a person must strive to receive God's grace by good deeds similar to a young monkey holding onto its mother as it is being transported.

Further reading: McGrath (1994); Olson (2007); Osborne (1990)

HARMONY

This concept is related cross-culturally to being in agreement, to concord, order, stability, and security. In some religious cultures, it assumes an even wider meaning, such as the ancient Egyptian notion of *Ma'at* that suggests what is straight, right, true, truthful, and righteous, and which also plays the role of an unchanging, eternal, and cosmic force established at the beginning of creation. *Ma'at* is a paradigm for a just and proper relationship on a broad plane that includes rulers, subjects, divine beings, and the cosmos.

Everything and everyone is subject to it. On Egyptian inscriptions, *Ma'at* is identified as the daughter of Re, the Sun **god**, or she is connected to Ptah, called the Great Artificer and famous as a god of law and order.

A similar concept is found in Zoroastrianism as *Asha* (**truth**, order of things, true order, or cosmic force) that functions as a norm for human behavior. Similar to *Ma'at* of ancient Egypt, *Asha* is personified as one of the six or seven "holy immortals" of the Best Order (Asha Vahishita), and serves as a member of the entourage of Ahura Mazdah, the godhead or an attribute of him, or as a creative agency of Vohu Manah.

Other ancient civilizations embody similar notions, such as *ṛta* (cosmic law) of ancient Indian Vedic **culture** or the *Logos* of Heraclitus of the pre-Socratic period of Greek philosophy. Heraclitus views the *Logos* as an ordering principle uniting all that exists into a coherent and enduring principle, and as possessing *alethia* (suggesting that which is unconcealed or revealed), which suggests that it represents the **truth** of things. Beneath the discord and conflicts of life, there is a hidden harmony identified with the *Logos*, which is both the cosmic order and the teleological orientation of the world. This Greek concept with its relationship to harmony, truth, and **revelation** exerts a powerful influence upon the early Christian movement, especially in the Fourth Gospel where Christ is identified as the *Logos* (word) in early church history; whereas in the letters of Paul it is the **power** of the Cross, which symbolizes Christ's sacrificial **love**, that holds together the universe (Eph. 3.18).

Ancient Chinese civilization is very preoccupied with harmony (*ho*) as manifested by its notions of mutually complementary opposites: *yin*, a female principle that is described as negative, receptive, passive, and low, and *yang*, a male principle that is defined as active, positive, aggressive, and high. The female principle is similar to **earth**, whereas the active male principle is akin to **heaven**. These principles operate in a cyclical pattern and alternate and complement each other during the course of a year. Although life is in a constant state of flux, it is derived from a blending and harmony of these two forces. Thus, humans have to take special precautions to protect themselves during periods, such as the summer and winter solstices, when *yin* and *yang* give way to each other and create a dangerous transitional period. Human life and affairs are more successful when they are in accord with these principles. In fact, state **rituals** are coordinated with the cycle of these cosmic forces to enhance successful results, and ideally humans form a triadic unity with **heaven** and **earth,** which they are called upon to imitate.

Consisting of *yin* and *yang* opposites, the *Dao*, a metaphysical principle, is the concept of harmony in ancient Daoism. Adherents are instructed to live in accord with the *Dao,* an all-embracing, impartial, simple, and unspoiled principle. Because of its mysterious nature, it is invisible, inaudible, subtle, and nameless, and it is called the **ancestor** and mother of everything because everything owes its existence to it. Because the *Dao*, representing a union of being (its function) and non-being (its essence), exemplifies the harmonious flux of the eternal principle, humans beings are instructed to conform to it in order to endure existentially and live in harmony.

Among the Native American Navaho of the southwestern part of North America, there is the notion of *Hozho*, which conveys the meanings of harmony, good, favorable, beauty, perfection, normality, well-being, and order. The prefix *ho* means a complete environment and also something abstract, indefinite, or infinite. This general and pervasive ordering principle can be disrupted, and order can become disorder. It is implied that the Navaho can attempt to maintain or restore it through **ritual**.

These various cross-cultural examples of different concepts of harmony enable a reader to recognize some common features in spite of conceptual differences. A common feature is the way that harmony is related to the natural cosmic order of everything. In addition to orderliness, harmony points to notions of rightness, **truth**, stability, security, and safety. It is thus important for humans to maintain it, restore it, or conform to it, depending on the religious tradition. The various examples also enable readers to recognize that harmony is either personified in the form of a deity or left abstract. It is, moreover, a cosmic and/or social force binding everything together.

Further reading: Boyce (1979); Needham (1969); Reichard (1950)

HEALING

Spurred by an ordinary cold, lung or heart disease, an accident that leaves a person crippled, mental illness, or the anxiety caused by the threat of eminent **death**, healing becomes a major concern for all religions. Sickness interrupts a person's life and everyday routine, disrupting personal assumptions about him/herself and the world in which he/she lives. Healing is directly related to concerns and uncertainties caused by illness.

There is a fundamental assumption among many religious cultures that physical health is connected to spiritual well-being or that health is somehow related to morality with the implication that illness is punishment for transgressions. Some cultures also assume that health is associated with a web of social relationships. When a person is sick, there is thus an assumption that there exists a disharmony between the sick person and the universe. Because sickness and healing are closely related to religious or moral concerns, healers often function as religious specialists, such as the **shaman**, spirit medium, **priest**, or other **holy person**.

The intimate connection between healing and religion suggests that illness is culturally defined and that illness possesses a **culture**-specific nature. Within the religious cultural context, a way is provided for a person to think about, have certain expectations, and deal with various forms of illness. It is the religious cultural context and assumptions made within such a situation that enables the healer to effectively treat patients. In other words, because the healer and patient share the same worldview, the former is able to work effectively by assigning a meaning to an illness.

The healer uses various possible rationales for a particular illness, such as the intrusion of an object into a sick person's **body**, **spirit** intrusion, the patient's loss of **soul**, or the use of sorcery to cause a disease. The various reasons for the causation of illness can be countered by methods such as confession by the patient, which is often done in public. This type of remedy presupposes a relationship between morality and illness, which can include a direct or indirect infringement of moral codes or violation of **taboos**, and it assumes that without confession healing cannot occur. By making the method public, the patient dispels negative thoughts and deeds, enabling the healer and community to deal with the underlying problems causing the illness. For the Ndembu of Zimbabwe, for instance, sickness is often related to the anger and aggression of male **ancestors**, who cause illness when a law or customary rule is broken. This type of illness is called *ihamba* and is identified with the central incisor of a dead hunter believed to possess the power to kill animals. The cure consists of a combination of confession by the victim and kin and removal of the *ihamba* by ritual. Among the Ndembu, it is presupposed that secrecy is not healthy.

Another major way to cure an illness is to transfer it from the patient to some object ritually, symbolically, or psychologically. The healer or ritualist works to condense, objectify, and bind the illness before it is dramatically destroyed or banished. Among the Yoruba of Nigeria, a healer performs a rite at a river after the patient strips naked and dons new white clothing. The sick person's head is shaved and cuts made in the scalp. After this action, the healer and patient go waist deep into the stream. The healer uses a dove as a sponge, wetting it and rubbing it over the patient's **body**. This procedure is intended to draw the illness out of the patient and transfer it to the dove, which is finally drowned and thrown downstream along with the disease. After a second dove is killed and its blood smeared on the head and upper body of the patient, the vitality and calmness of the bird is transferred to the patient. The patient,

HEALING

having been cleansed with water and rubbed with medicines, witnesses the killing of a third dove and the application of its blood onto his/her body. Before this third dove is thrown away, the patient stands on its body while an incantation is invoked.

Another means of healing is accomplished by **dance** and innate healing **power** among the Kung of the Kalahari Desert of southern Africa. Here the innate, latent healing power (*num*) must be cultivated by an individual, which often occurs within a **dance** context, giving birth to an altered state of consciousness (*kia*) that is a painful and frightening experience described as a **death**. The context for the work of the healer is the **dance** where the healer grinds up plants and places them into a turtle shell along with a hot coal that he waves over the patient. The healer may also place his hands on the patient in order to pull the sickness out.

The Navaho of the American southwest use **rituals** to restore the **harmony** lost by a sick person through what is called chantway. Although healing is considered the restoration of harmony within a sick person, the cause of illness must be determined by means of divination before the most appropriate chantway can be discerned. The Navaho believe that illness is caused when sorcerers shoot arrows, which are impure and **polluting**, into a victim's flesh. The polluting arrows can be removed by sweating as part of a larger ritual that can also include fasting and sexual abstinence. It is presupposed that the gods will only heal a patient when a patient is clean, pure, and holy. Therefore, for the Navaho, healing involves the expulsion of dirt and the creation of purity and harmony.

There is a twofold division of chantways: holyway and evilway. The fundamental distinction between these two types of chantways is that the holyway seeks to attract goodness and holiness, whereas the evilway tries to exorcise **evil**. Because the spiritual Holy People dislike impurity, the holyway procedure includes the purification of the patient's dwelling (*hogan*) by singers and **purification** of the patient by means of sweating and emetic **rituals**, such as induced vomiting. With preliminary aspects completed, the priest-singer chants hymns, **prayers**, and excerpts from Navaho **mythology** with the intention of visualizing certain deities or gradually identifying himself with a deity by describing it in detail and invoking the deity. Offerings of tobacco, cornmeal, and **prayer** sticks are made. More elaborate ceremonies involve sand paintings that depict a Navaho deity or mythical event. In the ceremony the patient sits on the figures obliterating them and the figures in the painting are transferred to the sick person.

Further reading: Gill (1981, 1982); Kinsley (1996); Sullivan (1989); Turner (1968)

HEAVEN

From a cross-cultural perspective, in the Western religious traditions, heaven is conceived as a location beyond the mundane world, whereas devotional Buddhism envisions Pure Lands located in a westerly direction. Whether East or West, heaven is usually conceived as a place of beauty, harmony, peace, and pleasure. Heaven stands in sharp opposition to hell, which is conceived as an absence of **reality** in comparison to heaven. Heaven is best grasped by a **metaphor**, such as a kingdom, temple, court, garden, city, or celestial sphere in Hebrew thought. Diverse religious traditions conceive of its particular aspects differently and use different **metaphors**.

During its historical development, the Christian tradition demonstrates a variety of opinions about the nature of heaven. Within the New Testament, it is not possible to find a single view about heaven or even much of a description of it. This is because the earliest Christian writers expected the imminent return of Christ and the end of the world, which renders superfluous any speculation about the nature of heaven. The apostle Paul stresses the present nature of heaven because Christ's salvific action is eternal. Following the Pharisaic Hebrew tradition, Paul envisions a delayed reunion with **God**, although the future promises a bodily resurrection. The resurrection of the **body**, a notion inherited from Jewish thought, conflicts with the immortality of the **soul** that comes from Greek influence. Although heaven might be theoretically universal, it is often conceived as a place of exclusion for those who do not accept Jesus as the Messiah, pagans, or sinful people.

The early Christian **church** father Irenaeus (*c.* 140–200), bishop of Lyons, capital of Gaul, conceives of heaven as a continuation and completion of a person's present life. This suggests that heaven resembles life on **earth** in a glorified material world. Once the earth is freed from the control of pagans, the righteous will live for a thousand years, a **millenarian** vision, and enjoy life under the earthly rule of Christ. Irenaeus also advocates a notion of compensatory paradise, which means that any new life after **death** is a compensation for persecuted Christians and a continuation and completion of the present life. Following the thousand-year reign of the kingdom of the Messiah, the kingdom of God will follow.

During the fourth century of the church and the growth of **monastic** life, the Christian heaven is conceived as an ecclesiastical **community**. Within the context of his early career, Augustine, bishop of Hippo in North Africa, conceives of heaven ascetically as an immaterial place, full of fleshless souls, resting, and finding pleasure in the presence of God in a theocentric heaven. Around 408, Augustine changes his view from souls related to God in ecstatic unions to the expectations of reuniting with family and friends in a new social milieu characterized by **love** (*caritas*) not lust (*cupiditas*), with all love directed to God.

Sparked by the urban revival in Europe, the medieval period conceives of heaven as an eternal city, a new Jerusalem, which is described as a city with golden streets, jeweled buildings, and richly dressed residents. The medieval heaven, a place of light, harmony, and contemplation, promised love and **knowledge** of God, which reflects a heaven conceived by educated, scholastic theologians. Heaven is also conceived as an empyrean, a place of light where the blessed and angels live with God. The empyrean heaven is characterized by a lack of active life and only contemplation of God that leads to the beatific **vision** of the divine.

The Islamic heaven is described in sensuous terms as a Garden (al-Jannah) or Paradise (Firdaus) characterized by rivers of water, milk, honey, and wine. It is a place where the faithful are content, peaceful, and secure; they enjoy gentle speech and pleasant shade. According to the Qur'an, the faithful drink and eat as they desire while seated on couches, robed in silk and brocade, and surrounded by gardens and fountains. Faithful males are promised *hūrs* (beautiful virgin maidens), rewards for a virtuous life (44.51–56).

Although it is not called by this term, the sensuous nature of heaven exists within Pure Land Buddhism, which adds the ubiquitous presence of jewels. While a person can hear the message of the Buddha throughout the land, a subject needs simply to wish to have one's hunger or thirst satisfied for it to be done. A person can also wish for pleasant odors and sounds. A major difference between the Buddhist Pure Land and other forms of paradise or heaven in other religious traditions is that there are no perishable items within the Pure Land.

Further reading: McDannell and Lang (1988); Olson (2005); Russell (1997)

HENOTHEISM

A concept developed by the German scholar and Oxford University professor Max Müller with the intention of distinguishing the belief in one **God** within a **polytheistic** context. Müller attempts to make sense of the many deities in the Vedic literature of ancient India and those hymns that focus on a single deity such as Agni, god of fire, and others. Although a religious tradition such as Hinduism possesses many deities, henotheism refers to situations when a person accepts one God among many to be one's personal deity and genuine God, even though one does not reject the other **gods** and **goddesses**.

Other scholars have attempted to refine or improve on the concept of henotheism by advocating monolatrism, which is the **worship** of one god at a time, and kathenotheism, worshipping one god after another and accepting a particular god as the most genuine for that moment. In comparison to monolatrism, henotheism is less exclusive because a person may **worship** any deity within an extensive pantheon. From a critical perspective, Axel Michaels finds Müller's term inadequate and substitutes the term "equitheism" because it includes the process of identification of a deity.

Further reading: Michaels (2004); Müller (1895–1898)

HERESY

A concept that is derived from the Greek term *hairesis* (choice), which implies adopting **beliefs** and practices that are deemed incorrect by the orthodox **community**. Thus, heresy is a relational term, with the decision about what is standard made by the group in **power** concerning the positions of an outside **community** or person, called a heretic, with the leader of a heretical group being labeled a heresiarch. Heresy, a value **judgment**, is impossible without an authoritative **body** of **doctrine** by which to measure a set of **beliefs** and practices. It is thus highly unusual for a person or group to call itself heretical.

Historically, heresy plays an important role in Christianity, which recognizes two types of heresy: formal, which is the willful persistence in error, and material, adhering to heretical views unknowingly. Arianism, Nestorianism, Donatism, and Pelagianism are deemed heresies by the early Latin **church**. Arianism denies that Jesus is God but is rather created by God, Nestorianism concerns the humanity of Jesus, Donatism adopts a contrary view of the **church** and **sacraments**, and Pelagianism emphasizes works and plays down the notion of divine **grace** giving the impression that an individual can merit **salvation**.

Heresy is less a problem in the East, although instances of it can be found with Hindus claiming that Jains and Buddhist are heretics because they reject the divine origins of the Vedic hymns, whereas Jains and Buddhism experience their own controversies over doctrine and practice that result in schisms. Heretics are recognized in Islam where the greatest violation that one can make is to deny the reality of **God** (*kāfir*) or to claim to be God, which is called *shirk*. By introducing any innovation of practice not divinely revealed in the Qur'an, this practice is called innovation (*bid'a*), while expressing contempt for the prophet is equally a heinous violation. Those deemed heretical by an orthodox group are designated as non-conformist and operate as **liminal** beings outside of the **orthodox** sphere.

Further reading: Betz (1965); Leff (1967); Troeltsch (1931)

HETERODOXY

A concept that originates from the Greek terms *hetero* (other) and *doxa* (teaching). A heterodox teaching deviates from the orthodox position but falls short of **heresy**. A heterodox position is often held in good **faith** and the holder of such beliefs is usually a member in good standing just as long as the individual's position does not contradict the **orthodox** standpoint.

Further reading: Leff (1967)

HOLINESS

It is derived from the Old English term *halignes* (without blemish). Within a **ritual** context, holiness presupposes a process of **purification**, which sets a person or thing apart as something special and without stain. In Judaism, Christianity, and Islam, **God** is identified as the most holy being and wholly other. In Judaism, God instructs His people to be holy just as He is holy (Lev. 19.2). Interpreted by the great Jewish thinker Maimonides, this means keeping the commandments given by God, whereas the Holy Spirit plays the role of sanctifier in Christianity. The apostle Paul instructs early believers to become temples of the Holy Spirit (1 Cor. 6.11). Holiness is used interchangeably with the **sacred** and is closely associated with **purification**.

HOLY PERSONS

This concept refers to all male and female figures considered set apart and special by virtue of their life and actions. It refers to a wide variety of historical figures that includes **shamans**, kings, monks, nuns, **mystics, prophets, saints, ascetics, martyrs,** Buddha, bodhisattva, or yogi. Not all of these figures, however, qualify as a holy person because such a designation is dependent on behavior. In many cultures, holy persons become paradigms upon which other people can model their own lives. In short, holy people exemplify the best practitioners of their respective religious traditions.

HOMOSEXUALITY

This notion means the same gender sexually, a term usually reserved for males but also applied to females, whereas lesbianism strictly designates female sexual relationships. Religious traditions do not usually devote much attention to homosexuality by condemning it or advocating it, although such behavior exists even within religious institutions. In the major **monotheistic faiths,** homosexuality is condemned as unnatural, deviant behavior, or contrary to **God's** laws.

Being based on the Torah, Judaism warns against behavior that compromises the clear distinction between male and female and their social roles. In Leviticus 18.22, homosexuality takes its place as an abomination alongside incest and eating unclean animals. In the narrative of Lot in Genesis (19), he decides not to give two male visitors to a gang demanding to have sex with them. Rather than being a party to homosexual rape, Lot gives his two daughters to the gang. In addition to citing these Jewish sources, many Christians agree that homosexuality is an abomination before God, as evident in the writings of the early Christian apostle Paul (Rom. 1.26–27; 1 Cor. 6.9–11), and that it can influence a person's **salvation,** although homosexuality is not a topic that occupies the attention of Jesus. In agreement with ancient Judaism and the early Christian Church, Islam forbids homosexuality in the Qur'an (4.16; 7.81; 20.28), and it is strongly condemned by the prophet Muhammad in Hadith literature. The major monotheistic faiths make it clear that heterosexuality within the context of marriage is the norm for sexual relationships. Such restrictions do not completely stop homosexuality, but it does drive it underground.

Eastern religions are equally conservative with respect to the issue of homosexuality. In Hinduism, the *Laws of Manu* (*c.* 100) condemns homosexuality and refers to fines and modes of **ritual** expiation, and it even more vehemently opposes lesbianism because of the importance attached to virginity at marriage. In contrast to *Manu*, the *Kamasūtra* of Vatsyayana (*c.* 300 CE), an ancient Indian sexual manual, tends to affirm homosexual experimentation with its ninth chapter on oral sexual behavior, its references to an independent woman, and a woman assuming the guise of a male. During the colonial period of British rule, the Indian Penal Code criminalizes homosexual relations by passing anti-sodomy laws.

Within the Buddhist tradition, homosexual, lesbian, and heterosexual relations are condemned for monks and nuns because they violate the vow of celibacy made by everyone entering **monastic** life. Moreover, any type of sexual relationship increases cravings, which is an obstacle to achieving **liberation** because the person loses control over his/her mind and body. By renouncing all sexual behavior, monks and nuns reject a biological family and enter the spiritual family of the Buddha embodied by the monastic **community**. Homosexuality develops in China and Japan between older and younger monks. The young boys are expected to assume a passive role in this age-structured practice in contrast to a relation structured by gender. Despite this type of practice, homosexuality is generally condemned in China and Japan for cultural reasons and the centrality of the family in these cultures. Monks violating their monastic code are said to be destined for rebirth in hell and suffer gruesome punishment.

Further reading: Boswell (1980); Dynes and Donaldson (1992); Foucault (1978); Kripal (2001)

IMAGES

The notion of images can be traced to the Greek term *eikon* (image) and the Latin *imago*, which denotes imitation, copy, or likeness. Images can assume the form of statues, paintings, or buildings that depict **gods, goddesses, holy persons**, or ideas. The image is usually a representation of a divine figure that is, for instance, identified by a halo around the figure's head in Eastern Orthodox and Roman Catholic Christianity. The study of images is called iconography, whereas iconoclasts destroy icons or images of the divine, an activity enacted by Protestants during the Reformation and Muslims during periods of their history. Along with Judaism, Islam rejects the use of images of **God** because of the mysterious and transcendent aspects of the divine nature. This prohibition against representation extends to the Prophet Muhammad whose face is left blank on paintings of him, a practice that does not extend to Sikhism where representational paintings of the faces of Gurus Nānak and Gobind Singh are prominently displayed at places of worship.

In contrast to Islam, Hinduism uses images extensively because it brings the divine closer to the devotee. Since Hindus believe that a god or goddess descends into the image and entrusts itself to the care of humans, it must be treated with the utmost respect as the deity is a sovereign. Although the image does not represent full divinity, a visual image objectifies the divine and enables ordinary people to see it. Images are incomplete, inadequate, and impermanent because they are believed to be created, live, die, and are replaced. Often images created for **festivals** are discarded at the end of the event. Many Hindu images are created with large eyes in order to stress the importance of a mutual process of **perception** between the divine image and the devotee.

In Buddhism, **symbols** associated with the Buddha are revered a few centuries before the advent of image **worship** between 100 BCE and 100 CE. There are three basic reasons for the creation of images of the Buddha: an image signifies the Buddha's presence without which **rituals** cannot take place because they would be rendered ineffective; an image discloses the Buddha's teaching; and it ensures the continuation of the **monastic** tradition. With kings playing the role of patrons of image, *stūpa* (memorial mound), and monastery construction, the installation of a new image involves a ritual, called either "eye opening" or consecration (*abhiseka*), to make the image holy by pouring water, connecting the rite to the life-giving force of water in a dissemination of **sacred power**. Typically, opening the eyes of the image brings it to life. Once the image is installed and consecrated, the image mirrors the Buddha in a mutual, self-reflexive act during which the Buddha recognizes the image as himself and vice versa.

In the current postmodern period, images and the representations of the divine that they depict are called into question by thinkers such as Jean Baudrillard, a postmodern cultural critic, who confesses to finding himself within a time of simulation. This artificial, malleable period tends towards equivalence that suggests faking that which one does not possess. This scenario suggests an absence rather than a presence, and it threatens the distinction between true and false, real and imaginary. What he calls the simulacrum opposes representation, terminates meaning, and simultaneously renders the real and illusory impossible because the latter is no longer possible without the latter. Within this confused context, the medium and the message also get befuddled because the former gets diffused, diffracted, and becomes intangible, which leaves the phantom of simulation, a hyper-real, and loss of history. The image created by Baudrillard reflects the reign of difference in which metaphysics is lost, exchange is annulled, and accumulation of wealth and **power** is terminated.

From a different postmodern perspective, Jean-Luc Marion draws a distinction between an idol and an icon with respect to their functions. While an idol, an object created for **worship**, restrains a person's gaze, an icon liberates the gaze and opens the mind of the viewer to imagination, which suggests that it opens potentialities in the viewer. This provocative nature of the icon provides a visible focus for the divine **reality** with the function of making invisible divine qualities accessible to some extent to the viewer. According to Marion, the icon renders itself visible by giving rise to an infinite gaze that suggests something beyond one's ordinary ability to conceptualize, whereas the idol functions like a mirror that reflects and limits the gazer's ability to conceive the unlimited divine.

Further reading: Baudrillard (1994); Besançon (2000); Freedberg (1991); Marion (1991); Schopen (1997); Strong (2004); Swearer (2004); Waghorne (1984)

INCARNATION

The derivation of this term resides with the Latin *in carne* (in flesh/body). This concept refers to a **God** becoming incarnate within a human **body**, representing a God-human being. The most famous incarnation in the West is Jesus, who is called the absolute paradox by the nineteenth century Danish thinker Kierkegaard; Krishna in Hinduism and the Buddha in Mahāyāna Buddhism are excellent examples in the East. Traditionally, Jesus' incarnation is interpreted as a gracious act of God intended to redeem humans from original **sin** by Jesus' sacrificial **death** on the cross. According to the *Bhagavad Gītā*, Krishna, assuming the guise of a warrior and teacher, becomes incarnate to fight against unrighteousness and to conquer the forces of evil. As the incarnation of the eternal Buddhanature, the historical Buddha brings wisdom to the world and the means of ending **suffering**.

Further reading: Pelikan (1971); Smith (1979)

INTERPRETATION/HERMENEUTICS

The technical term for interpretation is hermeneutics, which originates with the Greek term *hermēneuein* (to interpret). The term is also associated with the Greek **god** Hermes, who is identified as the messenger of the gods. Within a religious context, interpretation plays an essential role by making sense of and coming to understand the divine messages in oral form and those preserved in writing. As time evolves and historical circumstances change, the art of interpretation becomes a never-ending task for newer generations of a religious tradition seeking to make sense of their religious history and texts and those of others.

In the Jewish and Christian traditions, different methods of interpretation are applied to scriptures. The methods used include allegorical and grammatical means with the former seeking an external key to unlock meaning while the latter analyzes the structure of the text for its meaning. Rabbinic Judaism uses literalist interpretations and exegesis to discern a text. During the Middle Ages, Christian interpreters develop the fourfold meaning of a text following inspiration from the apostle Paul's distinction between the spiritual and the literal. Medieval interpreters find three senses in the spiritual: allegorical, anagogical, and tropological. The anagogical is concerned with the relation between the text and **faith**, whereas the tropological focuses on the moral meaning of the text. Later Protestant leaders insist on the literal interpretation of scripture, being convinced that the text interprets itself.

Hermeneutics changes dramatically with F. D. E. Schleiermacher (1768–1814), a German theologian, and Wilhelm Dilthey (1833–1911), a German philosopher. For Schleiermacher, interpretation is associated with the art of understanding that is both objective and subjective. The former dimension is grammatical, whereas the latter aspect involves a type of divination, a psychological feature of interpretation, which invites an interpreter to enter the subjectivity of an author. The grammatical and psychological aspects of interpretation both use a comparative method, but the psychological adds an intuitive divinatory aspect. From Schleiermacher's perspective, understanding reflects a dialogical relationship because there is a speaker and a hearer who hears the words and divines their meaning, which makes interpretation the art of hearing what the **other** is trying to say.

Dilthey makes interpretation a method for grasping artifacts of **culture**. He distinguishes between the human sciences and the natural sciences on the basis of their different objects of interest. If the natural sciences are focused on the external world, the human sciences are concerned with lived **experience** (*Erlebnis*), which is held together by a common meaning. This lived experience is not a physical action as much as an act of consciousness. Moreover, the goal of the natural sciences is explanation (*Erklären*), whereas the task of the human sciences is understanding (*Verstehen*), which opens an interpreter to the world of others and allows one to discover oneself in the others. What understanding grasps within the reciprocal interaction between the whole and its parts is meaning, which is a matter of relationship. Meaning is historical, which suggests that it changes with the passage of **time**. Thus, meaning is not something fixed, firm, or static.

The gist of Dilthey's program influences twentieth-century thinkers such as Martin Heidegger (1889–1976), Hans-Georg Gadamer (d. 2002), and Paul Ricoeur (d. 2005). In order to overcome the psychologism and subjectivity of previous theories of interpretation, Heidegger proposes developing a hermeneutical ontology that would be grounded in the existential situation of the interpreter, which frees interpretation from texts and transforms it into ontology. Heidegger argues that hermeneutics operates in a circle because any interpreter begins working from the standpoint of one's prejudices, pre-understandings, self-interests, and presuppositions. Thus, no interpreter begins within a neutral vacuum because there is always something that one brings to the act of interpretation. Gadamer also begins in the hermeneutical circle, and he retrieves the notion of prejudice in its original sense of being in relation to it and not detached from it. Gadamer recognizes that prejudgments play an important role in the art of interpretation along with historical context. An interpreter can understand an ancient text because that person is connected to an overall tradition, which links the interpreter in a process called "effective history." This type of history acknowledges that what happened in the past shapes later history, constituting a continuum with the past, which Gadamer calls the fusion of horizons. This goal of interpretation connects the horizon of the interpreter with the text of the past.

Among other things, Paul Ricoeur is concerned with getting beyond the hermeneutical circle, which he defines as believing in order to understand. Yet, by understanding, persons can believe. Thus, hermeneutics begins from a prior understanding of that which it attempts to understand. From this circle of believing and understanding, Ricoeur aims to move from the hermeneutical circle to re-enactment and ultimately to autonomous thought. How does this movement occur? Ricoeur transforms the hermeneutical circle into a wager that claims: I will understand better if I follow symbolic thought. Therefore, the wager opens the field of philosophical hermeneutics that seeks to speak to the human situation. Moreover, the hermeneutical situation and autonomy of the text owes its creation to the distance between the original author and interpreter.

From the postmodern perspective of Jacques Derrida (1930–2004) and his non-method of deconstruction, he sets forth to subvert texts by using them against themselves instead of attempting to interpret them. Influenced by Heidegger's term *"Destruktion,"* Derrida claims to be continuing a trend begun by the German philosopher and attempting to bring it to a conclusion by deconstructing the presence of the present. Deconstruction aims to disarrange the construction of terms in a sentence and disassemble the parts of a whole. For Derrida, this means to locate the otherness within a text that suggests a logocentric conceptuality and then to deconstruct this conceptuality by obtaining a position of exteriority, a kind of writing executed on the margins of the text. Derrida likens deconstruction to an *exergue*, an inscription on the face of a coin or at the beginning of a book, which involves making something evident. Deconstruction functions as a parasite by preying on other texts, readings, or interpretations in an endless process that attempts to overturn hierarchies by subverting them from the inside.

Further reading: Derrida (1976); Gadamer (1975); Heidegger (1962); Ricoeur (1976)

JUDGMENT

From very ancient times, many religious traditions conceive of some kind of final judgment usually based on a person's earthly conduct. The judgment is often determined by one or more supernatural beings or a legislative court of judges. The verdict rendered decides whether a person's fate involves reward or punishment. Therefore, judgment is often closely associated with concepts of the end of **time** and **heaven** or hell.

In ancient Mesopotamian religion, after the deceased is buried, the ghost of the deceased sets out for the netherworld, a land of no return, where the new arrival passes through seven gates guarded by seven fierce porters. The ghost makes offerings to the **gods** of the netherworld ruled by Queen Ereshkigal and her consort, Nergal. Although unconcerned with the earthly deeds of the deceased, the ghost is judged.

In ancient Egypt, the deceased reaches the hall of Osiris and gives a lengthy confession about sins that one does not commit during life. Then, the deceased is questioned by an assembly of gods about **knowledge** pertaining to the names of **powers**, before entering the presence of Osiris, lord of death, where the heart of the deceased (seat of human intellect and emotion) is weighted against a feather, which symbolically represents Ma'at (harmony and justice). If the heart weighs less than the feather, the deceased proceeds to the field of rushes.

Post-Exilic Judaism witnesses the prophets Jeremiah and Ezekiel, who assert that individuals are judged only for their own deeds. Ezekiel sees a **vision** of a valley of dry bones (37.1–14) and a revival of these lifeless skeletons by God. In another Hebrew text, individuals survive the grave to participate in God's final judgment and their own judgment (2 Macc. 12.43–45). The book of Daniel (11.2), moreover, affirms resurrection of the dead, which is combined with the affirmation of reward and punishment.

Ancient Greek **culture** presents at least two different accounts of the final judgment. According to the poet Homer, Minos, a son of Zeus and lord of the dead, does not determine one's fate, but rather settles disputes among the dead. In the *Gorgias* of Plato, Socrates relates a myth that describes the soul's judgment and its recompense for its deeds on **earth**. In this scenario, the **soul** is freed from the **body** and is judged by three sons of Zeus in a meadow from which two roads lead to either the Isles of the Blessed or Tartarus, a place of punishment.

Within the Christian Synoptic Gospels (Matt. 24.1–24; Mark 13.10–37; Luke 21.5–38), it is possible to find what is called the "Little Apocalypse," which is shaped by the book of Daniel in the Hebrew texts. These passages refer to a series of false **prophets** before the second coming (*parousia*) with the Son of Man riding on the clouds of heaven and angles gathering the elect. With the Son of Man seated on a throne of his own glory and the members of all nations gathered in front of him, the Final Judgment is rendered with the saved separated from the damned. Besides the Final Judgment, there is a particular judgment rendered immediately after death. The Gospel of Luke (16.19–23), for instance, refers to an immediate judgment when a poor man is said to be in a parable in the bosom of Abraham and a rich man in hell. Further evidence for an individual judgment is suggested again in Luke (23.43) when Jesus turns to one of the men being crucified with him and assures him of paradise.

The Day of Judgment in Islam is conceived to be a time of **chaos** and confusion when the sinners will be sent to a fiery Gehenna, whereas those magnanimous and subservient people to God's will are rewarded with a garden of paradise. This general judgment is combined with a judgment that begins at the grave when the deceased is visited by two angles and questioned about their **faith**. This theme of general and particular judgment is a feature of later Judaism, Christianity, and Islam.

Further reading: Griffiths (1991); Peters (2003)

KINGSHIP

The origin of kingship can take two forms: divine by nature and not divine by nature. In the first case, the king is considered to be an **incarnation** of a **god**, which serves to validate his **power** and authority. The king's divine nature reflects certain obligations, such as acting mercifully, being energetic and patient, acting wisely and being tactful when dealing with public affairs. Even though a king might not be divine by nature, he possesses access to supernatural powers. This gives him the ability to manipulate the gods for the good of his subjects and country. If the divine beings withdraw their support from the king, the result is drought, crop failure, wars, and epidemics. What happens when the king becomes old, feeble, ill, or sexually impotent? Since the king's **body** in many cases is conceived as the dwelling place of the gods, his infirm condition affects his people, who might be obligated for their own welfare to commit regicide.

The option of regicide is given to the Shilluk people of Africa, for instance, where the king serves as a **ritual** and political figure. The king's chief ritual function is to mediate between his nation and the forces of vitality controlled by Nyikang, the high god. The king also functions as the supreme judge and final court of appeal in cases of homicide, theft, incest, and other social transgressions. Even with all these functions, the king does not directly govern his people, which is a duty performed by a council of chiefs. Hence, the king is primarily a **priestly** figure who reigns but does not rule.

A different scenario is evident among another African people, the Nyakyusa, who presuppose that the proper operation of the natural order depends upon the **harmony** of the social order. In order to select the right person as king, this task is left to a group of hereditary priests, who take into consideration a candidate's character, fertility (proven by sons, cattle, and fertile fields), which suggests that a sterile person can never be chosen. Because kingly reigns are usually brief, men fear being chosen, and they must be literally seized and forced into the position. Once the selection is made, the king is secluded from his subjects and must adhere to various **taboos,** such as not walking in water, never bathing in a stream, not sitting on a green banana leaf that could cause bananas to fall prematurely, and never becoming ill, which would place the entire country at risk. When the king becomes ill he is killed by suffocation or being secretly buried alive along with living slaves place beneath him, while one or two wives and sons of commoners are buried above him. While still alive, priests remove the king's hair and nails, which are considered **relics** and are connected with the growth of crops.

Further reading: Evans-Pritchard (1956); Gluckman (1965); Wilson (1970)

KNOWLEDGE

A concept that can be traced in the West to the Greek terms *gnosis* and *episteme*. Within the context of religion, it is in tension or even conflict with the concept of **faith** because knowledge can provide an awareness of deep mysteries, and knowledge represents the cognitive aspect of religion. Although knowledge plays a role in faith-based religions, such as Judaism, Christianity, and Islam, its role is circumscribed to a degree because it is faith not knowledge that leads an individual to **salvation**, whereas non–faith-based religious traditions rely on some type of knowledge to achieve **liberation**. Certain types of Hinduism, Buddhism, and Daoism depend on knowledge for liberation.

In the Theravāda Buddhist tradition, genuine knowledge possesses no relationship to a subject/object type of knowledge, which is transcended by trance states to an intuitive insight into **reality**. Knowledge is also associated with knowing **doctrines** in a kind of intellectual knowledge. This is not considered a valid form of knowledge as it is regarded as being untrustworthy owing to its connection to distorting mental factors such as greed, hatred, and delusion. However, these can be controlled through meditative practice enabling a person to see things as they really are. The Sanskrit term for knowledge (*jñāna*) is often unfavorably compared to wisdom (*prajñā*), an intuitive type of knowledge. In Mahāyāna Buddhism, knowledge (*jñāna*) becomes a perfection that must be developed by the aspiring bodhisattva in order to attain a non-conceptualizing type of knowledge free of the subject/object dichotomy that is often synonymous with enlightenment.

In comparison to Buddhism, it is possible to find different accounts of knowledge in the Hindu schools of Sāmhkya and Advaita Vedānta. The Sāmkhya School argues that knowing the constituent elements of the world leads to an awareness of the absolute distinction between matter and the **self**, a fundamental reality obscured by an individual's ignorance. From another perspective, this process of knowledge implies an intuitive awareness of the distinction of pure consciousness from whatever is not consciousness that results in the awareness of a fundamental dualism of matter and spirit. The Advaita Vedānta position represents a non-dualism or monism because the aspirant realizes the absolute identity between Brahman (highest reality) and the Ātman (self) that is mutually defined as being, consciousness, and bliss. This type of intuitive knowing leads to liberation from the world and the cycle of existence because a person becomes identical to the single universal reality, while the Daoism type of knowledge leads to an aspirant becoming one with the universal Dao, mother and **ancestor** of everything that exists. By knowing the Dao, the sage becomes identified with it and assumes its attributes, which results in a state of namelessness, selflessness, changelessness, and speechlessness, and recognizes the unity within the multiplicity, or to see all things as one.

According to Jean-François Lyotard, a leading **postmodern** thinker, the quintessential form of knowledge is narrative, which reflects sensitivity to differences, enables us to tolerate the incommensurable, and is not an oppressive instrument of authorities. From Lyotard's perspective, this situation is a crisis that he traces to societies during the post-industrial age and **cultures** entering the postmodern period when knowledge – scientific, narrative, and common sense – becomes altered in such a way that it becomes a commodity to be produced and sold to consumers. When knowledge becomes a matter of production, this scenario possesses major consequences because it ceases to be an end in itself.

Further reading: Dubuisson (2003); Lyotard (1985); Olson (2005, 2007)

LANGUAGE

Human beings find themselves within a language that allows them to communicate with each other and to express their inner feelings and thoughts. Some of humankind's languages are considered **sacred**, such as Hebrew, Latin, Arabic, or Sanskrit. Within a religious context, language is used in **ritual**, **prayer**, praise of a divine being, confession, magical spells, **cursing**, chanting, and other forms, because in many instances it is believed to possess a **power** to transport messages or to make something happen in the case of a **performative** utterance. In the past century, the scholarly study of language developed semiotics, the science of signs, and semantics, the science of the sentence. Some theories of language reject these sciences of language because they do not address language as it is lived and used by people.

Hans-Georg Gadamer (d. 2002), a German philosopher, indicates the importance of living language and of human participation in it. Gadamer rejects the sign theory of language because when humans see that words are mere signs they rob words of their primordial power and make them into mere instruments. Language and its words are an expression of situation and being. Because language is an encompassing phenomenon, it cannot be grasped as a fact or fully objectified, which suggests that language is a medium and not a tool. Language not only discloses the human life-world, but it also makes it possible for humans to have a world. Hence humans exist in language and thus belong to it.

The emphasis of French philosopher Paul Ricoeur (1913–2005) is different to that of Gadamer. Ricoeur refers to language as discourse, but he shares with Gadamer an interest in how language is used and not with its linguistic structure. For Ricoeur, language constitutes a world of its own where items refer to each other, whereas discourse is the event of language by which he means that someone is speaking, whose message gives actuality to language. Because language pursues its own identity, it is not simply something transitory. Language is characterized by predication, an indispensable factor of a sentence because it tells a person something about the subject by designating quality, class, relationship, and action. Overall, discourse is comprehended as meaning actualized as an event.

Further reading: Gadamer (1975); Ricoeur (1976)

LAST THINGS

This refers to what happens at the end of **time**, and is more technically referred to as eschatology, a Greek term meaning the **doctrine** of last things. It is especially prominent among the major **monotheistic** faiths: Judaism, Christianity, and Islam.

In the ancient Jewish tradition, eschatological speculation begins with the Hebrew prophet Amos (8.2), who is the first prophetic figure to proclaim the end time is fast approaching. Later prophets expanded this type of proclamation by including a time for a final **judgment**. The eschatology of the Hebrew text is distinguished by its corporate nature, which implies that Israel is the people – an elected **community** – of **God**, that is destined to be restored at the end of time, a period both of judgment and **salvation**. The judgment is a decision based on historical action, while salvation represents a fulfillment or transfiguration of historical existence. Because the ancient Hebrews did not want to escape the world, time, and history due to potential salvific actions of God within time and place, their texts express an anticipation of a new world, a new time, and a new history (Isa. 65.17; 66.22). This new age represents a period in which people will live in unity under the rule of God in the Kingdom of God. The expected coming of the Kingdom of God is supplemented by the notion of a Messiah (an anointed one), who acts as a divine agent to accomplish renewal on earth, although ancient Hebrews conceived of the Messiah in several ways that included a person emerging from within the Jewish **community**, a figure of mysterious origin, or a divine being who would descends from **heaven**. It is also an expectation that there will be a gathering together of the dispersed Jews (Jer. 31.10), and the world will return to the peace of paradise (Jer. 31.12–14; Hosea 14.5–7; Zech. 8.12–13). With the book of Daniel, Hebrew eschatology becomes individualized because the text refers to the resurrection of the dead (Dan. 12.2), who will remain dead until the end of time. As the ancient Hebrew **faith** develops, this notion is extended to a general resurrection at the end of time at which the wicked receive final judgment and the righteous receive a reward for their faithfulness. The uniqueness of Hebrew eschatology is connected to salvation history because of the close connection between God's management of history by means of His providence and His election of the Jewish community as His chosen instrument by means of His **covenant** with them.

Eschatological scenarios often appear in apocalyptic literary speculations that are characterized by bizarre **visions**, strange symbolism and supernatural happenings. The term apocalyptic comes from a Greek term meaning to uncover, to reveal. The book of Isaiah (24–27) is often called, for instance, the little **apocalypse** in which the writer portrays the final judgment of God upon all nations as a cosmic catastrophe. Apocalyptic literature tends to be composed during periods of persecution, such as the Book of Daniel composed shortly after the outbreak of the Maccabean wars around 165 BCE; it uses a spiritual code language that makes it a sealed book (Dan. 12.4) to others outside the inner circle of **faith**.

Influenced by the Hebrew texts and ideas about the end of time, New Testament texts reflect an expectation of the imminent end of time and the arrival of the Messiah. Preceded by the proclamations of John the Baptist about the end of time (Mark 1.4–8; Matt. 3.1–6; Luke 3.7–9), many parables of Jesus also reflect an eschatological crisis (Luke 12.16–20, 13.6–9; Matt. 7.24–27). As a result of his crucifixion, resurrection, and ascension, the early Christian community understands Jesus as the long anticipated Messiah, a figure ushering in the new age. Jesus is described as the Alpha and Omega (Rev. 1.8), representing the first and last. Christians are urged to wait for his return (*parousia*) when the forces of **evil** dominating the world will be annihilated, the dead resurrected, and the entire creation judged and renewed. Therefore, the return of Christ brings not only the end of the world, but it also ushers in a new **earth** and a new **heaven** (2 Pet. 3.13). This kind of scenario suggests that the return (*parousia*) happens both in time and to time in the sense that it terminates the process of historical time while also transforming it.

The imminent return of the Messiah to the Christian community becomes a problem when the return is delayed, which facilitates a reinterpretation of the original Hebrew messianic eschatology. The Christian apostle Paul, for instance, changes his views of the end time from an earlier expectation of the impending arrival of Christ during Paul's own lifetime (1Thess. 4.14–17) to the possibility that he might not live to see the return of Christ (Phil. 1.19–25). Paul's writings reflect a tension between what has already happened and what is to come in the future (1 Cor. 15.24–28; 1 Thess. 4.13–17). The Gospel of Matthew (24.4–25) modifies the eschatological message in order to differentiate between the kingdom of the Son of Man (a present, morally mixed form of the **church**) and the kingdom of the Father that will purge all evil elements. The Gospel of Luke (21.9) and Acts (2.33; 3.20–21) alleviates the sense of urgency about the end of time by depicting Christ as already ruling at the right hand of God, whereas the Gospel of John shifts emphasis from a future fulfillment to the present availability of the age to come, emphasizing the eschatological time as a now moment.

During the formative period of Islam, the anticipation of the end time is a central part of Muhammad's message that contains information about the signs of the final hour: disruption of the natural order, a reverse process of creation, heaven would be destroyed, stars would fall and be extinguished, the sun and the moon would be covered resulting in no light on earth, the earth would shake, split apart, and be ground to dust, and the seas would become mixed creating a primordial chaos. In addition to these natural catastrophes, moral disasters would ensue with piety giving way to pride, truth giving way to lies, and public sex and licentious practices such as music, wine, drinking, adultery, and homosexuality would occur. Then, according to the Qur'an (27.82), the beast of the earth will arrive, who is identified as a false messiah and described as blind in one eye, reddish in color, and with the word unbeliever (*kafir*) written on his forehead. This false messiah possesses two primary functions: to lead Muslims away from the path of God and to establish a kingdom with himself as the ruler. Thereafter, two powerful giants named Gog (Yajūj) and Magog (Majūj) will appear (18.92; 21.96), and Christ appears once more on earth to purify the world. This entire scenario begins with Israfil blowing his trumpet, signaling the arrival of the final hour. The Qur'an refers to one blast (69.13) and two blasts (39.68) of the trumpet. The first blast signals the disruption of nature, whereas the second blast signals the dramatic cataclysm and extinction of all living things except God. Then, God resurrects the bodies of the deceased and joins them with their spirits. The general resurrection is followed by the Final Judgment when God appears with His angels and the book of deeds will be opened. At this point, an individual's own limbs will testify against a person (36.65). Those judged righteous will have the book placed into their right hands, while the unrighteous will have the book hung around their necks. Both the saved and the condemned must pass over a bridge, which is described as sharper than a sword and thinner than a hair by tradition, suspended over hell. The saved faithful will easily pass to heaven, whereas the condemned immediately fall into the fire of hell.

Further reading: Obayashi (1992); Peters (2003); Smith and Haddad (2002)

LAW

The concept of law includes principles, duties, and regulations that govern a religious **community** and obligate its members to obey and conform to its stipulations. The source of religious law is usually divine beings, a **sacred text**, tradition, or social custom. The laws can be enforced by a **god**, a body of elders, **ancestors**, communal pressure, or elected officials.

In ancient Judaism, the law is called Torah (teaching), and is connected to the **covenant** bond with Yahweh. There are two types of law found in the Pentateuch: conditional and absolute or apodictic. The formula for the conditional type of law expresses that if something happens then that will be the legal consequence. Each case contains numerous conditions. The absolute law is certain, meaning that it contains no "ifs" or "buts" about it, such as do not kill or steal. It is usually expressed in sharp, terse **language**. The Torah is intended for all humanity, but its purpose for Jews is to turn Israel into a nation of **priests** (Deut. 33.4), which amounts to a holy nation.

The centrality of the law in Judaism is matched by the role that it plays in Islam. The Arabic term for law is *shar'ia*, a term that originally means a path leading to water, that is, a way to the very source of life. Within a religious context, it means the way or the right path of action, the path ordained by God. The law, which makes all life and activity the sphere of

God's authority, is what God commands and what humans must obey. Islamic law is practical in the sense that it concerns human conduct, as well as **faith**. Moreover, along with personal behavior, Islamic law includes legal and social regulations. In short, law is a total way of life, an all-embracing **sacred** law.

There are four foundations of Islamic law: the Qur'an, the *sunna* of the **prophet**, *ijmā* (consensus), and *qiyās* (analogical reasoning). The Qur'an is the law directly revealed by God, whereas the *sunna* of the prophet refers to the authoritative decisions and pronouncements made by the prophet Muhammad during his life, but which after his death became infallible. The *sunna* ends with the passing of the Companions of the **prophet** and their generation. This is when *ijmā* begins, even though it includes *sunna*. *Ijmā* is the consensus of the Muslim community, and it possesses absolute authority. It is this communal consensus that determines the nature of *sunna* and the correct interpretation of the Qur'an. The term *qiyās* means analogical reasoning, which suggests that a legal expert can conclude from a given principle embodied in a precedent that a new case falls under this principle or is similar to this precedent on the strength of a common essential feature called the reason. Take for instance a case of unchastity, which demands a fourfold confession from the culprit before he/she incurs punishment by analogy with the four witnesses prescribed by the Qur'an. This type of process proceeds from a common element or the known to the unknown. Thus analogical reasoning becomes a provision whereby Islamic law is intended to cover situations analogous to, but not explicitly in, the Qur'an and tradition. Therefore, analogical reasoning serves as a bridge between prophetic *sunna* and consensual *ijmā*.

The concept of law also plays an important role in Christianity. Even after the dissolution of the Roman Empire, its legal system remains unbroken. With the development of Lombard towns during the twelfth century, there arises a demand for **knowledge** of the regulation of social life, which is met by a revived study of Roman jurisprudence. The center of this revival is Bologna, whose reputation is given to it by Irnerius, who separates the study of Roman law from rhetoric and fixes it as a subject for professional study. Irnerius is probably the first to use as his textbook the whole Justinian corpus. Adopting a method of giving texts for and against a particular opinion, Irnerius includes an occasional *questio* (question) which gives a firm decision on a doubtful point. He thus makes the study of law more scientific, systematic, and professional. The successors of Irnerius are called Glossators, those who establish the literal meaning of the law and perform a pioneer task of dialectical analysis.

In 1140, the *Decretum* of Gratian, a textbook, appears to enhance unity within the church as it seeks to reconcile the Roman and Franco-Germanic legal traditions. This work stimulates schools of canon law in France and England. Dating from about the thirteenth century, a faculty of canon law is a common part of the general studies of European universities. The Latin church begins to realize that Roman law can be exploited in the interests of the church. The church exploits several features of Roman law: its theory of law, its approach to justice, its understanding of contracts and pacts, and its maxims and reflect principles. The result of this exploiting is that civil law is almost a prerequisite for the study of canon law.

Canon law is based on sources in the Bible, the Church Fathers, the canon of Church councils and the decrees of the Popes, Lombard or feudal law, and Germanic law. Civil law is an actual source of canon law in the sense that the laws of Christian emperors become the law of both the church and the state. In a sense, canon law is an imitation of the civil law. In addition, canon law also represents a reaction against the civil code. In this opposing system, the Pope takes the place accorded by civil law to the Emperor.

Further reading: Berman (1983); Murphy (1997); Rawls (1999); Rosen (1989)

LIBERATION

A concept that means to attain freedom, emancipation, or enlightenment within the context of Eastern religious cultures. It is also associated with similar notions such as **salvation**, redemption, and absolution within a Western religious context. In both East and West, the concept of liberation carries **political** connotations. For the most part, it is more strictly used in an Eastern religious **culture**, such as Indian Hinduism, to refer to becoming liberated from the cycle of birth and **death**.

In Hinduism, the Sanskrit term for a liberated individual is *jīvanmukti* (one who is liberated while alive). Such a person reaches this condition by achieving the highest form of **knowledge**, after having renounced the world, following an **ascetic** life-style, and practicing **meditation**. The freedom of the liberated person can only be achieved while a person is alive, which implies that liberation from the cycle of life and **death** is not a post-mortem event. Thus it shares nothing with dying and then going to a place such as **heaven**. If a person does not achieve liberation during their lifetime, that individual is reborn after death. The *Brihadāranyaka Upanishad* (4.2.4) describes the liberated person as ungraspable, undecaying, and as nothing being able to cling to him. The liberated person lives in the world without sorrow or **pain**, unbound, free of fear, and unconditioned by the structure of the world. Devoid of desires or doubt, the liberated person lives simultaneously in **time** and eternity. By attaining this condition while alive, the liberated individual is considered among the living dead because such a person is literally dead to the world. Later Hindu thinkers refine the notion of the liberated person.

Further reading: Fort and Mumme (1996)

LIMINALITY

Liminality is a condition or status in which one finds oneself or attains by **ritual**. To be in a liminal condition means to find oneself in an ambiguous situation because one is neither here nor there and between positions assigned by **law**, custom, social convention, or ceremony. Someone in a condition of liminality completely lacks status or rank. Liminality is linked to such events as **death**, being in a womb, bisexuality, and invisibility.

According to the anthropologist Victor Turner, there are two main types of liminality: **rituals** of status elevation or life crisis rites (e.g. initiation, marriage, or **death**) and cyclical and calendrical rites. In the latter type of rites those of low status exercise ritual authority over supe-riors, who accept ritual degradation, which Turner calls rituals of status reversal. While life crisis rites pertain to the individual, calendrical rites tend to be collective in nature. In addition, life crisis rites are about status elevation, whereas calendrical rites may become rites of status reversal.

The liminal condition can give birth to what Turner calls *communitas*, a being with another that emerges where structure is lacking. *Communitas* represents an anti-structure, something that breaks through structure, or something beneath structure evoking a sense of inferiority. Ultimately, *communitas*, a relationship between individuals, is beyond structure, although it does not last for a long period of time, reverting dialectically back eventually to structure, which a society needs to function. The liminal nature of *communitas*, however, does contribute to the revitalization of society. Turner gives the annual Muslim **pilgrimage** to Mecca as an example, although other scholars dispute his claims using examples of pilgrimage from other cultures.

According to Turner, there are three basic types of *communitas*: existential or spontaneous, normative, and ideological. The last type is based

128

on existential *communitas*, and it represents a label for a variety of uto-pian models of **society**. Spontaneous *communitas* is a magical feeling of endless **power** that is an impermanent condition. Two good examples are the Franciscan movement, representing an embracing of poverty based on the model of Jesus and influenced by Joachim of Fiore's (d. 1202) **millenarianism** on its spirituality, and the Sahajīyā movement of Bengal in the sixteenth century and its inspirational figure Caitanya (d. 1533).

Further reading: MacAloon (1984); Turner (1969); van Gennep (1960)

LOVE

Although it is primarily a Western term, there are some close Indian equivalents with such terms in Hinduism as *bhakti, prema,* and *kama.* The ancient Greeks make a threefold distinction between types of love: *philia* (friendship), *eros* (an erotic and passionate type), and *agape* (pure, altruistic, and selfless). These Greek types can also be found in India with examples of friendship between Rāma and his younger brother Lakṣmaṇa and the monkey-general Hanumān in the epic *Rāmāyaṇa*. There is the friendship between Krishna and Arjuna, a warrior, in the massive epic the *Mahābhārata*. Erotic types of love are evident among Hindu Śaiva poets and the **saints** associated with Krishna devotion. The selfless type of love is expressed by numerous devotional poets and saints who are willing to give their lives to the devotion of **God**.

According to the Gospel of John (15.12–13), Jesus calls for loving a friend in a public way, and he serves as a primary example by calling his disciples to his ministry and being friends for a period of time (Luke 34.38–39). The *philia* type of love is essential for humans discovering a way to cope with the problems of life. Jesus' call to his disciples implies an ethical and moral injunction to assist others. The Christian apostle Paul emphasizes necessity of mutuality (Rom. 12.10), and he encourages the continuance of mutual love (Heb. 13.1).

Eros can be translated as desire, passion, or sensually erotic. *Eros* is reck-less, wild, voluptuous, mercurial, careless, overpowering, and overwhelm-ing. It is often metaphorically expressed as a burning **fire**, heat, or **pain** in a sadomasochistic sense. *Eros* may exceed the ability to control it, and becomes a means of transforming one into an unruly condition. But this type of love is limited to an object, and it does not reach far enough for the Christian who is instructed by scripture that God is love (1 John 4.16).

Jesus' crucifixion is the selfless example of *agape*, a higher love, which is unselfish, uncalculating, and sacrificial, and must not be confused with something instinctive or impulsive. *Agape* is also characterized by mutuality or equal regards of the other. The example of Jesus represents a pure **gift** because it is unmotivated, completely gratuitous, and demands nothing in return. The event of the cross for Christians symbolizes a perfect kind of love, which transcends all particular norms of historical justice. *Agape* is dynamic in the sense that God is identical to it, characterizes the action of God, and calls for a response from the faithful. The inherent incomplete and imperfect nature of erotic love is completed and perfected by *agape*. This selfless and self-sacrificial type of love is the most powerful form of love within the Christian tradition.

The highest type of Christian love (*agape*) is dialectically related to justice, which is historical, discriminating, and concerned with balancing interests and claims. Justice is a relational concept that represents a relative embodiment of love. Justice can only approximate love because the latter is both a fulfillment and a negation of justice. As it operates in the world, love demands justice, even though it always transcends justice and its tendency for calculation and discrimination. The redemptive nature of love enables it to fulfill justice, and it is able to encounter the other in his/her uniqueness. As many Christian **saints** and **mystics** demonstrate by their lives, love possesses the **power** to convey a person beyond themself and to their utmost potential.

Within the context of Hindu **culture**, the Sanskrit term *bhakti* is derived from the root *bhaj* (meaning "to participate," "to share," 'to worship," "to be devoted to"). When the term is used with persons it suggests a certain communion of heart and mind that manifests a loving relationship. If the term is used in a religious context, it conveys the sense of choosing, worshiping, and adoring a deity. In the *Bhagavad Gītā*, *bhakti* is devotion to God, and is both a path and the goal of a devotee of Krishna.

The Sanskrit term *kāma* is closer in meaning to the English term desire, which is mentioned as a legitimate end of life in the dharma literature of India. It is considered impossible to act without desire in such a text as the *Laws of Manu*. Desire is eventually defied and depicted as a deity (Kāma) with a flower bow and arrows used to pierce the hearts of victims, turning them into uncontrollable bundles of desire. The ascetic deity Śiva becomes the arch-enemy of desire, and even destroys it at one point before restoring Kāma to life. It is desire and ignorance that must be controlled and conquered by **ascetics**, if they are to win **liberation**.

A final term often translated as love in Sanskrit is *prema*. Within the school of Gauḍīya Vaiṣhnavism, Rupa Gosvāmī distinguishes two types of *bhakti* (devotion): *vaidhi* and *rāgānuga*. The first kind is based on scripture, whereas the superior second type is the deep love of God, which arises spontaneously by following one's **emotions**. This devotion is called an absolute *rasa* (sap, taste, essence), an active realization of God. Those members of the movement willing to risk everything for their love are the primary examples of pure love (*prema*), a selfless type of love similar to Christian *agape*.

Further reading: Gosvāmin (2003); Nygren (1953); Outka (1972); Watson (2000)

MADNESS

To be considered mad within a religious context does not mean that someone is clinically insane or mentally ill, although this could be the case. Since Religious Studies is a humanistic discipline, it is possible to view madness in a humanistic way. For someone to be perceived mad that person must act continuously abnormal, which implies that such a person must act contrary to accepted norms of behavior or what people expect of a normal and mentally healthy person. By deviating from the expected decorum of a person's social or religious role, such a person runs the risk of being labeled crazy. In other words, for someone to lack consistent intention, to act outrageously, to appear indifferent to what one says and does, and to behave in unpredictable ways are characteristics of a mad person.

There is a long tradition of mad figures within the context of the devotional Hindu tradition from Ālvār (one immersed in **god**) poets to saints such as Ramakrishna of the nineteenth century. Being separated from god is what drives the poet mad. Guṇḍam Rauḷ, a thirteenth-century saint of the Mahānubbāva sect of western India, often acts infantile, greedy, rude, excessively demanding, and petulant. Mīrābāī (1403–1470), a Rājput princess who refuses to commit *sati* (self-immolation on her husband's funeral pyre) after her husband's **death**, writes poems about how Krishna's flute drove her mad as does her separation from her deity. The Bengali saint Caitanya (d. 1533) is known to experience uninterrupted conscious separation from Krishna, a condition that drives him mad. He also experiences wide mood swings and incoherent behavior, and he manifests physical symptoms associated with madness. Within the Śaiva **ascetic** tradition, the Pāśupatas deliberately act mad in order to incur the censure of others for their crazy behavior, which helps an ascetic rid himself of negative karma and acquire positive karma on his path to construct a superhuman **body**, which would eventually equate him with his deity. Ramakrishna (d. 1886) would sit inert for long periods of time, exhibit wide mood swings, act like a demented person, converse with the image of Kālī, and feed the image. He performs unorthodox religious actions, and he is confused about his own identity by dressing, talking, and behaving like a woman or like Hanuman, a monkey god, by sitting naked in a tree. Moreover, Ramakrishna hears strange sounds and voices, experiences visions, and goes suddenly into trance states.

There are also some mad figures to be discovered within the Islamic, Eastern Orthodox and Latin Christian religious traditions. The Muslim Abū Yazīd al-Bistāmī (d. 874), for instance, once tells a pilgrim on the way to Mecca to circle him instead seven times, and he kisses a skull that he finds and alleges that it symbolizes Sufi annihilation (*fanā*). An even more controversial Muslim figure is al-Hallāj (d. 922) who dies as a Sufi **martyr** after he claims to be God and fails to recant his assertion. Symeon of Emesa of the Eastern Orthodox tradition lives on wild herbs and roots, wanders naked, enters the women's bath, and relieves himself in public, and allegedly carries the carcass of a dead dog in public. In addition, St. Francis of Assisi (1182–1266) is deemed mad by others and often driven away by stones and mud thrown at him. Obeying a remark made by Pope Innocent III, he rolls in the mud with a herd of pigs. As a young man, Francis renounces the world and his father's wealth to pursue a career of preaching and a life of poverty.

The Zen Buddhist master Ikkyū Sōjun (1394–1481) is renowned for his erratic and bizarre behavior even calling himself "Crazy-cloud." He acts contrary to the decorum expected of a Zen-enlightened master by frequently engaging his passion at brothels, where he claims great wisdom can be found, drinking wine to the point of intoxication, roaming the streets of the city with a dead dog tied to a string attached to a long bamboo pole, playing the role of a warrior by carrying a fake sword, and entering into a love affair late in his life with a blind poet.

These various examples of religious madness are very suggestive. Madness points to the freedom of the figure to act in unpredictable and tumultuous ways, and he/she is not encumbered by society because the madness places the person outside of the confining structure of the world and the social patterns of **society**. Thus the mad person is a social misfit. Within the context of the person's madness, the individual is free to **play**, a voluntary activity that is joyful and amusing. By breaking down boundaries, the mad figure surprises us, makes us laugh, and provides an opportunity for us to reflect on the folly of human existence. At the same time, madness embodies an iconoclastic and irrational spirit. Madness can be irresistible and contagious for the followers of such figures and unify them around the mad person. Therefore, madness can become a symbol of a holy person, a sign of religious realization, and points to the absurdities of conventional social life.

Further reading: Kinsley (1974); Olson (1990); Sanford (1981); Saward (1980)

MAGIC

The term can be traced back to the Greek *mageia* (Latin, *magia*) and beyond to the Persian *magos* (a **priest** or religious specialist). The ancient Persian meaning also implies a secret tribe or **society**, who are individuals responsible for royal **sacrifices**, funeral rites, divination, and interpretation of **dreams**. The magician is an expert technician of the sacred, especially with secret and mysterious words. These powerful words are used in rites intended to harm enemies, which also gives the practitioner access to higher spiritual **powers**. In ancient Greece, magic is viewed as a **gift** from the gods. By the end of the sixth century in Greece, magic acquires negative connotations that are suggested by the magician being described as a beggar priest, diviner, and wanderer of the night. Along with wizardry, magic represents the art of deception. In ancient Greece and Rome, the negative connotation is associated with its foreign origin in Persia. The foreignness of magic is emphasized by the magician's use of foreign names that represent a reversal of ordinary linguistic usage.

Contrary to some earlier theories, magic does not precede religion in some kind of evolutionary sequence, and it does not necessarily follow religion because religion contains magic. It is certainly true that as historically early as the Greek philosophers Heraclitus and Plato a dichotomy develops between religion and magic, with magic portrayed as attempting to persuade the gods, whereas religion allows gods free choice and humans characteristically submit to the will of the deities. This distinction points to the magician's coercion of the gods by invocation, a form of verbal compulsion, rather than using other methods at their disposal such as constraining the gods by trickery or extortion. These methods are combined with **knowledge** of divine nature that enables the magician to communicate with the gods, which demonstrates the close relationship between the magician and the deities, and it suggests the magician's ability to get the gods to behave favorably toward clients of the magician.

In ancient Rome, the magician performs two functions during an early period: **healing** and divination. In time, divination is transformed into harmful practices intended to harm others. Whatever the intention of a magical rite is its strange words are used because of their inherent power. Egyptian temple priests serve as freelance magicians, for instance, because they possess training in the written and oral use of words. The patron deity of these ancient priests is Thoth, **god** of writing and also magic. The magician might utter a **curse**, which represents automatically effective words, making the magician's pronouncement a **performative** utterance that by definition makes something happen. The magician may perform his rite or curse within the presence of a group of witnesses, operating as the sender and recipient of the rite, whereas a sorcerer performs the rite in isolation from any group.

Since magic and religion are often intertwined in a particular religious tradition in spite of an insistence on its foreignness, it is possible to find it in many religions. The Seal of Solomon is, for instance, a ring sent to the Hebrew king from God and delivered to him by the angel Michael, which enables the king to control **demonic** beings. The Metternich Stele contains an image of the **goddess** Isis teaching *heka* (magic) to selected people. The early Christian **church** makes an essential distinction between magic and miracle with the latter identified with divine powers that overrule the established natural order, whereas magic is associated with deceptive, fraudulent, or demonic activities in the view of church leaders.

In contrast to these negative connotations, the practice of magic presupposes an awareness of the interrelatedness of everything. Since everything is intimately interconnected, the magician can work on a subject from a distance or in direct contact. The interrelated nature of the world helps to understand the process of **healing** because an illness represents a break in the **harmony** of the world, while magical healing restores the original system. It operates within a religious **culture** to organize labor, solve social and legal disagreements, and preserves reliable knowledge.

The ancient Greek, Rome, and Christian churches' characterization of magic as something foreign to religion is echoed by nineteenth- and twentieth-century anthropological theorists. James Frazer considers it to be a pseudo-science, Tylor refers to it as a mistaken science, Durkheim calls it anti-religious, Lévy-Bruhl thinks that it is an example of prelogical mentality, and Malinowski distinguishes between magic and religion because magical rites are designed, for instance, to assure safety and success, while a religious rite represents an end in itself. Frazer views magic, for instance, in evolutionary terms as representing a period of human superstition, which gives rise eventually to religion and science. He identifies two fallacious laws underlying magic: similarity and contact or contagion. In the first case "like produces like" or what he calls homeopathic magic, whereas contact implies that things once in contact continue to act upon each other, which he calls contagious magic. With the homeopathic type, magic is produced by, for instance, injuring or destroying an image of a likeness of a person, whereas contagious magic operates by using bodily residues, such as hair or nails, against someone. The sharp contrast drawn between religion and magic by these theorists and others does not pertain to more current theory where they are interrelated more closely within a particular religion.

Further reading: Glucklich (1997); Luch (1985); Siegel (1993); Stutley (1980)

MARTYRDOM

This concept is derived from the Greek term *martus* (witness), and it specifically refers to an individual who suffers **death** for his or her **faith**. Christian martyrs are the first historically to be venerated as **saints**. From the second century, it is common for martyrs to be defined as those who imitate Christ and suffer as He does. During this process, the martyr becomes assimilated to Christ in the popular imagination. At the moment of the martyr's death, it is believed that Christ appears to the martyr and endures all suffering in the place of the martyr. Although a martyr is not to seek death, he or she is expected to submit passively to it. During the Middle Ages, Christian martyrs could expect **visions** and **dreams** that reveal the future and the **afterlife**. Not only are martyrs worthy of these visions and dreams, it is believed that they have a right to demand them and to converse with God. Besides its importance to Christianity, martyrdom plays an important role in Shi'ite Islam and mystical Sufism.

Further reading: Boyarin (1999); Davis (2003); Frend (1965); Gregory (1999); Le Goff (1984)

MATERIAL DIMENSION

This refers to the physical aspect of religion that can be divided into four major categories: artifacts, **art**, **architecture**, and landscapes. The objects associated with any of these categories provide insight into a particular religious world. Landscapes represent, for instance, a cultivation of nature by taking land and transforming it by means of roads, trees, houses, and churches. Landscapes are thus shaped by human intention in order to manipulate nature to express communal and personal values.

Because people interact with the material world, it is possible for this realm to communicate messages that include religious values, norms, actions, and attitudes. When studying objects for their significance it is import to pay attention to their form, function, mode of distribution, and the changes to the objects and their environment. How a sacred text is used and treated by people is instructive about their religion. It is also important for researchers to know how people interact with the material world and allow it to communicate its messages. It is possible, for instance, for religious objects to shape and to reflect religious beliefs and values. Although the materials are objective, they are not static because their meaning may change over time or people may alter their meaning.

Further reading: Lang (1997); McDannell (1995)

MEDITATION

A mental and subjective practice that is employed by a person to shape, control, and train their body, senses, emotions, and conscious and unconscious states of mind by means of an inward process of discipline. Christian and Jewish mystics use meditation to enhance their spiritual progress. Christian mystics meditate, for instance, on **prayer**, whereas Jewish Kabbalists meditate on the *merkabah* (chariot of **God**) with the purpose of having a **vision** of it. In Sufi Islamic **mysticism**, there is a twofold distinction on the path between stations (*maqām*) that are obtained by human effort, which represent the **ascetic** and ethical discipline of a Sufi, and the six states that are conferred by God that begins with meditation (*muraqaba*) and is followed by nearness to God, **love**, fear of God, contemplation, and certitude. The Sufi is instructed to redirect his thinking by the method of *dhikr*, which means thinking only of God.

Similar to the later Indian classical yoga system compiled by Patañjali, the *Maitri Upanishad* (6.18) promotes a sixfold path of yoga, involving breath control, withdrawal of the senses, and meditation, which enables a person to penetrate objects. This is followed by concentration on a single point in order to quiet and calm the mind. The meditator reaches a point of becoming conscious of consciousness before moving on to contemplation and finally absorption (*samādhi*), a non-dualistic **experience** of absorption and identity with Brahman, the lone **reality**.

As with the sixfold yoga of ancient Hinduism, meditation is the central practice in Buddhism for attaining enlightenment. The formative Buddhist tradition understands meditation (*dhyāna*) as a process of shaping, training, and controlling the **body**, senses, feelings, mind, and unconsciousness. A monk uses meditation to control his mind and to free him from the four cankers of sensual desire, craving for becoming or life, false views, and ignorance. Meditation also helps a monk overcome the latent dispositions of the unconscious and their unwholesome roots (greed, hatred, and delusion). Within the context of meditation, the calming of the mind (*śamatha*), a process that is necessary because of the normal state of flux of the mind caused by desires, delusions, and senses, frees the mind from distractions and mental impurities. Once the mind is calm, the meditator can achieve insight (*vipaśyanā*), which leads to an awareness of the **truth** of the Buddhist path and the three marks of existence: **suffering**, impermanence, and non-self.

Further reading: Eliade (1969); Olson (2005, 2007); Schimmel (1975)

MEMORY

A mental mechanism that enables humans to recall their past experiences. Memory is both collective and individual. The collective memory is a set of recollections that people share with **others**, which gives people access to past events and actions that are reconstructed, told to them, and held in common. Collective memories antedate individual memories of a childhood, family, and friends. Individual memories take shape against the backdrop of a collective memory. Memory is an essential attribute of human nature because without it there can be no history involving people. Memory not only possesses implications for history but is essential for **interpretation** and discerning collective and individual identities.

The collective and individual memories of religious traditions depend on their preservation and transmission from one generation to another. Memories die when there is no one to perpetuate them, but they can be restored to life if they have been preserved by a person or a text. Hagiographical accounts of **holy people** in the East and West are traditional forms of perpetuating memory of religiously paradigmatic people.

The Buddhist *Jātaka* tales of the Buddha's former lives are narratives that transmit Buddhist ethical values. Many Buddhist texts begin with the phrase "Thus have I heard," which reflects the importance of memory in the preserving, recalling, and sharing of the teachings of the Buddha. In contrast to the revealed literature of the Vedas in ancient India, the people accept a body of literature called *smriti* (that which is remembered), which is a humanly derived and constructed literary tradition grounded in the collective memory of the culture. Even the revealed Vedas are preserved for centuries by an oral tradition of memorizing these sacred texts. The same thing can be said for Judaism, Christianity, Islam, and other religious traditions.

Further reading: Ricoeur (2004)

METAPHORS

These are elements of **language** that allow humans to express something else because of resemblance and kinship. It is possible to find metaphors throughout the **sacred scriptures** of many religious traditions because they expand language by enabling a person to express a message using ordinary images that connote several layers of significance. The "throne of God" evokes, for instance, an image of majesty, royalty, and regal splendor with respect to a divine being with a metaphor taken from everyday life with which there are attached a number of cultural connotations. Metaphors are embraced by **mystics** cross-culturally to express **experiences** that cannot be put into words. The great Islamic Sufi poet Rumi (b. 1207) represents excellent examples of a mystical use of metaphor. He uses the game of polo to liken the ball to a lover without hands and feet and the stick that strikes the ball is **God**. He uses the metaphor of the rose to suggest the beauty and wrath (thorn) of God. Rumi's use of animal imagery is suggestive because the camel represents the spiritual journey, the lion is a model of the holy man, a parrot is eloquent and life-giving, and the falcon represent the **soul**; when the falcon's eyes are covered it suggest the soul's captivity to the world.

As evident in some of the examples from the poetry of Rumi, the philosopher Paul Ricoeur (1913–2005) observes that a metaphor is part of a **language** game that governs naming, but it does not give a person new information about **reality**. A metaphor manifests the phenomenon of predication because it only makes sense in a sentence. From one perspective, it is a calculated error that causes new meaning to emerge. It can thus tell others something new about **reality**.

Grounded in new research in cognitive science, the philosophers Lakoff and Johnson identify primary metaphors that are conventional, entrenched, and fixed aspects of the human conceptual system. These primary metaphors, such as "Life is a journey," form the basis for new metaphorical combinations that can be used for reasoning. Primary metaphors link human subjective experiences and judgments to the human sensory motor experience. The aptness of metaphors is measured by their ability to play a role in structuring our **experience**. Humans acquire metaphorical modes of thought automatically and unconsciously, which implies that humans have no choice whether to use them or not. What Lakoff and Johnson claim is that a system of primary and complex metaphors is part of the cognitive unconscious to which humans have no direct access or control over the way that it is used over time. In a practical way, metaphors define abstract concepts that make abstract scientific theorizing possible. By its ability, a metaphor is an embodied form of **truth** that originates in the unconscious of embodied human beings.

Further reading: Lakoff and Johnson (1999); Ricoeur (1977); Rumi (1968)

MILLENARIANISM

Owing its origins to an early Christian context, this concept refers to a thousand years during which the world will be at peace and its inhabitants perfectly good and happy. This social and spiritual bliss on earth is expected to arrive in the near future. Millenarianism is distinguished from eschatology (**doctrine** of **last things**) because it stresses a kind of paradise on earth, whereas the latter notion transfers its hopes for a better future to a hereafter. A distinction can also be made within millenarianism between pre-millenarianism and post-millenarianism with the former expecting Christ to return to earth and establish a millennial rule. The latter type believes that Christ will return to earth only after the **church** establishes the millennium. Another distinction between the two types of millenarianism relates to the lack of human effort associated with the coming of a messianic kingdom among the pre-millenarians, while human effort affects the progression toward such a kingdom after the church reforms the world. Whereas the post-millenarians see hope with possible political and social change, the pre-millenarians have a **vision** of the world getting worst until the advent of Christ.

Grounded in Christian expectations, millenarian movements developed in indigenous religions after their contact with Western **cultures**. These encounters are associated with disastrous events, such as detribalization, conquest of a country and people, destruction of indigenous cultures by white Europeans, collective deportations, or natural catastrophes. Any of these situations cause extreme distress, existential precariousness, and crisis. Thus millenarianism arises as an answer to a need for renewal, **purification**, and cultural catharsis. There are a wide variety of **cults** encompassed within the concept of millenarianism: nativistic movements, revivalistic movements, messianic movements, prophetic cults, cargo cults, and introversionist movements.

Nativistic movements stress the value of indigenous cultural elements and attempt to revive or perpetuate selected aspects of their culture. The Mau Mau Uprising in Kenya from 1952–1956 is a good example of this type in which political freedom is framed in traditional Kikkuyu moral and religious values, where the land serves a twofold symbolic function: it represents the living society and the historical identity of the people living on the land. Nativistic movements are similar to revivalistic movements, which represent an attempt to reinstate former customs and ways of life, and seek to stir religious **faith** among those who are indifferent. The Ghost Dance Religion of Native American Indians of 1870 and 1890 is an excellent example of this type. The movement anticipated the return of a Great Spirit to **earth** with the **spirits** of the dead **ancestors**, a great cataclysm would shake the **earth**, and white men would vanish, although their buildings and goods would remain for the Indians. These events produce an earthly paradise, but only the ancestors of those who believe would return to earth. The arrival of this event can be hastened with participation in a **ritual dance** in which the circle is open to allow for the entrance of ancestors. The 1890 Ghost Dance owes its origin to John Wilson, an adopted Indian known as Wovoka, who preaches a message of peace. A major innovation is the wearing of ghost shirts believed to possess supernatural powers and to be impervious to bullets. During the process of diffusion, Wovoka's peaceful message gets lost, and the movement ends in tragedy when Sitting Bull attempts to use the movement for his own restoration to power. He and many of his followers die at Wounded Knee Creek with many wearing the ghost shirts intended to make them invincible.

Messianic and prophetic movements form around a central figure and they sometimes overlap. A good example is The Church of Jesus Christ on Earth founded by Simon Kimbangu, who considered himself a prophet while his followers interpreted him as a messiah who brings redemption and **salvation**. Kimbangu sparks a nationalist movement that he neither intends nor can control. He dies in jail in 1951 hailed by his people as a black messiah. In contrast to the messianic movements, prophetic cults center around a divinely inspired individual whose leadership is confirmed by **visions**, **dreams**, or supernatural inspiration. The Milne Bay Prophet Cult in New Guinea begins with a native prophet, Tokerau, who foretells the approach of a terrifying cataclysm that will destroy everything and then be followed by a time of plenty and the return of dead ancestors. Because a plentiful supply of **food** is expected, the people are instructed to consume all garden produce and to slaughter and eat all their pigs. The people abandon their homes and follow their prophet inland to be safe from the predicted disasters.

Cargo cult is a term applied to millenarian movements on the Pacific islands. People believe that goods will arrive in the form of cargo consisting of Western commodities. They also believe that European ships, airplanes, trade articles, and military equipment could not be made by humans, but rather that they come from some supernatural source. Thus cargo cult **ritual** activity is designed to bring such goods to the cult members, who construct airstrips for planes and large storage houses to deposit the new supplies. The new order is inaugurated by a cataclysm that forces the whites to leave, be killed, or enslaved.

Because the world is alien and irredeemable, introversionist movements represent a withdrawal from the world. The Handsome Lake Movement of the Iroquois led by a Seneca prophet in 1799 is an example of this type. This particular movement synthesizes Indian and Christian elements. The Peyote cult among Native American Indians is another example in which the chewing of peyote, a non-addictive, hallucinogenic substance that grows at the roots of cactus plants, functions to provide **visions** and **healing power**.

Millenarianism is a religious movement determined by cultural and environmental factors. It is historically significant because it affirms a need for escape from the present, dire situation by attempting to abolish the present, return to a primordial **time** of peace and plenty, and renew and reform society. It accomplishes these types of things by reinterpreting the origin myth and projecting a return to origins into the future at which point the end time is realized and the world is renewed along with its culture, **society**, and political life.

Further reading: La Barre (1970); McGinn (1979, 1993); Ray (1976); Wilson (1973)

MODERNITY

This notion can be grasped as a contrast concept because it compares itself with what precedes it in a transition from the traditional to the new. This is embodied in its linguistic derivation from the Latin *modernus* that itself originally consists of *modo* (equivalent to nunc, now, new). Ninth-century Christians use the concept to differentiate historical periods. It is used in the thirteenth century by Christian theologians to compare their thinking with an earlier antiquity, and Enlightenment thinkers did the same thing with the Middle Ages, implying a decisive break with the past.

After the enlightenment in the eighteenth century, modernity is associated with what is progressive, innovative, and current. In such a context, modernity can be grasped as a process that includes the following types of elements: emergence of nation states; industrialization; market capitalism; democratization; rationalization; urbanism; and **secularization**. These features of modernity suggest that these characteristics not only coexist, but also generate counter-modernities, suggesting that there is no overarching modernity that applies to all situations. Thus it is best to become aware that there are many modernities. Recent theories offered by Giddens and Wagner discuss the process of separation and recombination of time and space and disruption of local social relations.

Further reading: Benavides (1998); Giddens (1990); Wagner (1994)

MONASTICISM

Christianity is open to the development of monasticism, Judaism rejects it, and Islam is suspicious of it. Monasticism develops gradually in some movements within Hinduism and is encouraged from the inception of Buddhism. In the West, the term originates with the Greek *monachos* (alone or solitary) with possibly an earlier meaning of **celibate**. Over time, monasticism refers to individuals who withdraw from society in order to devote full time to their religious life by praying, living a disciplined life, and practicing various forms of **asceticism**. Those choosing such a lifestyle can decide to live alone as an anchorite or adopt a cenobitic (living in **community**) way of life.

Although there are some references in the New Testament that suggest a monastic lifestyle (Mark 8.34; Matt. 19.12, 21; Luke 9.23; 14.26–27; 1

Cor. 9.26–27; John 12.25), monasticism begins around the third century in the Egyptian desert with St. Anthony, who begins to organize hermits. However, Christian tradition credits St. Pachomius (d. 346) as the first founder of monasticism by establishing monasteries in southern Egypt. St. Basil (*c*. 330-379) devises monastic rules known as Basilian, requiring a monk to lead a life of **prayer**, work, poverty, chastity, and obedience. These principles are practiced in hospitals, orphanages, and schools operated by the monks.

A simple, rustic, and largely uneducated **community** is envisioned by St. Benedict of Nursia (480–543) in order for a monk to live a quiet Christian life. From Benedict's perspective, it is not a monk's duty to reform the world but rather to reform himself. A basic presupposition of the monastic order is that it is impossible to live a Christian life in towns. The famous Benedictine Rule includes both an absolute obedience to God and the monastic community and a vow of stability, meaning that a monk is to remain in a particular monastery until **death**. A monk is forbidden to own anything and all property is to be shared. Letters and presents cannot be received without the abbot's permission, and he can allot such presents to other monks as he wishes. The over-arching ideal is humility, which one learns by praising God and working in the fields. It is not unusual for monks to view themselves as slaves of God. The Benedictine Rule seeks to create an ideal community within the **church** but it is exclusive in demanding of an individual permanent loyalty. Later Benedictines attempt to stimulate the scholarly and artistic life of the church from within it, while other monastic movements make other contributions to the development of the church.

The Dominicans, founded by Dominic (1170–1221), adopt the apostle Paul as their role model, and are convinced that they can win people to Christ by preaching. Dominic adopts the rule of St. Augustine and obtains approval for his order in 1216. Dominic's order adopts the principle of mendicancy, which means that members are to beg for their food. The constitution of the *Order of Preachers* specifies a master-general as head of the order chosen by the general chapter. The field is divided into provinces with a provincial prior in charge who is elected for a four-year term, while each monastery also elects a prior for four years. This system combines **church** authority with representative government.

The Franciscans are founded by Giovanni Bernadone (1182–1226) on February 24, 1208 after he hears words from the Gospel of Matthew (10.7–14) at a service that make him decide to preach repentance and the Kingdom of God. In addition to his preaching, Francis imitates Christ by taking a vow of absolute poverty, wearing plain garments, and practicing **love** like Christ. Francis sends his monks out in pairs, preaching repentance, singing, aiding peasants in their work, caring for lepers and outcasts, and begging for their sustenance. The organization of the order is left to others who devise the Rule of St. Francis, which make three spiritual demands: absolute poverty, refusal to solicit or accept ecclesiastical privilege, and renunciation of all human learning. These three demands are believed to prevent sources of spiritual corruption. In England, the Franciscans are known as the Grey Friars, whereas the Dominicans were called the Black Friars.

Other forms of Catholic monasticism promote different agendas. The Cistercian Benedictines want to reform the order by renewing the practice of rigorous **asceticism**. The Jesuits are founded to counter heretical (Reformation) teachings and to propagate the faith as missionaries, while the Trappists (a type of Cistercian order) want to practice a life of silent piety and prayer. Despite its members desire to live apart from society, monasticism makes significant cultural contributions in the West because monks help to preserve Latin classics and patristic writings by copying manuscripts, preserve the heritage of ancient science, and become superb illustrators.

These types of Western cultural contributions are also evident in Buddhism. Although Jesus never explicitly insists on monasticism, the historical Buddha does want a monastic **community** that is called the Samgha, a term that is synonymous with *gaṇa,* which indicates a political, professional, commercial group, or assembly of elders who govern tribal states. In Buddhism, the term possesses a narrower meaning of a fraternity of monks. The Buddhist monastic community can theoretically be without a leader because the teachings of the Buddha can guide it. The Buddhist Samgha is considered one of the three jewels (*triratna*) of the religion along with the Buddha and dharma (teachings), and everyone is encouraged to take refuge under the three jewels.

Buddhist monasticism is rooted in a wandering lifestyle typical of many **sects** and lone individuals. These wanderers have to contend with the annual monsoon season and this results in a break from their travels in what become rain retreats. Among the Buddhists, these rain retreats become more permanent locations as a congregation of fellow monks develop in either a town or the countryside. In time, monasteries (*leṇa,* private abode) develop and form a compact unitary establishment for a settled body of monks that is private in the sense that it is built to house a single monk fraternity.

Likewise, Buddhist monastic rules slowly evolve in response to incidents that occur and need a rule about whether or not the behavior is acceptable or contrary to monastic spirit. While the Buddha is alive, he functions as the voice of authority on matters of monastic discipline, but with his passing monks have to rely on past monastic precedents and teachings of the founder. The monastic order is united by its rules embodied in the *Pātimokkha*, which means bond. These various rules are committed to memory and periodically recited by the entire brotherhood. The Pāli canon contains 227 rules, the Chinese version 250 rules, and the Tibetan code embodies 253 rules. Divided into eight parts according to cases, the *Pātimokkha* elucidates, for instance, four cases that result in expulsion from the order: sexual intercourse, stealing, killing someone, hiring a killer or desiring the death of another. Less serious violations involve lighter sanctions, but the act of confessing violations remains intact. In addition to the *Pātimokkha* rules, the monastic community is guided by the *Vinaya Piṭaka*, a canon regulating monastic life for an individual and **community**. The term *vinaya* means literally "to lead away from" moral and ethical errors and transgressions. This code of discipline is intended to lead a monk or nun to **salvation** by attacking the false notion of ego-consciousness.

The lifestyle of a Buddhist monk is characterized by begging, a practice from which the term *bhikṣu* (beggar) for monk originates. Monks work, study **scripture**, copy texts, and **meditate** within the monasteries. Monks are only allowed to own a razor (to shave their face and head), begging bowl, three robes, a cord worn around the waist, a needle to mend their robes, water strainer, and a toothpick. Although Buddhist monks eventually settle into permanent communities, the wandering lifestyle never loses its allure. Becoming a monk involves a formal act of renouncing the world, accepting a life of poverty, adhering to the monastic code, and accepting a life of **celibacy**. When the renouncing of the world becomes ritualized a monk renounces his caste, kinship, and social mark, a ceremony that also includes accepting robes and a begging bowl. The intention of such a regimen is absolute detachment from the world, control of one's body and senses, and turning inward to achieve **liberation**.

Formative Buddhism recognizes two levels of ordination: novice and full ordination. The first level does not involve a formal affair, but an aspirant must be fifteen years old, recite the three refuges, shave his head, don robes, and resolve to abide by the ten precepts. There are eight requirements for full ordination: one must be a human being, be twenty years old, have the permission of parents or wife, be free of debt, free of disease, be a free man, not be in the employ of the government, and have one's own alms bowl and robes. If a candidate is eligible, he is presented to the assembly of monks, and it is necessary for ten monks to be present for a valid ordination. A senior monk asks three times whether the brotherhood favors admission. If there is no dissent, the aspirant is accepted into the brotherhood. Thereafter, the new monk selects a spiritual guide who must be a monk with ten years of experience.

The Buddha is opposed to the establishment of an order of nuns, but he eventually relents, but not before predicting the quicker demise of the monastic order if **women** are allowed to join. In addition to rules that apply to males, nuns are subject to additional monastic rules: nuns must treat every monk as a superior and pay homage and respect to all monks, nuns cannot admonish a monk, they cannot live in a location during the monsoon season where no monk is residing, nuns are administered a lecture twice a month by a monk after the rainy season, nuns are investigated for monistic violations, and guilty nuns are disciplined by both monastic communities and also ordained by both. This subordination of nuns reflects cultural attitudes about the roles of women and the dangerous nature of their **sexuality**.

The Buddhist monastic community is dependent upon the laity for its survival. This arrangement gives the laity an opportunity to earn merit, which improves their chances of obtaining a more favorable status in their next life, and it enables the monks to reciprocate by giving lay people the *dharma* (teachings). Thus both groups are mutually dependent on the other. By supporting the monastic community in thought, word, and deed, this scenario promotes the view that giving is beneficial to the lay person and healthful for the social order. In China at a later period, the spirit of giving enables monastic institutions to become very wealthy and powerful.

Further reading: Dutt (1962); P. King (1999); Laurance (2001); Schopen (1997)

MONISM

The **belief** that there is a single **reality** underlying the multiplicity characteristic of the cosmos and human life. Monism is exactly contrary to a position of pluralism. Monism is often referred to as a non-dualism. The best examples of monism are found in the East with the Advaita Vedanta philosophy of Śankara (788–820) and some forms of Buddhism, such as the Zen thought of Dōgen.

The term *advaita* means non-dualistic because the lone reality is Brahman, which possesses two aspects: without qualities (*nirguṇa*) and with qualities (*saguṇa*). The former aspect is defined positively as being (*sat*), consciousness (*cit*), and bliss (*ānanda*). Being pertains to the nature of Brahman in the sense of the negation of all empirical being. Being (*sat*) means that Brahman could not have originated from something else because Brahman alone is real. This position entails that the world does not have real being, implying that the world is essentially illusory (*māyā*) because its existence is sublated by Brahman. The conscious aspect of Brahman denies its opposite and suggests that consciousness is native to Brahman. The aspect of bliss introduces the principle of value and points to the fact that Brahman is free from birth and **death** and to realize it means to know it as blissful, which is an unconditional value. From an ultimate perspective, Brahman is indefinable, indescribable, impersonal, non-relational, and without qualities. The *saguṇa* aspect of Brahman refers to the lower aspect of reality because it is conditioned by limiting adjuncts such as ignorance, whereas *nirguṇa* (higher aspect) is free of limiting adjuncts and the object of liberating **knowledge**.

In contrast to Śankara's position on Brahman, Rāmānuja (1050–1137) promotes a position called *viśistādvaita*, which means qualified non-dualism because Brahman is not devoid of characteristics. In fact, Brahman is qualified by the *ātman* (**self**) and world (matter or *prakṛti*). For Rāmānuja, Brahman is a personal **God** equated with the personal deity Vishnu. Therefore, Rāmānuja rebutted the thoughts of Śankara by writing a commentary on the *Vedānta Sūtras* with the intention of defending the devotional position that he thought was threaten by Śankara. According to Rāmānuja, the *ātman* and world are modes of Brahman, who animates and supports them, and the self is a modification of Brahman which constitutes its **body**. Contrary to Śankara's position, the world is real for Rāmānuja, since the entire universe is incorporated by Brahman.

In contrast to these Hindu thinkers, the Madhyamika school of Mahāyāna Buddhism identifies emptiness (*śūnyatā*) as the non-dual reality. This line of thinking is embraced by the Zen thinker Dōgen and his notion of Buddha-nature, whose being is openly manifest and at the same time concealed. Dōgen equates all existence (including plant and animal life, and the inanimate world) with Buddha-nature, which is also being and being-itself. The absolute inclusiveness of Buddha-nature does not mean for Dōgen that it is immanent in all existence but that all existence is immanent in it. The inner aspect of Buddha-nature contains non-being, which is grounded in emptiness, the dynamic and creative aspect of Buddha-nature. Finally, Buddha-nature is impermanent because it is eternally coming into being and passing into non-being, which represents a single process of impermanence. This position implies that there is nothing static and immutable in the universe. This all-embracing, dynamic, creative, and impermanent Buddha-nature is the lone reality that a person must realize to become liberated.

Further reading: Dōgen (2007); Loy (1988); Rāmānuja (1971); Śankara (1968)

MONOTHEISM

Derived from the Greek terms *mono* (one) and *theos* (god), this is the **belief** in a single **God** in sharp contrast to **polytheism**, or belief in many deities. A religion that is monotheistic, such as Judaism, Christianity, or Islam, defines its singular God in a context of polytheism which it opposes. Although polytheistic religions do not assert their identity by opposing monotheistic religions, from the perspective of monotheistic faiths, the deities of polytheistic religions are false and cannot compete with the **power** of a singular God. The three major monotheistic religions – Judaism, Christianity, and Islam – are all based on revelation and not **rational** or empirical evidence. In the Qur'an, Allah is called al-Wahid (the One, 37.4), which eliminates any chance of pluralistic confusion with respect to the definitions of the deity and the cultural context for the understanding of His divine nature. The singularity of Allah represents the first article of the Islamic confession of faith (*shahada*: "There is no God but Allah and Muhammad is His messenger" (37.35). Overall, the monotheistic Gods tend to be extramundane and transcendent, whereas polytheistic deities tend to be more involved in the everyday lives of adherents, although both types are perceived as creator figures.

It is possible to find strands of monotheism within polytheistic religions. Hinduism is a good example of this phenomenon because when a devotee is worshiping his/her deity this god or goddess that is called the *iṣṭa deva* (personal deity) becomes the only genuine deity for that worshiper. The Oxford University scholar F. Max Müller (d. 1900) calls this development **henotheism** (etymologically derived from the Greek *hen* (one) and *theos* or deity). According to Müller, within a henotheistic context, many gods associate and cooperate with each other in an impersonal system in which one god assumes leadership of the pantheon for an unspecified period of time before relinquishing leadership to another deity, a pattern suggested to Müller by the Vedic pantheon of ancient India depicted in the Vedic texts. More recently, Indologist Axel Michaels gives three reasons why Müller's term is inadequate. First, there is basically no polytheism without henotheism. Second, to restrict henotheist variants to only particular divine beings is unjustified, because it is possible to discover the diffusion of numerous deities and prominent regional gods. Third, henotheism cannot grasp the complex connections related to inclusive ways of devotion between god and believer. Michaels substitutes the word "equitheism" for Müller's term henotheism. Occasionally, Michaels calls equitheism "homotheism." What he means is that either term denotes the idea of god as well as the fundamental process of identification.

Further reading: Michaels (2004); Müller (1895–1898); Peters (2003)

MUSIC

Within the context of time, music is the sound that expresses ideas and emotions created by instruments in rhythmical, melodious, and harmonious ways. The tempo for indigenous **dances** is maintained by music, the Christian mass is enhanced by music, and devotional emotions of Hindus are evoked by music. Muslims and Buddhist chant **scripture**, whereas Muslim Sufis use music to dance themselves into trance states. Some religious traditions do not place much value on music or even prohibit it for various reasons. Besides its ability to entertain, music can evoke powerful **emotions**, alter the moods of humans, and enable participants to praise and **worship God**. Music binds together musicians and listeners, and it is often integrated with dance. Religious music possesses the ability to transport listeners to a higher level of existence, and it enables them to communicate with higher beings.

From the time period of the early church, Christians are encouraged to sing hymns, psalms, and holy songs (Col. 3.16; Eph. 5.19). Several Christians recognize the salvific power of music. Boethius (*c.* 489–*c.* 524 CE), a Roman philosopher, statesman, and **martyr** for his Christian **faith**, writes *On Music* of which only the final part survives. In this work, he differentiates three kinds of music: that of the spheres (*musica mundane*), music reflecting the harmony of soul and body (*musica humana*), and music related to human voices or instruments (*musica intrumentorum*). A book with the same title as that of Boethius is composed by Augustine (354–430), a bishop of North Africa, in which he calls attention to the music of the **soul** in addition to cosmic and divine harmonies.

Within various traditions of the Christian church, plainchant (plain song), a monophonic and free rhythmic hymn, develops and becomes part of the **worship**. Examples of Christian hymns of praise are the so-called *Sanctus* and *Gloria*, which both express adoration of God. By the eleventh century, a more polyphony form is introduced coming to maturity by the fourteenth century. Before being used in worship, instrumental music is used to acclaim and praise members of the upper classes: the emperor, nobility, Pope, and bishops. During the eighth or ninth century, musical instruments are introduced into the liturgy. By 1300, many major churches in western Europe own an organ and attract those with the ability to play it. A noteworthy figure during the Middle Ages of Europe is Hildegard of Bingen (1098–1179), who creates a musical anthology from 1150–1160 called *Symphony of the Harmony of the Celestial Revelations*. Within her theology of music, Hildegard equates Adam's fall with that of music, which she imagines as a vehicle of grace that corrects the fall. According to Hildegard's interpretation of the Genesis narrative, the Devil's negative reaction to Adam's singing motivates him to corrupt the first man. Therefore, the Devil is not merely out of **harmony** with God, but the entire universe is also inherently musical. This type of sinful – anti-musical – condition, according to Hildegard's imagination, can be overcome by singing, a musical activity that reflects a celestial harmony and recalls the Incarnation of Christ. By making music, we unite **body** and **spirit**, reconcile the individual with the cosmos, and restore internal and external harmony. Thus, music can be grasped as an important feature on the path to **salvation**.

During the Reformation, music is used to tell biblical stories as evident in the compositions of Heinrich Schütz (1585–1672). Renowned composers are commissioned to write **church** music of wonderful quality and complexity, with men such as J. S. Bach (1685–1750) recalling the Passions according to the Gospels of Matthew and John. Others follow Bach, such as Haydn (1732–1809), Mozart (1756–1791), and Beethoven (1770–1827). In his compositions for the High Mass, Mozart often uses, for instance, drums and horn instruments, such as trumpets and trombones, to express adoration and celebration of God. Taking a basic musical key of the non-expressive C, Mozart lifts this part to the realm of the impassioned and trans-temporal. Mozart contrasts **heaven** and **earth** by moving from adoration to the *allegro* of jubilant praise. Christian music possesses the **power** to render words meaningless by synthesizing all texts into a single moment. Thereby, it transforms the whole liturgy into a single gesture of humility, respect, and adoration.

Confucians not only play a zither-like instrument like that in Daoism that is regarded as a way to realize the Dao, but Confucius also advocates music as an instrument of education and court ceremony. Drawing a distinction between popular and **ritual** music, Confucius thinks that music can help to develop a person's ethical character, as it represents the ultimate in **harmony**, beauty, and goodness. In ancient China, there is a close relationship between music and **ritual**. If ritual defines the external structure of the individual, music provides inner harmony. Moreover, the harmony of music is a microcosm of the harmony that exists between heaven and earth. Thus ritual and music are essential because they help one to understand both the distinction as well as the harmony between **heaven** and **earth**. The Confucian philosopher Hsün Tzu attributes cosmic symbolism to musical instruments: the drum represents a vast pervasiveness and heaven, bells represent fullness and earth, sounding stones stand for restrained order and water, mouth organs symbolized austere harmony and the **sun**, flutes signify a spirited outburst, the bamboo whistle is the breath of tone, the zither is gentleness, the lute manifests **grace**, and songs represented purity and fulfillment.

Hindu literature makes it clear that divine beings **love** music and are pleased by it. In fact, the patroness of music and arts is the **goddess** Sarasvatī, who is frequently depicted holding a stringed instrument identified as the *vina*. Because of their association with the **sacred** power of the goddess, instruments are treated with great respect by players, who often even worship their instruments and protect them from **pollution**. A musician is not the originator of the music because music exists eternally, making the musician its transmitter and preserver.

The Hindu conception of music is best grasped within a metaphysical context grounded in sound (*nāda*) that is either struck or unstruck. The latter form of sound represents a vibration of ether that permeates all space, although it cannot be perceived. A physical blow creates the struck sound, which consists of a temporary vibration of air. Ordinary people can hear the struck sound, which is a manifestation of the eternal sound. Because it can reveal the unstruck sound, the struck sound is not merely pleasing to hear, but it also can break down the cycle of earthly existence by putting a listener into contact with ultimate **reality**.

Further reading: Beck (1993); Collins *et al.* (1989); Shelemay (1986); Sullivan (1997)

MYSTICISM

This is a notion cloaked in mystery and leads to disagreement and even confusion among interested people. When something is called mystical it often suggests something vague, mysterious, or incomprehensible.

Mysticism is often confused with occult **experience**, trance states, hearing voices, speaking in tongues, extraordinary **visions**, prophetic utterances, or aesthetic sensitivity. Mysticism is also confused with conversion **experiences**, which can assume the form of a warm inner feeling, a tearful and joyful acceptance of **salvation**, or an awakening to moral and ethical principles. Although it may share some common features with these phenomena, mysticism is not precisely any of these phenomena. Another common error is to equate mysticism with the irrational. This is a mistake due in part to the mystic's penchant for expressing their experience in a contradictory manner because of an inability to find **rational** modes of expression that are adequate to express an experience.

The term mysticism is of Western origin, dating to Greek – Eleusinian, Dionysian, and Orphic – mystery **cults**. These cults are called *muein* (literally, to close the eyes) which suggest that they are hidden to the prying eyes of outsiders, although the rites and other mysteries are revealed to initiates. The Greek term probably owes its origins to the Indo-European root *muc* (mutter, mute, mystery), which is also associated with the term *muni* (silent one) in Sanskrit. The term *muein* (hidden or mysterious from a verbal root *muo*) is adopted by Christian writers who thereby apply the term to the mystery of Christ. Over a period of time, the term comes to denote a profound, deep, direct, personal, spiritual experience, although retaining its ancient meaning of secrecy and mystery. In fact, it is possible to find overt usage of the term in the sixth century by Pseudo-Dionysius, author of *The Mystical Theology*, emphasizing a *via mystica* (mystical path). By the seventeenth century, "la mystique" is a term used in France to designate a subjective experience that is independent of the Christian tradition.

Scholars of the subject have attempted to alleviate the confusion with more precise definitions. Many scholars agree that mysticism pertains to a profound religious experience that reflects a union, unity, or intimate relationship with something beyond and greater than oneself. In his classic work *The Varieties of Religious Experience*, the psychologist William James isolates four basic characteristics of mysticism: (1) ineffability; (2) noetic quality; (3) transiency; and (4) passivity. The ineffable quality of mysticism means that it cannot be adequately expressed in **language**; it can only be directly experienced and not transferred to another person. Its noetic quality means that the mystic thinks that their experience entails states of **knowledge**. By transiency, James wants to emphasize that the mystic cannot sustain his/her experience for a very long time, whereas passivity is indicative of the mystic's awareness of being grasped by a superior **power** over which he/she does not exercise control. Without recounting all the criticism of James's characteristics, it is useful to call attention to his notion of ineffability that excludes the possibility of cross-cultural comparisons of mystical experience because by definition ineffability already negates the possibility that an accurate description of mystical experience can be given by the mystic.

In addition to the characteristics identified by James, other scholars have attempted to define types of mysticism in order to further understanding of the subject. W. T. Stace differentiates two main types of mysticism: the extroverted and the introverted. The former type is characterized by: (1) the unifying vision; (2) experience is interpreted as having an objective reference; (3) apprehension of an inner subjectivity in all things; (4) feeling of blessedness, joy, or satisfaction; (5) a feeling that what is experienced is holy or sacred; (6) paradoxicality; and (7) ineffability of the experience. The introverted type of mysticism is characterized by: (1) void or empty unity; (2) being non-spatial and non-temporal; (3) a sense of objectivity or reality; (4) feelings of blessedness, joy, peace, or happiness; (5) the feeling that the holy is apprehended; (6) paradoxicality; and (7) ineffability. In contrast to Stace, R. C. Zaehner, an Oxford University professor, enumerates three types of mysticism: (1) panenhenic (nature); (2) **theistic**; and (3) **monistic**. Panenhenic mysticism is what Stace means by extrovertive mysticism, a type in which the mystic experiences **nature** in all things or of all things as being one. Zaehner equates theistic mysticism with various forms of Christian, Muslim, and Hindu devotional forms in which **love** and the **grace of God** are important features. A major characteristic of the theistic mystic is that he/she does not lose his/her individual personhood in God, whereas the monistic type of mystic does lose his/her identity in a greater **reality** or God. Another major difference between the theistic and monastic mystics is that the former depends on God for assistance, while the monistic mystic achieves the unitive experience by means of his/her own efforts. Ninian Smart agrees with Zaehner's distinction between panenhenic and monistic types of mysticism, but he questions Zaehner's differentiation between monistic and theistic types.

Are these types inadequate when applied to a cross-cultural perspective? Are these types too reductive and inflexible? If a person answers these questions positively, this means that such scholars are forcing multifarious and variegated forms of mystical experience into improper interpretative categories. Within anyone type, there are a number of varieties that promote the following danger: the uniqueness of a particular case could get lost or fundamentally important differences are obscured to the point of confusion. When Smart claims that all mystics share a similar experience, it becomes difficult to account for the differences, and it reflects an essentialist position that is associated with what is called a perennial philosophy (*philosophia perennis*), a way of thought that is basically the same and universal. Smart makes a distinction between the unitive experience itself and the mystic's **interpretation** of this experience in his/her writings. The distinction between experience and interpretation is not, however, very explicit because of the degree of ramification, which can be high or low depending on the concepts used by the mystic to describe the experience.

In response to the perceived need to typologize mystical experience, it can be affirmed that there is no pure mystical experience because every mystic is a product of his/her past religious experience, which includes the **belief** system, **symbols**, and **rituals** of his/her religious tradition. Thus every mystical experience is preconditioned by the mystic's religious history, the social structure of his/her culture, and by the expectation about what will be experienced, whether this is God, nirvāṇa, or Brahman. Not only is the experience of the mystic preconditioned by his/her history and **culture**, but it is also shaped by the language of the mystic by which he/she attempts to interpret and express his/her experience. Mystical language is often erotic by describing unitive experiences in terms of **sexual** ecstatic states or orgasm.

Historian Bernard McGinn calls into question the scholarly emphasis on experience of consciousness because he views such modes of spirituality as encounters with the presence of a living God. By emphasizing presence, McGinn moves from the subjective experience to the objective reality despite its transcendence that the mystic seeks. In brief, the mystic is a product of his/her religious culture, which does not mean that there is not room for uniqueness and creativity.

In addition to defining mysticism according to its type and stressing the unitive experience, the path of the mystic tends to be neglected by scholars. There are exceptions to this such as the work of Evelyn Underhill, who identifies five phases of the mystical path: (1) awakening or conversion; (2) self-knowledge or purgation; (3) illumination; (4) surrender or the dark night of the soul; and (5) union. These five phases are more accurately applied to Western forms of mysticism, but they need to be modified when applied to Eastern forms of mysticism. A preliminary form of such a modification notes a preliminary step taken by the aspiring mystic to turn away from or break with **society**. A particular mystic path is grounded in a regime of ascesis or self-discipline. The mystic path includes the following fivefold structure: (1) **purification**; (2) spiritual crisis or drama; (3) threshold experience; (4) symbolic **death**; and (5) unitive or ultimate experience. As a point of clarification, drama means the personal spiritual conflict and struggle that occurs within the individual. By participating in the drama, the mystic discovers his/her own personal narrative by simultaneously creating it. It is possible in many cases that the mystic realizes that he/she is the leading actor in a drama because he/she is so deeply absorbed in his/her role. The path of the mystic is not dramatic in the sense that it is playful or necessarily entertaining; it is rather dramatic in the sense that it redresses a personal, spiritual conflict within the individual. By comprehending the mystic path as a drama, it is implied that mysticism is not a static system; it is rather a disharmonic process characterized by intense conflict.

For many mystics, there is a return to society after their goal is achieved, a pattern that gives the mystical path a circular character. The basic pattern of the mystic path should not be construed as an inflexible sequence of steps because the fundamental phases of the path tend to overlap each other. It is preferable to view the path as an interconnected whole rather than as a series of steps that one must ascend, because, if the path is a series of steps, it would be easy to distinguish them, and this is not always the case. Viewed in its totality, the mystic path is a movement from multiplicity, ignorance, conflict, and flux to a position of unity, certainty, cohesion, and stability. As a point of clarification, the mystic path presupposes the practice of various forms of **asceticism**, which forms the foundation for the mystical quest. Despite the suspicions raised among orthodox adherents of faiths such as Christianity and Islam because of its being a potential source for **heresy** and schism, mysticism is a macro-concept because of its existence within a cross-cultural context.

Further reading: Hollywood (2002); James (1902); Katz (1983); Kripal (2001); McGinn (1993); Smart (1981); Stace (1961); Underhill (1911); Zaehner (1957)

MYTH

Derived from the Greek term *mythos* meaning word, utterance, or speech, myth is a **narrative** that embodies **knowledge** and wisdom about important events and actors, whereas mythology refers to the entire corpus of myths within a particular religious tradition. Myth is more specifically a narrative about what occurred at the beginning or end of time and exploits of supernatural beings or cultural heroes, other than tales of trivial events. These narratives concern substantial stories about such things as creation, life, and **death**. These primordial events are not only informative about what happened in the distant past, but they enable understanding about how those ancient events shaped our current **society** and individual lives.

For many religious cultures, it represents its **sacred** history and the rationale for present personal and social conditions. In many religions, myth also operates as an exemplary model for significant human behavior, such as rites and religious celebrations.

Mythic narratives, representing the primary stories of a religious **culture**, embody **violence, sexuality, pain,** desire, lust, life, death, **play** and **worldview**. The myth makers use elements from daily life to create their narratives and weave together an interconnecting web of these elements with human, heroic, or supernatural beings.

A particular myth may show evidence of additions and expansion as well as deletions, alterations, and substitutions as the cultural/historical circumstances change. This suggests that myth is a narrative in continual compositional process, development, and unfolding of the **truth**. This dynamic feature of myth is especially evident in oral cultures because the sharing of the myth by a storyteller influences its shape, the hearers may alter the story based on what they remember, and the storyteller may alter the story based on the reaction of the audience. The re-telling of a myth is sometimes restricted to certain times and places, whereas other religious traditions place no restrictions on the telling of a story. Restrictions on when a myth can be recited are directly related to its authoritative **language**, which enables a storyteller to simply present the story and not have to argue in a philosophical way for it. The telling of a myth is not only a social action that the storyteller shares with others, but it is also a **performative** act in the sense that the narrative is re-enacted and makes the mythical events recounted current again.

Mythic narratives are not merely entertaining, but they also represent worthwhile knowledge and serve as a form of knowing. The convincing nature of the myth gives hearers a secret knowledge about the origin of things that is otherwise inaccessible to ordinary people. If one knows the origin of something, this gives the knower **power**. Once one possesses this type of power, one can assume control of it, manipulate it, or reproduce it. When one knows a myth it is possible to repeat its actions in **ritual** and to re-enact ritually what occurred at the beginning of **time**. The knowledge gained from knowing a myth liberates one from having to think about certain things because the myth explains everything, can be taken for granted, not questioned, and frees us from the burden of thought. By knowing the myths of one's culture, this knowledge enables one to locate oneself in the world and the social order. A person knows to what group one belongs, the identity of the outsiders, and their relationship to one's religious culture. As useful tools of knowledge, myth establishes personal and cultural boundaries, enables one to make sense and interpret one's social and personal situation, and it thereby can guide one to properly adjust to normative attitudes, statuses, and roles.

Almost from their inception, myths are believed to refer to that which is fictitious or imaginatively invented by someone. Not only did Plato compare myth unfavorably to the **truth**, but the Romans classify it with *fibula* or that which is false. The association of myth with untruth persists for many centuries in the West until the eighteenth century when they are associated with true stories. According to the French thinker Voltaire (d. 1778), myth is, however, nothing more than superstition, historical distortion, and false fables. The modern notion of myth, its rediscovery, and invention can be traced to the scholarship of Gottlieb Christian Heyne, a German Hellenist scholar, who rejects assertions that myth is an absurd creation. Instead, he argues for its evidence as a form of primeval human thinking and ancient examples of human memory. Many other scholars follow Heyne's lead, developing elaborate and often conflicting theories about the nature of myth.

Myth is also viewed more favorably by the Italian thinker Vico (d. 1744) in his work *The New Science* in which he demonstrates the three ages of humankind that represent a gradual growth of maturity and **rationality** until a final stage of decline. The infancy of humankind is the age of myth, a time in which humans have not discovered themselves because they attribute all causal action to supernatural beings and express their understanding about the divine beings and their relations to them in oral narrations. Although myths have been subject to evolution and degeneration over time, there are original myths that embody a true account of the experience of humans which are later misappropriated, misunderstood, corrupted, and falsified. In order to understand myths, they must be placed in their historical context and reconstructed by semantic, etymological analysis by an interpreter.

Eighteenth-century German romantic figures, such as Herder (d. 1908) and Goethe (d. 1832), recognize myth as creative wisdom and a form of truth. Friedrich Schlegel (d. 1829), a revolutionary literary critic called the apostle of a new religion by Novalis (d. 1801), conceives of myth as a unity of thought, **art**, and **belief**. Calling for a new mythology because of its creative and dynamic nature, Schlegel thinks that myth possesses the ability to transform and transfigure the objective world. The German philosopher Shelling (d. 1854) also sees the potential of myth because of its metaphysical importance by serving as the key to the purpose of the Absolute Spirit. Moreover, myth reconciles the finite with the infinite and gives an individual an initial glimpse of the pre-established **harmony** of the real and ideal worlds because it corresponds to the lower principle in **God**. Myth is something experienced, lived, more primary than history, and an unfolding of the truth.

The contested scholarly conception of the nature of myth begins in earnest during the nineteenth century with such figures as Edward B. Tylor (1832–1917), Sir James George Frazer (1854–1941), and Friedrich Max Müller (1832–1900). Under the influence of Darwin's theory of evolution, Tylor uses elements of religion, such as myth, folklore, and customs, to construct an evolutionary model of the development of humanity. He identifies three stages: savage, or hunter-gatherer, barbaric, which is characterized by domestication of plants and animals, and civilized, which begins with the art of writing. With his preconceived plan, Tylor wants to re-establish the fundamental unity of humankind and to find survivals, which are processes, customs, and opinions carried by force of habit into a new state of society in distinction to the previous state. Tylor argues that myth is an elaboration of **belief** about gods and an explanation of the natural world, and it thus represents a history of errors of the human mind. Tylor's research is related to his attempt to develop a "science of **culture**" that would provide a history of the human mind. According to Tylor, myth and science contradict each other, with the latter replacing the former, resulting in the demise of myth, even though animistic beliefs that form the foundation of religion continue to exist.

In comparison to Tylor's evolutionary scheme, Frazer's sequence includes the following: **magic**, religion, and science. The final phase is equated with the truth, whereas religion is false. Magic is identified as more primitive than religion, a propitiation and conciliation of **powers** believed to be superior to humans. Magic is the mistaken application of powers believed to be superior to humans. Magic is also the mistaken application of an association of ideas and is thus necessarily false, whereas religion stands in fundamental opposition to magic and science. Myth is associated with magic, which cannot make fundamental logical distinctions, and it is thus irrational and false. Wanting to gain control of the natural world, magic makes practical use of myth in the form of **ritual**. Frazer envisions a time when humanity would reject magic, religion, and myth and embrace science, which he equates with knowledge and enlightenment. In the meantime, Frazer ties myth to ritual, which re-enacts myth and shapes it.

Frazer shares a similar conception of myth with members of the so-called myth-ritual school, which is advocated by such scholars as William Robertson Smith (1846–1804), Jane Harrison (1850–1928), and S. H. Hooke (1874–1968). Smith argues that myth is not autonomous because it is tied to ritual. Hence, all myths, which are actions, accompany rituals and vice versa. According to Harrison and Hooke, myth explains what happens in ritual, originates in ritual, and thus represents a secondary, later abstraction. Recent scholarship does not find a genetic connection between ritual and myth. When a myth migrates from one culture to another, for instance, it is not connected to any ritual.

If many of the scholars reviewed want to replace religion with something more enlightening, Müller calls for a science of religion, which is the last of the sciences to be developed. Müller's science of religion would be historical and trace the evolution of its subject, and it would also be inductive and adhere to the laws of causation. For Müller, the early development of religion is characterized by sacred human speech, giving religion and language an intimate connection. If there is thus a genetic relationship between languages, Müller thinks that the same should hold true for religions of the world. He is convinced that the language of religion possesses a dialectic nature that helps to explain the decay of religion. Therefore, myth represents a disease of language, which degenerates from an original **monotheism**.

A different perspective is offered by Lucien Lévy-Bruhl (1857–1939), who stresses the social nature of myth, which he thinks expresses the social solidarity of a group and that of surrounding groups. In addition to social solidarity, myth reflects a native imagination that is impressed by natural phenomena. Lévy-Bruhl is primarily concerned about myth for what it teaches about what he calls "primitive mentality," which he argues is different from that of Europeans because primitive minds are prelogical, or indifferent to the laws of logical contradiction. This means that so-called primitives possess minds that are concerned with collective representations, manifest a **mystic** mentality, and are pervaded by a sense of affectional participation, or a feeling of connectedness with other persons and objects that results in the data of **experience** flowing together and associating with each other in many complex ways rather than being regulated by strictly cause and effect relationships. There are, for instance, people who think of themselves as animals or birds, such as the Bororo of Brazil who call themselves parakeets and humans. Lévy-Bruhl argues that these kinds of people are not thinking metaphorically or symbolically, but their equation is actual participatory identity.

Philosophers of the nineteenth and twentieth centuries also make contributions to the conceptualization of myth. For the German philosophers Hegel and Marx, myth is false consciousness. Another German philosopher Friedrich Nietzsche argues that myth is a pragmatically necessary fiction, whereas the Neo-Kantian thinker Ernst Cassirer advocates myth as symbolic thought. Myth, an important life form for Cassier, is a major mode of cultural objectification and a form of thought and intuition.

In the twentieth century, Claude Lévi-Strauss, who devises the structural method to study his subject in a scientific manner that includes all its variants, identifies myth as a structured story. Myths are repetitive, which functions to expose its structure. Myth reveals the inner workings of a society by incarnating central contradictions of a social system. Myth also records and preserves the memories of primary systems of classification, which can be used to clarify the reasons for beliefs and customs. Moreover, myth enables one to discover operational modes of the human mind, which have remained constant over centuries. The ability of myth to reveal mind, which is autonomous and manifests nature, leads one to a natural reality, suggesting that myth is more than a simple story. Myth exemplifies logical thinking that is rigorous and concrete unlike the abstract modern mode of thinking, possesses its own end and inner drive, represents an autonomous mode of representation, and dies when its structure weakens.

By means of his method, Lévi-Strauss decomposes the mythical narratives by identifying and charting their most elementary constituent units called mythemes, which the myth maker assembles into meaningful wholes that manifest a dialectical organization of facts. The structuralist must analyze each myth individually by breaking down its story into the shortest possible sentences and to discern their bundle of relations. This gives the scholar a two-dimensional time referent: synchronic, which provides a horizontal axis that is non-reversible, and diachronic, which forms a vertical axis that is reversible and paradigmatic. It is the vertical axis that stands for the deep structure that reveals variations over a period of time. For Lévi-Strauss, the growth of a myth is continuous, but its structure remains constant. However, the overall purpose of myth is to provide a logical model capable of overcoming contradictions.

In addition to the structural and other approaches to myth, it is also conceptualized from a psychological approach, such as that of Sigmund Freud and his emphasis on the unconscious origins of myth that represent repressed wishes, and that of Carl Jung and his notion of archetypes that are buried in the unconscious and form a way for the collective unconscious to communicate with consciousness. Following Freud's theoretical thread, René Girard develops Freud's insights by applying them to biblical narratives, such as the story of Cain and Abel that suggests that Cain did not have a sacrificial outlet for his **violence**. Girard thinks that myth and ritual originate from generative violence, with the latter able to channel and control the violence of the community by directing it toward a victim.

Often confused with Jung because of the importance of archetypes in their theories of myth, Mircea Eliade is not a Jungian, but rather an historian of religion who advocates an encyclopedic approach to the study of religious phenomena. For Eliade, myth represents a primordial event that took place at the beginning of time, which makes the creation myth primary. Since myths narrate origin stories, they explain why the world, events, and humans are as they are at the present time. Moreover, myth is connected with ontology, embodies meaning, and speaks only of realities. It is the language of the sacred, and if the sacred is equivalent to the real, then the realities conveyed by myth are sacred realities. Therefore, activities done according to the mythical model or archetype belong to the sphere of the sacred and being. In this way, myths are social and personal heuristic devices and provide members of a society with **knowledge** of their identity, while also embodying a universal message.

Following Eliade at the University of Chicago, Wendy Doniger views myth as an inherently comparative form of narrative that is also interdisciplinary. Nonetheless, when studying a myth its context must be taken into consideration. Doniger's emphasis on the importance of context is stressed by her use of the **metaphor** of the "implied spider," which means that the author of a myth is implied by what the myth reveals about the author's experience. This suggests that it is possible for a scholar to witness the webs of significance, meaning, and culture that he/she leaves behind in the form of myths. The myth itself represents the shared experience, which is already narrative, of human beings with the culture.

Further reading: Doniger (1998); Doty (1986); Eliade (1963); Frazer (1994); Girard (1989); Lévi-Strauss (1963, 1970, 1973); Lévy-Bruhl (1985); Müller (1895–1898); Tylor (1871); Von Hendy (2002)

NARRATIVE

An oral or written story that can serve several purposes: pedagogical illustration, spiritual inspiration, behavioral motivation, moral or ethical example, or pure entertainment. The framework of a narrative is temporal in the sense of a chronological sequence, which implies that it can be historical. A narrative can, of course, be strictly fictional.

Narratives are both lived, which suggests that they are inherent in **culture** and history, and they are told, which reflects that narratives are imposed upon religious culture and history. The first perspective is that of the insider, whereas the second viewpoint is that of the outsider. Coming from within the tradition, the insider kind of narrative articulates a position that the tradition is normative, whereas the outsider accounts originate from within the context of that person's own discourses. Having made this distinction between insiders and outsiders, narratives still have the potential to overlap and borrow elements from each other, such as the ancient Hebrew borrowing from Canaanite religious culture.

In the current state of scholarship, it is possible to identify three positions on narrative: a narrative realist position represented by Alistair MacIntyre; a narrative constructivism expounded by Hayden White; and a narrativist position represented by Paul Ricoeur. The first position affirms that culture and history enact a lived narrative standpoint. Since all subjectivity represents a sequence of actions grounded in intentionality that forms a narrative, humans are authors and actors of their own narratives, which suggests that the stories are lived before they are told. MacIntyre indicates that humans are born into a set of pre-given narratives, although they can create something intelligible from these narratives even within their human limitations. According to White, scholars of religion construct the narratives that they present as facts from among a variety of cultural expressions, texts, and events, and they thereby construct religion by writing about it. This means that the narrative is imposed upon culture and history from White's perspective by an authorial voice that is powerful because of that person's ability to create the narrative. On the contrary, Ricoeur thinks that narratives are both lived and told, and not simply imposed upon a temporal sequence because narrative is a historical sequence. Ricoeur sees in narrative the importance of **time**, a central feature of human **experience**, that itself becomes human, on the one hand, when it is articulated through narrative and also attains full meaning when it becomes a condition of temporal existence. For Ricoeur, narrative can refigure both the past and the future in the human imagination, and is able to construct a coherent sense of identity for the narrator. What this means for scholars of religion is that they work by examining, studying, and critiquing other narratives from the perspective of their own narratives.

Further reading: MacIntyre (1981); Ricoeur (1984); White (2010)

NATURE

Rivers, mountains, seas, winds, trees, and other phenomena are parts of nature, which can be defined as the natural world, that in some religious traditions are considered **sacred**. The Native American Cree Indians conceive of the four winds, for instance, as brothers that form a circle around a hunter, with each wind associated with a specific type of weather, whereas the Navaho refer to wind **souls** born in a child that give it life and account for good and bad thoughts. From a cross-cultural perspective, poets have written about the beauty of nature. In short, nature provides the physical and spiritual material on which a religious culture can build. Nature also checks, transforms and canalizes already existing cultural forms. Nature can exercise either a direct or an indirect influence upon a **culture**. In the former case, nature operates independently of cultural activity, whereas an indirect influence is culturally conditioned. The direct influence tends to be more mechanical in the sense that the natural environment, for instance, can shape the economic system. Thus, due to the natural environment, nature might eliminate growing certain crops. With the indirect type of influence, culture produces the external physical conditions for nature to have an effect upon it. For the most part, nature does not disturb the cultural balance because any new impressions of nature are associated with already existing conditions.

Native American Indians of the western plains region identify with a cosmic totality, symbolized by the cross, circle, or world tree, and nature is a part of this totality. This does not mean that Indians exist in **harmony** with nature because they are both a part of nature and separated from it. This apparent paradox can be explained by the fact that Indians are alienated from nature because it is their economic source of life, which means that it is necessary to exploit it. At the same time, nature functions as the Indian's spiritual source of life. Indians thus manifest ambivalent attitudes towards nature: positive feelings associated with nature's bounty and negative feelings connected to the terrible and wrathful power of nature. In conjunction with these feelings, Indians generally recognize that they are dependent upon nature for their survival. In fact, some Indian societies, such as the Pueblo and Zuni, believe that they came from the **earth**.

Among Native American hunting societies, there is manifested a sense of kinship with the animals because they are equivalent to humans and guilt because Indians are destined to exploit their relatives in order to ensure human survival. The guilt associated with killing animal kin can be overcome by asking forgiveness for its destruction, which also includes the practice of burying the bones of the animal in anatomical order so that they can be resuscitated. Within the context of this type of practice, there is the belief in animal guardians, acting as supernatural rulers with the function of exercising stewardship over the world animals and thus protecting them. The animal guardian, with each species possessing their own, sees that animals get a correct burial, sanctions or prevents a hunter's slaying of them, and gives luck in hunting. The intimate relationship between an animal and a hunter suggests that the latter can take part in its **power**.

Native American Indians do not love the whole of nature, but they rather revere certain locations. This reverence for specific places is called geopiety. At these locations, Indians associate them with the **sacred** and power, with which they desire to live in close proximity. These places are sacred because the **spirits** of nature reveal themselves at them. This does not mean that Native American Indians indulge themselves in the beauty of nature, because their interests are more practical in the sense that they are interested in what nature can provide for their subsistence, although Indians do experience it as a realm of mystery.

In contrast to Native American Indian attitudes, Japanese Shinto and Zen Buddhism offer an alternative attitude towards nature. In the Shinto religion, nature is both an awesome power and beauty, and a manifestation of divine power. This attitude is expressed in a creation **myth** that recalls heavenly *kami* (spirits) dipping their long spears into the depths of the primal waters, with the mud that drips off their spears forming the islands of Japan. This early creation of the spirits is an exact replica of the heavenly abode, making Japan an earthly paradise. Since sacred power can be revealed through nature, the Japanese islands are also holy, beautiful, and pure.

Within the context of Zen Buddhism, when a person recognizes nature as what it is it becomes a part of that person. Thus I am in nature and nature is in me. Thereby, nature does not stand outside of me or opposes me. Therefore, the genuine Zen master is identified with nature. This fundamental Zen attitude finds expression in landscape gardens, which are similar to a three-dimensional painting modeled on Chinese Song dynasty ink paintings. From a theoretical perspective, everything that exists possesses some sense of awareness (*kokoro*), even rocks and trees. With Zen rock gardens, there is a dry landscape that strips nature bare to reveal its substance. These rock gardens are intended for meditation. Zen rock gardens evoke notions associated with rocks in ancient China that are believed to possess cosmic energy (*qi*), which animates the rocks and enables a person to receive beneficial effects by being in their presence. This Chinese attitude is combined with the Shinto belief that rocks are inhabited by *kami* (spirits), and helps form the background for the Zen attitude toward rock gardens. Overall, the Zen Buddhist attitude toward nature is less ambivalent than that of Native American Indians.

Further reading: Berthier (2000); Hultkrantz (1981); MacCormack and Strathern (1980); Suzuki (1959)

ORAL TRADITION

This concept refers to the transmission of various types of **narratives** from one generation to another by verbal means of transmission and preservation by **memory**. Oral traditions are evident in many cultures from ancient Vedic culture in India and the preservation of revealed hymns, to formative Buddhism, ancient Judaism, early Christianity, and Islam, whose teachings are preserved for centuries or years after the passing of the original historical figures and events associated with them. In many of these traditions, the preservation of an oral tradition in writing is perceived as a shortcoming of human ability.

In ancient India, for instance, writing is not considered a valued activity, which helps to account for the lower social status of scribes. According to the *Aitareya Upanishad* (5.5.3), writing appears on a list of polluting actions and activities that prevent a person from reciting the sacred Vedas. The importance of oral culture in India can be partly understood by the Indian stress on the significance of sound (*śabda*), which represents the powerful and dynamic aspect of a word. Moreover, alphabet characters of the Sanskrit language are considered a denigration and defilement of the **sacred** sound. The early Buddhist community is influenced by the wider Indian emphasis on oral communication, which is evident in such a phrase as 'Thus have I heard" that introduce many Pali texts and stress personal testimony of a person who receives an oral message.

Ancient Judaism is another excellent example of an oral tradition that is very instructive. Before the composition of the Jewish **scriptures**, its tradition experiences three centuries of oral transmission until the historical period of the monarchy of David. The preliterary period is characterized by bits of **memory** derived from a living situation associated with some action or event. Because the Jewish oral tradition represents **narratives** from different historical periods, various inconsistencies, repetitions, and stylistic differences serve as reflection about how the narratives are relived, reworked, and reinterpreted. This suggests that the Jewish oral tradition is marked by diversity within which it is possible to find narratives about creation, special locations, customs, tribal heroes, cultic practices, poems, songs, hymns of praise, and poetic aphorisms. This diverse oral tradition is a gradual process that unfolds over a long period of time.

Further reading: Dewey (1994); Lord (1991); Niditich (1996)

ORTHODOXY

This concept is derived from the Latin terms *ortho* (correct) and *dox* (doctrine). It is established by an organized group of believers about what beliefs or teachings should be accepted as authoritative in order to govern proper practices and **ritual**. What is orthodoxy is determined by often competing groups, with each pushing their **interpretations** about what is correct and each attempting to marginalize opponents. As with the examples of Roman Catholic and Eastern Orthodox forms of Christianity, it is not unusual to have competing forms of orthodoxy. The attempt to determine what precisely is the orthodox position of a particular religion often resorts to ancient authority, such as historical figures like Jesus, Muhammad, or the Buddha. The process of deciding the exact nature of orthodoxy follows a pattern of inclusion and exclusion of different opinions, interpretations, and ideology. Once orthodoxy is determined it becomes binding on all adherents and often assumes the status of **law**, and it thereby regulates the **belief** system and religious behavior of adherents while also legitimizing it.

In Western Christianity, orthodox **doctrine** assumes the forms of catechism and oral confessions of **faith** or creeds. The former takes the format of questions followed by answers in oral or written forms. A catechism is an official manual intended for popular instruction, which is a very systematic and standardized version of official **church** doctrine. The term creed is derived from the Latin *credo* (I believe) and is more a formal statement in summarized form of accepted beliefs and a genuine statement of doctrine. The Apostles Creed and the Nicene Creed are excellent examples of such documents.

Besides authorizing orthodoxies, creeds and catechisms are not remote from political necessity and expediency. The legislative bodies that determine orthodoxy are often influenced by the political climate of the historical period. Christian orthodoxy in the West is established by a number of councils over the centuries. A similar number of councils shaped Buddhist literature and doctrine. According to Buddhist tradition, the first council after the death of the Buddha was held at Rājagriha in order to establish his authoritative teachings on a site donated by King Bimbisāra. The second Buddhist gathering is the Council of Vaiśālī called for the purpose of confronting disputes about monastic discipline, which results in a split of the **community** into two sects: Sthavīras (Elders) and Mahāsaṃgikas (Great Assembly). Other councils would follow, but the scholarly debate about which councils actually occur and for what purpose continues in Buddhist scholarship.

Further reading: Berger (1979); Grant (2004); Olson (2005)

OTHER

This is a relational concept that refers to a researcher and his/her subject within the context of religious scholarship. The other is distinguished from the researcher by his/her different **worldview, society, religion, language**, and **culture**. From an even wider perspective, to be located in the world implies being in relationship to others. Some of these others are familiar to you because they live with you in the same **society**, whereas others are considered foreign or strange because they live in completely different cultures. To live with others who possess **language** suggests that communication between the **self** and others is possible. In order for communication to occur, the distance, which poses a potential danger, separating the **self** from the other must be bridged by both parties for a researcher to understand the religion of the other. The relationship between the **self** and other is a concern to Western, Eastern, and especially **postmodern** thinkers.

Some postmodern thinkers agree that the other exceeds my ability to grasp it, a claim that they stress by using the term alterity to point to radical otherness. The philosopher Emmanuel Levinas devotes considerable effort into understanding this radical otherness. Even though the other may resemble us, it is still external to us, and we encounter it as a mystery, which is identified with its alterity. Levinas stresses that the other assists the self arrive at its own self-understanding that occurs within a dialogical relationship. Nonetheless, the absolute otherness of the other is called infinity by Levinas in the sense that it is more than we can think. By thinking about the other, a thinker cannot extinguish or exhaust it, which suggests the excessiveness of the other. By being concerned with what overflows thinking, Levinas insists that we do not compromise the alterity of the other by thematizing it or interiorizing it. Since the other is beyond totality, possesses no place, and cannot be understood as a relation, the other is absolutely exterior to any totalizing intention of thought. By stressing the singularity and exteriority of the other, Levinas wants to protect it from being reduced to the same. He accomplishes this goal by calling attention to the face of the other. The face is an aspect of the other that cannot be conceptualized because of its overflowing nature. An encounter with the face of the other represents an ethical epiphany that obligates me and makes me responsible for the other. Nevertheless, it is impossible to fully grasp the nature of the face because it withdraws from me even as I encounter it.

Because of the fundamental and insuperable gap between the self and other, Jacques Derrida, a leading postmodern philosopher, asserts that their relationship represents both the possibility and impossibility of self-identity. The difference between the self and other combines and separates identity and difference. As a perpetual outsider, the other is always exterior to me and can never become interiorized. The other hovers around the margin of one's life, and this feature helps one to grasp it as an alternative to presence and absence. In other words, one's relation to the other makes the other possible and also impossible as presence, sameness, and assumed essence. This relation exceeds and overflows the present moment in the sense that the initial moment makes the other return to the same, whereas the second moment is no longer and never has been a present same. For Derrida, the other disturbs and shows the system of the same, and it forces it to become open to a difference that it did not anticipate. Thus the encounter with the other is neither a representation, nor a limitation, nor a conceptual relation.

Hindu and Buddhist thinkers present a very different view of the other in comparison to these selected postmodern scholars. In the Advaita Vedānta school, the Indian philosopher Śankara views the other as identical to the self from the standpoint of higher knowledge. In contrast to the postmodern thinkers, Śankara views the self as unrelated and relations as a hindrance to true selfhood. From the perspective of higher **knowledge** for Śankara, there is no other because the other is really not different than oneself.

Another non-dualistic position is offered by the Zen master Dōgen, who uses the term *dōji* to indicate that there is difference between the self and others. To truly practice *dōji* means that a person exists in **harmony** and unity with oneself and others. This virtue is grounded on the conviction that all things are interrelated. Both the self and other represent a complex web of relationships. Dōgen agrees with the postmodern thinkers that the relationality between the self and others is a reciprocal and horizontal type of relationship that stands opposed to hierarchical or vertical relations.

Further reading: Derrida (1976); Dōgen (2007); Levinas (1998); Śankara (1968)

PACIFISM

This concept reflects a conscious, willful, determined opposition to any **violence** or force to settle disputes. Based on strong moral principles or pragmatic concerns, pacifism advocates non-resistance and/or **non-violence**. Practitioners of pacifism with a religious foundation extend over the entire globe, and include figures such as the Buddha, Mahāvīra of Jainism, Jesus according to some interpreters, Daoist thinkers, Dorothy Day of the Catholic Worker Movement, Tolstoy, Gandhi, Martin Luther

King, Jr., the Dalai Lama, and the Vietnamese Buddhist monk Thich Nhat Hanh. In addition to these individuals, large groups also advocate pacifism, such as the Religious Society of Friends (Quakers), and the Amish, Mennonites, and Brethren.

Convinced that violence is inevitable in all societies, Jacque Ellul argues for a Christian Realism by which he means seeing the facts of a situation devoid of evasion or delusion and not recoiling in fear or horror as the result becomes evident. Christian Realism demands that a person be fully aware of what one is doing, why one is doing something, and what the result will be. Ellul wants to counter **violence** with what he calls the violence of **love**, which means to reject victory, exclude physical or psychological violence, and place one's **faith** in a miracle of the Kingdom of God.

Further reading: Ellul (1970); Gandhi (1986)

PAIN

A universal human, embodied **experience** that is without an object. Pain is distinct from **suffering** in the sense that pain is a sensation associated with tissue or bone damage. In contrast to pain, suffering is not a sensation but rather an emotional and evaluative reaction to any number of causes, and some of these causes are entirely painless. The loss of a love one is a common example of suffering for a survivor.

Pain can be involuntary or voluntary. The former type of pain can be the result of an accident or a disease such as cancer. The voluntary type of pain involves self-inflicted pain. Assuming that a subject is not sadomasochistic, self-inflicted pain is often practiced within a religious context by performing **ascetic** practices, **martyrdom**, or **pilgrimage**. Within the context of devotional religious traditions, pain may enhance a person's bond with their deity and other members of the **community**. Religiously related pain can also transform a person and provide insight into life, provide meaning, and possibly even **salvation**. The context in which pain occurs is suggestive with respect to interpreting its significance because it alters the meaning of the pain within a religious context, such as asceticism, martyrdom, initiatory ordeals, pilgrimage, or exorcism **healings**. Within a Christian context, ascetic, self-inflicted pain functions to **purify** a person from **sin**, and it should not be construed as something punitive.

From a negative perspective, pain can cause a person to become decentered leading to personal disintegration. A good example of disintegration is the Jewish figure Job, although not at the end of the **narrative**. Thus the powerful feelings induced by pain can affect a person's capacity to perceive and know **reality**. Pain also leads to psychological dissociation and can trigger very compelling **emotions**, which often become objectified and projected onto objects. But pain can also act as a mediating factor that makes the acquisition of reality possible. Along with these types of positive results, pain also possesses the ability to transform a person. Among the Kaguru people studied by the anthropologist T. O. Beidelman, pain is an essential feature within the context of **ritual** that transforms a person and enables that person to verify an invisible reality, which suggests that pain is equated with certainty. Pain is also related to imagination in the sense that easing of pain is related to cultivating social imagination. During the Sun Dance, the pain experienced by a Native American Indian is an appropriate example because the Indian's flesh is severed by breaking free from the leather thongs previously inserted under his back or chest muscles, signifying being released from ignorance. This painful experience also stimulates a native's personal and social imagination and gives one an insight into what he should do with his life.

Further reading: Beidelman (1997); Glucklich (2001)

PANTHEISM

A conception that is related to the relationship between **God** and the world. In pantheism, God is conceived as not merely immanent within the world, but God is also identical to the world, which is contrary to the **theistic** view of the wholly transcendent nature of God. When the world exists in God this represents a panentheistic position in which all **reality** is a part of God. Examples of either pantheism or panentheism are often discovered among poets and **mystics**.

A good example of pantheism in the Hindu tradition can be discovered in the thoughts of Rāmānuja where the world represents the **body** of the ultimate reality or Brahman, which is also transcendent. It is Neo-Platonism and its notion of emanation that provides the influence that shapes many Western and Arabic thinkers, such as al-Fārābī, Ibn Sīnā, and Ibn Rushd. The mystic Jakob Boehme and the philosopher Spinoza are seventeenth-century examples of pantheism in the West.

Further reading: Levine (1994)

PERCEPTION

A visual human ability that is more than an inherited biological ability to see objects in the world, although perception does occur within an embodied condition. It is a learned ability and a historically and socio-logically constituted form of behavior. Therefore, the ability to see happens within a cultural context and is shaped by that context. This implies that the act of perceiving is dependent on a wider apparatus beyond a particular individual that includes presuppositions, assumptions, inclinations, habits, historical associations, and distinct **cultural** practices. Within such a context, there is a close connection between the act of perception and **knowledge**. When humans see an object they come to know it, and are able to form a representation of it.

The act of perception is frequently referred to as the gaze, which is a visual field that includes seer, seen, and the act of seeing within a broader physical, historical, and cultural context. By means of the gaze, perceptual humans project cultural influences that allow the possibility of meaning, interrelationships among actors, and forms of **experience**. Thus, being in a European, Roman Catholic cathedral, a person sees, for instance, rows of pews, very high ceilings, stained glass windows, numerous statues of apostles and **saints**, and a large cross behind the altar. What a person perceives represents historical, cultural, and sociological elements of a person's religion that possess predetermined meaning and significance. Therefore, the gaze of the viewer is already shaped to a large degree, and what is seen is easily comprehended by the viewer because one is already inclined to see things in a certain way.

Perception represents a sensual aspect of religion that plays a vital role in all forms of religion. In India, the technical term, for instance, for seeing the **sacred** is *darśana*, a term with a twofold meaning: one sees the image of the deity and is seen by the deity. This type of mutual seeing represents a means of communication between an inferior subject and a superior divine being that allows a viewer to express their emotions. By seeing the image of the deity in one's home or in a temple, the viewer is also able to participate in the essence of the object being perceived by touching and knowing the image with one's eyes. In this process of perception, the viewer is not the initiator of the perceptual interaction because the act of seeing the divine image presupposes that the deity gives itself to be seen. By making itself visible, the transcendent deity condescends to descent to the threshold of human **experience** to allow humans to visualize it.

Further reading: Eck (1981); Gonda (1969); Morgan (2005)

PERFORMANCE

A concept derived from two Latin terms: *per* meaning through and *forme* meaning form. The concept implies role-playing before an audience and achieving something. Among the multiple connotations of the concept of performance, one refers to **ritual** that is enacted and performed. Within the context of ritual, an emphasis on performance attempts to overcome the theoretical bifurcation between thought and action.

The emphasis on performance is rooted in the linguistic philosophy of J. L. Austin and his investigation of performative utterance, which represents a close connection between the uttering of a word, phrase, or sentence and the occurrence of something. If a minister or priest says to a couple, for example, in a wedding ceremony: "I now pronounce you husband and wife." The saying of the words makes the man and woman a married couple. Austin's short book *How to Do Things with Words* proves to be influential beyond the realm of philosophy of **language**, as it affected anthropologists, such as Victor Turner, Stanley Tambiah, and Clifford Geertz.

Turner views ritual as a processual form of social drama that expresses cultural ideas and dispositions, whereas Tambiah views performance as a way to overcome the devaluation of action, common when it is compared to thought. Geertz argues that in order for an interpretation of ritual to be valuable it should be viewed as a game, a drama, or an ensemble of texts.

Reflecting on the works of these anthropologists, the ritual theorist Catherine Bell criticizes the performative turn in ritual theory because it does not offer a definitive **interpretation** of a set of ritual actions. Bell also contends that performative ritual theory gives ontological and analytic priority to actions. Using **metaphors** of performance, Bell does admit that such ritual theorists do offer something new by their holistic framework. Ronald Grimes critically responds to Bell that ritual and performance are substantively related but also significantly different.

Further reading: Austin (1962); Bell (1992, 1997); Geertz (1973); Grimes (1990); Tambiah (1990); Turner (1969)

PILGRIMAGE

The prevailing implication of the notion pilgrimage is an interior or external journey, or a combination of both types, to usually some place considered **sacred** within a pilgrim's religious tradition. Such a place would be Jerusalem for Jews, Rome and any place visited by the Virgin Mary, such as Lourdes or Fatima, for Christians, Mecca for Muslims, any of seven sacred cities for Hindus, locations associated with the life of the Buddha for Buddhists, or the Golden Temple in Amritsar for Sikhs. As with the John Bunyan's classic work *The Pilgrim's Progress*, the concept of pilgrimage is also used as a **metaphor** for a spiritual journey. An interior pilgrimage is often connected with a personal search for a person's true self, **God**, meaning, or a combination of these items. Many pilgrims journey to places associated with a **cult** of **relics** or a place considered sacred by the religious tradition because of paradigmatic historical events. Pilgrimage represents a break from ordinary life and assumes a joyful festive spirit as depicted in Chaucer's *Canterbury Tales*. Pilgrimage also often assumes the character of a **rite of passage** in some religious cultures.

As the anthropologist Victor Turner argues, pilgrimage and its resemblance to a rite of passage exhibits **liminality**, a time of withdrawal from normal modes of social action that represents a place and moment in and out of time. This implies that pilgrims are transitional persons because their character is characterized by ambiguity and paradox. Because pilgrims are structurally invisible, they are at once no longer classified and not yet classified. Being devoid of normal classification, pilgrims possess nothing and have no status; they are invisible and compared to being dead. According to Turner, pilgrimage exhibits a symbolic anti-structure that is often expressed as an existential *communitas*, a spontaneous, ephemeral **community**, even though normative *communitas* tends to reign in pilgrimage, which simply suggests that the original existential *communitas* is organized into a more enduring social system, such as Muslim pilgrimage to Mecca.

173

The annual pilgrimage (*hajj*) to the Ka'ba in Mecca, which is believed to have been built by Abraham and his son Isma'il, is arguably the most famous journey in any religious tradition because Muslims come from all over the world to attend this event. This pilgrimage is required of all Muslim males and females at least once in their lives, although a person must meet certain criteria: being of age (i.e. having reached puberty), being able to afford the trip, and being of sound mind. Prior to the journey, a pilgrim is required to assume a sanctified condition (*ihrām*) by performing a purifying ablution with water and donning an unsewn cloth garment made of two unsewn white sheets. All pilgrims must maintain a state of purity throughout the pilgrimage period. In addition to the **purification** requirements, there are particular prohibitions that must be observed: no cutting of hair and nails; no sexual intercourse; do not neglect one's daily toilet; avoid shedding of blood; no hunting, uprooting of plants, cutting of wood; no contracting of marriages; no acting as a witness; and no wearing of rings or perfume.

The Muslim pilgrimage begins with the lesser (*'umra*) pilgrimage to Mecca, which involves circumambulating the Ka'ba seven times and kissing the black stone, assuming that one can get near enough to it. Then, the pilgrims run seven times between the hills of Safā and Marwā. On the seventh day, the pilgrims listen to a sermon in the mosque at the Ka'ba; the eight day is called the "day of moistening" because the pilgrims provide themselves with water for the following days. The pilgrims proceed to Minā where they hear two sermons, and throw seven stones three times at a stone pillar representing Satan. On the tenth day at Minā, sheep or camels are sacrificed, and the pilgrims return the same day to perform another circumambulation of the Ka'ba. Between the eleventh and thirteen days of the pilgrimage, there is a respite for eating, drinking, and sensual pleasure at Minā. Upon resuming a consecrated condition, a pilgrim performs the final circumambulation of the Ka'ba. Afterwards, it is not unusual for pilgrims to visit the Prophet Muhammad's tomb in Medina. If a pilgrim dies during the annual event, the pilgrim is considered a **martyr**.

The Muslim pilgrimage allows a believer to present oneself before God. The attire and prohibitions associated with the event suggests that everyone is equal before God. By making the journey, a pilgrim imitates and repeats action performed by the Prophet Muhammad, and the journey thus enables a pilgrim to relive the past. Because the pilgrimage binds believers together in an annual congregation, it serves as a visible sign of religious unity and functions to solidify the religion. Finally, pilgrimage is not merely a journey to Mecca or another sacred location, but is also a journey home where a pilgrim can verbally share their experience with others.

Just as it does for Islam, pilgrimage plays an important role within Hinduism where is it called a *tīrtha-yatra* (meaning "undertaking journey to river fords"). *Tīrtha* implies crossing over as a verb and a crossing place as a noun. A pilgrim symbolically crosses over to **heaven**, an event symbolized by a ladder or a bridge, by journeying to a river that is believed to originate in heaven and flows down to earth. The **sacred** Ganges River is called, for instance, "the flowing ladder to heaven." Such waters are considered nourishing and purifying. When a person is purified he/she becomes a *tīrtha* for **others**.

Hindu pilgrimage is closely associated with the performance of life cycle rites at holy places where the rites bring greater bountiful blessings. In fact, ancestral and **death** rites are especially efficacious at these sacred locations where there is believed to be a connection between **earth** and heaven. Hindu pilgrimage can also become a substitute for other **ritual** activity. Moreover, from a social perspective, pilgrimage is where one can cross the boundaries between caste and sexual differences. Thus, pilgrimage is open and accessible to everyone. It also enables a pilgrim to cross beyond **sins**. The journey is both geographical and interior, a matter of the feet and the heart, and is associated with **truth**, charity, patience, self-control, **celibacy**, and wisdom.

Hindu pilgrims are motivated by a wide variety of reasons including: being part of a sacred geographical order: accumulating positive merit (good karma); the removal of sins; performance of important life-cycle rites (to be cremated in Benares is especially desirable because of the sacred nature of the city and its location on the banks of the sacred Ganges River); personal mundane reasons (e.g. desire for sons, higher business profits, better crops, or cure from an illness); social value for certain castes; and having a direct experience of the sacred. Because there is a hierarchy of sacred locations within the religious culture, not all places of pilgrimage in India are equal, but there are so many sacred places in India that the multitude of locations unites the country into an interconnected sphere of sacred locations. There are also different types of pilgrimages in India that depend on whether or not the places owe their sacredness to divine acts, destruction of **demons**, acts of **saints**, and those sanctified theoretically by the rulers of solar and lunar dynasties that pertain to the establishment of a temple by a king.

Further reading: Bhardwaj (1973); Eck (1981, 1983); Gold (1988); Morinis (1984); Peters (1994); Turner and Turner (1978)

PLAY

A distinction can be drawn between human forms of play, such as engaging in sports, games, and inter-human interactions, and divine play. The human type of play is not a serious activity; it is simply fun and enjoyable, although it embodies a sense to it by giving meaning to action. Play, a cultural concept, means something to members of a **society** and possesses a non-materialistic quality, even though it can transcend the immediate needs of life while also serving as a primary category of life. The play element of **culture** suggests that humans are not simply **rational** and serious creatures, because play is pervasive, possesses an irrational quality, and is not simply an opposite of seriousness, although play can be earnestly serious for participants. Play is also closely related to the notion of the comic, forming a subsidiary to play, but not in the sense that it is foolishness because play is beyond the antithesis of wisdom and folly. Finally, play is associated with the aesthetic beauty of the human **body** in motion saturated with rhythm and **harmony**.

These features of play do not suggest that it is easily susceptible to a precise logical, biological, or aesthetical definition. In his study of play, Johan Huizinga calls attention to eight general characteristics of the concept. (1) Play is a voluntary activity that manifests freedom and its superfluous nature, which suggests that it is never a task or form of work and it can be deferred or suspended at any time. (2) Play does not represent ordinary or real life because it gives participants an opportunity to step outside of life into a realm of pretending and fun. (3) Play is disinterestedness, which suggests that which stands outside of human desires and drives. Play, a temporary activity, functions as an interlude in our daily lives, while also being an integral part of life that enriches our existence. (4) Play is distinct from ordinary life in terms of locale and duration because it is performed within certain limits of **time** and place. This suggests that it contains its own repetitive course and meaning within a marked off space. (5) Play creates order, even though this order is temporary and limited, whereas any deviation spoils a game. Within the order of play, participants come under the spell of play in the sense that they are enchanted and captivated by a rhythmical and harmonious activity. (6) There is also a tension in play related to its uncertain, chancy nature, which introduces an ethical value by testing a player's ability. (7) Play possesses rules that are binding on all participants and eliminate doubt. If the rules are transgressed by a spoilsport, which robs it of its illusion, the play world collapses, revealing the relativity and fragility of that world. (8) Finally, play is secret because it is only for us and not for others. It gives us a chance to be different by playing another role. In his study, Huizinga connects play to ritual and war, and he indicates how they are bound by designated space and rules. He concludes that real civilization cannot exist in the absence of a certain play element. Divine play is evident within Hinduism with relation to its **gods** and **goddesses**. The Sanskrit term for play or sport is *līlā*, which suggests an activity that is intrinsically satisfying. This type of activity is unfettered and unconditioned, transporting the player from the confines of the mundane world to a kind of magical, superfluous place where a person can revel. The concept of divine play in Hinduism presupposes that gods and goddesses are complete in their nature, and they thus need and desire nothing, although they continue to act. This continuing action can be grasped as play, a purposeless, spontaneous activity that is not pragmatic. Divine play is directly connected to bliss (*ānanda*) in the sense that a god possesses bliss, and his nature is blissful. Therefore, Hindu gods are blissful when they **dance**, laugh, and sing. Their free spontaneous, superfluous actions are an aimless display that dazzles, sparkles, fascinates, and sometimes terrifies witnesses. From a macrocosmic perspective, the world is the play thing of divine beings. In fact, the world, a stage upon which the gods can play, dance, and dazzle, is created in the spirit of play. Divine play transforms the mundane, ephemeral world into a phantasmagoric display or magic show, and it overflows with divine bliss that humans can experience.

Although there are many divine players within the Hindu pantheon, Krishna is the player par excellence because he is depicted as the divine child, adolescent, and lover. The play of Krishna as a child expresses a spontaneous, pure mode of play when he crawls about aimlessly, plays tricks, and steals butter and sweets. As an adolescent, Krishna becomes the leader of a frolicking band of cowherd boys who engage in frivolous, merry, rollicking, free and wild play. Krishna's life and death struggles with **demonic** beings are performed in the spirit of play. As the divine lover, Krishna, an embodiment of beauty, grace, and charm, plays with the cowherd women (*gopīs*) or with Rādhā, a favorite cowherd female. Krishna calls the women to play with him by means of his flute, an extension of his beauty and anarchical instrument that calls into question and breaks down social norms of behavior. As the divine lover of Rādhā, their playful love is more personal and complex, whereas Krishna's love relationship with the other cowherd girls is riotous, festive, and secretive because he induces them to surreptitiously leave their families and steal into the forest to play with him. This play often assumes the form of a circle dance (*rāsa-līlā*) during which Krishna stations himself between every two girls, giving each of them the impression that the god is next to them. The dance and frolicking are performed in the spirit of play and are forms of play.

The spirit of play is also evident among Hindu holy men, such as Rāmakrishna, a nineteenth-century Bengali saint and devotee of the goddess Kālī. He usurped the role of women at times by playing the role of a nurturing mother figure and he played with the icon of the goddess Kālī by feeding, speaking to and dancing with it. He assumed the persona of the monkey deity Hanuman by sitting naked in a tree, eating fruit, and tying a cloth around his waist to form a tail.

The pervasive nature of play in a cross-cultural context, and the contributions of Victor Turner have inspired some anthropologists to propose using it as a method with which to study religion. According to André Droogers, play – methodological ludism – can operate as a mediator between analytical and synthetic approaches that characterize the left and right hemispheres of the brain. The method of play can help a researcher overcome **reductionism** and the distinction between the insider and the outsider because play possesses the capacity to deal simultaneously and subjunctively with two or more ways of classifying **reality**. By means of play, a researcher can enter playfully into the **experience** of the **other** without bracketing out their religious reality and **experience** that reality in an inter-subjective relationship with the people being studied. In other words, a researcher plays with the informants in an attempt to reach understanding without converting to the reality of the informants. Therefore, the subjunctiveness of play is used to develop an understanding of a different reality, although this procedure is also subversive and connected to **power**, which can be distinguished from play or merged with it in a power game. Power can frustrate play or stimulate it, while play can articulate the ambiguity of reality. The liminal nature of play invites inversion, experimentation, a new mode of thinking, an inner dialogue of contrasting views that can simultaneously embrace different orders of the normal and abnormal, the usual and the exceptional and other opposites.

Jonathan Z. Smith, a historian of religions, is another scholar interested in methodological aspects of play in the sense that he views religion and the study of religion as an oscillation between play and not-play. Smith focuses, for instance, on incongruity between elements within which religion plays rather than overcoming them. It might be the case that a scholar of religion must attempt to reconcile two or more irreconcilable positions. The scholar attempts to reconcile them by playing between positions rather than seeking to overcome the differences. In this case, play represents a boundary that manifests alternatives that it governs itself.

Further reading: Cox (1969); Droogers (2006); Handelman and Shulman (1997); Huizinga (1955); Kinsley (1975); Olson (1990); Smith (1978, 2004)

PLURALISM

This refers to the cross-cultural realization that there are many religions around the globe and even within particular countries. It is basically synonymous with religious diversity. Pluralism is a contributing factor in the rise of **secularization** because the wide variety of religions gives rise to a subjective feeling that one's inherited religion cannot be a plausible explanation of **reality**, if one compares it to other religions. Recognition of pluralism tends to also promote tolerance.

More recently, pluralism conveys a more ideological meaning because of a growing conviction that every religion possesses a right to its own doctrinal position, historical traditions, ritual practices, and spiritual attitudes. If pluralism is accepted ideologically, this entails practicing tolerance and mutual acceptance of different religious positions.

POLITICS

A concept that is derived from the Greek term "*polis*," meaning city or state, becomes "politics" during the use of Middle English in Europe. It generally refers to a process whereby groups of people make decisions, and is also connected to the struggle for influence and **power**. From the time of ancient Egyptian pharaohs, who are considered both human and divine, politics and religion have been intertwined by religious **symbols**, integrated practices, and a mutual striving for power.

In ancient Judaism, the notion of a **covenant** between a superior **God** and His chosen people is not only religious, social, and economic, but is a political agreement between unequal parties. Although some scholars depict Jesus as a political revolutionary, others say he is not that focused on politics because he expects the end time at any moment, and it is more important for a person to prepare for the final moment instead of the ongoing political realm. As the early Christian Latin **church** develops, the political sphere of the state enters into a more intimate and supportive relationship with the church, especially with the rise of Constantine (312–327), who espouses Christianity as the official religion in order to control the church and to enhance his own political power. A reaction to such a movement is made by St. Gelasius, who serves as Pope from 392 to 396, with his doctrine of the two swords: secular power of the emperor and the spiritual power of the church. During the Middle Ages, the Latin church advocates a theocracy, with the state in an inferior position to the church. After the Reformation, the state controls the church, a position that dates to the work of a Swiss theologian named Thomas Erastus and called Erastianism after its author.

Other religious traditions develop their own responses to the political realm with Islam advocating a total way of life combining the secular and the religious under one **God**, although not all Muslim thinkers advocate a theocracy and view the origins of politics from within the **community** instead of a divine source. In contrast to Islam, Buddhism teaches the importance of renouncing the world and politics, but the monastic **community** becomes dependent upon the political realm for its survival, and political rulers receive their legitimacy by their generosity to, and protection of, the monastic community. In Asia and other areas over time, religious processions with their royal ceremonial symbolism assume political significance because kings use these events to demonstrate publicly territorial ownership and control.

During the contemporary era, politics plays an essential role in developments such as black theology, feminist theology, and liberation theology. They all share a desire for freedom from bias, prejudice, discrimination, and political bondage. In contrast to these liberal forces, conservative religious forces with roots in Pentecostalism in America support the right wing of the Republican Party to push its agenda of opposition to abortion, homosexuality, gay marriage, and support of prayer in public schools. Suppression of religion can be witnessed in Communist countries, such as Russia, Albania, China, Cambodia, and Cuba; while in America, there have been slow growths of what have been called the "civil religion," a synthesis of Christian religious symbols and themes with the history and identity of the nation. These modern examples point to the continued intimate relationship between religion and politics.

Further reading: Asad (1993); Bellah (1970); Chidster (1988); R. King (1999); Lincoln (1991, 2003); McCutcheon (1997); Wasserstrom (1999)

POLLUTION

Pollution suggests being in a wrong condition with respect to **others**, social norms, and **cultural** mores. Pollution also means to be defiled, sullied, or dirty. It is possible to become polluted by personal actions, coming into contact with a defiled person, or having contact with a dirty substance, such as some form of bodily waste product. In order to correct or overcome one's polluted condition, it is necessary to practice some form of **purification**. This implies that pollution is best understood in relation to forms of purification.

As the anthropologist Mary Douglas demonstrates, pollution involves dirt of some kind. Dirt is misplaced matter that offends against order, which is symbolized by **purity**. Dirt is never a unique, isolated event because it always presupposes an ordered **symbolic** system and a systematic ordering and classification of matter, whose boundaries are culturally determined. Moreover, pollution is a type of danger that can result in disorder, and it can be committed intentionally or inadvertently. In order to remove the actual or potential danger of pollution, purification is absolutely necessary under certain circumstances.

Pollution, a kind of genetic uncleanness, can be caused by blood, spittle, semen, and decaying flesh. Hebrew scripture mentions, for instance, skin diseases (Lev. 14), bodily discharges (Lev. 15) and corpses (Num. 19.11–16). Within Greek culture and Hinduism, birth, sex, and **death** are also associated with pollution. The Christian tradition views **sin** as a form of transgression and defilement, a form of pollution. After being infected by sin, a person represents a danger to his/herself and others and needs to remove the pollution, which can be accomplished by atonement in the form of confession.

Within the context of the Hindu religious tradition, menstruation is a major form of pollution on the village level of Indian society. During their menstrual period, **women** are required to leave the house and live an **ascetic** lifestyle for five days. Husbands are forced to assume female household duties during this time while wives enjoy a kind of vacation from normal chores. Death is another major source of pollution in Hinduism, and is considered a type of defilement transmitted by genealogical linkage. A general rule is the following: the closer the deceased is genealogically to the survivors the greater the pollution for them. A third major form of pollution is birth, which is called happy pollution, a form that is transmitted through kinship, although it involves a smaller group of kinsfolk than death pollution. While the mother is polluted for three months, the husband is polluted for eleven days. Other types of pollution within Hinduism for upper caste members include bodily emissions, contact with leather, sexual relations, shaving, cutting of hair, and paring of nails. These are all forms of impurity, and a person also becomes impure after a solar or lunar eclipse. An unusual type of defilement within Hinduism is respect pollution, which is an intentional type of pollution. Intentional pollution is performed to show deference and respect to such as one's guru (teacher). By doing what one would not do under normal circumstances, one expresses one's inferior position. Examples include washing a superior's feet or touching the feet of an exalted person.

On the village level of existence in India, pollution ideas are directly related to supernatural beings because the high gods maintain the highest state of purity, whereas spirits are innately impure and malevolent and local deities are not as consistently protected from impurity. If the local village deities are maintained in a field of purity, they are useful to people by granting desires, whereas impurity can elicit their malevolent aspects. Within Hinduism, areas of purity exist like islands in an ocean of impurity, which suggests that purity is artificially created and maintained. Hence, purity is not an absolute condition because it is always temporary and relative. Thus, the simple opposition between pollution and purity does not hold in Hinduism, in part because purity is a **ritual** state of being that must be continuously renewed.

Finally, the evidence from Hinduism allows us to recognize that pollution can flow, directly or through a conductor, from one being to another. In contrast to pollution, purity cannot flow from person to person, although it can be lost by contact with a defiled person. Purity is an impermanent condition that can be easily lost but never transferred.

Indian cultural attitudes towards pollution call for experts in dealing with pollution, such as washers and barbers, although the greatest amount of pollution is removed by Untouchables or Dalits because of their activities associated with village sanitation, scavenging, deposing of animal carcasses, and working in leather. These occupations protect upper caste members from pollution by performing defiling tasks, such as plowing fields, making **blood sacrifices** to demanding local deities, sweeping public roads, and disposing of dead animal bodies. This type of situation in village India suggests that higher castes need the assistance of lower castes because the formers' states of purity are dependent upon a division of labor among castes.

Further reading: Babb (1975); Douglas (1966); Turner (1967)

POLYTHEISM

Although this concept is ordinarily defined as the worship of many (*poly*) gods (*theos*), this definition is too simplistic because historical evidence elucidates that the oneness of **god** plays an important role in polytheistic religions such as Egyptian, Babylonian, Indian, Greek and other religious traditions. From the perspective of the major **monotheistic faiths** – Judaism, Christianity, and Islam – polytheism is called idolatrous and pagan as a way of distinguishing a religion's monotheistic position. These major monotheistic religions arise within, and react against, prevailing polytheistic religions, even though the term polytheism is not prevalent before the seventeenth century.

Some important distinctions can be drawn between these two types of religion. In comparison to monotheism, polytheism is less polemical and less apt to call attention to its differences with monotheism. Polytheism views the cosmos as a more cooperative process between gods and other supernatural beings or between gods and humans. The many gods are usually arranged in a hierarchically structured pantheon with the highest god conceived as the creator, such as Marduk in Babylonia, Re and later Amun-Re in Egypt, and Zeus in Greece. The hierarchical structure of the pantheon often serves as a mirror image of the mundane political structure of a **culture,** with the king representing the highest god on **earth.** Although the notion of divine unity is not totally missing from polytheistic religions, the many deities are clearly differentiated with their own personal names, shape, and function. If the monotheistic Gods are transcendent, the polytheistic deities are more imminent, closer to people, and more apt to animate the world from within it. Gods and **goddesses** of villages, towns, and cities in India and China are good examples of these figures, as are Marduk and Babylon, Ptah and Memphis, and Athena and Athens. If considered over a period of historical development, polytheistic religions tend to be more ethnocentric. These religions tend to be less concerned about orthodoxy (what is to be believed) and more about orthopraxy (what is to be done).

Further reading: Burkert (1983, 1985); van der Leeuw (1963)

POSSESSION

This is a complex, multivocal, and ubiquitous phenomenon evident around the globe. It can be defined as an integration of spirit and matter that represents a force, **power** or corporeal **reality.** A subject can become possessed either suddenly or gradually. I. M. Lewis, writing about the Tungas of the African Zambesi valley, identifies two psychosocial loci of possession: central, which is highly valued because it supports prevailing **political,** moral, and religious **beliefs** and whose **spirits** are sympathetic to these beliefs; peripheral, which represents an intrusion of **evil,** amoral **spirits** that is considered undesirable and dangerous. The central type of possession occurs among persons of higher social status and power, whereas the peripheral type happens to people lacking power and status.

In India, it is possible to find something similar with a distinction between two Sanskrit terms *āveśa* (entrance into) and *praveśa* (to enter toward). The former is a friendly, benign, and self-motivated form of possession that is voluntary, while the latter representing possession from outside is involuntary and executed by a malevolent being.

For the insider or person possessed, it is an ontological **reality** that is self-validating and thus cannot be doubted. Possession is also grasped as a modification of one's personality that is a traumatic **experience** and a state of tension. The possessed person manifests a liminal state of mind because the individual's social status recedes into **liminality**, an ambiguous status, when a person is possessed.

Possession, a form of social control and **political power**, is self-contained in the sense that it is limited by the boundary of the **body**. Possession also acts like a **ritual** by representing a structure of resistance implying a disruption of the psychological, social, and political fabric of **society**. It is also **performative** in the sense that it is a public event that can be openly verified by anyone observing the behavior of the possessed person. Within the context of a disjunctive and disjointed world linked to transvestism, sexual conflict, powerlessness, sexual abuse, or illness, possession can heal a person. From a psychoanalytic perspective, Karkar interprets possession as a self-induced mechanism for psychic release or a mental **healing**.

Because in many religious **cultures** more **women** than men become possessed, some observers have commented on the **gendered** nature of possession. Oppressed and marginal women perform their possession, which empowers them and gives them authority and status within the context of a male-dominated patriarchal society. This scenario is not the threat to the established order that one might assume because possessed women tend to maintain the cultural power structure.

Further reading: Caldwell (1999); Kakar (1982); Lewis (1971); Smith (2006)

POSTMODERNISM

This is a difficult concept to define with complete accuracy because it means different things to the writers who consider themselves postmodern. The roots of postmodernism are equally imprecise, but can be traced to changes in architectural design, philosophical attitudes expressed in the thought of Nietzsche, advocating a reign of frivolity with its return to the artistic, the erotic, and the playful, and to the German philosopher

Martin Heidegger and his vision of the end of metaphysics. According to some postmodern thinkers, postmodernism represents the completion of the Enlightenment project, whereas others claim that it is a reaction against the position of the Enlightenment with its Cartesian and Kantian perspectives.

Generally, the thinkers of the Enlightenment stress the importance of liberty, equality, tolerance, and common sense. Along with a conviction that a natural law prescribes the pursuit of pleasure, profit, and property, there is a strong **belief** in the natural goodness and perfectibility of human nature. Moreover, the period exemplifies a **secularization** of **knowledge** and thought. A fundamental assumption of the Enlightenment thinkers is that **rational** reflection is liberating.

In response to the Enlightenment intellectual thrust, postmodernists are critical of the static world envisioned by its thinkers, stressing instead becoming, contingency, relativity, chance, and difference. This impetus rejects imitation of models or conforming to models. Postmodernists acknowledge that there is no place from which one can begin and no place at which one will arrive in the future. Within the world of flux, there are no universal and timeless **truths** to be discovered because everything is relative and indeterminate, which suggests that our knowledge is always incomplete, fragmented, and historically and culturally conditioned. Therefore, there can be no foundation for philosophy or any theory, and it is wise to be suspicious of any universal claims to validity made by reason. Moreover, there is no center of the individual, **society**, **culture**, or history. There is instead a postmodern emphasis on **pluralism** that is, for instance, expressed by artists deliberately juxtaposing different styles from diverse sources in the way that the *bricolage* reconfigures different objects or images. The postmodern use of irony exemplifies a preference for aesthetic categories and a different style of writing that attempts to extend itself to the very limits of human **experience**.

The postmodern period is characterized by discontinuity, irregularity, rupture, decenteredness, and lack of hope for any type of utopia. There is also no transhistorical value for many postmodernists because of the **death** of **God**, an example of the postmodern iconoclastic spirit. Within this type of context, anyone who can write can become a revolutionary, although writing involves a wandering, erring, marginal lifestyle in which one experiments with words and thoughts. According to some postmodernists, this wandering, errant lifestyle is destined to end in decadence.

Among the experiments conducted by postmodern thinkers are a series of experiments within **time** that emphasizes the present moment. Many postmodern thinkers tend to problematize time because they are uncomfortable with the past that tends to embody the roots of logocentrism, metaphysics of presence, and other undesirable things, like authority, the scientific worldview, hierarchy, hegemony, and grand **narratives**. Postmodernists stress the present over the past and future, reflecting their convictions that the future offers little hope for realizing utopian dreams and that the past is associated with authority, hegemony, and ideology. Postmodernists desire to be free of tradition to view indifferently the play of heterogeneous discourses.

Further reading: Derrida (1976); Lyotard (1985)

POWER

The concept of power is a ubiquitous feature of religions viewed cross-culturally, although it appears under different names with distinct meanings. In Japan, the *kami* are spiritual forces vaguely associated with various types of natural and supernatural powers. Chinese Daoism holds Dao to be a mysterious power because of its invisible, inaudible, and subtle nature, and De (virtue, power) is a force within things, which differentiates one thing from another. The major **monotheistic** religions of Judaism, Christianity, and Islam agree that **God** is all-powerful and the source of power. The Qur'an, for instance, affirms that Allah is all-powerful and possesses power over everything (6.17). Moreover, the Arabic term *barakh*, which means literally blessing, is a mysterious power possessed by the prophet Muhammad and to a lesser degree by Muslim saints. Among North American Native Indians, power is associated with the *manitou* among the Algonquian people, *orenda* among the Iroquois, and *wakan* among the Sioux. Numerous other examples could be recited from other past and present religious traditions. The possibility of a precise definition of power, however, is a challenge for scholars.

In *Religion in Essence and Manifestation*, Gerardus van der Leeuw (1890–1950), a Dutch phenomenologist of religion, argues that power belongs to both the subjective and objective aspect of religion. He stresses the impersonal, potent, and dangerous nature of power. When a powerful person or thing is revealed it is set apart and distinguished from everything else. This distinguishing indicates that the powerful person or thing is dangerous and thus taboo, a warning that the powerless person should maintain his/her distance and secure protection. When power is revealed in a person or thing it is being authenticated. Power can become collective in the sense that actions, thoughts, and principles of human beings can represent a collection of power, even though it may be independent of its bearer. The accumulation of power constitutes an effective potency, which can benefit an individual or group in an impersonal or personal way. In the final analysis for van der Leeuw, power is the essence of things and humans. Because of its dynamic nature, it tends to expand and deepen into a universal force.

Mircea Eliade (1907–1986), a Romanian historian of religion, states that power is equivalent to being, and it conquers non-being and makes life possible within the context of a religious way of life. It is power that renders possible the being of things – animate and inanimate – and determines the structure of things. Power is something in which humans can participate and share with others. Power is meaningful and gives meaning to life. In fact, power challenges us to find our center of being, helping a person become master of his/her world. Power is, however, ambivalent because it can be both creative and destructive. The encounter with power demands care, if one is not to be overwhelmed and overawed by it.

In sharp contrast to the concept of power within the theories of van der Leeuw and Eliade, a more recent conception is offered by Michel Foucault (1926–1984), a poststructuralist thinker, who disputes their essentialist grasp of the concept and emphasizes that power is a relation between forces. A force is not singular because it always exists in relation to other forces and possesses no other subject or object than itself. Foucualt suggests that power is something that circulates over a wide area, implying that power is a complex web of interconnections, never localized in a particular place, and cannot become the possession of any single person. Power is also multi-directional because it operates both from the top down and from the bottom up, although Foucault is more interested in the ascending nature of power.

Despite the wide circulation of power and its integration into the fabric of a **society**, it only exists when it is put into action. The exercise of power, a form of action, is a way that certain actions modify other actions. Foucault defines power in a non-confrontational and non-adversarial way, while still recognizing that a power relationship involves potentially a strategy of struggle. An important relationship for Foucault exists between power and **knowledge** in the sense that power produces knowledge and knowledge is power, which suggests that they are integrated and create each other.

In addition to these three theorists, it can be added that power possesses a drive, impulse, or tendency, which can be associated with its ability to empower. This suggests that power generates, gives, increases, and enhances itself. This inner dynamic drive of power is often manifested as degrees of power that can only be measured when one encounters it, but one can never be certain in one's final calculations because power always remains ultimately mysterious and elusive. Its dynamic

187

nature implies that power influences things and people by forcing them to move or behave in a certain manner. The dynamic and energetic force of power possesses a compulsive aspect because it can potentially coerce certain actions and results and even prohibit them. This suggests that power is an exercise of force over something with the potential of compulsion. The compulsive aspect of power gives the owner control over his/herself, **others**, and possibly the cosmos. To gain control is an instance of power extending beyond itself.

Further reading: Eliade (1959); Foucault (1994); van der Leeuw (1963)

PRAYER

Prayer can be comprehended as a form of communication between humans and higher **powers**. The word is derived from a Latin term *pre-care* (to beg or entreat). Prayer is also evocational in the sense that it calls forth a network of **symbols** related to sense **experiences**, moods, **emotions**, and values. This aspect of prayer is associated with rhythmic repetition, symbolic **language**, sounds, sights, **ritual** gestures, and **dance** movements. Prayer is a ritual act that possesses a pragmatic character. It also represents a **performative** utterance, suggesting that the reciting of the words of the prayer is the doing of an action that makes something happen, such as **healing** or wish fulfillment.

Within many religions, there are preparatory procedures that a person intending to pray must perform before uttering a word. Roman Catholics, for instance, make the sign of the cross on their bodies with their right or auspicious hand. Orthodox Jews cover their head and secure the *tefillin* (phylacteries), which involves binding two leather boxes containing scriptural passages (Exod. 13.1–19, 13–16 and Deut. 6.4–9; 11.13–21) around one's head and left arm by means of leather straps. Muslims **purify** themselves with water, or clean sand if no water is available, by washing their hands, arms to the elbow, face, and feet before entering a mosque to pray. Within Islam, there are two forms of ablutions recognized: lesser ablution (*wudhū*) and the greater ablution (*ghusl*). The lesser example involves washing both hands to the wrists with water, rinsing one's mouth three times, taking water into the nostrils three times, washing the face three times, washing both arms to the elbows, wiping the forehead once with the right hand, wiping the ear lobes once, wiping the head and neck once, and washing both feet to the ankles. The greater ablution includes washing the entire **body**, which is done following any major **pollution**. Since the place of prayer must also remain clean, worshippers must leave their shoes outside of the mosque.

Muslim prayer is not merely recited but also performed by a series of *rak'ah* (bowings), which culminates in kneeling on the floor and touching one's forehead to the floor. The performance of prayer involves seven basic movements: standing and reciting "Allah akbar" (**God** is great); reciting the opening chapter of the Qur'an, followed by another verse, while standing upright with hands placed before the body; bowing from the hips while placing the hands on the knees; straightening up; prostrating by gliding to the knees, putting the nose and forehead on the ground; sitting back on the haunches and reciting "God is great"; and prostrating once again. Muslim **performance** of prayer is a sign of submission and an act of homage to God, a taking refuge in God that is expressed verbally by a believer. By performing prayer in a communal setting, a believer comes to recognize that he/she is part of the **community** of God.

In Islam this prayer of several bowings represents institutional prayer (*salāt*, an Aramaic term meaning bowing) that is an obligation and thus a fulfillment of a duty to God. Its legal basis implies that it is a performance of what God has established in the past. To neglect or abandon it results in the forfeiture of Islamic status. The second type of prayer in formative Islam is spontaneous (*du'ā*), which a believer can recite at any time of the day. The institutional form of prayer is ideally performed five times a day: daybreak, noon, mid-afternoon, after sunset, and early evening. In addition to the two major forms of Islamic prayer, giving thanks for life, praise of God, penitence, and supplication, there is also remembrance (*dhikr*) of God, which plays an important role in Sufism, a Muslim form of **mysticism**. Overall, Muslim prayer can be construed as a witness to the fundamental truth of the faith: there is no God but Allah.

Besides the Muslim distinction between prayers, there are many different types of prayer in Christianity. Christian prayers are identified as petition, intercessory, thanksgiving, theurgical, liturgical, and thaumaturgical. Among Christians, the best known prayer is the Our Father, which is adopted from Jewish religion via the ministry of John the Baptist. Although he might not be mentioned in a prayer, it is accepted that the name of Jesus makes the prayer effective. In fact, Jesus is the archetypical model of the performer of prayer for Christians, which implies that by performing prayer an individual models their behavior on that of Jesus. Christian prayer is, moreover, scriptural in the sense that it is connected to biblical texts and contexts. The success of prayers depends on **faith** and God's will. As Christian prayer loses its thaumaturgical and theurgical settings, it becomes liturgical, or a part of the regular **ritual** observances without the expectation that miracles or angels would appear.

189

Many Christian prayers end with Amen (truly, yes), a Hebrew term connected historically with legal disputes and military command.

Prayer plays a central role in the religion of the Navaho Indians living in the North American southwest where the singer of the prayer is also the master composer in that his performance represents his moment of composition. The Navaho distinguish among eight types of prayer: (1) blessing prayer acts, used with ceremonies for blessing a new home, a girl's puberty rite, or weddings; (2) lifeway prayer acts, which are intended to restore someone to health; (3) enemyway prayer acts, whose purpose is the expulsion of malevolence; (4) uglyway prayer acts that focus on the expulsion and dispersion of native malevolence; (5) holyway prayer acts that call for the removal of the power of Holy People and its disorder; (6) liberation prayer acts that are recited to recover the lost means of a healthy life; (7) protection prayer acts, whose purpose is to procure protection against an attack upon one's health; and (8) remaking prayer acts that are intended to remake and restore Holy People. A holyway prayer is repeated, for instance, several times, and it includes the names of the Holy People, reference about making and offering and the preparation of a smoke offering, beseeching the Holy People to remake the person praying, a passage that describes the removal and dispersion of the inflicted spell, a statement about the recovery occurring, and concludes with a description of an accomplished state of pleasantness. If the prayer is successful, the sick person gains a state of *hózhqí*, a condition of the pristine beauty of creation.

Further reading: Denny (1985); Gill (1981)

PRIEST

The primary function of the priest is the conduct of **worship**, although he also serves as the guardian of the traditions of his religion and keeper of the **sacred knowledge**. As the guardian of his culture's religious tradition, the priest may also be called to assume the roles of advisor, educator, philosopher, judge, administrator, scholar, or interpreter of the holy law. The ancient Vedic priest of Indian religion is a good example. Among the Vedic priestly caste (Brahmin), priests specialize during **ritual** services. The Brahmin insures the success and protects the effectiveness of the **sacrifices** by overseeing the entire rite and eliminating errors by reciting **sacred** mantras (repeated formulas). In order to successfully perform these various functions, the office of the priest presupposes preparation and education. In some cultures, the office is inherited, as in India, or a person may feel called to the office.

The basis of priestly existence and activity is communion with the divine, with the priest playing a mediating role between **god** and humans. The Hogan (priest) of the Dogon people of Africa mediates the deity Lebe's life-giving force, which is signified by his tunic and trousers that symbolize the four cardinal directions and four elements. The Hogon's sandals represent the ark of the deity Nomo that brings humankind to earth at the beginning of time, whereas his cylindrical-shaped headdress is woven in a spiral pattern which corresponds to the path followed by the original cosmic seed. The priest's association with the divine sometimes obligates him to interpret the divine will for the people.

In some religious cultures, the priest formulates rules of conduct and enforces their observance. Among the African Nuer people, the priest protects the killer in a case of homicide from any danger associated with revenge by giving him/her sanctuary. The priest may, for instance, negotiate a settlement by offering compensation to the family of the deceased. Then, the priest performs a **sacrifice** to enable normal social relations to resume, and he rehabilitates the slayer. The Nuer priest also presides over the taking of oaths, which involves licking a spear or a metal bracelet as a sign of telling the **truth**.

Priestly administrative duties are derived from his cultic activities, which is evident by his supervision and maintenance of sacred buildings, religious instruments, and finances. His authority for these types of responsibilities rests within his office. By virtue of his office, he dispenses **salvation** by submitting his will to the divine, whereas, in contrast, a magician seeks to force the deity to obey him.

Along with his many functions and responsibilities, a priest is subject to many restrictions with respect to lifestyle, diet, and **sexuality**. Certain taboos associated with the priestly office emphasize the necessity to maintain holiness. Members of the Brahmin priestly caste in India observe a vegetarian diet, whereas Roman Catholic priests must take a vow of **celibacy**. Due to his association with the **earth**, the Nuer, leopard-skin priest does not approach people when they are making pots to protect the pots from cracking. Various **taboos** can enhance the efficacy of priestly action. Along with his attire, taboos set the priest apart from other members of a **society**, although the distinctiveness of the priest from others does not affect his followers who tend to be regular and stable. In his distinctive role, a priest's influence exceeds the religious and moral realms to include social, cultural, and political spheres.

Further reading: Evans-Pritchard (1956); Leopold (1973); Osborne (1988)

PROPHET

The most distinctive characteristic between a **priest** and a prophet is the personal call received by the latter, although some priests feel called to their office. This call experienced by the prophet forms the basis for his authority, which is ultimately derived from a divine being. Another important distinction between a priest and a prophet is the personal charisma of the latter, whereas the priest possesses office charisma, a Greek word meaning favor, **gift**, or gift of **grace** in the New Testament. In short, it is a personal magic of leadership that gives the owner the ability to persuade others of their message, gets others committed to their cause, and motivates them to act upon the message. There are two basic types of charisma: office and personal. The former type tends to be more **rational** and demands tempered obedience, whereas personal charisma is due to personal qualifications that appeal more to the **emotions** of **others**, claiming complete loyalty and even individual surrender.

A prophet is usually called to do something, such as proclaim a religious doctrine or divine commandment. The Jewish prophet Jeremiah, for instance, calls for a new **covenant** (31.31–34) that would fulfill the intention of the original Sinai covenant made with Moses that is now broken. It is important to recognize that the prophet is conscious of being the organ, instrument, or mouth piece of the divine will (Sam. 28.6, 15). This implies that a prophet's authority is secondary or derived from a higher source. During the process of receiving a message, prophets encounter **visions**, voices, **dreams**, and trances, which can be revelations that arise spontaneously and are received passively by the prophet. The Islamic prophet Muhammad, who is considered the seal of the prophets after having received the final and most perfect revelation according to the Islamic tradition, even refers to messages deposited on his heart. Whatever the modes of message, they are not self-induced by the prophetic figure. And unlike a priest, a prophet receives no monetary rewards for his work, propagating ideas for their own sake.

The Islamic doctrine of the role of the prophet teaches that **God** never leaves humankind without a prophet, and sends them to all peoples. The Qur'an refers to a line of prophetic figures from Noah, Abraham, Moses, David, Solomon, Jonah, and Jesus. The message of these prophets and Muhammad, last of them, is essentially the same, although there is a gradual evolution of the messages towards the final and perfect revelation. The Qur'an lists four qualities of a prophet: truthfulness, fidelity,

PSYCHOLOGY

propagation of God's message, and intelligence. From the Muslim perspective, the prophet is endowed with immunity from error and **sin**. The prophet Muhammad does not function as a mediator between God and humankind, he possesses no superhuman status, and he is certainly not divine, but is simply God's prophet, having been chosen by God for a task on earth that involves proclaiming the divine word.

Further reading: Denny (1988); Peters (2003); von Rad (1965)

PSYCHOLOGY

With its roots in the Greek terms *psyche* (mind) and *logos* (doctrine), it is the science of the conscious and unconscious mind, although there is no consensus on a specific definition just as there is no single universal definition of religion. Educated and employed at Harvard University, William James (1842–1910) is credited with publishing the first truly significant book on the psychology of religion *The Varieties of Religious Experience*, whose contents date to the prestigious Gifford Lectures at Edinburgh University in Scotland from 1901–1902. James is more concerned with consciousness than the unconscious. According to James, religion, a strenuous mode of life because it involves self-sacrifice, courage, overcoming hardships and obstacles, is indicative of a radical transformation of one's existence, freedom, and the presence of a transcendent **power** beyond oneself. These primary modes of **experience** are the sources for religion, whereas secondary features such as **theology** and dogma degenerate and decline over time. James draws a few distinctions such as that between healthy-minded and unhealthy-minded or sick souls. The initial distinction represents the "once-born," which is characterized by optimism, whereas the opposite "twice-born" is pessimistic because they **experience** a second birth by dying from their unreal life.

Another major figure approaching religion through the lens of psychology is Sigmund Freud (1856–1939). Freud associates religious people with neurotics, with both parties practicing patterned behavior that leads to feelings of guilt when one deviates from the path. Because religion demands repression of one's basic instincts, and psychological neuroses originate from repressed fundamental instincts, there is a resemblance between religious behavior and mental illness by manifesting a universal obsessional neurosis of our frustrated instincts. Freud also

193

associates religion with a projection of infantile dependencies onto external reality. Grounded in his theory of human development, Freud identifies the Oedipus complex with the origins of religion, which necessitates the son killing his father in order to gain access to the women of the tribe. Feeling remorse and guilt, the son finds a substitute of the father in the totem animal, which it is agreed would not be killed and instead worshipped. This dead father figure is projected into **God** by the son. With the publication of *Future of an Illusion* in 1927, Freud argues that religion is not revealed by some deity, its claims cannot be scientifically verified, and it does not represent logical conclusions. Because people want religion to be true, religious **beliefs** are illusions, which cannot be proven or refuted.

Many working in the field of the psychology of religion describe Freud's work and that of Carl Gustav Jung (1875–1961) as speculative. Jung does not, however, agree with Freud on some important issues such as the Oedipus complex, the inevitably of sexual conflict between father and son, and rejects the notion of the mother as an object of incestuous desire. Instead of Freud's unconscious, Jung envisions a collective unconscious, which is defined as impulses to action devoid of conscious motivation. Within the collective unconscious, Jung locates archetypes that are the product of recurring experiences of life, such as birth, **death**, danger, and attempts to satisfy desire for sex and **food**. Jung understands this as a process in which religion, an archetypal requirement for human nature and a numinous conscious **experience**, plays an important role. In contrast to Freud, Jung thinks that the presence of religion is not a sign of neurosis, but its absence might be a sign of neurosis especially later in life.

In addition to James, Freud, and Jung, many more theorists make contributions to the psychology of religion by developing the insights of these early pioneers or attempting to move in a more scientific and a less speculative direction. These three early examples of scholars of psychology continue to manifest the inability of the field to operate with a unified body of theory and method. These approaches also illustrate the continued use of empiricism, **reduction**, and an anti-religious bias in many cases. Moreover, the psychological approach to religion is criticized for being insensitive to historical development and the contents of religion such as **symbols**, **myths** and **rituals**.

On a more positive note, psychologists of religion study religion as a way of coping with everyday stress, health issues, drug-induced religious experience, and the effects of **meditation**.

Further reading: Freud (1919, 1975); James (1902); Jung (1969)

PURGATORY

The concept of purgatory, an intermediate place between **heaven** and hell and the **death** of a person and the final **judgment**, does not become firmly established in Christianity until sometime between 1150–1200 CE. Purgatory is a place for those Christians tainted by **sin** at the end of their lives who are not yet worthy of heaven, and is thus related to ideas of individual free will and responsibility along with a final judgment of the dead. In Christianity, purgatory is related to notions of **fire** and **purification**.

Clement of Alexandria (*c.* 150–*c.* 215) and Origen (d. 253/254), Greek theologians, are the presumptive founders of purgatory. They borrow the Hebrew Bible notion that **fire** is a divine instrument, use the New Testament idea of baptism by fire, and the notion of a **purification** trial after death from the letters of Paul. Clement distinguishes two types of sinners: incorrigible ones and sinners who can be corrected. The latter type of sinner can benefit from education, whereas the incorrigible need punishment. In the afterlife, the incorrigible are consumed by a devouring fire, whereas the correctable sinner encounters a fire that sanctifies and does not consume. For the first time in Christian history, Origen states that the **soul** can be purified in the other world after death, while also making a distinction between mortal and venial sins.

The mature concept of purgatory is historically preceded by personal **visions** and stories about spiritual journeys outside of the human **body**. There are also tales of the dead being punished in purgatory, and asking the living for help or warning them to mend their ways. The development of the notion of purgatory manifests the influence of the twelfth-century notion of justice, which implies that the inequalities and injustice of the present life are supposed to be corrected in the next life. Another influential factor in the evolution of purgatory is the distinction made by Anselm (*c.* 1033–1109), Archbishop of Canterbury, between voluntary **sins** that are subject to damnation and venial sins due to weakness of the flesh. In short, the souls in purgatory are among the elect, and thus they are ultimately destined to be saved. Moreover, a soul can be reprieved from punishment by virtue of outside intervention and not its good conduct. By the end of the thirteenth century, purgatory is conceived as a place and **time**: a place of limited duration and a time of sin and purgation. The concept of purgatory is popularized by preaching friars, and they evoke hope with their preaching.

The many fragmentary themes related to purgatory are woven together by Dante (1265–1321) in his *Divine Comedy*, which is divided into three books of thirty-three cantos each. The Trinitarian symbolism is obvious, and it represents the deepest universal truth. Dante's **narrative** assumes the form of a personal vision expressed as a voyage during which Dante travels himself with the assistance of three guides: Beatrice, Virgil, and St. Bernard. The poem is set in holy week from Maundy Thursday to Easter Sunday, a pilgrim's journey similar to the journey of Christ on earth, to hell, to purgatory, to **heaven**, and finally back to **earth**.

Dante locates purgatory on the earth in the form of a mountain diametrically opposite Jerusalem. Rising toward heaven, an earthly paradise is located at its summit at the level of innocence that is situated between the peak of **purification** in purgatory and the beginning of the glorification of heaven. In Dante's conception, purgatory comprises seven circles arranged one above the other with circumferences that diminish as one moves closer to the summit. Souls are purged of one of the seven deadly sins in each of the circles: pride, envy, wrath, sloth, avarice, gluttony, and lust. The elected are purged and become more pure as they progress to the summit of the mountain by three basic means: punishment, **meditation** on the sin to be purged and its correlative virtue, and **prayer**. It is **love** that serves as the governing principle for the souls in each of the circles until the love of God is restored in the soul.

Dante's purgatory contains certain structural features such as a narrow gate that stands in contrast to the wider gate of hell. Three different colored steps lead to purgatory, and they represent the three acts of the **sacrament**: contrition (white), confession (causes the penitent to turn a deep purple with shame), and satisfaction (a flaming red of love by which one is motivated). Throughout the journey through purgatory, hope reigns supreme, although the soul's progress depends on help from the living. The progress of the soul is marked by time whose maximum length of stay is the interval between death and the Last **Judgment**.

Further reading: Le Goff (1984)

PURIFICATION

To purify something means to transform it into something holy or **sacred** from its former status as profane or possibly polluted. Purification sets an object apart from others, making it complete, whole, unified, and distinct. Before performing some religious action, it might be necessary to purify an instrument to be used, a place for a rite, or oneself. Before a Muslim enters a mosque to pray, he purifies himself, for instance, with water or clean sand, if he is in a remote location.

Purification removes the unclean dirt that is equated with **pollution**. Though they are not simply opposites, in order to grasp the nature of purification, it is necessary to know about the nature of pollution. They do, however, represent an interconnected notion, although pollution is a dangerous condition and purity a higher ordered condition more akin to rightness. In comparison to pollution, purity is temporary and unstable, and does not flow directly or indirectly like pollution.

Diverse religious cultures have devised different means to perform purification. Water is probably the most common means of purification. Bathing in a sacred river is a common form of purification in Hinduism, while washing one's clothes and taking a bath is the remedy for an ancient Hebrew having contact with a person with a venereal disease (Lev. 15). Even though it can pollute a person in some contexts, **blood** is another liquid that can also be used to purify; for instance, a house infected by mole or a person of leprosy (Lev. 14). The blood of a sucking pig is used in ancient Babylon to cure a person possessed by evil **spirits**. Within the context of ancient Indian Vedic culture, **fire** is used to purify an area to transform it into a sacrificial plot. Those possessed by ghosts in ancient Babylon are purified by sulfur, an agent also used to purify a blood-stained house in Homer's Greek epic of the *Odyssey* (22.481–494).

Three basic methods of purification are used among different Native American Indians. Plains, southwestern, and eastern woodland Indians pour water over hot stones within an enclosed space or sweat lodge. Alaskan Eskimos and Pacific Northwestern California Indians light fires within closed spaces, while the Pueblos employ heating ducts from an outside chamber. The general purpose of the sweat lodge is a spiritual and physical purification. The Sioux sweat lodge is related to the goodness of the **earth** and symbolically represents its womb. A participant crawls in and out of the lodge like a baby from a place within which one is reborn.

Other forms of purification are evident among other Native American groups. For instance, the Creeks drink a liquid called the black drink, which functions as a strong emetic and causes a drinker to vomit and cleanse themselves. This drink purifies one of all **sins**, leaves one in a state of perfect innocence, makes one invincible in war and cements friendship, benevolence, and hospitality. Among the Zulu of Africa, spitting is a method of purification, which helps one to cleanse oneself of anger. When a male Zulu fears being secretly treated by certain medicines that can prove harmful to him, he can sleep with a woman not his wife and emits his semen and thus expel his evil into her.

Further reading: Babb (1975); Berglund (1989); Douglas (1966)

RATIONALITY

The concept of rationality represents the foundation of much of Western epistemology that can be traced to ancient Greek philosophers, and the claim that humans are innately rational. Rationality is grounded in reason, a mental **power** used to form **judgments**, make inferences, reach conclusions, and construct arguments. If an individual possesses a **belief** and needs to defend it, that individual can resort to reason to support, justify, or explain their position. To be declared lacking in reason by others means that an individual is stupid, irrational or insane. Western theologians use reason to support their positions on the doctrine of **God, faith,** and **revelation** during the Middle Ages by arguing in part that **theology** is rational and that theological issues do not contradict reason.

In the West, rationality arguably reaches its pinnacle of influence during the Enlightenment, which is called the "Age of Reason," and which holds the promise of freedom from **myth**, superstition, and a **belief** in mysterious **powers** by using critical reasoning. Immanuel Kant attempts to use reason to critique itself, in the sense of determining its own limits, and to develop rational rules by which to adhere to these restrictions. Kant not only distinguishes reason (*Vernunft*) from understanding (*Verstand*) and sensibility (*Sinnlichkeit*), he distinguishes theoretical – which determines or constitutes the object given in intuition and applies categories to the data of sense intuition – from practical reason, in which reason functions as the source of its objects in order to determine its moral choices in accordance with a law that originates from itself. By relying solely on concepts gained by such **knowledge** based on principles, a person can apprehend the particular contained in the universal and the former can then be deduced from the latter, which indicates that knowledge gained through reason is very different from knowledge obtained by principles of understanding. But by accepting the concepts and judgments of the understanding, reason attempts to unify these multiple phenomena according to a higher principle. Therefore, reason seeks that which is unconditioned, something not given in sense **experience**, and unity. Because knowledge is limited to the sphere of experience, knowledge of things-in-themselves is not possible. The possibility of synthetic a priori knowledge, **truths** that can be known independently of experience, is only transcendentally possible by arguing from the categories of rationality, innate ideas, or pure concepts of understanding. Kant's notion of the law of reason requires us to seek unity.

The influence of Enlightenment rationality shapes the scholarly approach to the study of religion beginning with the nineteenth-century studies by anthropologists such as James Frazer, Edward Tylor, and Lucien Lévy-Bruhl. In their studies of technologically simple, indigenous religious cultures, Frazer and Tylor characterize their mentality as irrational, whereas Lévy-Bruhl argues for a "prelogical mentality." E. E. Evans-Pritchard disputes Lévy-Bruhl's claim by arguing in part that indigenous religious cultures think empirically to solve everyday problems. Along similar lines, Claude Lévi-Strauss, father of structuralism, extends rationality to all the human sciences by extending structural modes of linguistics to cultural analysis, which enables him to grasp a mode of logic in **myths**. In contrast to the **belief** about a universal rationality, other scholars have pushed for relativist rationalities by being sensitive to cultural contexts. Warning about using Western rationality to make **judgments**, Stanley Tambiah, an anthropologist, rejects radical relativism because it makes critical judgments impossible, whereas the anthropologist Clifford Geertz argues for the universality of cognitive processes and the need to protect cultural diversity.

From another perspective, rationality has been used to dismiss religion because it hinders the development of reason. In his *Leviathan*, political philosopher Thomas Hobbes dismisses religion as "ignorance," and this agrees with David Hume's assessment of religion that no human testimony is adequate, for instance, to account for something like a miracle. Another philosopher, Ludwig Feuerbach, argues that gods, who are idealized conceptions, are the creation of human imagination. The psychologist Sigmund Freud calls religion "illusion" and a "neurosis" that modern people must overcome in order to be cured. While other examples can be added, the general consensus is that religion lacks genuine rationality. These types of attitudes contribute to predictions about the imminent demise of religion. In fact, religion is doomed because it cannot survive the assault of **secularization, pluralism**, science, and technology. And yet religion persists because it responds to fundamental emotional and social needs that people must satisfy in order to live a healthy and meaningful life. There is even speculation that humans may be genetically inclined to be religious.

A focus on rationality is not confined to the West because it is possible to find it stressed by Indian schools of philosophy such as the Nyāya and Vaiśeṣika with their acceptance of an atomic theory of matter, a conviction about the **reality** of the world, a **belief** in the plurality of selves, and an active interest in investigating the fundamental categories of reality by carefully considering issues of epistemology, logical analysis, and rationality. Adopting the pluralistic realism of the Vaiśeṣika school in the third century CE, the Nyāya philosopher, Akṣapāda Gotama, introduces a method of inferential reasoning to support the pluralistic reality. In Indian Buddhism, two philosophical schools – Svātantrika and Prāsangika – argue about the possibility of establishing the truth of emptiness (*śūnyatā*) with the former represented by Dharmakīrti during the seventh century CE and the latter by Candrakīrti (*c.* 650). Being convinced that logical arguments can provide certainty, Dharmakīrti develops notions of cognition and meaning from the Buddhist philosopher Dignāga (480–540 CE), whereas Candrakīrti argues that the **truth** of emptiness can only be established by an argument based on a reduction to absurdity and the ability to witness the inherent contradictions present within any logical and rational attempt to support the truth.

Among other Eastern religious movements, Zen Buddhism calls rationality into question because it is associated with a representational mode of thinking that is captive to a subject/object type of thinking. Zen wants to retrieve a mode of thinking that is pre-reflective and not captive to rationality by using, for instance, *kōans* (enigmatic statements that are nonsensical and paradoxical) to jolt a person into a non-thinking mode of consciousness, using the Zen master Dōgen's terminology, that is the most fundamental mode of consciousness and devoid of any intentional attitude.

Along with Zen Buddhists, **postmodern** thinkers are also dissatisfied with rationality, and their approaches to it by, for instance, rescuing reason or by embracing the irrational. Jean Lyotard, for instance, makes a distinction between a rationalist and a post-rationalist path by drawing out their political consequences. If the rationalist path suggests a desire to preserve existing rules that conform to the dictates of capitalism, the post-rationalist path leads to destabilization and the unbalancing of the structures needed for the **performative** functioning of knowledge, an example of **power** and capitalist rationalization. Lyotard wants to save reason and to free it and knowledge, which is nothing more than a product to be sold, from the bondage of capitalist authorities.

Further reading: Evans-Pritchard (1965); Geertz (1973); Lévi-Strauss (1962); Lyotard (1985); Olson (2000); Tambiah (1990)

REALITY

What is genuinely real as it is captures the sense of reality. Within many religious traditions, reality is often identified with the high God, or it is equated with a more abstract reality such as Brahman in some forms of

Hinduism, nirvāṇa in Theravāda Buddhism, emptiness in Mahāyāna Buddhism, Buddha-nature in Zen Buddhism, or the Dao in Daoism. Reality is often defined as that which is permanent, although there are exceptions in Eastern forms of thought.

In the major **monotheistic** traditions, Christian thinkers agree, with the exception of process theologians, that God is permanent because of God's immortal status as compared to the finite and transitory nature of human life. Likewise, in Islam, Allah is defined as the real, the one with ninety-nine beautiful names in the Qur'an (7.179; 17.11). Muslim interpreters insist that the ninety-nine beautiful names of God are not mere attributes, but they are rather realities. Moreover, Allah is completely transcendent so that "sight reaches him not" (6.101). If God is wholly other than humans, He is considered over humans who are under His rule and they are expected to be obedient.

In the Indian religious tradition, a Hindu thinker such as Śankara defines Brahman, a non-dual, ultimate reality, as not this, not that (*neti, neti*), suggesting that there is nothing in the world that defines or resembles it. For Theravāda Buddhist, nirvāṇa is defined negatively as the extinction of craving, uncompounded, unconditioned, absence of desire, cessation, end of becoming, causeless, whereas more positive modes of expression include absolute freedom, deathless calm, the unborn, undecaying, unaging, undying, and the truth that is beyond duality. In Mahāyāna Buddhist thought, emptiness (*śūnyatā*) is defined by the philosopher Nāgārjuna as empty. When an aspirant sees all things as empty that person's prior erroneous viewpoint is overcome and he/she can see things and events as they truly are, which implies seeing them as devoid of any essence or permanence.

As defined by the Zen master Dōgen, Buddha-nature is impermanent because it is being-time, which suggests that a person experiences temporal existence. In other words, when a person experiences a phenomenon just as it is such a person overcomes the perception of a thing in terms of a sequence of past-present-future. Since every moment contains all of reality and is complete in itself for Dōgen, a person **experiences** things in the right-now (*nikon*) of being-time.

Likewise, the mysterious Dao of Daoism is always in motion with being and non-being representing its phases or its movement. Being, which is equivalent to the named, refers to the function of the Dao, whereas non-being, which is equated with the nameless, represents its essence. Non-being of the Dao represents the beginning and end of all things, which means that it is the co-principle and repository of being, the identity of all opposites, and the ultimate aspect of the Dao within its pure motion. This motion moves from the Dao to non-being, evolves to being, reverts back to non-being and finally returns back to the Dao. In this scheme being and non-being give birth to each other in a never ending cycle, although non-being is prior to being and thus more powerful because non-being makes being function. If one takes the example of a wheel, it is the emptiness (non-being) of the hub that allows the spokes to unite and form a wheel.

Further reading: Dōgen (2007); Lao Tzu (1963); Śankara (1968)

REDUCTIONISM

Reductionism is of some importance for those methods used for coming to grips with various aspects of religion. More specifically, it is the rendering of data into a presupposed perspective. The tracing of the origin of religion in **animism**, the evolution of religion from **magic**, the reduction of religion to feelings, the attribution of religion to mass neurosis, and the reduction of religion to the distinction between the **sacred** and profane are some random examples of reductionism. The major methodological problem with reductionism is that it injects uncritical presuppositions, biases, and unexamined judgments on religious phenomena, and it is used to reduce religion to a sociological, **psychological**, or **economic** phenomenon that destroy its complexity, resulting in an incomplete perspective on the subject. Those scholars accused of reductionism often insist on the necessity of an anti-reductionism standpoint. There are other scholars that argue that all methods are to some degree reductionistic, and presuppose the limited standpoint of the scholar. These critics claim that to argue for the irreducibility of religious phenomena is to engage in reductionism.

Further reading: Baird (1971); Fenton (1970); Segal (1983)

RELICS

The English language derivation of the term comes from the Latin *relinqueure* ("to leave behind"). There are two Sanskrit terms that have a different connotation than the English term: *śarīra* (**body**, bodily structure) and *dhātu* (constituent part, ingredient, element, primordial matter). Christian relics that have consisted of bodily parts or items associated with a **holy person** have enjoyed popularity from ancient times to the present. The Christian veneration of relics is closely associated and influenced by the **cult** of **martyrs**. The influence exerted by the Christian cult of relics changes notions of who is and who is not **dead**. In fact, martyrs, witnesses to their faith, are not dead because they continued to live in their relics. The Christian cult of relics in Europe manifests political and **economic** significance for rulers and towns because it legitimates rulers who protect the relics, and it provides economic benefits for towns in which relics are located when pilgrims journey to visit the various sites. The **saint** or martyr may be dead, but their relics are alive and **powerful** with the ability to perform miracles. The relics of many saints and martyrs are housed under altars, a custom that proliferates between the fifth and ninth centuries for both symbolic and practical reasons. The multiple altars symbolize the presence of saints because of the relics that they house, and create a symbolic **community** of saints. Moreover, the multiple altars enable the practical simultaneous celebration of many masses.

Besides Christianity, Buddhism is another religious tradition in which relics play a significant role in any of their three types: body relics (hair, nails, teeth, or bones); contact relics (bowls, robes, robe fibers, or bodhi trees); dharma relics (whole texts, or a dharma verse). Buddhist relics embody the qualities of the historical Buddha, are considered alive, own property, and perform miracles. Although relics are not precisely the Buddha, they render him present. In addition, relics are expressions and extensions of the Buddha's biography by telling a narrative and embody the whole of the Buddha's coming and going in a threefold sequence: his descent from heaven to earth to be born, his decision to preach, and the collection of his relics, which is the third coming into the world. This scenario suggests that the Buddha's relics are spreaders and continuators of his presence, and serve as a historically effective means for spreading Buddhism to those countries where it is not known. The biographical aspects of the Buddha's relics are episodic in nature by recalling particular events in his life. By also referring to the process of achieving enlightenment, the relics recall for devotees the entire biography of the Buddha.

The Buddha's relics and those of Buddhist saints embody and objectify charisma, and this occurs in three ways: the importance of lineage as, for instance, with the bodhi tree; the **performance** of miracles; and an esoteric strategy of charisma that revolves around keeping the relics hidden.

In the final way, the *stūpa* (memorial mound) assumes the charismatic focus. By journeying to a *stūpa* or temple that holds a relic, a devote Buddhist can receive *darśan* (seeing) of the relic and the consequent merit that accompanies such an act. In addition to power, relics are performative acts that possesses **political** (e.g. legitimate kingship, guarantee law and order, justify war, enhance peace, and promote rain), social (affirm existing social structure), and **economic** (attract pilgrims and created merit for devotees) consequences.

Further reading: Brown (1981); Strong (2004)

REVELATION

This concept, derived from the Latin *revelare* (to unveil), suggests the unveiling of something secret or hidden and its communication to others, such things as truths that would otherwise remain hidden. It is possible to make a distinction between natural and general revelations. The former refers to **truths** within the natural order that can, for instance, be discerned by reason and empirical observation, whereas general revelation tends to refer to a supernatural revelation derived, for instance, from a divine being, which often assumes the form of a **God** using **language** to communicate. The concept of revelation can be discovered cross-culturally.

The Torah (Law) of Judaism, the Gospels and other texts of Christianity, and the Qur'an of Islam are considered texts based on divine revelation. The process of revelation in Islam is called *wahy* in Arabic; it embodies the connotation of verbal inspiration through the mind or heart in the Qur'an (25.193–195), representing the eternal word of God. Orthodox Muslims believe that it is based on a heavenly book that is preserved in the presence of God, and it is called the "Mother of the Book" (43.1–4). The aim of the Qur'anic revelation is intended to function as a warning to hearers, and what is revealed is the order (*amr*) or command of God. The command is revealed in Arabic, a believed divine language, to facilitate understanding by humans. The preferred way for a person to receive the message is to memorize it, a practice that keeps the revelation alive in that person's mind.

The Muslim and Jewish conception of revelation shares three features: God's oral communication with a chosen messenger (Muhammad or Moses); the public proclamation of the message by the prophet; the oral preservation of the message and finally its being written down for the benefit of future generations. The revelation from God most often assumes an oral form, although the law is written in stone in the case of

Moses. Those not directly receiving the revelation frequently ask for something to authenticate it, which often takes the form of a miracle. Moses is able to perform miraculous deeds that slowly convince people, but Muhammad asserts that his only miracle is the Qur'an and challenges his listeners to produce another such text (2.23; 10.38).

The ancient Indian religious tradition holds the Vedas to be revealed (*śruti*). Some Vedic seers attach their names to poems, but this is not indicative of a claim of authorship because it is merely an acknowledgement of the identity of the person who receives the revelation. Needless to say, the divinely revealed origin of the Vedas gives this literature an unquestionable authenticity and authority over other bodies of literature that historically follow it.

Further reading: Olson (2007); Peters (2003)

RITES OF PASSAGE

These rites mark important periods of human life that are considered dangerous, such as birth, initiation, marriage, and **death**. The rites are performed to ensure safe passage from one mode of life to another. Rites of passage manifest a threefold pattern: separation (preliminal), transition (liminal), and incorporation (postliminal).

Rites of separation involve being separated from one's former condition, such as parents or **society**. During birth rites, separation is marked by cutting the umbilical cord along with other features, such as one's first hair cut, shaving of the head, or donning clothes for the first time. In some religious **cultures**, a pregnant woman is isolated. During the initiation ceremony of the Bambara of Mali, young boys wear white gowns, and they are led out of the village single file to the initiation grove, a journey toward the West, direction of the setting **sun**, and symbolic death. A more dramatic scenario is enacted by the Murring of Australia with women sitting on the ground with their young boys, who are covered with a blanket in front of their mothers. Running men approach the women and boys, suddenly seize the boys, and run off with them.

Transition rites represent the movement from one position to another, such as from infancy to childhood, from adolescence to adulthood, from unmarried to married, or from alive to dead. During initiation rites, the young person's personal and social status are totally changed and he/she becomes a person with **knowledge**, equality, and responsibility. Transition rites include segregation, initiatory ordeals, symbolic death, instruction, and regeneration. While segregated apart from society in the bush or forest, the ordeals refer to bodily operations performed on the novices. Among Native American Indians, Tewa Pueblo and Hopi novices are whipped by a masked man impersonating a **god**, an act that signifies the symbolic death of the novices, whereas the Bambara of Mali whip the novices with thorn branches and flail them with burning torches. The boys symbolically regress to an infant stage as a prelude to being reborn. Among the Dogon of Africa, initiation involves circumcision because the prepuce of the novice's penis represents his female **soul,** which must depart in order to free the novice from the element of femininity. The Mukanda rite of the Dinka people of Africa is also a rite of circumcision and is an absolute necessity because without the circumcision the dirt beneath the foreskin is a permanent source of **pollution** and a boy is considered lacking whiteness or purity. Among the Dinka, circumcision is a symbolic death that reveals the hidden manhood of the novice.

There is a direct association between the transition stage and **liminality**, which is a time of withdrawal from normal modes of social action. Liminality represents a threshold, a place and moment in and out of time. Therefore, an initiate is between one state and another or on the periphery of normal life because he/she is a liminal being. The liminal novice, who is ambiguous and paradoxical, eludes normal classification because they have no possessions or status.

Rites of incorporation refer to a return and adoption into one's society. The Bambara of Mali lead the newly initiated through a hole in the **earth,** representing a burrow of a hyena that incarnates wisdom, toward the sunlight at the end. Among some societies, incorporation rites may include washing or **fire** that function to purify the initiate of his acquired **sacred power** and protect members of society.

Further reading: Eliade (1958); van Gennep (1960)

RITUAL

The concept originates with the Latin terms *ritus* and *ritualis* that are connected to the structure of a ceremony and the text that defines the structure. The concept is revived around the 1890s in conjunction with the quest for the origins of religion when it stands for repetitive and symbolic action. The revival of an interest in ritual coincides with the emergence of anthropology as a scholarly discipline within a cultural environment in which Protestants mistrust ritual.

The centrality of ritual for religion is argued by turn of the century scholars such as William Robertson Smith (1846–1894) and Edward B. Tylor (1832–1917). The former argues that **sacrifice** is fundamental because it focuses on the relationship between humans and their totems, whereas Tylor uses the **gift** model to comprehend ritual sacrifice, arguing that humans make offerings to **ancestors** in return for blessings.

Similar to Smith, the anthropologist James George Frazer (1854–1941) thinks that sacrifice is the primary ritual, functioning as the primary source of many forms of **culture**. Due to the social context of ritual, these scholars emphasize the central part that ritual plays in **society**, and they stress its social function. According to Frazer, ritual represents an enactment of the **death** and resurrection of a **god** or divine being, which is symbolically connected to fertility and human welfare. Joining with Frazer and others to form the so-called Myth and Ritual School, Jane Ellen Harrison argues that ritual is a source of **myth**, rendering myth a secondary position to ritual, which correlates to the actions narrated in myth. But in the wider view, rituals tend to die before myths, which often continue to exist after the extinction of a ritual. At a later date, the anthropologist Clyde Kluckhohn reacts to the claims of the Myth and Ritual School by stating that not all myths are connected to ritual because it is possible to discern a variety of relations between myth and ritual.

In France, the sociologist Emile Durkheim (1858–1917) connects rituals with rules of conduct governing human society, and he argues that ritual internalizes gods into a society. French sociologists Henri Hubert (1872–1927) and Marcel Mauss (1873–1950) attempt to isolate the structure of rites, whereas René Girard (b. 1923) stresses the way that rites, especially sacrifice, operate to control the flow of **violence** in a society. Instead of society destroying itself in an orgy of collective **violence**, members kill a designated scapegoat that functions to channel violence in a safe way and preserve society. In Germany, Walter Burkert (b. 1931) focuses on the anxiety and aggression associated with ritual activity.

According to the Dutch phenomenologist Gerardus van der Leeuw (d. 1950), a ritual is a drama and a game governed by rules with the intention of gaining control over the vicissitudes of life and to draw power from it. Sacrifice, for instance, preserves the cycle of **power** by strengthening the power of the **community** and binding its members firmly together into a more powerful group. The acquisition of power enables a person or group to dominate the world by utilizing the potency inherent with the natural powers. Thus it is ritual that enables religious people to develop power and exercise it. On the other hand, Mircea Eliade (d. 1986), a historian of religions, discusses ritual in terms of its ability to symbolically repeat paradigmatic actions of the gods embodied in myths, and this repetitive action gives their actions meaning. Ritual also helps to relate the **sacred narrative**. In sharp contrast to Eliade, Jonathan Z. Smith, another historian, emphasizes the importance of context, which often assumes a dramatization about how life should ideally be and not what it is in fact. By periodically reaffirming the existing cosmic and social order, ritual keeps **chaos** from overwhelming the cosmos by creating wide patterns of order and meaning.

The anthropologist Victor Turner (1920–1983) breaks new theoretical ground with a theory of ritual by viewing it as a social process with a dramatic structure. Turner seeks to stress the dynamic aspect of ritual by focusing on its process. Ritual represents five aspects of a dramatic **performance**: playing of roles, use of a rhetorical style of speech, an audience, knowledge and acceptance of a single set of rules, and a climax. Rituals are also social dramas of either harmonic or disharmonic process. These dramas arise in conflict situations, and they adhere to a pattern of conflict: breach, crisis, redressive action, and reintegration. During the conflict, social contradictions are masked from view. The ritual drama provides a symbolic unification which temporarily bridges factionalism and schismatic rifts in a society. Ritual is thus a symbolic layer on real social processes. Turner also identifies a fourfold structure of ritual: symbolic, value, telic (purpose), and role. The symbolic structure of ritual means that it is an aggregation of **symbols**. Value stands for information expressed in actions and gestures that are regarded as authoritative, valid, and axiomatic. The telic structure underlies the observable structure, with each phase containing an explicitly stated aim, such as getting rid of evil or to benefit the people with abundant crops or health. The role structure refers to the interaction between human actors.

In a provocative essay, the Indologist Frits Staal claims, after investigating an ancient Hindu sacrifice, that rituals are meaningless. Devoid of any aim, function, or goal, rituals are pure activity and orthopraxis. He phylogenetically asserts that human rituals are often modeled on ritualized animal behavior. Ritual, a pure activity for Staal, constitutes its own aim, and thus its essence is meaninglessness.

Instead of a lack of meaning, the anthropologist Roy Rappaport stresses the non-instrumental aspect of ritual, which suggests that it operates to regulate the relationship between people and their natural resources, resulting in the maintenance of an environmental balance. Although ritual is a social process, it also represents a connection to a cultural ecosystem and a formality discovered in all human behavior. By means of its formal features, ritual can communicate its meaning instead of relying on its symbolic or expressive aspects. Rappaport calls attention to five features of ritual: (1) encoding by others than performers, which means that performers do not determine all acts and utterances because they have already been established; (2) formality, which suggests adherence to form in the sense of punctilious and repetitive behavior within a specific context; (3) invariance means that there is no ritual without some variation and choice about participation; (4) performance; and (5) formality versus physical efficacy. The formal element refers to ritual decorousness, punctiliousness, conformity, repetitiveness, regularity, and stylization.

Ritual includes a wide variety of physical actions, styles, and cognitive sensibilities for more recent scholars. The ritual specialist Ronald Grimes catalogs many ritual components that includes action (e.g. movement, **dance**, **performance**, mime, **music**, rhythm, gesture, and **play**), **time** (e.g. season, holiday, or repetition), objects (e.g. masks, customs, icons, and **art**), **symbol** and **metaphor**, divine beings (e.g. **gods**, **goddesses**, **demons**, and **ancestors**), and **language** (e.g. sound, song, poetry, story, and **myth**). Types of ritual can be classified into the following: **rites of passage**; **festivals**; **pilgrimage**; **purification**; exchange; **sacrifice**; **worship**; **magic**; **healing**; interaction rites; meditation rites; rites of inversion; and ritual drama. Catherine Bell offers a pragmatic approach to categories of ritual with her six open-ended types: calendrical rites; rites of passage; rites of exchange and communion; rites of affliction; fasting, feasting, and **festivals**; and political rites. Rites of affliction seek to mitigate, for instance, spirits believed to be harming humans by healing, exorcizing, protecting, or purifying people to alleviate their suffering.

Bell calls attention to linguistic **performance**, which focuses on the action of the **body**. If all action is strategic and situational, ritual action construes its situation in terms of overt submission to the authority of transcendent modes of **power** and the humans accepted as spokespersons for such power. Strategy is associated with deft bodily moments, marking off space and time, and acts of kneeling or procession. It is the human body that initially defines ritual **space** and **time**, and thereafter dramatically reacts to it. Hence ritual does not control a person, but it rather constitutes a specific dynamic of social empowerment.

Somewhat akin to Bell, Stanley Tambiah, an anthropologist, takes a performative approach to ritual by arguing that rituals accomplish or perform something. As a symbol of communication, ritual causes a transformation of its participants. Ritual is a culturally constructed system, according to Tambiah, that represents a symbolic communication, which consists of a patterned and ordered sequence of words and activity whose context and arrangements are characterized by formality, rigidity, fusion, and repetition. Rituals are performances in three fundamental senses: (1) saying something is doing something; (2) a staged performance that uses multiple media; and (3) indexical values being attached to and inferred by actors during the performances.

Most of the theorists would agree that ritual is a way of communicating with the divine for the purpose of changing or maintaining, assuming that it is a positive condition, the human situation. Ritual actions accomplish practical things, such as curing illness, increasing fertility, defeating enemies, changing one's social status, removing impurity, or revealing the future. Ritual also informs us why a particular group communicates with the divine beings, settles moral conflicts, manipulates sacred power, and controls and renews the flow of **time**. Ritual accomplishes these things often periodically at, for instance, the start of the agricultural cycle, marking the end of the harvest, or the formation of a community. The Bladder festival of the Alaskan Eskimo attempts to repair relationships between hunter and game owners for the next hunting season. Inflated, painted bladders, which symbolize the souls of all birds and animals slain during the year, are returned to their spiritual homes by either being placed on a fire or in a hole in the ice. In contrast, the Ihamba rite of the Ndembu of Africa is intended to cure illness caused by neglecting a deceased relative, who punishes the victim by inflicting him/her with an invisible tooth under the skin. The ritual consists of washing the body of the victim with medicines and using cupping horns to suck out the tooth of the dead person.

Further reading: Bataille (1962); Bell (1992, 1997); Gill (1982); Girard (1989); Grimes (1990); Humphrey and Laidlaw (1994); Rappaport (1999); Staal (1989); Tambiah (1990); Turner (1967, 1968, 1969)

SACRAMENTS

The word sacraments comes from the Greek *mysterion* that is translated into Latin as the term *sacramentum*. Although it is thus a Western notion, it is possible to find a rough equivalent in Hinduism. Within the Christian context, sacraments are considered visible forms of invisible **grace** by Augustine, Bishop of Hippo in the fourth century. Although there is historically some disagreement about the precise number of sacraments, their number is fixed at seven by the time of Peter Lombard in the twelfth century: baptism, Eucharist, confirmation, penance, extreme unction, ordination, and marriage. In theory, these sacraments are grounded in actions by Jesus in the New Testament.

According to Roman Catholic sacramental theology, the sacraments operate and confer grace *ex opera operato*, which means by the work performed or by force of the action itself. In short, the sacraments are effective because of divine **power**. This implies that the effect of the sacraments is not dependent upon the worth of either the minister or recipient. The recipient must, however, be receptive in the sense of *non ponentibus obicem* (in the case of those who place no impediment). This formula means that the recipient must not place an obstacle arising from free will, such as a lack of **faith**, in the way of the operation of the sacrament. This type of obstacle would block the reception of grace. Sacraments are remedies for an individual's weakened intellect and will, which might be tainted by **sin**, and they are thus remedies for weakness caused by sin. The administrator of the sacraments must intend what the **church** does by its giving of the sacraments and what the rite means. Otherwise, the sacraments are invalid. Moreover, in principle, the validity of the sacrament does not depend upon the faith or moral character of the minister.

Sacraments have character, a distinctive mark, which implies a certain likeness to **God** and especially to Christ. This distinctive mark distinguishes between believers and unbelievers. In this sense, sacraments consecrate a person to God. This is especially true of baptism, confirmation, and ordination because these unique sacraments cannot be repeated.

The rite of baptism in the ancient church is full of symbolism signifying such things as a return to paradise. In some baptistries, symbols of deer with serpents in their in mouths appear and this can be traced to an ancient belief that deer can eat snakes; the often octagonal shape of the baptistery is related to the number eight, a **symbol** of the resurrection, that an initiate enters upon baptism. Those to be baptized are stripped of their **clothing** before the actual rite; this signifies replacing the old person, a symbol of sinfulness and mortality, with the same nakedness of Christ on the cross and returning to innocence. The initiate is next anointed with oil, which is intended to **heal** the person and the **soul** and to strengthen the initiate for his/her struggles with **demons**. A triple immersion in the baptismal pool is a symbolic **purification** from **sin** and imitation of the burial of Jesus for three days and nights, rendering the waters of baptism a tomb in which the old person is buried. But the waters are not merely a tomb because they also enable one to be reborn. Immersion also signifies communication with the Holy Spirit. The initiate is finally clothed in a white garment, signifying the purity of the soul, incorruptibility of the **body**, and resurrection of the body. The white clothing also suggests a return to paradise and embodies an eschatological meaning (Rev. 3.5) that those who triumph over the Devil by **martyrdom** are clothed in white. Finally, the giving of the *sphragis*, marking of the sign of the cross on the forehead of the initiate, comes often after the conclusion of the formal rite. The *sphragis* is a seal used to impress a mark on wax, or it is used by an owner to mark one's possessions such as sheep. In fact, the Roman army marks

211

recruits on the hand or forearm with an abbreviation of the name of the general. Within the context of baptism, it signifies that the initiate belongs to Christ. It is not merely a sign of ownership by Christ because it is also a guarantee of the protection of the shepherd, which enables one to repel demons. Moreover, the sign of the cross imprints on the soul the image of God.

It is believed that after baptism something is still lacking, and it is identified with perfection which consists in the **gifts** of the Holy Spirit. Since the Holy Spirit is already given in baptism, a new outpouring of the spirit takes place with confirmation, which involves being anointed with perfumed oil and sharing in the anointing of Christ by the Holy Spirit after baptism. Confirmation represents the development of **faith** into **knowledge**. If one is an infant at baptism, when one is confirmed one becomes an adult member of the church. Confirmation can be grasped as a strengthening of one's spiritual life.

At the heart of the entire sacramental system of the Catholic Church is the Eucharist rite that consists of a threefold structure: a preparation called offertory, **sacrifice**, and distribution of the consecrated elements at the communion. The altar for the **sacrifice** symbolizes the body of Christ. After preparation of the offerings, there is the washing of the hands and kiss of peace. The former signifies that one should be pure of all sin, and the kiss is a sign of peace. The sacrifice is introduced by the priest saying *"Sursum corda,"* which means a person should stand in the presence of God with fear and trembling and that one is no longer on earth but is transported to **heaven.** After the priest consecrates the bread and wine, they become the body and **blood** of Christ. By eating the sacramental bread, a person becomes immortal. Overall, the mass is a sacramental representation of the sacrifice of Jesus on the cross and a sacramental participation in the heavenly liturgy.

Although it is not an exact translation of the English sacrament, the Sanskrit term is *saṃskāra*, a notion related to verbs meaning composing, making perfect, or preparing correctly. There are sixteen widely accepted rites, although some authorities have more, beginning with conception and ending with death. Each *saṃskāra* is a ritual action that transforms the person, and it removes defects from a person's body. For young children, parents often combine the rites for reasons of **economy** and convenience.

The primary sacraments today are initiation, marriage, and **death**. Details of the marriage ceremony differ, for instance, according to various religious authorities and they manifest regional differences as well. A highlight of the wedding occurs when the bride steps with her right foot on a millstone, a symbol of firmness, to the north of the sacred **fire.** This act is symbolic of the bride's devotion and fidelity to her husband. Since females are excluded from the normal initiation ceremony, marriage functions as their passage into adulthood.

Further reading: Davis (1991); Pandey (1969); Shurden (1999); White (1999)

SACRED

This concept possesses Latin roots with terms such as *sacer* (holy), *sacrare* (to devote), *sancire* (to make holy), and *hieros* (holy or sacred). In the early Jewish tradition, it signifies something that is set apart from other things. There are not necessarily precise equivalent terms in the language of other cultures, although there are similar concepts.

In his work on the sociology of religion entitled *The Elementary Forms of the Religious Life* (1912), Emile Durkheim (1858–1917) defines religion as the sacred, which is something completely set apart from its exact opposite the profane and eventually equated with society. A different line of conceptualization is evident in the studies of religious phenomena by Mircea Eliade (1907–1986), a historian of religions, who conceptualizes the sacred as something supernatural. Before defining the sacred further, Eliade begins by indicating that it is qualitatively different from the profane. Eliade continues to unravel the nature of the sacred by indicating that it is that which is strong, efficacious, durable, real, powerful, and wholly **other**. Moreover, the sacred is equivalent to a **power**, is saturated with being, and is equated with **reality**. According to Eliade, the sacred is dialectical because it represents a reality not of this world yet is manifested in things of this profane world, and possesses the power to transform a natural object into something else. If one considers a sacred object, it possesses this exalted status because its source is a superior force and it shares in the power of this source. Thus, every sacred object is based on a hierophany, a manifestation of the sacred, and every hierophany is a kratophany, a manifestation of power. Particular instances of the sacred and power are part of a total system. A religious person wants to be near the source of power, to participate in it, and to be immersed in it because proximity to the sacred sustains a person's existence and benefits the welfare of others. Once the sacred is established by revealing itself, it makes special orientation possible, which suggests that it establishes the world by fixing limits and establishing order. Nonetheless, the sacred is also ambivalent because it both possesses the ability to attract and also repel a person. It is thus useful and dangerous.

Examples of objects considered sacred in other cultures do not fully support Eliade's definition of the sacred. Among Native American Indians cultures, the pipe bundle is considered sacred by many tribes, such as the Blackfoot. A typical Blackfoot bundle contains numerous objects: a sacred pipe, skins of certain animals and birds, tobacco placed in bird skins, a rattle wrapped in the skin of a prairie dog. Many of these items are painted red. The bundle owes its existence to two sources: **vision experiences** of the original owner and similar experiences of successive owners. Opening the pipe bundle involves a **ritual** procedure and process of **purification** for the owner.

Among the Native American Crow, bundles are mostly associated with warfare and are believed to bring their owners success in battle and good fortune in life. Another sacred object among the Crow is their shields, which owe their origin to **dreams** or waking **visions**. These shields are considered powerful but are not taken into battle because they are too bulky and heavy. A part of the shield, such as a feather, or a miniature reproduction of the shield, tied to the hair or suspended around the neck of a warrior, can be taken into battle. Elements constituting the shield symbolically signify certain aspects of life, such as: a green border associated with summer; dark drown lines on the shield representing bullets or projectiles bouncing off of it; or feathers from the owl and eagle ñ two powerful birds – signifying the power of vision because the owl is believed to be able to see the future and an eagle is believed to fly the highest and thus able to view the entire earth. The entire shield represents the buffalo.

Among the Native American Sioux Indians, there is nothing more sacred than the sacred pipe, which is used on ceremonial occasions and handled with great care and respect. The bowl of the pipe symbolizes the **earth**, the carved buffalo calf represents all animals, while its feathers hanging from the stem signified the eagle and all winged creatures. Finally, the seven circles symbolically represent the seven rites of the Sioux. Thus, the sacred pipe embodies in a single object some of the fundamental values of the people.

In contrast to Native American Indians, classical Hindus uses a few terms that are generally equated with the sacred, such as *pavitra* (pure, clean), *divya* (holy), *śuddha* (clean, pure), although there is no precise equivalent of the English term. Hindus do not believe that anyone possesses ownership of the sacred, which is understood as ubiquitous and amorphous. Because it is so ill-defined, the sacred is best grasped within certain contexts in which it is encountered. Unlike Durkheim and Eliade's definition of the sacred, the Hindu conception does not include the distinctive separation of the sacred from the profane. Hindus conceive of the sacred and profane more as a continuum. A notion such as *pavitra* is closer in meaning to physical cleanliness and purity usually secured by ritual means and bathing. This also implies that sacredness is a condition that is temporary and needs to be retrieved continually.

Further reading: Caillois (1959); Durkheim (1915); Eliade (1959); Girard (1989); Harrod (1987)

SACRIFICE

Even though it is practiced around the globe by diverse religions from ancient times to the present, the name for this concept originates in the West. The term is derived from the Latin word *sacrificium* (*sacer* means holy and *facere* means to make), which suggests that it implies a consecration, transforming something previously profane into something **sacred**. To sacrifice means to kill or destroy an animal, object, grain, or vegetable product, although the centrality of killing is called into question by some scholars. Sacrifice is a personal act in the sense that a sacrificer gives his **self** or a part of himself. The Sun Dance of the Sioux, an indigenous Native American Indian society, is a perfect example of sacrificing oneself because the **dancer** gives pieces of his flesh, which symbolizes ignorance, to the spirits. In this scenario, the dancer gives parts of himself for the benefit of the people.

When a person performs a sacrifice, or is a patron of a sacrifice performed by **priests**, one is establishing communion between humans and divine beings, which establishes a two-way transaction with each party giving to the **other**. In cases of benefits already received, humans may offer a free-will thank offering in a spirit of gratitude. A sacrifice often regenerates a cycle of unending birth and **death**. When a cycle of **time** comes full circle and the cycle of time and the cosmos are waning, sacrifice sets it going again, a feature that is indicative of the circularity of form and intention in sacrifice.

In many cultures, sacrifice is closely intertwined with anxiety and aggression. Hunting and farming occupations are surrounded by anxiety because of the danger, for instance, of the **food** supply being depleted, danger of a hunter losing his life, scarcity of food can lead to competition, and the very existence of a **society** can be endangered. The aggression that is associated with hunting must be controlled; otherwise uncontrolled and undirected aggression along with anxiety can destroy a society. Sacrifice redirects aggression and anxiety onto a victim, and it thereby protects a society by ensuring that a society avoids becoming its own victim. Sacrifice operates to replenish the food supply with the assistance of supernatural beings, and thus guarantees the continual life of a society. By channeling aggression and anxiety, sacrifice does not allow them to reach dangerous levels because aggression is focused on the victim and anxiety is overcome with a successful outcome. Thus anxiety can be transformed by a sacrificer becoming anxious to give and not to lose something. Being anxious to give something, the sacrificer receives an adequate return on his generosity. By overcoming and transforming anxiety and aggression, the group is more closely united by their efforts, and this helps to prevent greediness associated with competition for sparse food supplies.

The sacrificial victim or scapegoat is the central actor and focal point of the sacrifice because it is around the victim that action occurs and to which it is directed. The victim is both innocent and guilty. Because the conflicts or problems are not its fault, the victim is innocent, whereas it is guilty because a victim is required to atone for those very conflicts and problems. For example, the Native American Skidi Pawnee performs a human sacrifice by capturing a girl from an enemy village, who is then **purified** with smoke, painted red, and dressed in black. After being lifted onto a scaffold and tied into position, her captor shoots her through the heart with a **sacred** arrow and bow, another participant strikes her on the head with a sacred war club, a priest cuts open her chest and smears his face with the victim's **blood**, a captor catches the falling blood on dried buffalo meat and corn seeds, and finally all male members of the society shoot arrows into victim's body. The innocent female victim carries away the **pollution** of the **community**, and her blood ensures fertile crops and abundant buffalo. The Pawnee victim mediates between the human and divine worlds, and she links them together. This scenario suggests that the divine becomes subject to human control or coercion in order to receive necessary mundane benefits for survival.

Cross-cultural incidents of sacrifice tend to conform to a threefold structure: consecration, invocation–immolation, and communion–purification. The first phase involves making **sacred** the location of the sacrifice, its time, the victim, and all participants. Among the Native American Sioux a sweat lodge is used to purify and revivify persons in a formal rite, Inipi. The darkness of the interior of the lodge after the door is closed is symbolic of a return to the womb where participants will be reborn. While participants are seated in the tent, water is sprinkled over the hot stones causing steam to raise, heat the interior of the tent, and purify the participants.

The invocation–immolation phase suggests that the sacrificer speaks to **god**, and he states the intention of the sacrifice. Immolation is the actual killing of the victim by cutting its throat, cutting its chest open, decapitation, or suffocating it as in the ancient Vedic cult of India. Within the context of the Ogun sacrifice of the Yoruba of Africa, the invocation involves splitting apart kola nuts and casting them before the god's shrine to ascertain his will, whereas the immolation entails cracking open a snail's shell and pouring its contents onto the god's stone. Then, a pigeon's head is wrung off and a priest drips its blood on the stone. Finally, a dog is beheaded and its blood is sprinkled on the stone.

The communion–purification phase begins with the sharing of the victim's flesh, which confirms the spiritual bond between the sacrificer and divine being. Communion also reinforces the moral and social bonds of the participants. A final purification of the participants enables them to return safely to society and normal social interaction. This final act presupposes that the participants have become dangerous to other social members because they have been in a sacred condition, performing sacred acts, and in direct communion with supernatural beings, which means that ordinary citizens are at risk from the **power** inherent in the acquired sacredness. Thus, this final purification protects the non-sacrificial members of society. Among the Yoruba, communion involves sharing the consecrated flesh of the dog, which renews the bonds of unity among participants and reinforces god's relation to the group.

Further reading: Burkert (1983); Detienne and Vernant (1989); Girard (1989); Hubert and Mauss (1964); Widengren (1969)

SAINT

This concept can be traced to an ancient Greek term *hagios* and the later Latin term *sanctus* that are both originally used to mean a **holy person**. Greeks and Romans use these terms broadly to refer to emperors, **gods**, and deceased relatives. Later Christians use the terms in the plural to refer to the faithful on **earth**, those in **heaven, martyrs**, monks, and clergy. Developing the technical meaning of the term, the Latin **church** offers three general definitions (identified respectively as moral, theological, and liturgical): a person who leads or has led a life of heroic virtue, a person who goes to heaven (regardless whether or not this fact is recognized), or a person who by virtue of the church's **judgment** resides in heaven and is canonized, making that person a legitimate object of **worship**.

During the Patristic period of Christianity (*c.* 200–500 CE), the popular veneration of saints begins in the West with St. Polycarp of the second century recognized as an early saint because of his **martyrdom**. Those individuals who suffer but do not die for their **faith** are called confessors. Beginning in the sixth century, diptychs (lists of names) of martyrs and confessors find a place in the liturgy of the Latin church, and the lives of saints are retold during matins from the eight century. By the late twelfth century, the Pope begins to exercise control over sainthood by claiming sole authority over it instead of the previous popular acclamation of a person made by ordinary people. Christian saints manifest contemplation on the presence of God, a life of **asceticism**, which possesses a purgative affect by ridding a person of vices and passions, and action such as helping others. The candidate for sainthood is expected to endure suffering and pain, often self-inflicted, that can take the form of wearing hair-shirts or by self-flagellation. The various features constituting a saint are determined by whether or not they imitate the life of Christ.

The other major monotheist religions are suspicious of saints. In Judaism, the saint is incompatible with the Jewish emphasize on the people. The Muslim Qur'an does not refer to the holiness of persons but only of God. A term that later refers to a saint (*walī*) in the Islamic tradition means friend, patron, benefactor, protector, or helper in the Qur'an. From the Islamic perspective, a **prophet** is superior to the saint because he is bearer of a special message from God to humankind, is sinless, and performs different types of miracles. The miracles performed by a prophet are called *mu'jizāt* and confirm his mission, and those performed by a saint are called *karāmāt* or **gifts** of **grace**. It is believed that God selects those to become saints. In Muslim history, saintliness and Sufism, Islamic **mysticism**, are closely related, and the shrines of such saints are locations of **pilgrimage**.

From the perspective of ordinary people, the saint is a wholly **other** person unlike others. The saint also gives the impression of existing on a different plane of **reality**. Traditionally, saints have inspired admiration and veneration more than imitation. Within the Christian and Islamic traditions, saints function as patrons, protectors, wonder-workers, and intercessors with God. Moreover, the relics of saints in Christianity and Islam are associated with **healing**.

The lives of saints are preserved in literature called hagiography, which functions to preserve the memory of the sacred figure. In the Christian context, these stories are considered most effective if they imitate the life of Christ. This suggests that hagiographers borrow from a common cultural source of religious motifs and patterns to construct their tales. By using historical, mythical, and legendary elements in the construction of their **narratives**, hagiographers create "mythohistorical" products that are invitations for others to imitate and/or revere the depicted subject. These sacred narratives can be found cross-culturally, although their different context does not free them from becoming stereotypical descriptions of sacred persons. It is thus difficult to discern a chronological account of a subject's life because the subject's virtues and religious achievements tend to be emphasized by the composer. What a reader receives is an ideal portrait of a subject bereft of personal faults and weaknesses. Rather than a complete and objective portrait, the composer stresses the sanctity of the subject. Because hagiographies are embellished, pious narratives, it is impossible for a reader to grasp their accuracy and truthfulness, although the stories are realistic in order for readers to feel comfortable with them and to be able to relate them to their current world.

Hagiography provides a paradigm for a particular type of religious figure. These narratives also function didactically in the sense of precisely demonstrating ideal models for religious life within a particular tradition, employing cosmologies and teachings already accepted by followers. Hagiographical literature combines paradigmatic thinking that provides a system of categories and concepts with narrative thinking that depicts experience by locating it in particular times and places. These two types of thinking complement each other because paradigmatic thinking produces a whole system, while narrative thinking generates particular stories. Within a particular hagiography, paradigmatic and narrative thinking reinforce and legitimate each other.

Upagupta and Śāriputra are two Buddhist monks who exemplify Buddhist virtues and **truths**. Śāriputra, who is considered second in stature and authority to the Buddha during their lives together, is depicted as a paragon of humility, compassion, wisdom and patience. He is also remembered and depicted as an expert in the more philosophical Abhidharma literature. Upagupta, a very handsome man, is depicted as an accomplished monk able to resist the entreaties of the most beautiful harlot in the area. After she is severely punished with disfigurement for the murder of a lover, Upagupta demonstrates his compassion by teaching her the Buddhist **doctrine**.

The term hagiography is criticized by some scholars because the stories are glowing, mixed with **mythical** and legendary elements, and contain uncritical descriptions of a person without much trustworthy historical content. These scholars want to replace the term with "**sacred biography**" in order to escape the negative associations characteristic of hagiography. Other scholars want to retain hagiography for **narratives** about saints, mystics, **prophets**, and other charismatic figures, while saving sacred biography for stories initiated by followers or devotees of a religious founder.

Further reading: Brown (1981); Cunningham (1980); Heffernan (1988); Reynolds and Capps (1976); Schimmel (1985); Weinstein and Bell (1982)

SALVATION

The concept is rooted in the Latin term *salus* (sound, safe). This ubiquitous religious concept presupposes two things: being saved from some
situation on earth and a process by which this can happen. Various religions offer different answers, and some traditions provide multiple
responses, although salvation can be viewed as the goal of most religions.
Depending on the religion, the problematic nature of the human situation
that hinders the achievement of salvation is traced to such conditions as
sin, disobedience to **God's** commandments, failure to follow the **laws** of
God by ignoring them, ignorance, desire, rebirth, and **suffering**.

Jews are part of a **covenant**, for instance, initiated by God, who
will save the faithful at the end of time. Christians are born into original sin from which they will be saved by **faith**. Muslims have been
given a straight path by Allah, and those chosen by God will be saved
at the conclusion of history. Buddhists can follow a path of ethical
behavior, **asceticism**, and **meditation** to reach nirvāṇa that is free of
rebirth and suffering. If one takes the text of the *Bhagavad Gītā* as
representative of Hinduism, this work provides three paths to salvation: **knowledge** (*jñāna yoga*), good works (*karma yoga*), and devotion (*bhakti yoga*). In general, devotional types of religion that require
faith usually promise salvation in some kind of paradise that is free of
pain and **suffering**.

Further reading: O'Flaherty (1980); van der Leeuw (1963)

SANCTIFICATION

This means to make holy (to be without a blemish). The source of sanctification in Judaism and Islam is **God**, who is defined as the most holy,
whereas Christianity locates the source of holiness with the Holy Spirit,
which is part of the Trinity. The term sanctification possesses strong
Western connotations associated with the preparation for reading the Torah
in Judaism, preparing for prayers in Islam, and becoming a **priest** in Latin
Christianity, but it also plays an important role in other cultures with, for
instance, Buddhist ordination. Sanctification is directly connected to the
concept of **purification** and removal of **sin** in many contexts.

Further reading: Rappaport (1999)

SCRIPTURE

This concept is derived from the Latin *scripto* ("I write") to refer to texts in various world religions. Many of these scriptures are preceded by an often long period of oral transmission before assuming a written form, and they are considered **sacred** by believers because the scriptures are revealed to humans by a divine being. This point is true of Judaism, Christianity, Islam, and ancient Vedic Hinduism. The believed divine origins of these scriptures give them authority over other forms of written works such as novels, diaries, or travelogues.

The scriptures of ancient Judaism consist of twenty-four separate books that are eventually called the Bible from the Greek term *biblia* (books). These discrete books recall the **narrative** concerning **God's** interaction with His chosen people. Within the context of this drama, the major themes of Jewish faith are contained, including the promise of the ancient patriarchs to be faithful to their deity, the divine deliverance of the people from Egypt, divine guidance while wandering in the wilderness, the bestowing of the **law** at Sinai to the **prophet** Moses, and the inheritance of the Promised Land. These events are often abbreviated to the "Exodus event," which depicts God's redemptive work for His people. Since God acts in history for His chosen people, history is meaningful and informs the Jewish people about what God did (past), what God is doing (present), and what God will do in the future, representing a unity of time.

Ancient Jews refer to their scripture as Tanakh, an acronym for its three major divisions: Torah (Law), Nevi'im (prophets), and Kituvim (hagiographia). The most authoritative division is the Torah, consisting of the Five Books of Moses or the Pentateuch: Genesis, Exodus, Leviticus, Numbers, and Deuteronomy. The Torah represents God's **gift** to the people of Israel. The gift is, however, conditioned upon the people's acceptance of, and obedience to, the divine commandments.

Once it is collected, edited, and written to preserve it, Christian scripture represents the "Good News" of Jesus, which is especially true of the so-called Synoptic Gospels (Mark, Luke, and Matthew). The historically earliest Christian writings are the letters of Paul that are preserved and gathered into a collection by the end of the first century, which are called "letters to the seven churches," because seven is a symbol of wholeness in the ancient world and in this context implies the entire **church**. Although Paul's letters are addressed to particular congregations and their problems, Paul's message that he claims comes directly from Jesus is intended for a wider audience within the hostile socio-cultural milieu of the Graeco-Roman world.

In contrast to Paul's letters, the Gospels are more narratives and interpretations of the life and teachings of Jesus. The authority of these texts is grounded in the words and deeds of Jesus, which are preserved by **memory** and transmitted orally before being composed by anonymous authors. During their formative period, the Gospels are considered historical testimonies, even though there are some striking differences between the texts; it is not until later that they are considered scripture. In addition to the Gospels and letters of Paul, what comes to be called the New Testament includes several other works such as the Acts of the Apostles, the letters of Peter, James, and Jude, and the Book of Revelation.

When he reaches forty years of age Muhammad begins to have strange **experiences** in **visions, dreams**, and a feeling that words are written on his heart. When he receives his first **revelation** (96.1–5), Muhammad is commanded to speak by a heavenly messenger. This message and others are preserved on any available material. The early messages concern the power and mercy of **God**, the coming final Day of **Judgment**, the need for humans to respond to God with fear, gratitude, and **worship**, and his vocation as a **prophet** of God. These various messages from God over a period of years represent the eternal word of God that eventually assumes the written book form of the Qur'an. From an orthodox Muslim perspective, the prophet Muhammad is not the author of the uncreated word; he is merely its recipient. Muhammad's illiterate status (7.157–158) testifies to his inability to compose the text. Muslim tradition testifies to others writing the words of the revelation after being recited by the prophet after he receives them from the angel Gabriel. Because many reciters of the revelation are killed at the battle of Yamanah, not long after the death of the prophet, the second caliph, Umar ibn al-Khattab, arranges to have the revelation collected and written down to preserve it. The divine origin of the Qur'an guarantees its status as a sacred scripture.

Within the cultural context of ancient India, the Vedas are conceived as revealed scriptures, whereas other scriptures are considered traditionally remembered literature (*smti*) and include such works as the Dharma Sūtras (approximate dates of composition 600–200 BC), the epic *Mahābhārata* (dates to between 300 BC–AD 300), the epic *Rāmāyaṇa* (composed between 200 BC–AD 200), and the vast body of Purāṇas, which begin to be composed around AD 400. The Vedas consist of four collections: Rig, Sāma, Yajur, and Atharva. Each of these four revealed collections is further divided into four sections: Samhita (*mantra* or sacred formula/utterance collection), Brāhmaṇa (theological and ritual commentaries), Āraṇyaka (forest or wilderness texts), and the Upaniṣads (speculative and secret philosophical texts). This revealed body of scripture is believed to have been revealed to ancient sages, who preserve them by memory, and pass on the hymns by means of oral transmission before being written. The divinely revealed origin of the Vedas gives them an unquestionable authenticity and authority similar to the major **monotheistic** tradition of Judaism, Christianity, and Islam, and gives them greater prestige over other bodies of scripture within India.

Siddhārtha Gautama (fifth century BCE), who becomes the historical Buddha (enlightened one), has an approximately forty-year teaching career, and his discourses on various subjects are preserved orally before being collected and retained in written form. After the death of the Buddha, the Council of Rājagṛha is established to determine the authentic teachings, and divides the Buddha's discourses into initially two baskets (*piṭakas*) called the *Sutta Piṭaka* (Basket of Discourses) and the *Vinaya Piṭaka* (Basket of Monastic Discipline) and later a third collection called the *Abhidhamma* (Basket of Higher Teachings). A senior monk, Kaśyapa supervises the council, and he utilizes the memory of a monk and close companion of the Buddha named Ānanda to recall the actual sermons. Scholars call into question this traditional account because internal evidence suggests a later date for the scriptures. Early Buddhist schools claim that the canon is closed, but the Mahāyāna schools argue for its openness and periodically add texts.

The early Buddhist tradition traces the origins of its scripture to the personal **experiences**, insights, and teaching of a historical person. Therefore, formative Buddhist scripture is not divinely revealed but becomes a sacred body of literature due to its origin in the authoritative utterances of the Buddha. Nonetheless, Buddhist scripture is not unique because what the historical Buddha discovers is merely a rediscovery of that of previous Buddhas. The Buddhist conception of scripture is grounded in its understanding of **language**, which is identified as an impermanent human creation. If language like everything else within the world is impermanent, it does not possess an enduring structure or metaphysical status. Lacking any intrinsic value, the words of scripture are only valuable in an instrumental way, which suggests that the value of the Buddha's discourses have value to the extent that they accomplish something, such as helping a person achieve enlightenment.

The five examples of scriptures from Eastern and Western religious traditions are all distinctive, but they do share something in common: the importance of performing their scripture. In other words, they shared a **performative** intention to make something happen by reciting the words in a public forum: the oral performance of Paul's letters in the early church, Hindu and Buddhist reciting of *mantras* (sacred formulas), and also the public performance of their scriptures by Jewish rabbis and Muslim mullahs and reciters. In addition, whether scriptures are divinely inspired or originate with a historical person as in the case of Buddhism, they are eventually accepted as authoritative by the respective traditions.

Further reading: Coburn (1984); Denny and Taylor (1985); Levering (1989); Smith (1993); van der Leeuw (1963); Widengren (1969)

SECTS

Sects are usually religious groups that create a separate identity from established institutions because of dissatisfaction with, alienation from, or criticism of a fixed group. This usually occurs when the established group is facing a crisis and the old order is collapsing. This scenario represents an attempt by the sect members to integrate itself into a new **community**. In contrast to being born into a **church**, a person voluntarily joins a sect in which there is often an emphasis on right behavior. The selective sect places intensity and commitment above universality for its members and tends to maintain uncompromising radical attitudes. Placing a high regard for charismatic authority and feeling of privilege due to membership in the truly saved or true group, it prefers isolation to compromise. In comparison to a church, a sect is not only usually smaller, less stable, and more exclusive, but it also tends to reject or qualify the prevailing values of a church or the larger **society**.

Historically, sects have been transient, and they often evolve into denominations in the West with a more enduring structure and organization. They have also been world-affirming or world-denying. A latter example would be the Branch Dravidians lead by David Koresh, which derive from Seventh Day Adventists influence and end in tragedy at their center in Waco, Texas, whereas the former attitude is exemplified by the Rādhāsoāmī Satsang founded in 1861 in North India with branches around the world today and belief that one can be saved by the Satguru (primal teacher).

Further reading: Wach (1944); Yinger (1970)

SECULARIZATION

A concept that can be traced back to the Latin term *saeculum* (world, century, age), suggesting a process that replaces religious **beliefs** and modes of behavior with worldly ways of thinking and behaving. During this process, the significance of religion is greatly reduced and replaced with other convictions. Secularization is both private and public in the sense that it alters one's way of understanding oneself, life in general, and one's **worldview**, and it affects how one conducts oneself in public.

In its ecclesiastical literature, the Western **church** distinguishes between members that are regular or secular, creating an opposition between them. The secular refers to worldly affairs that are outside the confines of the church, whereas regular designated members are subject to rules of the internal **monastic** order. Within the context of Protestantism, some sociologists, such as Max Weber and Bryan Wilson, agree that reformed Christianity embodies secularizing elements within its ethos because it promotes **rationalization** that necessarily leads to disenchantment of the religious world, and it encourages scientific explanations that lead to the questioning and undermining of religious justifications for the world. The sociologist Peter Berger adds that Protestantism divests itself of the concomitant elements of the **sacred** by rejecting mystery, miracle, and **magic**, and it polarizes a radically transcendent deity and fallen humankind. Moreover, Protestantism subverts mediators between **God** and humans, such as **sacraments**, intercession of **saints**, and miracles, which throws humans back upon their own coping devices.

In the modern world, there are many reasons for the process of secularization besides rationalization that disrupts **faith**. This process also includes industrialization, social differentiation, individualism, differentiation, societalization, diversity, relativism, pluralism, modernization, technology, and egalitarianism. These factors and others combine to undermine religion. Charles Taylor identifies, for instance, three meanings of secularity: (1) that understood in terms of public space that is emptied of God or any reference to ultimate reality, even though many people still believe in God; (2) the decline of religious beliefs and practice with people turning away from God and not attending services; (3) with its connection to the initial two senses of secularity, its final meaning consists of a situation in which belief in God is understood to be one option among many others. Intending to focus on lived **experience**, Taylor points to the loss of immediate certainty and the option of humanism with its localization of alternatives. Secularization is indicative of a disenchanted world because of the absence of God within a pattern of religious life that is characterized by destabilization and decomposition.

Industrialization takes a person from the home in order to perform impersonal tasks for which one is paid a wage that enables families to thrive economically, but it creates a wedge between family life and economic life outside of the home. Industrialization demands specialization of economic roles that results in the fragmentation of home life. Social differentiation grows in concert with economic growth of industrialization and specialization as socio-economic classes become more separate. Workers are often distinguished into white collar and blue collar types of employment. As a consequence of economic progress, mass education becomes a necessity for an expanding work force and new types of jobs, which contributes to the spread of literacy and more independent modes of thinking. This scenario makes people less willing to blindly accept **beliefs** and follow religious leaders.

The emphasis on individualism creates an autonomous status for the person and enhances the importance of the individual over the **community**, which along with social differentiation tends to subvert small communities. Individualization tends to make religion something private, a matter of choice, which lacks a binding quality and results in religion becoming public rhetoric and private virtue. Differentiation makes one aware that there are different peoples, **cultures**, and religions, which tends to reduce the plausibility for an all-encompassing religious system. Within a pluralistic context, a person recognizes that their religion is not unique, which gives rise to questions and doubts, makes one's allegiance to a religion voluntary, and encourages a person to chose among competing religions based on personal preference. Within particular religions, disagreements for a wide variety of reasons give rise to schisms and new **sects**, which increases the competing choices for a person. This pluralistic situation demands ecumenicity and the necessity to collaborate.

Societalization refers to the organization of life by the nation state, which replaces the role of religion in such an endeavor. This results with the larger **society** becoming the focus of the individual rather than the smaller religious community. If the nation state assumes the previous role of religion, it becomes the force that legitimates the world.

The diversity of religious cultures suggests relativism, which can result in a conviction that there is no single **truth**. With many religions espousing paths to **salvation**, the need for the transmission of **orthodoxy** is undermined. Diversity of, and relativism among, religions calls for tolerance to ensure social **harmony**, but it also subverts the certainty promised by religion. In America, religious freedom and diversity involve the separation of church and state.

Modernization and technology disrupt communal bonds, traditional employment patterns, and social status, and they give a person a sense of increased **power**. Their promise is so strong that they reduce the need for a person to turn to religion for answers to the problems of life. There is no need to depend on religion because contingency is reduced and certainty heightened by relying on modern technology. Personal **faith** is

226

placed on scientific technology to offer solutions, and divine intervention is limited to extraordinary occasions.

These various factors that contribute to secularization foster an egalitarian spirit that in some cases lead to the rejection of religion by some people, while others adapt the old values to certain circumstances thereby creating newer values. Those of a more intransigent demeanor refuse to change or alter their prior convictions. These types of people reaffirm the traditional beliefs and modes of life by turning inward, becoming more exclusive, and possibly embracing fundamentalism. The turn to terrorist tactics by Muslim extremists, for instance, represents an attempt to preserve an old way of life and reject secularization of their communities.

Further reading: Barker *et al.* (1993); Berger (1969); Crimmins (1989); Dobbelaere (1999); Smith (2003); C. Taylor 2007); Weber (1963); Wilson (1982)

SELF

In the West, the concept of the self suggests personal identity, uniqueness, a self-related and self-conscious being. In modern terms it also recognizes relationship with others and coming to recognize one's identity in a relational way. In Eastern cultures, the self is usually defined more impersonally and often in isolation from the **other**, or it is identified with the other. Even taking into consideration these fundamental cross-cultural distinctions, many paradigms of the self have been proposed by different thinkers.

The Danish thinker Søren Kierkegaard defines the self as a combination of **body**, **soul**, and **spirit**. The soul is the animating faculty that enables one to make choices defining who we are but the spirit is identified with the self. More precisely, a self is a relationship that is related to itself, but it is not the relationship itself, because it is rather the aspect of the relationship by which the relationship is related to itself. The self is a relationship because a person is a synthesis of infinite and finite, eternal and temporal, and freedom and necessity. As long as a person remains only a synthesis between two such antitheses, such a person is not yet a self, which implies that a third element is needed to place the two opposites in a relationship, This third element is the self that is related to itself. Kierkegaard argues that a person can be tricked out of selfhood by the crowd, which emerges out of de-personalization. It is the crowd that swallows up the single one, engenders moral corruption, and destroys one's relationship with **God**.

What defines the self for Kierkegaard are the choices that it makes and its relationship to God divorced from the crowd.

For the Jewish thinker Martin Buber, the self is defined in a triadic relationship between self, God, and **other**. Similar to Kierkegaard, Buber stresses achieving authentic being, which is possible when a person becomes an I through the Thou, which is characterized by mutuality, directness, presentness, intensity, and ineffability. The I of the primary I–Thou relationship, which stands in contrast to the potentially exploitive I–It relation, achieves its personhood by meeting with the Thou with the whole of one's being. The Thou can be another person, God, objects of nature, or animals. For Buber, real living takes place through encountering others and engaging in dialogue with them, although a real relationship to others is possible only in terms of a real relationship to God. The self is unique and personal for two basic reasons: its relation to others and its relation to God. Thus, this triadic relationship is grounded in history and **society**, which means that the self is personal, historical, and social by nature.

In contrast to Kierkegaard and Buber, the Buddha taught that there is no permanent self because we are captive to the cycle of causation, thus impermanence, and ignorant cravings that endlessly drive the cycle. The assumption that a person can satisfy their self or ego is a false notion that represents a fundamental misconception because there is no self or ego to satisfy. The Buddha refers to this teaching as the *anatta* (non-self) doctrine. What a person mistakenly assumes to be a self is actually a group of five aggregates that consists of matter, sensations, **perceptions**, impulses to action, and consciousness, which are in a constant state of flux and impermanence. In the *Milindapañha*, the monk Nāgasena compares the five aggregates to a chariot and its parts, which represent nothing substantial. When a person dies the five aggregates completely dissolve and leave no distinctive physical or mental identity that endures. Therefore, complete detachment from the five aggregates is essential for escaping the world of suffering and **pain**. Unenlightened people are prone to cling to the five aggregates that give them an illusion of a self and keep them caught in the cycle of death and rebirth.

Centuries after the death of the historical Buddha, Dōgen, a Zen Buddhist master, writes about the authentic and inauthentic self. The latter arises from the human tendency to superimpose the following onto **experience**: patterns of thinking, categories, and concepts. This is done in order to manipulate experience with the inauthentic conveying itself out to the experience and imposing meaning on it. The authentic self is the exact opposite because it results from things advancing to the self. The authentic self is concrete because it represents the immediacy of experience, whereas the inauthentic self is abstract because it arises from the self's **memory** of past concrete experiences. This implies the inauthentic self is a product of the mind's own self-image. The authentic self is liberated from clinging to life and fearing **death**. The inauthentic self fails to realize its own impermanent nature and ignorantly believes that it is a self. Dōgen states that the self is authenticated by enlightenment in a process in which one forgets the self. A person comes to recognize that the self is impermanent, a series of selves that come into momentary existence in the form of unified experience and successively perish as experience changes. An authentic self is equated with Buddha-nature, which means that the self is both permanent and impermanent and is authenticated by enlightenment, which does not mean that the self transcends the world. For Dōgen, the authentic self is dynamic and active, profoundly immersed in the worldly experience, and relational. It is the other in the sense that the self is experienced as encompassing the **other** as a self, which implies that the authentic self is not isolated and aloof from the world and the other.

A different conception of the self is evident in the Advaita Vedānta thinking of Śankara, who identifies the self as Ātman or *jīva*, corresponding respectively to higher or lower forms of **knowledge**. The Ātman is defined as self-luminous, timeless, not subject to birth and **death**, spaceless, a state of being, and finally unthinkable. The Ātman is non-different from Brahman, the highest **reality**, whereas the *jīva* is the individual existing in the world that in essence is one with the Ātman, but the *jīva* is limited by adjuncts such as ignorance, which implies that it is a mere reflection of the Ātman, just as the appearance of the **sun** in a pool of water is a mere reflection and nothing real. Śankara examines the nature of the *jīva* according to four states of consciousness: waking, **dream**, deep sleep, and transcendental. The Ātman represents the single consciousness in each of the four states of consciousness, constituting pure undifferentiated consciousness. From the perspective of the highest reality or Brahman, there is no separate entity called the *jīva*.

A reaction to Śankara's non-dualistic concept of the self is made by Rāmānuja in India with his qualified non-dualism. Rāmānuja agrees with Śankara that the essential nature of the Ātman is **knowledge**. They differ when Rāmānuja refuses to identity the self with pure consciousness, which is always qualified and possesses specific attributes. There is also an important relationship between the Ātman, matter, and God because they form a unity. This means that the Ātman and **body** are interdependent because the **body** is a mode of the Ātman and sustains it, whereas the Ātman is the ground of the body by animating, guiding, and supporting the body. The body and Ātman are modes of God, who animates and supports them. Since the Ātman and body (matter) constitute the body of God, they are teleologically orientated toward the realization of Brahman or God. Unlike the position of Śankara, there is no absolute identity between the self and God because Brahman is qualified by the matter and the Ātman that constitute its body.

From the perspective of **postmodernism** and arguably its most famous representative Jacques Derrida, the self is disappearing in Western thought. Previous conceptions of the self from Derrida's perspective conceive of the self as a presence. Using his deconstructive method on the statement "Here I am," Derrida thinks that the statement does two things: it effaces the present nature of any such exactly duplicate quotation, and it indicates that the self is not present as itself and cannot make itself present to itself. Moreover, Derrida connects the self to a trace, which represents the erasure of selfhood. Since the self is a genuine trace, there can be no presence of the self because a trace possesses the ability to inscribe itself as a difference between the breaches it creates in space. The dual powers of repetition and erasure make full presence impossible for the self. In addition, Derrida thinks that it does not really matter if one thinks that the self is different from God or whether the self is identical to God because the name of God is a mere trace, and it thus does not designate anything permanent. Derrida probably possesses more in common with the Buddha with his emphasis on impermanence than with the other thinkers cited on the problem of the self.

Further reading: Buber (1958); Derrida (1976, 1978); Kierkegaard (1980); Olson (2005, 2007)

SEXUALITY

If sex is determined by anatomical differences between men and **women**, the concept of sexuality is determined by **culture**. Various religious cultures attempt to define sexuality, control it, and channel its energy. In some instants, religions encourage sexual behavior, such as Judaism and Islam, while other religious cultures espouse a more ascetic lifestyle, such as Buddhism and Jainism. Christianity and Hinduism both encourage and discourage sexuality in certain contexts and for certain people.

Although Buddhism contains no systematic discourse on sex, there is, however, an element of general discourse on desire or **power**. Buddhists tend to focus on desire because it represents a basic problem with respect to achieving **liberation**. Desire is considered thus one of the three poisons (hatred, ignorance, and desire) that pollute and maintain the cycle of human existence and **suffering** associated with it. Desire is not limited to sexual desire because it encompasses all sensual desire. Carnal desires are commonly associated with hunger and thirst, whereas chastity, vegetarianism, and sobriety are forms of non-desire. What drives humans is desire during life and to rebirth after death. The Buddhist monk seeks to control desire by following **monastic** regulations and practicing the Eightfold Path prescribed by the founder.

By adhering to the path, a monk not only seeks to quell his desire, but he must also control his **body**, which is described as an impure entity, as with the following negative set of images: nine open sores leaking putrid stuff; a boil filling with overflowing pus; or an infected wound that never heals. In short the human body is foul, and the female body is even worse, being described as a razor coated with honey, a cave filled with snakes, or poisoned creepers. An emblematic aspect of female defilement is menstruation, whose cyclical nature reminds an individual of changes and decline. Texts continuously remind and warn monks about the dangers of female attraction, which undermines any chance of attaining **liberation**.

Since Buddhist texts are written by males and manifest a predominately male viewpoint, their discussion about sexuality focuses primarily on males. In conjunction with the Buddhist teachings about desire and the human **body**, heterosexual activity is strictly prohibited for monks, and it is reason for expulsion from the monastic order. Bestiality is actually less reprehensible than heterosexual relations, but it can still get a **monk** expelled from the order, as it does for the recorded tale of a monk who trains a monkey, which is only discovered when the monkey offers herself to other monks. Monastic texts also have a regulation against eunuchs because monks must be capable of performing sexually while also controlling their desire. In addition, trans-sexuality is not encouraged, but it is not condemned by monastic rules, even though it is judged weird and pitiful. A serious offense for monks is masturbation, which can lead to temporary exclusion from the order, although nocturnal emissions are not considered equivalent to masturbation. The intention to have a wet dream is an offense. Nuns are given detailed warnings about masturbation that includes not inserting any object into their vaginas.

In India, generally speaking, homosexuality is associated with decline and decadence, but it is widespread among the Chinese and Japanese. Japanese monks keep young boys, a practice called *nanshoku* (male love), which is an essentially age-structured rather than a gender-structured practice with older monks having relations with young boys. The Japanese make a distinction between active and passive with the latter designation reserved for women and young boys (*chigo*). The passive role does not carry any negative connotations, although the practice of homosexuality is generally condemned. Homosexuality is obscured by a secret language as, for instance, chrysanthemum (*kiku*), which is a metaphorical expression for anus and by extension male love. The Chinese use the term *jijian*, which literally means chicken lewdness. The term also conveys the meaning of sodomy because of a common belief that domesticated chickens act in this way.

In comparison to Buddhism, the major **monotheistic** faiths – Judaism, Christianity, and Islam – encourage sexual relationships within the confines of marriage. The early primary texts of these traditions have little to say about **homosexuality** or lesbianism. The story of Lot in the Hebrew Bible (Gen. 19) tells the subject's horror about the possibility of homosexuality; whereas the book of Leviticus makes it clear that sodomy is an abomination, although homosexuals do not violate Jewish law if they remain **celibate**. The orthodox Jewish attitude towards homosexuality is that it is unnatural. The Christian apostle Paul (Rom. 1.26) seems to assert that lesbianism is also unnatural. In the Qur'an (4.16; 7.81; 29.29; 7.72), there are some passages that apparently condemn same sex relationships. In the Islamic legal tradition, there is no ambiguity about same sex relations because they are strongly prohibited by legal scholars.

Judaism and Islam do not advocate the development of monastic orders, although mystical movements do develop in each religion that compromise the original allowance for sexual relations between a man and a woman to some degree. A strong monastic trend develops in Christianity that dictates the necessity for **celibacy**, which is traceable to the letters of Paul and his dualism between spirit and flesh. The general Christian attitude toward sex is that it is natural and necessary for the future social life of the **community**, but many writers urge moderation of sexual activity during marriage. From within the context of Christian marriage, the proper role of sexuality is not pleasure but rather the propagation of the species.

Further reading: Boswell (1980); Brooten (1996); Faure (1998, 2003a,b); Gulik (1961); Hollywood (2002); Kripal (2001); Urban (2006)

SHAMANISM

A shaman is a master of ecstatic trance states and can be either male or female, although most of them are men. Being able to enter into an ecstatic trance state allows the shaman to travel to or commune with spirits in order to cure the sick with the help of the **spirits**, or to find hidden things. A shaman receives **power** directly from the **gods** and spirits, acquiring his/her status through personal communication with the supernatural. A shaman's status is not determined by **knowledge of ritual**, but rather his/her authority is based upon personal charisma.

A shaman treats two types of illness: an intrusion into a patient's **body** of a spirit or an object, and **soul** loss. In the first type of case, the object that causes the disease is often transmitted by a spirit or an **evil** person, such as a sorcerer or witch. Even though there are no obvious changes in the patient's consciousness, the afflicted person **suffers** from external injuries or internal **pains**. In order to cure a patient, the shaman must remove the object, initially determining the object's location and its nature, and then extract it by sucking it out, blowing it away, or massaging it away. In cases of soul loss, the patient's soul may leave the body freely or by the force of evil spirits, who carry it away. Either type of scenario calls for the shaman to retrieve the loss soul, a condition that renders the afflicted delirious and unconsciousness, and return it to the body of the patient and restore that person to health. In order for the shaman to journey to the land of the dead to retrieve a patient's soul, he/she enters into an ecstatic trance state, and releases his/her soul from the body, which crosses over to the invisible world. Then, the shaman's objective is to establish contact with the patient's soul, to retrieve it, and to replace it into the body of the sufferer, which cures the patient.

There are three primary ways in which shamans are recruited: spontaneous vocation in the form of a call or election to the position, by hereditary transmission of the profession, and by personal quest. The last type is generally considered less powerful because the shaman is self-made. In central and northern Asia, once the shaman is recruited he/she must be initiated, a process that involves torture and violent dismemberment of the body, scraping away of flesh until reduced to a skeleton, and substitution of internal organs and renewal of his/her **blood**. After this initiatory procedure, the shaman descends to the underworld to be educated by the souls of former deceased shamans and **demons,** and then ascends to **heaven** to gain consecration from the divine powers.

Besides the ability to enter into ecstatic trance states, the shaman possesses the ability to see spirits and contact souls of the dead, which presupposes dying in order to encounter these souls. A shaman may also have helping guardian spirits, who are divine beings peculiar to the shaman and are unknown to the rest of the community. These guardian spirits often assume animal form, and only the shaman offers them **sacrifice**. It is possible for others to know that these animal spirits are present because the shaman imitates animal cries or behavior. In addition, the shaman possesses a secret **language** that often represents an animal language, which can be learned from a teacher or by means of the shaman's own efforts. Knowing such a language enables the shaman to know the secrets of **nature** and be able to prophesy. The shaman is also able to communicate with his drum and rattle, which assists in summoning helping spirits or frightens away evil spirits. Among the Iroquois of northeastern America, some shamans wear false faces as part of their costume.

A good example of the way a shaman operates is evident in the spirit lodge ceremony (*yuwipi*) among the Sioux of the northern plains of North America. Situated within a teepee, the shaman (called a medicine man among Native American Indians) is tied to the base of the lodge pole, while spirits enter through the smoke hole at the top of the teepee. When the spirits enter the teepee it begins to shake, a sign that they are present, whereas other phenomena also testify to their presence, such as light **visions**, voices, tapping sounds, articles being thrown around, and the **liberation** of the shaman from his bonds. In what is called the rope-binding trick, the shaman may disappear. It is common for the shaman to go into a trance while his soul leaves his body with the purpose of curing the patient.

Besides their ability to cure the sick, shamans assume other important roles in their religious cultures. They play a leading role in ceremonies and rites, serve as an authority on the **sacred** tradition of a tribe, insure **economic** success, play the role of a rain maker, attract animals for hunting using magical means, control winds, enhance female fertility, create war medicine, fight **evil** powers, or even paradoxically produce evil. In general, the shaman protects the **community**, and gives it assurance that at least one of its members can assist the community in a crisis, which helps the community to feel secure.

Further reading: Eliade (1964); Lewis (1971); Powers (1982); Winkelman (1992)

SIN

An inadvertent or willful transgression of a religious norm that is established by an authoritative figure, divine being, or established doctrine. In the major **monotheistic** religions of Judaism, Christianity, and Islam, sin is often defined as the purposeful disobedience of **God's** will. Pride, self-centeredness, and greed are also human conditions that contribute to sinful action in these religious traditions. The concept of sin is a Western notion, but, although in the East there is nothing approaching the Christian doctrine of original sin, the doctrine of karma approaches its meaning. In this an individual's **evil** deeds follow them like an unshakable shadow that determines in what condition they will be reborn.

In ancient Judaism, sin is traced back to the paradigmatic act of disobedience by Adam and Eve. Sins committed after the Abrahamic **covenant** are violations of a **sacred** contract. The Torah refers to such violations as *het* ("missing the mark") and later Rabbinic thought calls them *averah* ("crossing the line"). The book of Numbers (15) draws a distinction between unconscious and conscious sin, whereas later rabbis draw a distinction between grave and light offenses, which become the mortal and venial sins of later Christian theologians.

Christian thinkers also draw a distinction between original and actual sins. Humans are born with original sin, but actual sin refers to transgressive deeds, words, or thoughts, which call for atonement by suffering punishment, remorse, or penance. Actual sins are further subdivided into mortal or venial, a distinction that relates to degrees of human awareness, severity, and deliberateness. Actual sin is also divided into material and formal. The former type of actual sin is a wrongful act contrary to God's **law**, but the sinner is not culpable because the subject is unaware of the transgression, whereas a formal sin is a direct violation accompanied by awareness that it is a transgression.

From a **symbolic** perspective used by the philosopher Paul Ricoeur (1913–2005) in his book *The Symbolism of Evil*, sin is a symbolic defilement or stain that assumes two traits: it objectively infests and it subjectively inflicts dread upon a sinner. The consciousness of sin leads a person to an awareness of his/her guilt and motivates confession by the sinner. In summary, sin is not merely personal; it is also communal.

Further reading: Eichrodt (1961); Peters (2003); Ricoeur (1967); von Rad (1965)

SOCIETY

This dialectical phenomenon is a human product that also produces an individual, in the sense that an individual becomes a person through a social process acting upon its original producer. This dialectical process, according to the sociologist Peter Berger, operates in three stages: externalization (a physical and mental outpouring of the individual into the world); objectification (attained by products of the activity of externalization); internalization (transformation of objective social **reality** to subjectivity of individual).

The reciprocal relationship between humans and society is also evident in the relation between religion and society, in that the existence of social groups is often founded upon religious motivation with the development of religious concepts, rites, and institutions dependent upon the necessities, desires, and ideals of social groups. Therefore, religion and society tend to conserve and strengthen each other to such an extent that their goals and values often appear to be identical. Social groups interwoven by religious and natural bonds create a strong cohesive force. In concert with this cohesive effect, religion gives to society a sense of its own significance and self-identity.

Society teaches the individual how to come to grips with its **body**, **sexual** roles, and mental modes by serving as a model for proper behavior. Religion can also satisfy a social person's material needs, desires, and cognitive requirements by fulfilling a person's desire to know, understand, and find meaning. A **belief** in supernatural beings and performance of **ritual** can operate to alleviate desires for such essential things as rain, crops, victory in war, or healing. In addition to relieving such substantive desires, religion reduces expressive desires such as fear and anxiety by providing a minimum level of psychological security. Moreover, religion spurs a release of communal energy for coping with social problems. The creation and maintenance of means of coping with social problems, such as hunger, illness, or homelessness, provides a basis for social stability and integration.

If religion can act as a cohesive force within a particular society, it can also function as a disruptive, destructive, and disintegrating force. Wars sparked by religious motives around the globe have been sources of widespread suffering and senseless devastation. Even within particular social groups, religious motives cause disagreements, dissent, and divisions. A potential development is the creation of secret societies within the context of larger societies.

A secret society is an undeveloped form of religious organization that is not necessarily united by **blood**, age, or **gender** status. Members usually share a common religious **experience**, or they join seeking such an experience, although membership is usually by selection or election. Admission into the group often follows a period of instruction about the aim and purpose of the group and initiation symbolized by **death** and rebirth. Once a person becomes a full member of a secret society he/she takes a vow of silence concerning its teachings and **rituals**.

Illustrative examples of secret societies are the mystery **cults** of ancient Greece: Eleusinian, Orphic, Dionysian, and Mithraism, with the origin of such societies usually attributed to a mystical founder. Although they accord and even preserve the prevailing social structure, they tend to develop on the basis of popular dissatisfaction with the traditional modes of religious observance. The Greek mystery cults are voluntary associations rather than socially constituted groups. Their **doctrines** are esoteric, often direct their devotion to **ancestors**, and possess an experiential character that gives members a more direct contact with the divine. The cult of Mithras, for instance, symbolically expresses group fellowship by sharing a **sacrament** of bread and wine.

Further reading: Berger (1969); Bourdieu (1990); Rappaport (1999); Wach (1944); Weber (1930, 1963); Yinger (1970)

SOUL

Westerners owe the concept of the soul (*psyche*) to the ancient Greeks, where Plato sharply distinguishes it from the **body**. The soul is immortal and transmigrates to a new body when it perishes at **death**. A more ambiguous conception of the soul is evident among ancient Hebrews who do not sharply distinguish the body and soul. The Hebrews refer to three terms that provide something similar to a soul: spirit (*ru'ah*), animating breath (*nefesh*), and vitality (*neshāmah*), which early Christians transform into the Greek *psyche* (soul) and *pneuma* (spirit). In contrast, the Buddha teaches that there is no permanent soul that transmigrates from one life to another, as the Hindus believe in the ancient Upanishadic texts.

Many religions believe that an individual consists of multiple souls An example is the Yoruba of Africa with their belief in a life-breath given by god at one's birth, a shadow soul that leaves the body during sleep, and the *ori* (literally head). The *ori* contains two complementary aspects: the *ori* located in the head constitutes the essence of one's personality or ego and another one, located in the heavens, constitutes one's guardian soul called the guardian **ancestor**. It is the ancestor *ori* that chooses one's destiny before birth, determines one's character, occupation, success in life, and time of **death**.

Likewise, the Native American Sioux believe in multiple souls: breath (*ni*), which leaves the body at death; guardian spirit (*sicun*), which is a **power** possessed by all supernatural beings and animate and inanimate objects; and the shadow or shade (*nagi*). The guardian spirit, a kind of potency, is an immortal aspect created in every animate object, which helps one to ward off **evil** and returns to the supernatural beings at **death**. It is possible for one person to borrow the *sicun* of another person, which can be invested through **ritual** and be accumulated and shared with others. The shadow (*nagi*) is an eternal counterpart of all animate and inanimate objects, which lingers after death upon a person losing their breath.

After death, the *nagi* can become a *wanagi*, or dangerous ghost, that grieves for its loved ones and attempts to entice family members to join it. In order to appease the *wanagi*, relatives keep it for one year by feeding it. Thereupon, the *wanagi* departs to the south along the ghost road (equated with the Milky Way) where it meets an old woman who assesses its deeds on **earth**. Those souls judged good pass to a place that reflects their life with their *ni*, whereas bad souls are pushed over a cliff and roam the earth as evil **spirits** where they endanger the living.

Further reading: Levison (1997); Perrett (1987); Peters (2003); Powers (1977)

SPACE: SACRED AND PROFANE

The basic distinction between profane and **sacred** space is implied in the work of Emile Durkheim (1858–1917), father of sociology, and is developed more fully by Mircea Eliade (1907–1986), a historian of religions. For Eliade, profane space is neutral, homogeneous, without structure or consistency. This amorphous mass, which is experienced by humans as **chaos**, is relative and lacks orientation. For ordinary profane space to become sacred, it must be transformed by the appearance of a deity or consecrated by **ritual** means. Within the homogeneity of undifferentiated profane space, sacred space represents a radical break in such space because it provides orientation and a fixed point, which implies being able to establish a world and order in which to live safely. According to Eliade, this is accomplished by humans following the paradigmatic model of the creation **myth**, resulting in the transformation of profane space into something sacred along a horizontal point of reference and a vertical axis of communication that consists of the central axis of the world.

Among the Tewa Pueblo of the North American southwest, sacred and profane space is a bit more complicated than suggested by Eliade's basic distinction because their creation myth relates that they lived under a lake with animals and **gods**. There are two co-mothers of the people: Blue Corn Mother (associated with summer) and White Corn Woman (associated with winter). A man is sent forth to examine the world, and he finds that it is green or unripe. A further journey above witnesses him encounter predatory animals, which initiate him and accept him by giving him things necessary for hunting. The original man returns to his people as the Hunt Chief to lead his people to the surface of the **earth** where they have adventures and suffer from illness. The Tewa world consists of a concentric scheme with the sacred center in the village, dance plazas, shrines, sacred flat-topped hills, and sacred mountains. Beyond the mountains is profane space, whereas horizontal space corresponds to the levels of being of the **culture** and vertical space represents three cosmic levels: below, middle, and above. The below and above are like the middle. This is a cosmos born from its center and expanding outwards.

Further reading: Eliade (1959); Ortiz (1969)

SPEECH ACTS

This notion is elucidated by the philosopher J. L. Austin in his book *How to Do Things with Words* and is developed further by John Searle in his work *Speech Acts*. **Performative language**, which involves uttering words, is directly connected to the doing of an action. In other words, perfomative language makes something happen when it is verbally expressed. If a governor of a state cuts a ribbon across a highway that runs over a bridge, and proclaims, for instance, "I now declare this bridge open," the bridge is open and cars can now pass over it. Austin develops a threefold classification of speech acts: the locutionary act of saying something with a certain sense and reference, for example, the act of saying, "the automobile is not running," with reference to a particular auto; the illocutionary act of doing something in the act of saying something, for example, in saying, "Start the auto," a person performs the act of giving an order; and, finally, the perlocutionary act of accomplishing something by the act of saying, for example, "Turn the engine off." There are also certain conditions that are necessary for a performative utterance to be successful, which include an accepted conventional procedure and result within a certain context. The persons and circumstances must be appropriate for the invocation of the particular procedure utilized. A final criterion involves the complete and correct execution of the procedure by all participants.

Austin's theory of performative utterance is criticized by Jacques Derrida, a postmodern philosopher, because Austin does not consider a pre-existing system of predicates that Derrida calls graphematics. Derrida claims that Austin also blurs the differences between original event-utterances and citational utterances because Austin misses the iterable marks that introduce a split into the utterance. In addition, Derrida claims that the utterance can never be completely determinable because it is necessary for conscious intention to be present and immediately apparent to itself and the **other**. Finally, Derrida asserts metaphysics reigns within Austin's work.

Regardless of Derrida's criticism of him, Austin's theory of speech acts as performative utterance manifests a major impact on **ritual** theory. Anthropological representatives include Gilbert Lewis, Victor Turner, and Stanley Tambiah. In addition to the ritual context, performative utterances also play a role in a religion such as Zen Buddhism and its use of unusual teaching methods. There are numerous examples of a word or shout being uttered and triggering an enlightenment **experience**. The same result is evident with beatings administered by enlightened masters upon students, the raising of a fly whisk, or a single finger. If the student is prepared, any of these performative utterances or actions can elicit a spiritual breakthrough.

Further reading: Austin (1962); Derrida (1976); Lewis (1971); Searle (1969); Tambiah (1990); Turner (1967)

SPIRITS

In comparison to personalized and individualized **gods**, spirits usually represent a collective group that is often large. Being usually below the gods in rank and owning their origin to gods, spirits are often closer to the everyday life of a people as protectors or as inflictors of punishment for some transgression. Sometimes, specific spirits separate from the group and assume temporary or permanent abode in a specific place or object. Spirits play roles in religious traditions around the globe, especially at the local level of a tradition where they come into close contact with ordinary people.

Among Native American Indians, there are numerous categories of spirits, with the master of animals considered among the most important. Ruling over all animals or a single animal species, the master of animals sees that no animals are killed unnecessarily and insures that they are treated with care. After an animal is killed, it must be buried with appropriate rituals as in the Bear Ceremony of the Northern Saulteau. As part of this ceremony, a hunter addresses the bear before killing it to apologize for the **violence** that is about to occur, and explains the rationale for the killing to the animal. Afterward, the hunter dresses the bear in fine clothing, and erects a pole upon which are hung the bear's skull, skin, and its ears. This ceremonial pattern is a means of showing respect for the bear and for the master of species. As a consequence of this respect, future game and continued success in hunting are assured. The ritualistic respect given to the bear implies treating it like a person with whom the hunter is related in a personal way.

In addition to the master of animals, Native American Indians recognize **nature** spirits. The Dakota and Cheyenne revere the Black Hills as the homeland of the spirits, and Yellowstone Park is believed to be inhabited by spirits. The Shoshoni assume that rock cravings in the mountains are made by spirits and the Pueblo venerate lakes and other apertures in the **earth's** surface from which their ancestors emerged. More specifically, Indians recognize spirits in rocks. For instance, Inyan is a term for all rocks among the Sioux, and is considered the oldest divinity and ancestor of all things and all gods. Particularly large boulders are decorated with paint to call attention to their significance, whereas **prayers** and dog **sacrifices** are also addressed to them. Animal-shaped stones are kept by the Crow Indians as powerful medicine. Indians also identify spirits of water such as seas, lakes, springs, or rivers as guardian spirits.

American Indians also believe in personal guardian spirits that can be given at birth or later acquired by an individual. Among the Pueblo, Santa Ana comes at birth and is believed to prevent a person from committing a wrong action. This spirit receives food sacrifices before each meal by the person that it guards. Acquired guardian spirits are obtained through **visions** in secluded places. These spirits often appear in animal form, and they endow their protégé with some kind of capacity, such as strength or wisdom; or the spirit might give a person a medicine bundle that includes animal parts, pipes, rattles, or corn cobs and is believed to possess **healing** magic. If a person transgresses a **taboo**, the guardian spirit may then leave the guilty person. During the course of their relationship, an individual acquires the characteristics and possibly the name of the guardian spirit, and he paints tattoos on his **body** to resemble the spirit and decorates his clothes and weapons with, for instance, the claws, feathers, and fur of the animal.

If one concentrates on a single **society** such as the Ojibwa, it is possible to witness the complexity of spirit beliefs. According to the Ojibwa, the source of Indian existence can be traced to manitos, which are powerful beings. The four winds are responsible for seasonal changes and weather, whereas underwater manitos are composed of two beings: underwater lion and horned serpent. This composite spirit influences the abundance and availability of land and sea animals. The underwater manitos also cause rapids and stormy waters. Thunderbirds are hawk-like birds that manifest themselves through thunder and lightning and control various types of winged animals; they are considered powerful guardian spirits that are sought in visions. The owners of nature are the spirits of each species, who control animals and demand respect and offerings from Indians, and the owners of **sacred** places are identified with, for instance, springs and waterfalls. Finally, the windigo is a spirit identified as a giant cannibal made of ice, which is symbolic of winter and starvation, and prefers to eat human flesh.

The Nuer people of Africa make a clear distinction between spirits of the air above and spirits of below. The former type of spirit is represented by the **sun**, a craftsman of God, who can twist the bodies of humans and deform them. Other spirits are associated with cattle, rain, lightning, rivers, and wild animals. There is also a spirit of war, who is connected with clan spear names and thunder. A female spirit is associated with rivers and streams. The colwic spirits are former people who may have been struck by lightning. Although they retain their personal identity and often attach themselves to individuals of their own families or lineages, these former humans are believed to be chosen by god and become a part of god. The colwic spirits, who delight in **blood** and battle, may possess people or make them sick. The lower spirits are believed to have fallen from above, and there are four major types of them: totemic spirits, totemistic spirits, nature sprites, and fetishes. The first type refers to the relationship between a spirit and a social group, whereas the second type indicates a relationship between a spirit and an individual. Nature sprites attach themselves to objects, and fetishes are pieces of wood, which are very dangerous, but function as medicines that can communicate. These amoral fetishes can be acquired by purchase or inherited.

From these types of examples, it is possible to recognize that spirits are often treated like gods by demanding sacrifices and **worship**. They act in ways that recall the behavior of gods, such as providing assistance to humans or punishing them. In many cultures, the spirits are considered relationally closer to the people and more caring than gods.

Further reading: Beattie and Middleton (1969); Evans-Pritchard (1956); Gill (1982); Hultkrantz (1992, 1997); Lewis (1971); Smith (2006)

SUFFERING

Suffering is a global **experience** of physical and mental **pain** directly caused by **violence**, anxiety, fear, loss of a loved one, loneliness, vulnerability, or simply frustration of desires. The **reality** of suffering gives rise to attempts to reduce it, raises questions about its fairness, especially in light of a **God** who is supposed to be merciful, good, and just, and calls into the question the purpose and meaning of life. Religious traditions have come to grips with suffering by attempting to place it into a comprehensive context of universal understanding, and have endeavored to find ways to alleviate or to escape suffering. Often, these two fundamental responses overlap.

In Judaism, suffering arises from the finite human condition, which is more directly caused by **sin**, a willful disobedience of God's commandments, or ignorance of the right religious path. Suffering can be construed as negative because it is a punishment for transgressions but in a more positive way it helps to educate a person. According to ancient Jewish texts (Deut. 4.20; Isa. 48.10; Jer. 11.4), suffering is also a means of refinement and **purification**. Moreover, suffering can help a person gain insight into human existence and help that person gain a sense of empathy toward **others**. It is also possible that a person can suffer by behaving virtuously, as evident with Job as the primary paradigm in the Jewish tradition. Disobedient or virtuous persons are not the only sufferers in the Jewish tradition because God is also said to suffer due to His concern for the afflictions of His people (Gen. 6.5–6; Isa. 63.9).

Similar to the Jewish position, the Christian apostle Paul teaches that suffering is punishment for sin (Gal. 6.7), which makes it inevitable because of sinful human nature. At the same time, suffering is welcomed because it directly assists in building a person's character, endurance, and hope (Rom. 5.3–4) with the model being the suffering servant, Jesus, who himself suffered for the sins of humankind in an act of vicarious atonement. In fact, the early Christian community is historically nurtured in suffering for their **faith** from their Roman persecutors. Those Christian sufferers who pay the ultimate, **violent** price for their faith become heroic **martyrs** who immediately gain entry into **heaven**.

Suffering plays a definitive role in Buddhism because it represents the First Noble Truth of the Buddha's teachings: All life is suffering (*dukkha*). This fundamental truth is based on the Buddha's empirical observations about life with its sickness, old age, and death, but it needs to be grasped in a wider context that includes the cycle of causation, which necessarily means that everything within the world is causally conditioned or produced. The notion of suffering includes the notions of imperfection, impermanence, emptiness, and insubstantiality. If the root meaning of *dukkha* (suffering) is examined, it suggests that life is dislocated in its present condition because of ordinary suffering, suffering produced by change, and suffering inherent in conditioned states. If ordinary suffering is obvious, the second type refers to the fact that within the pleasant and joyous moments of life there is suffering because such moments do not last and their passing causes sorrow. Inherent suffering is related to the changing nature of things and a person's tendency to cling to **self**, I, or ego and to ignorantly assume that it is possible to satisfy the self when in fact it does not even exist because it is a heap of ever-changing elements that does not endure from one moment to the next. The only way to end suffering, which is tied to rebirth, is to attain nirvāṇa by following the Noble Eightfold Path of the Buddha, which takes a person outside of the cycle of causation.

As in Buddhism, Jains believe that suffering is inevitable because joy and happiness are impermanent, whereas violence, cruelty, and injustice dominated life within the world. In the Jain **worldview**, an omniscient and merciful god is unnecessary because it is the law of karma, which is the concept of cause and effect, that explains the fate of individuals at **death** based on one's deeds, and the **reality** of **evil** and suffering. If suffering is inevitable in the Jain perspective, suffering can still be grasped as a test of a person's actions and that person's potential for **liberation**.

Further reading: Bowker (1970); Cort (2001); Olson (2005)

SUN

The sun is arguably the most visible object in **nature**. It is absolutely necessary for life and embodies great **power** and religious significance, such as **truth** and justice. In ancient times, the sun was deified by many religious cultures around the globe.

In ancient Mesopotamia, the sun **god** is Šamaš, a masculine figure conceived as a judge, punisher of transgressions, fighter of injustice, and helper of those in need. He is described as uttering oaths and becomes the patron god of soothsayers. Every evening he descends in the west to the realm of the dead. Ancient Egyptians identify the sun god by at least three names: Re conceived as a falcon is the most common; Atum is located in the city of Heliopolis and represents the evening sun that sinks; the morning sun is Kheprer who is represented by a sun-disk believed to be the right eye of Horus. Among ancient Iranians, Mithra is associated with the sun by means of his origin. In South America, the tribal god of the Incas is Inti, a male figure, considered the mythical ancestor of the political dynasty. In ancient India, the sun is called Sūrya, and the most sacred Vedic hymn is address to the sun deity called Savitri. The deity Vishnu is also a solar figure who possesses great importance for later Hinduism. In ancient Japanese cosmogony, the husband of the primordial pair produces the sun (female) and moon (male) from, respectively, his right and left eyes. The sun is identified as the **goddess** Amaterasu, who represents light and purity, whereas Susano-o-no Mikoto stands for **violence** and **death**. Both figures represent complementary aspects that are necessary for life on earth.

Further reading: Aldhouse-Green (1991); Hultkrantz (1981)

SYMBOLS

A concept that can be traced back to the Greek term *sumbolon* (sign, token, pledge), implying that it points to something beyond itself. A flag is, for instance, a sign symbolizing a nation, the cross a symbol of the Christ event. In his theory of the symbol, Mircea Eliade (1907–1986), a historian of religions, stresses that a religious symbol is multivalent because it can express several meanings simultaneously. The symbolism of the moon suggests fertility, recurrence of life, time, destiny, and change. An inaccessible modality of the real is expressed to ordinary people by symbols. The manifestation of **power** can be expressed by a symbol, which can also be revealed in **myth**, a **narrative** form of a symbol. This point indicates the ability of symbols, which precede **language** and discursive reason, to reveal deeper layers of **reality**. Moreover, symbols can express paradoxical situations. Symbols have a logic, which means that they can fit together diverse realities into a coherent system, and possess a history in the sense that a symbol may have spread from a specific cultural center.

According to the philosopher Paul Ricoeur (1913–2005), symbols possess three dimensions: cosmic, oneiric, and poetic imagination. With the cosmic dimension, a person understands the **sacred** as, for instance, an aspect of the world in sky, **sun**, and moon symbolism. Having innumerable meanings, these unified significations give rise to speech. Thus the manifestation of a thing and its meanings are contemporaneous and reciprocal. The oneiric dimension refers to manifesting the sacred in the human psyche during **dream** states, delving into the inner depths of the imagination that is common to all religious **cultures**. Finally, the poetic imagination forms the complement of the cosmic and psychic dimensions. The poetic modality of symbols puts **language** in a state of emergence.

245

If a symbol is a sign that communicates meaning, it also possesses a double intentionality, according to Ricoeur. The first kind is the literal sense that refers to something beyond itself as with defilement, for instance, and its sense of stain. This literal meaning points towards a second intentionality as when the notion of stain refers to an existential situation that is directly associated with being defiled or impure. This suggests that the literal meaning "stain" is opaque because it points analogically to a second meaning. Thus, by living in the literal meaning, a person is lead to the symbolic meaning in which that person lives and participates. Since the symbol is the very movements of the primary meaning, it enables a person to share in its hidden meaning.

Further reading: Eliade (1963); Ricoeur (1967)

TABOO

Taboo refers to that which is forbidden. It can be traced to the Tongan **language** of Polynesian culture and the term *tapu*, or the Fijian word *tabu*, meaning prohibited, not allowed, or forbidden. It is closely associated with what is **sacred** and is surrounded by custom and **law**. Taboos include certain dietary restrictions (vegetarianism in Hinduism and Buddhism, non-consumption of pork products in Judaism and Islam), **sexual** restrictions (prohibitions against adultery, **homosexuality**, incest, or sex with children, animals, or the dead), bodily restrictions (prohibitions against taking certain drugs, spitting, flatulence, burping), and taboos associated with abusive language, **death**, and dress. The Eskimo, for instance, observe taboos associated with food whereby one does not mix caribous and seal meat because hunting the former is a summer activity and hunting the seals takes place in the winter. Just as eating their meat together is forbidden, so is the wearing of **clothing** made from the skins of these animals at the same time also prohibited.

Further reading: Lévi-Strauss (1962); Turner (1975); Wagner (1972); Webster (1942)

THEATRICAL PERFORMANCES

Various religions use theatrical performances to convey their message by re-enacting **narratives** from their tradition for a public audience. From approximately the fourth century, Christianity stages passion (from the Latin *passio*, suffering) plays that recount the final days of the life and **suffering** of Jesus with narrative and **music**. Later developments include the addition of poems, hymns, and chorales, which include singing by the audience. Two Passion works by J. S. Bach are especially famous: the *St. John Passion* (1721) and *St. Matthew Passion* (1729).

Shi'ite Muslims re-enact their own passion play that commemorates the **martyrdom** of al-Husain at Karbalā called the *ta 'ziya*. According to Shi'ite tradition, the prophet Muhammad gave al-Husain the key to heaven and appointed him an intercessor to serve as a rescuer of sinners. The public re-enactment of the suffering of al-Husian is commemorated by male believers marching through the street and flagellating themselves with metal-tipped whips upon their backs or cutting their foreheads to elicit blood in order to share in the suffering of their martyr and his redemptive promise.

In India, popular devotion offered to Krishna and Rāma is often expressed by theatrical performances (*rāsa līlā*) given by itinerant troupes of young boys who **play** male and female parts. These richly colored, costumed, youthful actors imitate the divine beings by staging a drama that is also a liturgy; this is enhanced by the waving of camphor lamps at the beginning and end of a **performance**. A performance commences with a **dance** followed by a one-act play based on the deeds of Krishna or Rāma. The play is intended to encourage an audience to participate in whatever mood is depicted in the drama by enabling a viewer to feel indirectly the **emotions** of another person. These public plays evoke emotions with visual, oral, and aural experiences. The Rāma plays contain political messages because they depict a wisely governed kingdom characterized by justice, order, and prosperity, an ideal ruler, and a vision of a utopian kingdom.

Further reading: Hawley (1981); Hein (1972); Kinsley (1974)

THEISM

A concept derived from the Greek term *theos* (**God**). In the Judeo-Christian-Islamic tradition, it refers to a transcendent and personal deity who creates the world from nothing, sustains it, and governs it. This type of God is defined as omnipotent, omniscient, eternal, immutable, a necessary being, and all good. The theistic deity reveals something about itself and its message about the proper human–divine relationship. Theism should not be confused with Deism, a defense of the **rationality** of religion in light of Newton's scientific theories. Deism denies that God personally governs the world, and it denies **revelation**, miracles, and divine providence because these features are irrational. Moreover, the deity of Deism creates the world and institutes the **laws** governing it, and this deity then allows the world to follow its own course without divine intervention.

Further reading: Beaty (2003); Powers (1977)

THEOLOGY

This concept is historically based in Western thought dating back to the Greeks where the term is derived from *theos* (**God**) and *logos* (word or discourse). Theology is thus a discourse about God in the sense of being a reflection on a supreme being. The Greek term *theologia* is adopted by Christian **churches** to account for God's purpose and activity in biblical **narratives** concerning God's relationship to humanity.

From its early association with Greek **myths**, the early Latin church fathers adopt *theologia* to emphasize praise of God, although it does not possess a separate and distinct status as a discipline at this time. As Christianity historically develops, theology is nurtured in European monasteries in association with so-called rural schools, focusing on issues of **prayer** and **worship** in addition to the nature of God. During the Middle Ages, the growth of cities is accompanied by the creation of cathedral schools intended to train diocesan clergy. In the twelfth and thirteenth centuries at the University of Paris, due to the influence of Peter Abelard and Gilbert de la Porrée, theology changes to a more systematic study of the **faith** at the university level and broadens its scope from the doctrine of God to the whole of Christian **doctrine**. At this time, theology, a form of **sacred** learning and wisdom, becomes the so-called "Queen of the Sciences." The status of theology as a science becomes a contentious issue because its status as a form of rational **knowledge** relying on its own first principles is called into question by Enlightenment philosophy that recognizes the limits of human knowledge. Losing its status as a leading science, theology finds a place in the modern university in 1809 at the University of Berlin where a debate about its status in the university curriculum takes place between J. G. Fichte and F. D. E. Schleiermacher. The former thinker argues that theology has no place in a modern university because it violates norms of **rationality**, whereas the latter figure affirms that rationality does not compete with theology. It is still possible to find courses in theology at major universities but it tends to be treated more as intellectual history. The primary locations for the teaching of theology are now for the most part in Catholic and Protestant seminaries, which are schools for pre-professional training, and at church-affiliated institutions that still have departments of theology or a combination and integration of theology and religious studies. There is a vocal voice within the academy for not teaching theology within the setting of the modern university because it is not scientific and thus not a rigorous discipline.

There have evolved four traditional fields of theology: systematic, historical, pastoral, and philosophical. Systematic theology is theoretically founded on biblical scholarship. Historical theology calls attention to the historical nature of Christian theological discourse and its time and place in an attempt to elucidate the relationship between the development of ideas and their context. A historical theologian might, for instance, be interested in how the socio-economic situation influences the doctrine of salvation in liberation theology in Latin America. Historical theology is subversive in the sense that it can expose how foreign notions get incorporated into Christian thought. Pastoral theology is primarily concerned with nurturing and care for the souls of local parishioners and other issues associated with ministry, whereas philosophical theology uses philosophical rationality to support religious positions. An excellent example is the five arguments for the existence of God by Thomas Aquinas who incorporates the philosophy of Aristotle into his theological reflections. In some cases, as with the twentieth-century theology of Paul Tillich, systematic theology uses philosophical insights to raise existential questions about the human condition, and theology responds with answers to these human problems in what Tillich calls the method of correlation because philosophical questions and theological answers are in mutual interdependence.

Since the Enlightenment, there have been numerous types of theologies: liberal, modernism, neo-orthodoxy, feminism, **narrative**, liberation, process, and **postmodern**. Even though its precise origins are complex, liberal theology is often traced to the work of Schleiermacher with his emphasis on human feeling and condition. Within a cultural context of scientific optimism, technological progress, and economic prosperity, liberalism attempted to bridge the gap between **faith** and scientific **knowledge** by reassessing **doctrines** such as original **sin** and the identity of the historical Jesus. Modernism is a Roman Catholic school that took a critical and skeptical view of traditional church doctrine, although its versions in different European countries do not allow it to form a school because of a lack of commonality. Modernism can partly be grasped as a late response to the Enlightenment. Neo-orthodoxy is given impetus in the aftermath of World War I, and it represents a rejection of liberal theology because it seems to the best exemplary Karl Barth (1886–1968) to be more about human experience than a God-centric theology. Rather than the human-centric theology

249

of liberalism, Barth stresses the total otherness of God and the need to grasp the self-revelation of God in Christ. Feminist, black, and Hispanic theologies are examples of **liberation** theology that protest historical, economic, social, sexual, and racial disparities and other forms of oppression. They tend to look to the Bible for models of **liberation** among **prophetic** figures and Jesus. **Narrative** theology points to the importance of stories used in the Bible to convey important messages. Scholars indicate the roots of narrative theology in the work of Barth with his emphasis on scripture and in H. Richard Niebuhr's book *The Meaning of Revelation* (1941) that stresses that stories are a proper way to express God's revelation. Process theology is inspired by the philosophy of Alfred N. Whitehead (1861–1947), which emphasizes that God exists within the process of becoming and is in fact identical to it, a dynamic process that governs the entire universe. Using the non-method of Jacques Derrida, postmodern theology deconstructs Christian theology in order to expose its internal contradictions. According to Mark C. Taylor, the concepts of God, **self**, history, and book are interconnected and fall together, resulting in the **death** of God, disappearance of the self, the end of history, and the closure of the book (revealed **scripture**). A so-called deconstructive a/theology represents a reformulation of theology in postmodern terms and restores what is lost in the deconstruction, which includes the death of God yielding to writing as a divine milieu, the self reappears as marking and trace, the teleological history of salvation is replaced by mazing grace, and the closed book opens out into an unfinished, errant, endless scripture.

In addition to the Christian tradition, theology has played an important role in the development of Islam, where it begins under the impact of Greek thought, indirect influence encountered with Christian theology, and local issues that spring from early political issues over succession to the **prophet** and religious controversies. The Arabic term for theology is *kalam* (speech, oral discussion) and its practitioners are called *mutkalimūn* (literally means speaker), which means in a theological context a person who introduces a dogma or a controversial theological problem into a topic for discussion. The Muslim theological tradition begins essentially by accepting revelation and then applying reason to revelation in order to interpret, defend, justify, and solve problems arising from revelation, even though the primary concern of the theologian is reaching understanding and interpreting revealed scripture.

During the formative years of the development of Islam, there arise four major schools of theology: Khārijites, Murji'ites, Mu'tazilites, and the Ash'arites. The Khārijites insist that the only valid **judgment** comes from God, which entails that every Muslim must follow the teachings of the Qur'an. Since the judgment of God is already clear and known, it simply remains for humans to execute it. This position implies a righteous **community** of **saints** that knows the divine **law** and practices it. This type of **society** opposes communities that do neither. Thus **salvation** is achieved through membership in the righteous **sect** that is called the People of Paradise, in sharp contrast to the People of Hell. If a member of the former group associates with anyone from the latter group, that person imperils the **salvation** of the entire community. In contrast to this position, the Murji'ites want to postpone judgment until the last day when a sinner's fate is decided by God, which implies that one should desist from passing judgment on the grave sinner. Taking a neutral position between the prophet's grandson Ali and his opponents, the Mu'tazilites reject the deterministic interpretation of the Qur'an in order to save God's goodness and to make an individual responsible for their deeds by arguing for free will. Since an individual's actions emanate from oneself, the individual is a responsible being. If an individual does not have free will, it is unjust for God to hold one responsible for a person's actions. A consequence of this argument is that God, who is necessarily just, cannot do what is unreasonable and unjust. This suggests that divine omnipotence is limited by the requirements of justice as in the doctrine of promise and threat, which means that God can neither pardon an evil-doer and violate His threat nor punish the righteous person and violate His promise. This type of theological position leads to the law of compensation that rewards those unjustly enduring **pain** and **suffering** on earth and compensates them in paradise. Finally, the Ash'arite school argues that all human acts are created by God, but the acts attach themselves to the will of an individual who thus acquires them. This line of argument results in the conviction that all **power** rests with God while all responsibility remains with human beings.

Further reading: Hick (1973); Küng (1976); McGrath (1994); Rahman (1966); Smith (1963, 1981)

TIME

An elusive and mysterious concept that is difficult to define, although it is possible to see evidence of time in **nature** with old trees, old homes, and old people. Finding themselves within and subject to time, humans attempt to measure it using clocks, but this type of measurement of time is not lived time. Three moments of time can be identified – past, present, and future – with the present representing the now moment, the past what has been, and the future what will be.

According to the theory of religion of Mircea Eliade, a historian of religions, there are two kinds of time: **sacred** and profane. The latter is ordinary temporal duration that is measured by clocks into units of seconds, minutes, and hours. In contrast, sacred time is the period of religious **festivals** and **rituals**, which represents a succession of eternities. The major difference between sacred and profane time is that the former is reversible, which suggests a cyclic concept of time, because the events can be repeated each year, whereas the latter is an irreversible duration. From Eliade's perspective, a religious festival repeats a sacred event that occurs in primordial mythical time, which is recoverable and indefinitely repeatable. Sacred time is a time-out-of-time that represents an interruption of ordinary linear time. By returning to the time of origin, time is regenerated and humans are reborn, and become contemporary with the **gods** and their original creative acts.

Eliade's theory is helpful to a degree, but indigenous religions of Africa and Native American Indians help one to realize that time is even more complex because they indicate that their concept of time is local and foreshortened, representing a microcosmic and not a macrocosmic vision. In this conception of time, there is no indefinite future because time is episodic and discontinuous. If time is not linear or unitary, there is no absolute clock or single time scale, which leaves these peoples with a variety of times associated with different kinds of natural phenomena and human activities. These multiple forms of time can be **mythical**, historical, **ritual**, agricultural, seasonal, solar, or lunar.

In retrospect, everyone is subject to linear time, which possesses a beginning and a conclusion. In contrast to linear time, cyclical time is suggested to humans by the **earth** revolving around the **sun**, the alternation of day and night, phases of the moon, and the seasons. If life and **nature** suggest a cycle, linear time is also concerned about the cycle of life and its accompanying rites to mark important occasions, such as birth, marriage, initiation, and **death**. Within this scenario, there exists no simple opposition between sacred and profane time because these types of time are integrated within the life of a religious person.

Further reading: Eliade (1954)

TOTEMISM

Referring to a **belief** that manifests itself in group behavior, totemism is more specifically a relationship between a group and an animal or plant species. Members believe that they are descendents of some animal, which results in the group assuming the name and identities of some mythical animal of whom living animals are their offspring. In practical terms, this means that members of the bear clan, for instance, do not kill bears, although they may use the meat and hide of the animal if someone from another clan kills the bear. Not only are totem animals held in reverence, they are also called upon in critical situations by members because they are believed to offer protection.

Totemism attracts the attention of Émile Durkheim (1858–1917), a French sociologist, because he is interested in its social implications. A clan's identification with a totem animal means that no one can eat the totem, and a member cannot marry within the clan because of their relationship to the totem. Thus beyond **blood** relationships there are wider clan relations with totems that have to be considered. Durkheim finds totemism a **rational** belief, even though it is mistaken because there cannot be a physical kinship between humans and totem animals.

Further reading: Durkheim (1915); Frazer (1910); Freud (1919); Lévi-Strauss (1962)

TRUTH

By revealing itself as it is, this simple definition obscures its complexity and diversity in a cross-cultural context. Different religious traditions identify the truth with their **God**, highest **reality, doctrines,** or **beliefs.** The truth is often cross-culturally associated with absolute certainty, human **experience,** value, accurate **knowledge, reality, harmony, salvation,** or **liberation.** In short, each particular religion thinks that its position represents the absolute truth, while other religions are either false or represent a relative form of truth.

In recent intellectual history, the general religious claim that truth is certain, absolute, and possesses an essence is disputed by postmodern thinkers. From the perspective of Michel Foucault, truth is produced through **power,** and there is no way to exercise power except by means of truth. Other postmodern thinkers view truth as epistemologically and ontologically relative because of the contextual nature of meaning and the relational nature of being. The postmodern philosopher Jacques Derrida does not presume to disclose the truth in his works because they are prefatory in nature, and they are thus an impossible means of revealing the truth in a conclusive sense. Since there is no truth as such for Derrida, truth cannot be singular; it can only be plural.

Further reading: Allen (1993); Blackburn and Simmons (1999); Derrida (1976); Foucault (1994); Hill (2002); Lynch (2001)

VIOLENCE/NON-VIOLENCE

The concept of violence is a relative concept that refers to acts that injure, cause harm or **pain**, or destroy an object, animal, or person. Non-violence is also a relative notion that means the opposite of violence. Within a particular **culture**, it is difficult to find members characterizing their actions as violent because harsh actions tend to be equated with justice, a righteous war, heroic actions, **martyrdom**, or **ritual**. Those external to a religious **culture** are apt to view violence within a religion in a negative way. From cultural insiders, violence tends to get **rationalized** and thus justified. From a cross-cultural perspective, violence and non-violence are relative concepts because the degrees of acceptability are different among diverse religions and even within particular religious cultures. Moreover, the acceptability of violence or its opposite is often different within changing historical periods and circumstances.

Violence is most evident within a religious context with the **performance** of a **sacrifice**, which basically calls for something to be killed or destroyed. The ancient Vedic sacrificial **cult** of India is a complex system, suggesting a mixture of violent and non-violent elements within a particular rite. Within the context of an animal **sacrifice**, priests ask the gods permission to use the animal, participants turn their faces away from the victim, give excuses for its **death**, lament its demise, suffocate or strangulate the animal so that it does not make a sound, and killing is even denied by the sacrificer. As the religious culture evolves, texts present evidence of two movements within the sacrificial **cult**: a growing embarrassment about violence and a move towards **symbolic performances**. This symbolic sacrifice can be found in the ancient human sacrifice and the various forms of self-sacrifice performed by **ascetics** by turning within themselves and using their mind to execute the rite. In ancient India, the violence associated with sacrifice is used metaphorically to depict the self-sacrifice of a warrior on a battlefield.

Reacting in part against the Vedic sacrificial system, Buddhism and Jainism advocates non-violence for everyone. The Buddha makes non-violence part of his Eightfold Path to liberation and a major ethical precept, which presupposes a respect for all life, a universal moral imperative. Buddhism does not think that all life is equally valuable because it measures a creature's ability to attain nirvāṇa or final release. Additional criteria depend on whether or not something possesses a karmic life, which in turn depends on two criteria: sentience and ontological individuality. A cow or a horse is ontologically distinct from bacteria or micro-organisms. Moreover, only sentient life is karmic and possesses intrinsic worth, whereas non-karmic life is merely instrumental. Because of their conviction that all things possess **souls**, Jains practice non-violence to all living things. Jain monks, for instance, filter their drinking water in order to avoid consuming any small bodies, and they sweep the road along which they are walking to avoid harming any creature. It is this spirit of non-violence that later influences Mahatma Gandhi's advocacy of the practice within the struggle for independence.

According to the Christian realist Jacques Ellul, violence is pervasive in all cultures and time periods because all states are founded by violence and maintain their existence through it. He agrees with Thomas Hobbes's belief that violence is the natural condition of **society**. Ellul expounds five laws of violence: (1) certainty; (2) reciprocity, which means that violence begets more violence; (3) sameness, which means that one cannot distinguish between justified and unjustified violence; (4) violence begets violence and nothing else; and (5) a person who uses violence always attempts to justify both it and themselves. To counter this pervasive violence, Ellul offers the violence of **love** that demands that the **other** live, rejects victory, excludes physical or psychological violence, and is based on a **faith** in the possibility of a miracle.

In contrast to the hopeful position of Ellul for combating violence, René Girard perceives an inseparable relationship between violence and the **sacred**. Since humankind is by nature violent and vengeance characterizes human relationships, it is essential for the survival of society to find a process which can break the repetitive and destructive cycle of violence. It is religion in the form of sacrifice, a faithful replica of an original act of violence, which shelters humans from violence by channeling it toward a victim whose **death** provokes no reprisals or recurrent reciprocal violence. Thus, by means of sacrifice, a community is able to subdue the destructive forces that can potentially pull apart the social fabric.

Human violence and killing of some victim is grounded in mimetic desire, which suggests that humans do not know what to desire, and they turn to others to help them decide from Girard's perspective. This process of imitation creates the potential for violent conflict because of competition for the same object. Thus society controls individual desires either negatively by means of prohibitions and taboos or positively by the intrinsic desirability of certain objects and forms of behavior. Violence is a continuation of mimetic desire. It is religion that channels violence and protects the **community** from self-annihilation.

A postmodern theory of violence is offered by Jacques Derrida, an advocate of the method of deconstruction, who does not think that it is possible to avoid violence. This is especially true of the process of writing, which can be identified with three moments: (1) the original violence of writing; (2) violence of metaphysics; (3) violence associated with the deconstructive method itself. The second moment of violence attempts to suppress the violence of writing, whereas deconstruction makes it possible to return to original violence, although it is not truly a method. Deconstruction is, however, parasitic and violent because it preys on the text, other readings, and other interpretations. **Language** is thus a battlefield where violence is committed.

Further reading: Burkert (1983); Derrida (1978); Ellul (1970); Gandhi (1986); Girard (1989); Lincoln (1991)

VISIONS

From a cross-cultural perspective, visions are mental and visual representations of humans, animals, ghosts, **spirits**, or other forms of supernatural beings. Visions are a broad concept that can include hallucinations, **dreams**, unusual auditory or visual stimuli, **possession**, and trance states. Visions are considered valid and real when a person is either in a wakeful or a sleep condition. Scholars identify ecstatic, which implies being out of oneself, experience as also a condition during which people have visions. Some visions appear suddenly, while others may involve a long, arduous process. In general, there are three methods for inducing a vision from a cross-cultural perspective: (1) rhythmical stimulation by means of drums as among Siberian shamans and Inuit Eskimo; (2) sensory deprivation as among the Shakers; and (3) isolation and fasting as among the Oglala Indians. Seekers of visions are driven by a quest for the truth or knowledge.

Among Native American Indians, it is common to seek visions during times of crisis – war, disease, **death** – or as an act of thanksgiving. By seeking visions during periods of stress, this gives three fundamental results: (1) acquiring **ritual** privileges; (2) receiving advice; and (3) acquiring **power**. Within Native American Indian culture, there are two phases of a vision: quest and action. The action phase enables a person to legitimatize one's vision, whereas the quest phase refers to the methods used to acquire a vision that usually involve isolation in a remote location and self-mortification of various kinds. It is possible to identify a common pattern among Indians: (1) preparation by purifying baths; (2) sacred smoking; (3) nightly vigil; (4) **meditation**; and (5) vision. Only those Native Americans deemed worthy by supernatural **spirits** would receive a vision, a scenario that implies that some seekers are unsuccessful. The visions themselves can be benign or horrific. An example of the latter is the vision recorded of the nineteenth-century Bengali saint Rāmakrishna, observing the goddess Kālī rise from the Ganges River as a beautiful woman, giving birth to a child, nursing it, turning into a horrible hag, and then proceeding to eat the newborn. In response to this vision, Rāmakrishna is left astonished and speechless. While lying gravely ill on May 13, 1373, the anchoress Julian of Norwich of the Christian tradition receives a series of sixteen revelatory visions. In her initial vision, Julian sees the red **blood** flowing from the crown upon Christ's head until the sixteenth vision that confirms the previous fifteen visions. These waking visions are followed by a vision of the Devil when she falls asleep. In summary, visions have existential, social, and psychological consequences for the person having a vision because it can transform a person's life, unify the individual with the wider **society**, and relieve or promote psychological turmoil.

Further reading: Couliano (1984); Goodman (1988); Holmes (1982)

WOMEN

According to feminist scholars, the concept of women does not merely refer to females, but is a socially constructed concept created by and within a patriarchically dominated **culture**. Patriarchy refers to a cross-cultural pattern of behavior that is historical, social, political, and institutional, all of which are reflections of male **power**. Patriarchy results in female inferiority, domination, subordination, and marginalization. The all-embracing specter of patriarchy is supported by male sexism that involves the ideology of male superiority. The inferiority of women in comparison to men is evident in the East and the West.

In traditional Chinese religious culture, a woman is inferior by nature, which helps to explain why she is described as dark as the moon, as changeable as water, jealous, narrow-minded, indiscreet, unintelligent, and dominated by **emotion**, whereas a woman's beauty is a snare for the unwary male. In fact, her lowly status is reflected in the cosmic order. The feminine *yin*, for instance, is identified with the earth and all things lowly and inferior; it is also characterized as yielding, receptive, and devoted. Although inferior to the masculine *yang* force, the *yin* is still indispensable to the proper workings of the universe, rendering women the complementary opposite of males.

The Chinese character for a wife shows a woman with a broom, which exemplifies her domestic role. Within their natal families, Chinese women do not have much status because they are destined to join the ranks of another family at marriage. Women are educated at home in order to prepare them for their future roles as wives and mothers, learning good manners and domestic skills such as sewing and weaving. At the age of fifteen, a young girl receives a hairpin that marks a coming-of-age ceremony, but by the age of twenty, she is expected to marry. Once married, a woman's duty is to serve her husband, whereas a husband's duty is to manage his wife, although married couples are expected to show each other mutual respect. Couples are expected to restrict their intimacy because too much familiarity can lead to excessive lust and anger. A proper relationship of a married couple is based on **harmony**. An aspect of this harmony obligates a wife to be responsible for her husband's moral character by monitoring and nurturing it. Women are also expected to be chaste not simply with respect to sexual continence but in a wider sense of integrity and honor.

As in Indian culture, Chinese women are considered sources of **pollution** for two basic reasons: they emit unclean substances and their connection with birth and **death**. The unclean substances are various types of bodily fluids and substances. Female bodily fluids are associated with dangerous **powers** that suggest that menstrual **blood**, for instance, creates babies, although semen begins the growth of a child. A woman's value and status are enhanced when she gives birth to a son who represents the generational line of descent and performs the necessary ancestral rites.

There are many similarities between traditional Chinese religious culture and formative Muslim religion with respect to the role of women. According to the Qur'an (4.38), women are to be managed by men, should be obedient, and can be beaten for rebelliousness. Qur'anic verse (2.228) also makes it clear that men are superior to women, and they are the protectors of women (4.34) because this situation is **God's** preference and because men provide support for women. Such scriptural passages justify the male role as the head of the household, make a male the final decision maker, render a male the spiritual authority of his wife and family, make women subordinate to men, and consider women incapable and unfit for public duties. Nonetheless, women are still part of the Muslim **community**, and believing women are offered the reward of paradise. The Qur'an (2.223) also instructs males to consider women fields that need to be plowed, a passage that suggests that a woman's value can be measure by her fruitfulness.

The traditional inferior status of women in Islam involves disadvantages for women in issues such as marital infidelity and divorce. A husband needs no justification for divorce, having the right to repudiate his wife at any time. This right is not accorded to the wife, although she is allowed to divorce her husband when she adopts Islam and he fails to convert. The right of custody of the children goes to the father. An important innovation in the Qur'an is the permission for women to inherit and own property, although there is no **community** property between a husband and wife.

The Islamic tradition depicts Muhammad as allowing women to pray with him and declaring that women could go to the mosque regularly if their husbands permit. After the rise of the legal tradition, legal scholars rule that women cannot pray in a mosque with men, and they are expected to rather pray at home, whereas women participate fully with men in all activities of **worship** and **prayer** in the early community in Medina. With respect to women in the public sphere, the Qur'an does not state that women should completely cover themselves, and it does not affirm anything about face veils, although women of pre-Islamic Arabia wear veils in the urban areas and remain unveiled in the desert. There is, however, evidence of Muhammad commanding his wives, daughter, and the wives of believers to wear long veils in public, although the practice becomes more widespread during the period of early conquests when Muslims are coming into contact with other religious cultures. The particular evidence might be different, but it is possible to find similar examples of the inferior status of women in Christianity, Judaism, Hinduism, and Buddhism, as evident in classical Chinese and Islamic cultures.

Further reading: Falk and Gross (1980); Holm and Bowker (1994); King (1987, 1995); Mernissi (1991); Sharma (1987)

WORLD RELIGIONS

The notion of world religions is a recent development that begins around the late nineteenth century, and it owes its origin to scholars of religion, during the period of colonialism and Western domination and exploitation of Third World countries. It also develops during the period of **comparative religion**, a scholarly activity reflecting a Christian bias and feelings of religious superiority. In order words, other religions are compared to Christianity with the purpose of demonstrating their inferior nature. This concept also hides a Christian and European universalism under a new banner because a Christian and European viewpoint represent the standard by which other religions are judged and deemed worthy of inclusion among other world religions. Unfortunately, there are some religions, such as Shinto that is indigenous to Japan, that are mistakenly included among the world religions. The concept of world religions' evolution and broad acceptance in the West becomes institutionalized on college campus and departments of religious studies with offerings of such broad survey courses to large numbers of undergraduates. Often, these courses include religions that are not truly speaking "world religions." There are some scholars who think, given the historical origins and cultural context of such a concept and its development into college courses, that the concept and its embodiment within college courses have outlive their usefulness and pedagogical value.

Further reading: McCutcheon (1997); Masuzawa (2005); Smith (1998)

WORLDVIEW

Virtually, all religions have some conception of the world, which provides a religious **culture** with its basic orientation and defined location within an all-encompassing view of the world and itself. The worldview of a culture is often associated with a culture's creation **myth**. The classical Christian worldview includes **heaven** above, **earth** in the middle, and hell below the earth. This is distinctly different from the contemporary worldview of astronomical science. A worldview is something lived in and acted out by embodied beings. A worldview is not something static but rather something open that advances in concert with its environment and transforms itself according to changing circumstances, a feature that suggests a continual interplay between the world and human experience. A worldview functions as the fundamental conceptual framework for a religion for integrating diverse elements within it and any new additions.

In classical China, the cosmos is spontaneously self-generating, impersonal, and naturalistic, which means that it is characterized by regularity and lacks a creator deity, ultimate cause, or will external to itself. The world is composed of a vertical axis connecting a zenith and nadir and framed by the four quarters. **Heaven** is described as round and encloses the **earth**, which is square. Each of the four quarters and center are associated with a color, taste, sound, and **symbol**. China is located at the center of the world with its capital at the center of the middle kingdom. Likewise, the royal palace is at the center of the capital and represents the center of the world. This is the precise location for communication between **heaven** and **earth**. In turn, the capital possesses a **ritual** palace that is built on a square base representing the earth, and it is covered by a round thatched roof that symbolizes heaven. As the year progresses, the emperor follows the flow of **nature** and moves from one part of the palace to another in order to place himself at the quarter of the palace dominated by the calendar. Thus the emperor successively inaugurates the seasons and the months, and he incarnates the center of the world, serving as the connection between heaven and earth.

The classical worldview of China involves a triad of heaven, earth, and human beings implying that humans are called to imitate the behavior of heaven and earth. The cosmos teaches three lessons: (1) heaven and earth are life-giving, nurture and sustain life, and bring it to completion; (2) everything in life is relational because nothing comes into being in isolation and nothing survives in isolation within a hierarchical structure in which the context of heaven is superior and creative and earth is inferior and receptive; and (3) the cosmos operates orderly and with **harmony**, with each part acting for the good of the whole and observing a deference for each other, such as the **sun** dominating the daytime and yielding its place to the moon at night. This cosmic order is the primary source for a divine revelation and serves as a model of human **society**.

Classical Islam divides the world into two parts: unseen and visible, with **God** reigning over both and humans over the latter. The Qur'anic world is also divided into present and after world with humans living in the present, lower world, whereas the after world, which stands in sharp contrast to the first world, is that location to come in the future. Both of these worlds are connected by the Last Day or Day of **Judgment**. Moreover, the after world is divided into two entities: the Garden and Hell **Fire**. This structure allows one to notice that the Qur'anic worldview is based on a conceptual opposition.

This structure of opposition can be witnessed with other aspects of the Islamic worldview. Although there is an ontological relation between God and humans, humans owe their existence to God, which implies that humans are infinitely inferior to God. It is God that stands at the center of this world of being with humans serving as God's creatures. Therefore, the ontological world is theocentric in its structure. The relational aspects of the Islamic worldview are also evident in the two kinds of communicative relations: verbal and non-verbal. The communication of God to humans assumes the form of **revelation**, whereas **prayer** is the means of communication of humans to God. The non-verbal form of communication from God to humans takes the form of signs, while humans communicate with God by means of **ritual worship**. There is also the Lord–servant relationship that emphasizes God's majesty, sovereignty and absolute **power**, which stands in sharp contrast to the status of the servant, who is humble, modest, and absolutely obedient. The ethical relation points to two different aspects of God: infinite goodness, mercy, and forgiveness, which is balanced by His wrath and strict justice. The corresponding human relation is thankfulness and fear. Furthermore, the Muslim community is divided into the people of the book (those with revealed **scripture**) and the people without the book, which suggests a distinction between believers and unbelievers. Jews and Christians are accounted among the people of the book. The Islamic worldview is an excellent example of a concept that helps to meditate notions of difference and commonality. The common features are a **belief** system, **mythic** elements, and **ritual**.

Worldviews set boundaries for a religion and suggest the importance of its social dimension. Worldviews are not static concepts because they are known to change over time. The Vedic worldview of ancient India, with its threefold structure of the sky (masculine), the atmosphere, and earth (feminine), and embodying a distinction between being and non-being, which is located beneath the **earth**, is different from the later purāṇic view. This later view is of a world shaped like an egg of seven concentric circles within which the earth is located at the center and India represents the center of the earth with Mt. Meru rising from its center. Different worldviews call attention to the diverse geographic and cultural distinctions among religions. A religious worldview is not merely something cultural and geographic but also historical and social. Worldviews enable students to witness how **language** organizes **reality**, classifies things within the world, integrates the various aspects of the world, and interprets its world and new events. The worldview of a religion gives one a possible insight into how that religion might deal with change, or internal or external challenges.

Further reading: Izutsu (1966); Paden (1988); Smart (1995, 1996)

WORSHIP

An act of devotion that is usually directed to a **god, goddess, sacred** person, or **sacred** object that is assumed to be more real and superior to the devotee. In addition to devotion and adoration, worship also includes words of praise or homage to the subject of the action. Worship takes place within a context that includes the **myths, doctrine,** and **ethics** of a particular religious tradition that shape the form of the activity. Often, worship is intermixed with other types of devotional activities, such as petitions and expiations.

An excellent example of worship is the Hindu practice of *pūjā* that embodies ancient Indian notions of hospitality, with its emphasis on greeting a guest and offering **food** and drink, entertaining stories, possibly a change of clothing, and water to wash and cool oneself. When *pūjā* is performed in the home the deity is considered a guest in one's home, and the divine being is treated according to traditional rules of hospitality. *Pūjā* is also performed daily in the temple by **priests** who are paid for their services. Whether performed in the temple or at home *pūjā* represents a series of acts of service or respect. Beginning in the morning with the awakening of the deity, other activities include washing the divine image, offering **food** and drink, clothing the image in a new garment and **sacred** thread, anointing it with sandalwood paste or unguents, offering it flowers, incense, and perfumes, and waving a lighted lamp. Other actions may include a full prostration before the **image** of the deity, a circumambulation of the image, praising the deity, and finally bidding the deity farewell or goodnight.

Hindus draw distinctions between temple and home worship, with the former type performed for the benefit of the world and the latter form performed for the welfare of a particular household. Within the context of a temple, priests play the primary role of performing worship, while this is performed in the home by a household member or a priest hired specifically for the task. The temple form of worship is considered effective whether or not there are observers. At the end of the temple ceremony a camphor flame, which represents the embodiment of the deity within the **image** and its transcendence with the flames rising and disappearing, is waved by the priest before the image, an act that unifies the worshiper and deity. This represents a unity that is signified by devotees taking the flames by waving their hands through them and touching their eyes with their fingertips and transferring the **power** of the flames to their bodies. Within the Pāli Buddhist tradition, worship is directed to either images of the Buddha or *stūpas* (memorial mounds), which are considered merit-making activities. Both types of worship involve certain prohibitions that are related to not covering one's head, sitting with legs extended toward the object of devotion, spitting, or yawning. It is also necessary to purify oneself with water and remove one's shoes before worship. The central act of *stūpa* worship involves circumambulating the structure in a clockwise direction with the right side of one's **body** always directed toward the object. The worship of an image of the Buddha is very similar to Hindu worship of a divine image.

Other types of religious movements direct their worship at different types of objects. During the thirteenth century in Japan, the Nichiren movement, named for its **prophet**, directs its devotion to the text of the *Lotus Sūtra*, a document believed by its adherents to embody the most perfect message of the Buddha and the sole means to **salvation**. In a similar fashion, the Sikhs revere the *Ādi Granth*, a text embodying the revelation and presence of God. Before he died, it is believed that Guru Gobind Singh designated that this text would be his successor. Although these **sacred** texts stand within a broader context of **belief**, they focus the devotional attention of devotees and their worship.

Further reading: Babb (1975); Faure (2003a,b); Fuller (1992); Ostör (1980); Peters (1994); Smart (1996); Teiser (1988)

BIBLIOGRAPHY

Aberle, David F. (1991) *The Peyote Religion among the Navaho*. Norman, OK: University of Oklahoma Press.

Adams, Doug and Apostolos-Cappadona, Diane (1990) (eds.) *Dance as Religious Studies*. New York: Crossroad Publishing.

Aldhouse-Green, Miranda (1991) *The Sun-Gods of Ancient Europe*. London: B. T. Batsford.

Allen, Barry (1993) *Truth in Philosophy*. Cambridge, MA: Harvard University Press.

Anderson, Bernhard W. (1967) *Creation versus Chaos*. New York: Association Press.

Ariès, Philippe (1981) *The Hour of Our Death*. New York: Alfred A. Knopf.

Asad, Talad (1993) *Genealogies of Religion: Discipline and Reason of Power in Christianity and Islam*. Baltimore, MD: Johns Hopkins University Press.

Austin, John L. (1962) *How to Do Things with Words*. Oxford: Clarendon Press.

Babb, Lawrence A. (1975) *The Divine Hierarchy: Popular Hinduism in Central India*. New York: Columbia University Press.

Baird, Robert D. (1971) *Category Formations and the History of Religions*. The Hague: Mouton.

Barker, Eileen, Beckford, James, and Dobbelaere, Karel (1993) (eds.) *Secularization, Rationalism, and Sectarianism: Essays in Honor of Bryan R. Wilson*. New York: Oxford University Press.

Barnhill, David Landis and Gottlied, Roger S. (2001) (eds.) *Deep Ecology and World Religions: New Essays on Sacred Ground*. Albany, NY: State University of New York Press.

Barrett, Justin (2000) "Exploring the Natural Foundations of Religion." *Trends in Cognitive Sciences* 4/1: 29–34.

Bataille, Georges (1962) *Death and Sensuality: A Study of Eroticism and the Taboo*. New York: Walker and Company.

Bataille, Georges (1991) *Visions of Access: Selected Writings, 1927–1939*. Trans. by Allen Stoekl. Minneapolis, MN: University of Minnesota Press.

Baudrillard, Jean (1994) *Simulacra and Simulation*. Trans. by Sheila Faria Glaser. Ann Arbor, MI: University of Michigan.

Beard, Mary (2004) "Writing and Religion." In *Religions of the Ancient World: A Guide*. Edited by Sarah Iles Johnston. Cambridge, MA: Harvard University Press, pp. 127–138.

Beattie, John and Middleton, John (1969) (eds.) *Spirit Mediumship and Society in Africa*. New York: Africana Publication Corp.

Beaty, Michael (2003) (ed.) *Christian Theism and the Problems of Philosophy*. Notre Dame, IN: University of Notre Dame Press.

Beck, Guy L. (1993) *Sonic Theology: Hinduism and Sacred Sound*. Columbia, SC: University of South Carolina Press.

Beidelman, T. O. (1997) *The Cool Knife: Imagery of Gender, Sexuality, and Moral Education in Kaguru Initiation Ritual*. Washington, DC: Smithsonian Institution Press.

Bell, Catherine (1992) *Ritual Theory, Ritual Practice*. New York: Oxford University Press.

Bell, Catherine (1997) *Ritual Perspectives and Dimensions*. New York: Oxford University Press.

Bellah, Robert (1970) *Beyond Belief: Essays on Religion in a Post-traditional World*. New York: Harper & Row.

Benavides, Gustavo (1998) "Modernity." In *Critical Terms for Religious Studies*. Edited by Mark C. Taylor. Chicago, IL: University of Chicago Press, pp. 186–204.

Berger, Peter I. (1969) *The Sacred Canopy; Elements of a Sociological Theory of Religion*. Garden City, NY: Doubleday.

Berger, Peter I. (1979) *The Heretical Imperative*. Garden City, NY: Doubleday.

Berger, Peter I. (1997) *Redeeming Laughter: The Comic Dimension of Human Experience*. New York: Walter De Gruyter.

Berglund, Axel-Ivar (1989) *Zulu Thought-Patterns and Symbolism*. Bloomington, IN: Indiana University Press.

Berking, Helmuth (1999) *Sociology of Giving*. Trans. by Patrick Camiller. London: Sage.

Berman, Harold (1983) *Law and Revolution: The Formation of the Western Legal Tradition*. Cambridge, MA: Harvard University Press.

Berthier, François (2000) *Reading Zen in the Rocks: The Japanese Dry Landscape Garden*. Trans. by Graham Parkes. Chicago, IL: University of Chicago Press.

Berthrong, John and Tucker, Mary Evelyn (1998) (eds.) *Confucianism and Ecology: The Interrelation of Heaven, Earth, and Human*. Cambridge, MA: Harvard University Press.

Besançon, Alain (2000) *The Forbidden Image: An Intellectual History of Iconoclasm*. Trans. by Jane Marie Todd. Chicago, IL: University of Chicago Press.

Bettelheim, Bruno (1962) *Symbolic Wounds: Puberty Rites and the Envious Male*. New York: Collier.

Betz, Hans Dieter (1965) "Orthodoxy and Heresy in Primitive Christianity." *Interpretation* 19: 299–311.

Bhardwaj, Surinder Mohan (1973) *Hindu Places of Pilgrimage in India*. Berkeley, CA: University of California Press.

Blackburn, Simon and Simmons, Keith (1999) (eds.) *Truth*. New York: Oxford University Press.

Blair, Sheila S. and Bloom, Jonathan M. (1995) *The Art and Architecture of Islam 1250–1800*. New Haven, CT: Yale University Press.

Bloch, Maurice and Parry, Jonathan (1982) (eds.) *Death and the Regeneration of Life*. Cambridge: Cambridge University Press.

Boswell, John (1980) *Christianity, Social Tolerance and Homosexuality*. Chicago, IL: University of Chicago Press.

Bourdieu, Pierre (1990) *The Logic of Practice*. Trans. by Richard R. Nice. Cambridge: Cambridge University Press.

Bowker, John (1970) *Problems of Suffering in the Religions of the World*. Cambridge: Cambridge University Press.

Boyarin, Daniel (1999) *Dying for God: Martyrdom and the Making of Christianity and Judaism*. Stanford, CA: Stanford University Press.

Boyce, Mary (1979) *Zoroastrians: Their Religious Beliefs and Practices*. London: Routledge and Kegan Paul.

Boyer, Pascal (1994) *The Naturalness of Religious Ideas: A Cognitive Theory of Religion*. Berkeley, CA: University of California Press.

Brooten, Bernadette J. (1996) *Love between Women in Early Christian Responses to Female Homoeroticism*. Chicago, IL: University of Chicago Press.

Brown, Peter (1981) *The Cult of Saints: Its Rise and Function in Latin Christianity*. Chicago, IL: University of Chicago Press.

Brown, Peter (1982) *Society and the Holy in Late Antiquity*. Berkeley, CA: University of California Press.

Buber, Martin (1958) *I and Thou*. Trans. by Ronald Gregor Smith. New York: Scribners.

Buckser, Andrew and Glazier, Stephen D. (2003) (eds.) *The Anthropology of Religious Conversion*. Landham, MD: Rowman & Littlefield.

Bulkeley, Kelly (2008) *Dreaming in the World's Religions: A Comparative History*. New York: New York University Press.

Burkert, Walter (1983) Homo Necans: *The Anthropology of Ancient Greek Sacrificial Ritual and Myth*. Trans. by Peter Bing. Berkeley, CA: University of California Press.

Burkert, Walter (1987) *Ancient Mystery Cults*. Cambridge, MA: Harvard University Press.

Butler, Judith (1990) *Gender Trouble: Feminism and the Subversion of Identity*. London: Routledge.

Bynum, Caroline Walker (1987) *Holy Feast and Holy Fast: The Religious Significance of Food to Medieval Women*. Berkeley, CA: University of California Press.

Caillois, Roger (1959) *Man and the Sacred*. Trans. by Meyer Barach. Glencoe, IL: Free Press.

Caillois, Roger (1961) *Man, Play, and Games*. Trans. by Meyer Barach. New York: Free Press.

Caldwell, Sarah (1999) *Oh Terrifying Mother: Sexuality, Violence and Worship of the Goddess Kāli*. New Delhi: Oxford University Press.

Callicot, J. Baird and Ames, Roger (1989) (eds.) *Nature in Asian Traditions of Thought: Essays in Environmental Philosophy*. Albany, NY: State University of New York Press.

Capps, Walter H. (1995) *Religious Studies: The Making of a Discipline*. Minneapolis, MN: Fortress Press.

Chapple, Christopher Key and Tucker, Mary Evelyn (2000) (eds.) *Hinduism and Ecology: The Intersection of Earth, Sky and Water*. Cambridge, MA: Harvard University Press.

Chidster, David (1988) *Patterns of Power: Religion and Politics in American Culture*. Englewood Cliffs, NJ: Prentice Hall.

Clark, Elizabeth A. (1986) *Ascetic Piety and Women's Faith: Essays on Late Ancient Christianity*. New York: Oxford University Press.

Coburn, Thomas B. (1984) "'Scripture' in India: Towards a Typology of the Word in Hindu Life." *Journal of the American Academy of Religion* 52: 435–459.

Cohn, Norman (1993) *Cosmos, Chaos and the World to Come: The Ancient Roots of Apocalyptic Faith*. New Haven, CT: Yale University Press.

Collins, Mary, Power, David, and Burnim, Mellonee V. (1989) (eds.) *Music and the Experience of God*. Edinburgh: T & T Clark.

Colson, Elizabeth (1962) *The Plateau Tonga of Northern Rhodesia, Social and Religious Studies*. Manchester: Manchester University Press.

Combs-Schilling, M. E. (1989) *Sacred Performances: Islam, Sexuality and Sacrifice*. New York: Columbia University Press.

Coomaraswamy, Ananda K. (1941) "Līlā." *Journal of the American Oriental Society* 61: 98–101.

268

Cort, John E. (1996) "Art, Religion, and Material Culture: Some Reflections on Method." *Journal of the American Academy of Religion* 64/3: 613–632.

Cort, John E. (2001) *Jains in the World: Religious Values and Ideology in India*. New York: Oxford University Press.

Couliano, Ioan Petru (1984) *Expériences de l'extase*. Paris: Payot.

Cox, Harvey G. (1969) *The Feast of Fools: A Theological Essay on Festivity and Fantasy*. Cambridge, MA: Harvard University Press.

Cragg, Kenneth and Speight, Marston (1980) *Islam from Within: Anthology of a Religion*. Belmont, CA: Wadsworth.

Crimmins, James (1989) (ed.) *Religion, Secularization and Political Thought: Thomas Hobbes to J. S. Mill*. London: Routledge.

Cunningham, Adrian (1990) "Religious Studies in the Universities: England." In *Turning Points in Religious Studies: Essays in Honour of Geoffrey Parrinder*. Edited by Ursula King. Edinburgh: T & T Clark, pp. 21–45.

Cunningham, Laurence (1980) *The Meaning of Saints*. San Francisco, CA: Harper & Row.

Davidson, Donald (1980) (ed.) *Essays on Action and Events*. Oxford: Oxford University Press.

Davis, Joyce M. (2003) *Martyrs: Innocence, Vengeance, and Despair in the Middle East*. New York: Palgrave.

Davis, Richard H. (1991) *Ritual in an Oscillating Universe: Worshiping Śiva in Medieval India*. Princeton, NJ: Princeton University Press.

Davis, Richard (1997) *Lives of Indian Images*. Princeton, NJ: Princeton University Press.

Dean, James and Waterman, A. M. (1999) *Religion and Economics: Normative Social Theory*. Boston, MA: Beacon.

De Groot, J. J. M. (1969) *The Religious System of China*. 6 Vols. Taipei: Ch'eng-wen Publishing Company.

Deleuze, Gilles and Guattari, Félix (1983) *Anti-Oedipus: Capitalism and Schizophrenia*. Trans. by Robert Hurley *et al*. Minneapolis, MN: University of Minnesota Press.

Deleuze, Gilles and Guattari, Félix (1988) *A Thousand Plateaus: Capitalism and Schizophrenia*. Trans. by Brian Massumi. Minneapolis, MN: University of Minnesota Press.

Delphy, Christine (1993) "Rethinking Sex and Gender." In *Sex in Question: French Materialist's Feminism*. Edited by Diana Leonard and Lisa Adkins. London: Taylor & Francis, pp. 30–41.

Denny, Frederick M. (1985) *An Introduction to Islam*. New York: Macmillan.

Denny, Frederick M. (1988) "Prophet and Walī: Sainthood in Islam." In *Sainthood: Its Manifestations in World Religions*. Edited by Richard

Kieckhefer and George D. Bond. Berkeley, CA: University of California Press, pp. 69–97.

Denny, Frederick M. and Taylor, Rodney L. (1985) (eds.) *The Holy Book in Comparative Perspective*. Columbia, SC: University of South Carolina Press.

Derrida, Jacques (1976) *Of Grammatology*. Trans. by Gayatri Chakravarty Spivak. Baltimore, MD: Johns Hopkins University Press.

Derrida, Jacques (1978) *Writing and Difference*. Trans. by Alan Bass. Chicago, IL: University of Chicago Press.

Derrida, Jacques (1992) *The Gift of Death*. Trans. by David Wills. Chicago, IL: University of Chicago Press.

Derrida, Jacques (1998) "Faith and Knowledge: The Two Sources of 'Religion' at the Limits of Reason Alone." In *Religion*. Edited by Jaques Derrida and Gianni Vattimo. Stanford, CA: Stanford University Press, pp. 1–78.

Detienne, Marcel (1989) *Dionysus at Large*. Trans. by Arthur Goldhammer. Cambridge, MA: Harvard University Press.

Detienne, Marcel and Vernant, Jean-Pierre (1989) (eds.) *The Cuisine of Sacrifice among the Greeks*. Trans. by Paula Wissing. Chicago, IL: University of Chicago Press.

Dewey, Joana (1994) "Orality and Textuality in Early Christian Literature." *Semeia* 65:1–216.

Dobbelaere, Karel (1999) "Towards an Integrated Perspective of the Processes Related to the Descriptive Content of Secularization." *Sociology of Religion* 60: 229–247.

Dōgen (2007) *Shōbōgenzō: The True Dharma-Eye Treasury*. 4 Vols. Trans. by Gudo Wafu Nishijima and Chodo Cross. Berkeley, CA: Numata Center.

Doniger, Wendy (1998) *The Implied Spider: Politics and Theology in Myth*. New York: Columbia University Press.

Doty, William C. (1986) *Mythography: The Study of Myths and Rituals*. Tuscaloosa, AL: University of Alabama Press.

Douglas, Mary (1966) *Purity and Danger: An Analysis of Concepts of Pollution and Taboo*. New York: Praeger.

Droogers, André (2006) "The Third Bank of the River: Play, Methodological Ludism, and the Definition of Religion." In *Playful Religion: Challenges for the Study of Religion*. Edited by Anton von Harskamp *et al.* Delft: Eburon, pp. 75–96.

Dubuisson, Daniel (2003) *The Western Construction of Religion, Myths, Knowledge, and Ideology*. Baltimore, MD: Johns Hopkins University Press.

Durkheim, Emile (1915) *Elementary Forms of the Religious Life*. Trans. by Joseph Ward Swain. London: George Allen & Unwin.

Dutt, Sukumar (1962) *Buddhist Monks and Monasteries of India*. London: George Allen & Unwin.

Dynes, Wayne R. and Donaldson, Stephen (1992) (eds.) *Homosexuality and Religion and Philosophy*. New York: Garland.

Eck, Diana L. (1981) *Darśan: Seeing the Divine Image in India*. Chambersburg, PA: Anima Books.

Eck, Diana L. (1983) "India's Tīrtha's 'Crossings' in Sacred Geography." *History of Religions* 20: 323–344.

Eichrodt, Walther (1961) *Theology of the Old Testament*. 2 Vols. Trans. by J. A. Baker. Philadelphia, PA: Westminster Press.

Eickelman, Dale F. (1976) *Moroccan Islam: Tradition and Society in a Pilgrimage Center*. Austin, TX: University of Texas Press.

Eliade, Mircea (1954) *The Myth of the Eternal Return*. Trans. by Willard R. Trask. New York: Pantheon Books.

Eliade, Mircea (1958) *Rites and Symbols of Initiation*. New York: Harper & Row.

Eliade, Mircea (1959) *The Sacred and the Profane*. Trans. by Willard R. Trask. New York: Harcourt Brace.

Eliade, Mircea (1963) *Myth and Reality*. Trans. by Willard R. Trask. New York: Harper & Row.

Eliade, Mircea (1964) *Shamanism: Archaic Techniques of Ecstasy*. Trans. by Willard R. Trask. New York: Pantheon Books.

Eliade, Mircea (1965) *Mephistopheles and the Androgyne: Studies in Religious Myth and Symbol*. Trans. by J. M. Cohen. New York: Sheed & Ward.

Eliade, Mircea (1969) *Yoga: Immortality and Freedom*. Trans. by Willard R. Trask. Second Edition. Princeton, NJ: Princeton University Press.

Ellul, Jacques (1970) *Violence: Reflections from a Christian Perspective*. London: SCM Press.

Evans-Pritchard, E. E. (1956) *Nuer Religion*. Oxford: Oxford University Press.

Evans-Pritchard, E. E. (1965) *Theories of Primitive Religion*. Oxford: Oxford University Press.

Falk, Nancy Auer and Gross, Rita M. (1980) (eds.) *Unspoken Worlds: Women's Religious Lives*. Belmont, CA: Wadsworth.

Faure, Bernard (1998) *The Red Thread: Buddhist Approaches to Sexuality*. Princeton, NJ: Princeton University Press.

Faure, Bernard (2003a) *The Power of Denial: Buddhism, Purity and Gender*. Princeton, NJ: Princeton University Press.

Faure, Bernard (2003b) (ed.) *Chan Buddhism in Ritual Context*. London: Routledge.

271

Fenton, John Y. (1970) "Reductionism in the Study of Religions." *Soundings* LIII/1: 61–76.

Feuerbach, Ludwig (1967) *Lectures on the Essence of Religion*. New York: Harper & Row.

Fischer, Kaus (1979) *Erotik und Askese in Kult und Kunst der Inder*. Cologne: Dumont.

Fort, Andrew O. and Mumme, Patricia (1996) (eds.) *Living Liberation in Hindu Thought*. Albany, NY: State University of New York Press.

Foucault, Michel (1978) *The History of Sexuality, Vol. 1: An Introduction*. Trans. by Robert Hurley. New York: Vintage/Random House.

Foucault, Michel (1994) *Essential Works of Foucault 1954–1984*. 3 Vols. Edited by Paul Rabinow. New York: The New Press.

Frazer, James G. (1910) *Totemism and Exogamy*. 4 Vols. London: Macmillan.

Frazer, James G. (1994) *The Golden Bough: A Study of Magic and Religion*. Oxford: Oxford University Press.

Freedberg, David (1991) *The Power of Images: Studies in the History and Theory of Response*. Chicago, IL: University of Chicago Press.

Frend, W. H. C. (1965) *Martyrdom and Persecution in the Early Church*. Oxford: Oxford University Press.

Freud, Sigmund (1919) *Toten and Taboo*. Trans. by A. A. Brill. London: Routledge.

Freud, Sigmund (1975) *The Future of an Illusion*. Trans. by James Strachery. New York: Norton.

Fuller, C. J. (1992) *The Camphor Flame: Popular Hinduism and Society in India*. Princeton, NJ: Princeton University Press.

Gadamer, Hans-Georg (1975) *Truth and Method*. New York: Seabury Press.

Gandhi, Mahatma (1986) *The Moral and Political Writings of Gandhi*. 3 Vols. Edited by Raghavan Iyer. Oxford: Clarendon Press.

Geertz, Clifford (1973) *The Interpretations of Cultures*. New York: Basic Books.

Gelpi, Donald L. (1998) *The Conversion Experience*. New York: Paulist Press.

Giddens, Anthony (1990) *The Consequences of Modernity, Self and Society in the Late Modern Age*. Stanford, CA: Stanford University Press.

Gill, Sam (1981) *Sacred Words: A Study of Navajo Religion and Prayer*. Westport, CT: Greenwood Press.

Gill, Sam (1982) *Native American Religions: An Introduction*. Belmont, CA: Wadsworth.

Gill, Sam (1994) "The Academic Study of Religion." *Journal of the American Academy of Religion* LXII/4: 865–975.

Girard, Rene (1989) *Violence and the Sacred.* Trans. by Patrick Gregory. Baltimore, MD: Johns Hopkins University Press.

Girardot, N. J., Miller, James, and Xiaogan, Liu (2001) (eds.) *Daoism and Ecology: Ways within a Cosmic Landscape.* Cambridge, MA: Harvard University Press.

Glucklich, Ariel (1997) *The End of Magic.* New York: Oxford University Press.

Glucklich, Ariel (2001) *Sacred Pain: Hurting the Body for the Sake of the Soul.* Oxford: Oxford University Press.

Gluckman, Max (1965) *Politics, Law, and Ritual in Tribal Society.* Chicago, IL: Aldine.

Godelier, Maurice (1999) *The Enigma of the Gift.* Chicago, IL: University of Chicago Press.

Gold, Ann Grodzins (1988) *Fruitful Journeys: The Ways of Rajasthani Pilgrims.* Berkeley, CA: University of California Press.

Gonda, Jan (1969) *Eye and Gaze in the Veda.* Amsterdam: North Holland.

Goodman, Felicitas (1988) *Ecstasy, Ritual, and Alternate Reality.* Bloomington, IN: University of Indiana Press.

Gosvāmin, Rūpa (2003) *The Bhaktirasāmṛtasindhu of Rūpa Gosvāmin.* Trans. by David Haberman. New Delhi: Indira Gandhi National Centre for the Arts and Motilal Banarsidass.

Gottlieb, Roger S. (1996) (ed.) *The Sacred Earth: Religion, Nature, Environment.* New York: Routledge.

Graber, David (2001) *Toward an Anthropology of Value: The False Coin of our own Dreams.* New York: Palgrave.

Grant, Robert (2004) *Augustus to Constantine.* Louisville, KY: Westminster John Knox.

Gregory, Brad S. (1999) *Salvation at Stake: Christian Martyrdom in Early Modern Europe.* Cambridge, MA: Harvard University Press.

Griaule, Marcel ((1965) *Conversations with Ogotemmêli: An Introduction to Dogon Religious Ideas.* London: Oxford University Press.

Griffths, John Gwyn (1991) *The Divine Verdict: A Study of Divine Judgment in the Ancient Religions.* Leiden: E. J. Brill.

Grimes, Ronald L. (1990) *Ritual Criticism: Case Studies in Its Practice, Essays on Its Theory.* Columbia, SC: University of South Carolina Press.

Gulik, R. H. van (1961) *Sexual Life in Ancient China.* Leiden: E. J. Brill.

Hallowell, A. Irving (1975) "Ojibwa Ontology, Behavior, and World-View." In *Teachings from the American Earth: Indian Experience and*

Philosophy. Edited by Dennis Tedlock and Barbara Tedlock. New York: Liveright, pp. 141–178.

Handelman, Don (1981) "The Ritual Clown: Attributes and Affinities." *Anthropos* 76: 321–370.

Handelman, Don and Shulman, David (1997) *God Inside Out: Śiva's Game of Dice*. New York: Oxford University Press.

Hanna, Judith Lynne (1987) *To Dance Is Human: A Theory of Nonverbal Communication*. Chicago, IL: University of Chicago Press.

Harper, Edward B. (1964) "Ritual Pollution as an Integrator of Caste and Religion." In *Religion in South Asia*. Edited by Edward W. Harper. Seattle, WA: University of Washington Press, pp. 151–196.

Harpham, Geoffrey Galt (1987) *The Ascetic Imperative in Culture and Criticism*. Chicago, IL: University of Chicago Press.

Harrod, Howard L. (1987) *Renewing the World: Plains Indian Religion and Morality*. Tucson, AZ: University of Arizona Press.

Harvey, Graham (2006) *Animism: Respecting the Living World*. New York: Columbia University Press.

Harvey, Peter (2000) *An Introduction to Buddhist Ethics: Foundations, Values and Issues*. Cambridge: Cambridge University Press.

Hawley, John Stratton (1981) *At Play with Krishna: Pilgrimage Dramas from Brindavan*. Princeton, NJ: Princeton University Press.

Heffernan, Thomas J. (1988) *Sacred Biography: Saints and their Biographers in the Middle Ages*. New York: Oxford University Press.

Heidegger, Martin (1962) *Being and Time*. Trans. by John Macquarrie and Edward Robinson. New York: Harper & Row.

Hein, Norvin (1972) *The Miracle Plays of Mathurā*. New Haven, CT: Yale University Press.

Heusch, Luc de (1985) *Sacrifice in Africa: A Structuralist Approach*. Bloomington, IN: Indiana University Press.

Hick, John (1973) *God and the Universe of Faiths*. London: Fount.

Hick, John (1989) *An Interpretation of Religion: Human Responses to the Transcendent*. New Haven, CT: Yale University Press.

Hill, Christopher S. (2002) *Thought and World: An Austere Portrayal of Truth, Reference, and Semantic Correspondence*. New York: Cambridge University Press.

Himmelfarb, Martha (1993) *Ascent to Heaven in Jewish and Christian Apocalypses*. New York: Oxford University Press.

Hollywood, Amy (2002) *Sensible Ecstasy: Mysticism, Sexual Difference, and the Demands of History*. Chicago, IL: University of Chicago Press.

Holm, Jean and Bowker, John (1994) (eds.) *Women in Religion*. London: Printer.

Holmes, Nils G. (1982) (ed.) *Religious Ecstasy*. Stockholm: Almqvist & Wiksell International.

Hubert, Henri and Mauss, Marcel (1964) *Sacrifice: Its Nature and Function*. Trans. by W. II. Halls. Chicago, IL: University of Chicago Press.

Huizinga, Johan (1955) Homo Ludens: *A Study of the Play-Element in Culture*. Boston, MA: Beacon Press.

Hultkrantz, Åke (1981) *Belief and Worship in Native North America*. Edited by Christopher Vecsey. Syracuse, NY: Syracuse University Press.

Hultkrantz, Åke (1983) "The Religion of the Goddess in North America." In *The Book of the Goddess Past and Present: An Introduction to Her Religion*. Edited by Carl Olson. New York: Crossroad, pp. 202–230.

Hultkrantz, Åke (1992) *Shamanic Healing and Ritual Drama: Health and Medicine in Native North American Religious Traditions*. New York: Crossroad.

Hultkrantz, Åke (1997) *Soul and Native Americans*. Woodstock, CT: Spring.

Humphrey, Caroline and Laidlaw, James (1994) *The Archetypal Actions of Ritual: A Theory of Ritual Illustrated by Jain Rite of Worship*. Oxford: Oxford University Press.

Humphrey, Caroline and Piers Vitebsky (1997) *Sacred Architecture*. London: Duncan Baird.

Husserl, Edmund (1958) *Ideas: General Introduction to Pure Phenomenology*. Trans. by W. R. Boyce. London: George Allen & Unwin.

Hyers, M. Conrad (1969) "The Comic Profanation of the Sacred." In *Holy Laughter: Essays on Religions in the Comic Perspective*. Edited by M. Conrad Hyers. New York: Seabury Press, pp. 9–27.

Hyers, M. Conrad (1981) *The Comic Vision and the Christian Faith: A Celebration of Life and Laughter*. New York: Pilgrim Press.

Hynes J., William and Doty, William G. (1993) *Mythical Trickster Figures: Contours, Contexts, and Criticisms*. Tuscaloosa, AL: University of Alabama Press.

Izutsu, Toshihiko (1966) *Ethico-religious Concepts in the Qur'an*. Montreal: McGill University Press.

James, William (1902) *The Varieties of Religious Experience*. 2nd Edition. New York: Longman, Green.

Johnston, Sarah Iles (2004a) "Magic." In *Religions of the Ancient World: A Guide*. Edited by Sarah Iles Johnston. Cambridge, MA: Harvard University Press, pp. 139–152.

Johnston, Sarah Iles (2004b) "Mysteries." In *Religions of the Ancient World: A Guide*. Edited by Sarah Iles Johnston. Cambridge, MA: Harvard University Press.

Jordan, David K. (1969) *Gods, Ghosts, and Ancestors: The Folk Religion of a Taiwanese Village*. Chicago, IL: University of Chicago Press.

Jung, Carl G. (1969) *Psychology and Religion: East and West*. 2nd Edition. Princeton, NJ: Princeton University Press.

Kakar, Sudhir (1982) *Shamans, Mystics and Doctors: A Psychological Inquiry into India and Its Healing Traditions*. New York: Alfred A. Knopf.

Katz, Steven T. (1983) *Mysticism and Religious Traditions*. New York: Oxford University Press.

Khare, R. S. (1992a) "Annambrahman: Cultural Models, Meanings, and Aesthetics of Hindu Food." In *The Eternal Flood: Gastronomic Ideas and Experiences of Hindus_and Buddhists*. Edited by R. S. Khare. Albany, NY: State University of New York Press, pp. 201–220.

Khare R. S. (1992b) "Food with Saints: An Aspect of Hindu Gastrosemantics." In *The Eternal Flood: Gastronomic Ideas and Experiences of Hindus and Buddhists*. Edited by R. S. Khare. Albany, NY: State University of New York Press, pp. 27–52.

Kierkegaard, Søren (1954) *Fear and Trembling*. Trans. by Walter Lowrie. Garden City, NY: Doubleday.

Kierkegaard, Søren (1980) *The Concept of Anxiety: A Simple Psychologically Orienting Deliberation on the Dogmatic Issue of Hereditary Sin*. Edited and trans. by Reidar Thomte. Princeton, NJ: Princeton University Press.

King, Peter (1999) *Western Monasticism: A History of the Monastic Movement in the Latin Church*. Kalamazoo, MI: Cistercian.

King, Richard (1999) *Orientalism and Religion: Postcolonial Theory, India and "The Mystic East"*. London: Routledge.

King, Ursula (1987) (ed.) *Women in the World's Religions, Past and Present*. New York: Paragon House.

King, Ursula (1995) (ed.) *Religion and Gender*. Oxford: Blackwell.

Kinsley, David (1974) "'Through the Looking Glass': Divine Madness in the Hindu Religious Tradition." *History of Religions* 13/3: 271–286.

Kinsley, David (1975) *The Sword and the Flute: Kālī and Krsna, Dark Visions of the_Terrible and the Sublime in Hindu Mythology*. Berkeley, CA: University of California Press.

Kinsley, David (1995) *Ecology and Religion: Ecological Spirituality in Cross-Cultural Perspective*. Englewood Cliffs, NJ: Prentice Hall.

Kinsley, David (1996) *Health, Healing, and Religion: A Cross-cultural Perspective*. Upper Saddle River, NJ: Prentice Hall.

Knipe, David (1975) *In the Image of Fire: Vedic Experiences of Heat*. Delhi: Motilal Banarsidass.

Kramrisch, Stella (1946) *The Hindu Temple*. 2 Vols. Calcutta: Motilal Banarsidass.

Kripal, Jeffrey John (2001) *Roads of Excess, Palaces of Wisdom: Eroticism and Reflexivity in the Study of Mysticism*. Chicago, IL: University of Chicago Press.

Küng, Hans (1976) *On Being a Christian*. Trans. by Edward Quinn. Garden City, NY: Doubleday.

La Barre, Weston (1970) *The Ghost Dance: Origins of Religion*. London: George Allen & Unwin.

Lakoff, George and Kovecses, Zoltan (1983) *The Cognitive Model of Anger Inherent in American English*. Berkeley, CA: University of California Press.

Lakoff, George and Johnson, Mark (1999*) Philosophy in the Flesh: The Embodied Mind and Its Challenge to Western Thought*. New York: Basic Books.

Lamb, Ramdas (2002) *Rapt in the Name: The Ramnamis and Untouchable Religion in Central India*. Albany, NY: State University of New York Press.

Lang, Bernhard (1997) *Sacred Games: A History of Christian Worship*. New Haven, CT: Yale University Press.

Lao Tzu (1963) *The Way of Lao Tzu (Tao-te-ching)*. Trans. by Wing-tsit Chan. Indianapolis, IN: Bobbs-Merrill.

Laurence, Clifford H. (2001) *Medieval Monasticism: Forms of Religious Life in Western Europe in the Middle Ages*. London: Longman.

Leff, Gordon (1967) *Heresy in the Later Middle Ages*. Manchester: Manchester University Press.

Le Goff, Jacques (1984) *The Birth of Purgatory*. Trans. by Arthur Goldhammer. Chicago, IL: University of Chicago Press.

Leidy, Denise Patry (2008) *The Art of Buddhism: An Introduction to Its History and Meanings*. Boston. MA: Shambhala.

Leopold, Sabourin (1973) *Priesthood: A Comparative Study*. Leiden: E. J. Brill.

Levering, Meriam (1989) (ed.) *Rethinking Scripture*. Albany, NY: State University of New York Press.

Levinas, Emmanuel (1998) *Entre Nous: On Thinking-of-the-Other*. Trans. by Michael B. Smith and Barbara Harshau. New York: Columbia University Press.

Levine, Michael P. (1994) *Pantheism: A Non-theistic Concept of Deity*. New York: Routledge.

Levison, John R. (1997) *The Spirit in First Century Judaism*. Leiden: E. J. Brill.

Lévi-Strauss, Claude (1962) *The Savage Mind*. Chicago, IL: University of Chicago Press.

Lévi-Strauss, Claude (1963) *Structural Anthropology.* Trans. by Claire Jacobson and Brooke Grundfest Schoepf. New York: Basic Books.

Lévi-Strauss, Claude (1970) *The Raw and the Cooked: Introduction to a Science of Mythology: 1.* Trans. by John and Doreen Weightman. London: Jonathan Cape.

Lévi-Strauss, Claude (1973) *From Honey to Ashes: Introduction to a Science of Mythology: 2.* Trans. by John and Doreen Weightman. London: Jonathan Cape.

Lévy-Bruhl, Lucien (1985) *How Natives Think.* Trans. by Lillian A. Clare. New York: Alfred A. Knopf.

Lewis, I. M. (1971) *Ecstatic Religion: An Anthropological Study of Spirit Possession and Shamanism.* Middlesex, UK: Penguin Books.

Lincoln, Bruce (1991) *Death, War, and Sacrifice: Studies in Ideology and Practice.* Chicago, IL: University of Chicago Press.

Lincoln, Bruce (2003) *Holy Terror: Thinking about Religion after September 11.* Chicago, IL: University of Chicago Press.

Ling, T. O. (1962) *Buddhism and the Mythology of Evil.* London: Allen & Unwin.

Long, Charles H. (1963) *Alpha: The Myths of Creation.* New York: George Braziller.

Lord, Albert Bates (1991) *Epic Singers and Oral Traditions.* Ithaca, NY: Cornell University Press.

Loy, David (1988) *Nonduality: A Study in Comparative Philosophy.* New Haven, CT: Yale University Press.

Luch, Georg (1985) Arcana Mundi: *Magic and the Occult in the Greek and Roman Worlds.* Baltimore, MD: Johns Hopkins University Press.

Lynch, Michael P. (2001) (ed.) *The Nature of Truth: Classical and Contemporary Perspectives.* Cambridge, MA: Harvard University Press.

Lynch, Owen M. (1990) "The Social Construction of Emotions in India." In *Divine Passions: The Social Construction of Emotion in India.* Edited by Owen M. Lynch. Berkeley, CA: University of California Press, pp. 3–34.

Lyotard, Jean-François (1985) *The Postmodern Condition: A Report on Knowledge.* Trans. by Geoff Bennington and Brian Massumi. *Theory and History of Literature Vol. 20.* Minneapolis, MN: University of Minnesota Press.

MacAloon, John (1984) (ed.) *Rite, Festival, Spectacle.* Philadelphia: Institute for the Study of Human Issues.

McCauley, Robert (2000) "The Naturalness of Religion and the Unnaturalness of Science." In *Explanation and Cognition.* Edited by Frank Keil and Robert Wilson. Cambridge, MA: MIT University Press, pp. 61–86.

MacCormack, Carol P. and Strathern, Marilyn (1980) (eds.) *Nature, Culture and Gender*. Cambridge: University of Cambridge Press.

McCutcheon, Russell T. (1997) *Manufacturing Religion: The Discourse on Sui Generis Religion and the Politics of Nostalgia*. New York: Oxford University Press.

McDannell, Colleen (1995) *Material Christianity: Religion and Popular Culture in America*. New Haven, CT: Yale University Press.

McDannell, Collen and Lang, Bernhard (1988) *Heaven: A History*. New Haven, CT: Yale University Press.

McGarth, Alister E. (1994) *Christian Theology: An Introduction*. Oxford: Blackwell.

McGinn, Bernard (1979) *Visions of the End: Apocalyptic Traditions in the Middle Ages*. Ithaca, NY: Cornell University Press.

McGinn, Bernard (1993) *The Foundations of Mysticism: Origins to the Fifth Century*. New York: Crossroad.

McGinn, Bernard (1994) *Antichrist: Two Thousand Years of the Human Fascination with Evil*. San Francisco, CA: Harper San Francisco.

MacIntyre, Alasdair (1981) *After Virtue*. Notre Dame, IN: University of Notre Dame.

Mandel, Oscar (1970) "What so Funny: The Nature of the Comic." *The Antioch Review* 30: 73–89.

Marion, Jean-Luc (1991) *God without Being*. Trans. by Thomas Carlson. Chicago, IL: University of Chicago Press.

Markarius, Laura (1970) "Ritual Clowns and Symbolic Behaviour." *Diogenes* 69: 44–73.

Martin, Luther H. (1996) (ed.) "The New Comparativism in the Study of Religion: A Symposium." *Method and Theory in the Study of Religion* 8/1: 1–49.

Masuzawa, Tomoko (2005) *The Invention of World Religions Or, How European Universalism Was Presented in the Languages of Pluralism*. Chicago, IL: University of Chicago Press.

Mathews, Charles T. (2001) *Evil and the Augustinian Tradition*. New York: Cambridge University Press.

Mauss, Marcel (1990) *The Gift: The Form and Reason for Exchange in Archaic Societies*. New York: W. W. Norton.

Mendenhall, George (1953) *Law and Covenant in Isreal and the Ancient Near East*. Philadelphia, PA: Westminster John Knox Press.

Merleau-Ponty, Maurice (1962) *Phenomenology of Perception*. Trans. by Colin Smith. London: Routledge and Kegan Paul.

Mernissi, Fatima (1991) *Women and Islam: An Historical and Theological Enquiry*. Trans. by Mary Jo Lakeland. Oxford: Oxford University Press.

Michaels, Axel (2004) *Hinduism: Past and Present*. Princeton, NJ: Princeton University Press.

Miller, Barbara Stoler (1977) (trans.) *Love Song of the Dark Lord: Jayadeva's Gitagovinda*. New York: Columbia University Press.

Mithen, Steven (1996) *The Prehistory of the Mind: The Cognitive Origins of Art, Religion, and Science*. London: Thames & Hudson.

Morgan, David. (2005) *The Sacred Gaze: Religious Visual Culture in Theory and Practice*. Berkeley, CA: University of California Press.

Morinis, S. E. Alan (1984) *Pilgrimage in the Hindu Tradition: A Case Study of West Bengal*. Delhi: Oxford University Press.

Morreal, John (1983) *Taking Laughter Seriously*. Albany, NY: State University of New York Press.

Morrow, Lance (2003) *Evil: An Investigation*. New York: Basic Books.

Müller, Max (1895–1898) *Chips from the German Workshop*. 2 Vols. New York: Scribner.

Murphy, Joseph M. (1983) "Oshun the Dancer." In *The Book of the Goddess Past and Present: An Introduction to Her Religion*. Edited by Carl Olson. New York: Crossroad, pp. 190–201.

Murphy, Tom (1997) *The Oldest Social Science: Configuration of Law and Modernity*. Oxford: Oxford University Press.

Needham, Joseph (1969) *Science and Civilization in China, Vol. 2: History of Scientific Thought*. Cambridge: Cambridge University Press.

Niditch, Susan (1996) *Oral World and Written Word*. Louisville, KY: Westminster John Knox Press.

Nygren, Anders (1953) *Agape and Eros*. Philadelphia, PA: Westminster Press.

Obayashi, Hiroshi (1992) (ed.) *Death and Afterlife: Perspectives of World Religions*.Westport, CT: Praeger.

O'Flaherty, Wendy Doniger (1976) *The Origin of Evil in Hindu Mythology*. Berkeley, CA: University of California Press.

O'Flaherty, Wendy Doniger (1980) (ed.) *Karma and Rebirth in Classical Indian Tradition*. Berkeley, CA: University of California Press.

Ogden, Daniel (2002) (ed.) *Magic, Witchcraft, and Ghosts in the Greek and Roman Worlds*. Oxford: Oxford University Press.

Olson, Carl (1983) (ed.) *The Book of the Goddess: An Introduction to Her Religion*. New York: Crossroad.

Olson, Carl (1990) *The Mysterious Play of Kālī: An Interpretive Study of Rāmakrishna*. Atlanta, GA: Scholars Press.

Olson, Carl (2000) *Zen and the Art of Postmodern Philosophy: Two Paths of Liberation from the Representational Mode of Thinking*. Albany, NY: State University of New York Press.

Olson, Carl (2003) *Theory and Method in the Study of Religion: A Selection of Critical Readings.* Belmont, CA: Wadsworth/Thomson.

Olson, Carl (2005) *The Different Paths of Buddhism: A Narrative-Historical Introduction.* New Brunswick, NJ: Rutgers University Press.

Olson, Carl (2007) *The Many Colors of Hinduism: A Thematic-Historical Introduction.* New Brunswick, NJ: Rutgers University Press.

Olson, Carl (2008) (ed.) *Celibacy and Religious Traditions.* New York: Oxford University Press.

Opler, Morris Edward (1965) *An Apache Way of Life.* New York: Cooper Square.

Ortiz, Alfonso (1969) *The Tewa World: Space, Time, Being, and Becoming in a Pueblo Society.* Chicago, IL: University of Chicago Press.

Osborne, Kenan B. (1988) *Priesthood: A History of the Ordained Ministry in the Roman Catholic Church.* New York: Paulist Press.

Osborne, Kenan B. (1990) *Reconciliation and Justification: The Sacrament and Its Theology.* New York: Paulist Press.

Östör, Ákos (1980) *The Play of the Gods.* Chicago, IL: University of Chicago Press.

Otto, Rudolf (1928) *The Idea of the Holy.* New York: Oxford University Press.

Outka, Gene H. (1972) *Agape: An Ethical Analysis.* New Haven, CT: Yale University Press.

Paden, William E. (1988) *Religious Worlds: The Comparative Study of Religion.* Boston, MA: Beacon Press.

Pandey, Raj Bali (1969) *Hindu Samskaras.* Delhi: Motilal Banarsidass.

Parry, Jonathan P. (1994) *Death in Benares.* Cambridge: Cambridge University Press.

Parsons, Elsie Clews and Beads, Ralph I. (1934) "The Sacred Clowns of the Pueblo and Mayo-Yaqui Indians." *American Anthropologist* 36/4: 491–514.

Parsons, Talcott (1967) *Sociological Theory and Modern Society.* New York: Free Press.

Patton, Kimberley C. and Ray, Benjamin C. (2000) (eds.) *A Magic Still Dwells: Comparative Religion in the Postmodern Age.* Berkeley, CA: University of California Press.

Pelikan, Jaroslav (1971) *The Christian Tradition: A History of the Development of Doctrine, 1: The Emergence of the Catholic Tradition (100–600).* Chicago, IL: University of Chicago Press.

Pelikan, Jaroslav (2003) *Credo: Historical and Theological Guide to Creeds and Confessions of Faith in the Christian Tradition.* New Haven, CT: Yale University Press.

Perrett, Roy W. (1987) (ed.) *Death and Immortality*. Dordrecht: Martinus Nijhoff.

Peters, F. E. (1994) *The Hajj: The Muslim Pilgrimage to Mecca and the Holy Places*. Princeton, NJ: Princeton University Press.

Peters, F. E. (2003) *The Monotheists: Jews, Christians, and Muslims in Conflict and Competition*. 2 Vols. Princeton, NJ: Princeton University Press.

Petruccioli, Attilio and Khalil Priani (2002) *Understanding Islamic Architecture*. London: Routledge.

Porterfield, Amanda (1998) *The Power of Religion: A Comparative Introduction*. New York: Oxford University Press.

Powers, William K. (1977) *Oglala Religion*. Lincoln, NE: University of Nebraska Press.

Powers, William K. (1982) *Yuwipi: Vision and Experience in Oglala Ritual*. Lincoln, NE: University of Nebraska Press.

Proudfoot, Wayne (1985) *Religious Experience*. New York: Oxford University Press.

Radin, P. (1956) *The Trickster: A Study in American Indian Mythology*. New York: Philosophical Library.

Rahman, Fazlur (1966) *Islam*. New York: Holt, Rinehardt and Winston.

Rāmānuja (1971) *Vedānta Sūtras with the Commentary of Rāmānuja*. Trans. by George Thibaut. Sacred Books of the East. Volume XLVIII. Delhi: Motilal Banarsidass.

Rambo, Lewis R. (1993) *Understanding Religious Conversion*. New Haven, CT: Yale University Press.

Rappaport, Roy A. (1999) *Ritual and Religion in the Making of Humanity*. Cambridge: Cambridge University Press.

Rattray, R. S. (1969) *Ashanti*. Oxford: Clarendon Press.

Rawls, John (1999) *The Law of Peoples*. Cambridge, MA: Harvard University Press.

Ray, Benjamin C. (1976) *African Religions: Symbol, Ritual, and Community*. Englewood Cliffs, NJ: Prentice Hall.

Reichard, Gladys A. (1950) *Navaho Religion: A Study of Symbolism*. Bollingen Series XVIII. Princeton, NJ: Princeton University Press.

Reynolds, Frank E. and Capps, Donald (1976) (eds.) *Biographical Process Studies in History and Psychology of Religion*. The Hague: Walter de Gruyter.

Reynolds, Frank E. and Waugh, Earle H. (1977) (eds.) *Religious Encounters with Death*: *Insights from the History and Anthropology of Religions*. University Park, PA: Penn State University Press.

Ricketts, Mac Linscott (1966) "The North American Trickster." *History of Religions* 5/4: 327–350.

Ricoeur, Paul (1967) *The Symbolism of Evil.* Trans. by Emerson Buchanan. New York: Harper & Row.

Ricoeur, Paul (1976) *Interpretation Theory: Discourse and the Surplus of Meaning.* Forth Worth, TX: Texas Christian University Press.

Ricoeur, Paul (1977) *The Rule of Metaphor.* Trans. by Robert Czerny. Toronto: University of Toronto Press.

Ricoeur, Paul (1984) *Time and Narrative.* 3 Vols. Trans. by Kathleen McLaughlin and David Pellauer. Chicago, IL: University of Chicago Press.

Ricoeur, Paul (2004) *Memory, History, Forgetting.* Trans. by Kathleen Blamey and David Pellauer. Chicago, IL: University of Chicago Press.

Riesebrodt, Martin (2004) "Uberlegungen zur Legitimität einer universalen Religionsbegriffs." In *Religion im kulturellen Diskurs: Festschrift für Hans G. Kippenberg zu seinem 65. Geburtstag.* Edited by Eugene Luchesi and Kocku von Stuckrad. Berlin: Walter de Gruyter.

Ringer, Fritz K. (1969) *The Decline of the German Mandarins: The German Academic Community 1890–1933.* Cambridge, MA: Harvard University Press.

Rosen, Lawrence (1989) *The Anthropology of Justice: Law as Culture in Islamic Society.* Cambridge: Cambridge University Press.

Roux, Jean-Paul (1988) *La sang: Mythes, Symboles et réalités.* Paris: Fayard.

Rumi, Jalal al-din (1968) *Mystical Poems of Rumi.* Trans. by A. J. Arberry. Chicago, IL: University of Chicago Press.

Russell, Jeffrey Burton (1977) *The Devil: Perception of Evil from Antiquity to Primitive Christianity.* Ithaca, NY: Cornell University Press.

Russell, Jeffrey Burton (1981) *Satan: The Early Christian Tradition.* Ithaca, NY: Cornell University Press.

Russell, Jeffrey Burton (1984) *Lucifer: The Devil in the Middle Ages.* Ithaca, NY: Cornell University Press.

Russell, Jeffrey Burton (1986) *Mephistopheles: The Devil in the Modern World.* Ithaca, NY: Cornell University Press.

Russell, Jeffrey Burton (1997) *A History of Heaven: The Singing Silence.* Princeton, NJ: Princeton University Press.

Saler, Benson (1993) *Conceptualizing Religion.* Leiden: E. J. Brill.

Sanford, James (1981) *Zen-Man Ikkyū. Studies in World Religions 2.* Chico, CA: Scholars Press.

Śankara (1968) *Vedānta Sūtras with the Commentary of Śankarācārya.* Trans. by George Thibaut. Sacred Books of the East Vols. XXIV, XXXVIII. Delhi: Motilal Banarsidass.

Saward, John (1980) *Perfect Fools: Folly for Christ's Sake in Catholic and Orthodox Spirituality*. Oxford: Oxford University Press.

Schimmel, Annemarie (1975) *Mystical Dimensions of Islam*. Chapel Hill NC: University of North Carolina Press.

Schimmel, Annemarie (1985) *And Muhammad Is His Messenger: The Veneration of the Prophet in Islamic Piety*. Chapel Hill, NC: University of North Carolina Press.

Schopen, Gregory (1997) *Bones, Stones, and Buddhist Monks: Collected Papers on the Archaeology, Epigraphy, and Texts of Monastic Buddhism in India*. Honolulu, HI: University of Hawaii Press.

Searle, John R. (1969) *Speech Acts: An Essay in the Philosophy of Language*. London: Cambridge University Press.

Segal, Robert A. (1983) "In Defense of Reductionism." *Journal of the American Academy of Religion* 51: 97–124.

Sharma, Arvind (1987) (ed.) *Women in World Religion*. Albany, NY: State University of New York Press.

Sharpe, Eric J. (1986) *Comparative Religion: A History*. 2nd Edition. La Salle, IL: Open Court.

Shelemay, Kay Kaufman (1986) *Music, Ritual, and Falasha History*. East Lansing, MI: Michigan State University Press.

Shilling, Chris (2005). *The Body and Social Theory*. 2nd Edition. London: Sage.

Shulman, David and Stroumsa, Guy G. (1999) (eds.) *Dream Cultures: Explorations in the Comparative History of Dreaming*. New York: Oxford University Press.

Shurden, Walter B. (1999) *Baptism and the Lord's Supper*. Macon, GA: Mercer University Press.

Siegel, Lee (1993) *Net of Magic: Wonder and Deceptions in India*. Chicago, IL: University of Chicago Press.

Slotkin, James Sydney (1975) *The Peyote Religion: A Study in Indian–White Relations*. New York: Octogon Books.

Smart, Ninian (1981) *The Religious Experience*. New York: Macmillan.

Smart, Ninian (1995) *Worldviews: Crosscultural Explorations of Human Beliefs*. 2nd Edition. Englewood Cliffs, NJ: Prentice Hall.

Smart, Ninian (1996) *Dimensions of the Sacred: An Anatomy of the World's Beliefs*. Berkeley, CA: University of California Press.

Smith, Christian (2003) (ed.) *The Secular Revelation: Power, Interests, and Conflicts in the Secularization of American Life*. Berkeley, CA: University of California Press.

Smith, Frederick M. (2006) *The Self Possessed: Deity and Spirit Possession in South Asian Literature and Civilization*. New York: Columbia University Press.

Smith, Jane Idelman and Haddad, Yvonne Yazbeck (2002) *The Islamic Understanding of Death and Resurrection*. Oxford: Oxford University Press.

Smith, Jonathan Z. (1978) *Map Is not Territory: Studies in the History of Religions*. Leiden: E. J. Brill.

Smith, Jonathan Z. (1982) *Imagining Religion: From Babylon to Jonestown*. Chicago, IL: University of Chicago Press.

Smith, Jonathan Z. (1987) *To Take Place: Toward Theory in Religion*. Chicago, IL: University of Chicago Press.

Smith, Jonathan Z. (1990) *Drudgery Divine: On the Comparison of Early Christianities and the Religions of Late Antiquity*. Chicago, IL: University of Chicago Press.

Smith, Jonathan Z. (1998) "Religion, Religions, Religious." In *Critical Terms for Religious Studies*. Edited by Mark C. Taylor. Chicago, IL: University of Chicago Press, pp. 261–284.

Smith, Jonathan Z. (2004) *Relating Religion: Essays in the Study of Religion*. Chicago, IL: University of Chicago Press.

Smith, Wilfred Cantwell (1963) *The Meaning and End of Religion*. New York: Macmillan.

Smith, Wilfred Cantwell (1979) *Faith and Belief*. Princeton, NJ: Princeton University Press.

Smith, Wilfred Cantwell (1981) *Toward a World Theology: Faith and the Comparative History of Religion*. Philadelphia, PA: Westminster Press.

Smith, Wilfred Cantwell (1993) *What Is Scripture? A Comparative Approach*. Minneapolis, MN: Fortress Press.

Spencer, Paul (1985) (ed.) *Society and the Dance*. Cambridge: Cambridge University Press.

Sperber, Dan (1996) *Explaining Culture: A Naturalistic Approach*. Oxford: Oxford University Press.

Srinavas, M. N. (1952) *Religion and Society among the Coorgs of South India*. Calcutta: Asia Publishing House.

Staal, Fritz (1989) *Rules without Meaning: Ritual, Mantras and the Human Sciences*. Bern: Peter Lang.

Stace, W. T. (1961) *Mysticism and Philosophy*. London: Macmillan.

Stark, Rodney and Bainbridge, Williams Sims (1985) *The Future of Religion: Secularization, Revival and Cult Formation*. Berkley, CA: University of California Press.

Storm, Perry (1987) *Functions of Dress: Tool of Culture and the Individual*. Englewood Cliffs, NJ: Prentice Hall.

Stringer, Martin D. (1999) "Rethinking Animism: Thoughts from the Infancy of our Discipline." *Journal of the Royal Anthropological Institute* 5/4: 541–556.

Strong, John S. (2004) *Relics of the Buddha*. Princeton, NJ: Princeton University Press.

Stutley, Margaret (1980) *Ancient India: Magic and Folklore – An Introduction*. Boulder, CO: Great Eastern.

Sullivan, Lawrence E. (1989) *Healing and Restoring: Health and Medicine in the World's Religious Traditions*. New York: Macmillan.

Sullivan, Lawrence E. (1997) "Enchanting Powers: An Introduction." In *Enchanting Powers: Music in the World's Religions*. Edited by Lawrence E. Sullivan. Cambridge, MA: Harvard University Press, pp. 1–14.

Suzuki, D. T. (1959) *Zen and Japanese Culture*. New York: Pantheon Books.

Swearer, Donald K. (2004) *Becoming the Buddha: The Ritual of Image Consecration in Thailand*. Princeton, NJ: Princeton University Press.

Tambiah, Stanley Jeyaraja (1970) *Buddhism and the Spirit Cults in North-East Thailand*. Cambridge: Cambridge University Press.

Tambiah, Stanley (1990) *Magic, Science, Religion, and the Scope of Rationality*. New York: Cambridge University Press.

Tarlo, Emma (1996) *Clothing Matters: Dress and Identity in India*. Chicago, IL: University of Chicago Press.

Taves, Ann (1999) *Fits, Trances & Visions: Experiencing Religion and Explaining Experience form Wesley to James*. Princeton, NJ: Princeton University Press.

Taves, Ann (2009) *Religious Experience Reconsidered: A Building-Block Approach to the Study of Religion and other Special Things*. Princeton, NJ: Princeton University Press.

Taylor, Charles (1985) *Philosophical Papers I: Human Agency and Language*. Cambridge: Cambridge University Press.

Taylor, Charles (2007) *A Secular Age*. Cambridge, MA: Harvard University Press.

Taylor, John H. (2001) *Death and Afterlife in Ancient Egypt*. Chicago, IL: University of Chicago Press.

Taylor, Mark C. (1984) *Erring: A Postmodern A/theology*. Chicago, IL: University of Chicago Press.

Taylor, Mark C. (2007) *After God*. Chicago, IL: University of Chicago Press.

Teiser, Stephen F. (1988) *The Ghost Festival in Medieval China*. Princeton, NJ: Princeton University Press.

Tiele, Cornelis P. (1897, 1899) *Elements of the Science of Religion*. 2 Vols. London: William Blackwood & Sons.

Titiev, Mischa (1972) *The Hopi Indians of Old Oraibi: Change and Continuity*. Ann Arbor, MI: University of Michigan Press.

Toomey, Paul M. (1992) "Krishna's Consuming Passions: Food as Metaphor and Metonym for Emotion as Mount Govardhan." In *The Social Construction of Emotion in India*. Edited by Owen M. Lynch. Berkeley, CA: University of California Press.

Troeltsch, Ernst (1931) *The Social Teachings of the Christian Church*. 2 Vols. London: George Allen & Unwin.

Turner, Victor (1967) *The Forest of Symbols: Aspects of Ndembu Ritual*. Ithaca, NY: Cornell University Press.

Turner, Victor (1968) *The Drums of Affliction: A Study of Religious Processes among the Ndembu of Zambia*. Oxford: Oxford University Press.

Turner, Victor (1969) *The Ritual Process: Structure and Anti-structure*. Chicago, IL: Aldine.

Turner, Victor (1975) *Revelation and Divination in Ndembu Ritual*. Ithaca, NY: Cornell University Press.

Turner, Victor and Turner, Edith (1978) *Image and Pilgrimage in Christian Culture: Anthropological Perspectives*. New York: Columbia University Press.

Tylor, E. B. (1871) *Primitive Culture: Researches into the Development of Mythology, Philosophy, Religion, Art, and Customs*. London: J. Murray.

Underhill, Evelyn (1911) *Mysticism: A Study of the Nature and Development of Man's Spiritual Consciousness*. London: Methuen.

Urban, Hugh B. (2006) *Magia Sexualis: Sex, Magic, and Liberation in Modern Western Esotericism*. Berkeley, CA: University of California Press.

Van der Leeuw, G. (1963) *Religion in Essence and Manifestation*. 2 Vols. New York: Harper & Row.

Van Gennep, Arnold (1960) *The Rites of Passage*. Trans. by Monika B. Vizedom and Gabrielle L. Caffee. Chicago, IL: University of Chicago Press.

Vecsey, Christopher (1983) *Traditional Ojibwa Religion and Its Historical Changes*. Philadelphia, PA: The American Philosophical Society.

Von Hendy, Andrew (2002) *The Modern Construction of Myth*. Bloomington, IN: Indiana University Press.

Von Rad, Gerhard (1965) *Old Testament Theology*. 2 Vols. New York: Harper & Row .

Wach, Joachim (1944) *Sociology of Religion*. Chicago, IL: University of Chicago Press.

Waghorne, Joanne Punzo (1984) *Gods of Flesh/Gods of Stone: The Embodiment of Divinity in India*. Chambersburg, PA: Anima.

Wagner, Peter (1994) *A Sociology of Modernity: Liberty and Discipline*. London: Routledge.

Wagner, Roy (1972) *Habu: The Innovation of Meaning in Daribi Religion*. Chicago, IL: University of Chicago Press.

Walls, Andrew F. (1990) "Religious Studies in the Universities: Scotland." In *Turning Points in Religious Studies: Essays in Honour of Geoffrey Parrinder*. Edited by Ursula King. Edinburgh: T & T Clark, pp. 32–45.

Wasserstrom, Steven M. (1999) *Religion after Religion: Gershom Scholem, Mircea Eliade, and Henry Corbin at Eranos*. Princeton, NJ: Princeton University Press.

Watson, Francis (2000) *Agape, Eros, Gender: Toward a Pauline Sexual Ethic*. Cambridge: Cambridge University Press.

Weber, Max (1930) *The Protestant Ethic and the Spirit of Capitalism*. New York: Scribner.

Weber, Max (1963) *The Sociology of Religion*. Boston, MA: Beacon Press.

Webster, Huttton (1942) *Taboo: A Sociological Study*. Stanford, CA: Stanford University Press.

Weinstein, Donald and Bell, Rudolf M. (1982) *Saints and Society: The Two Worlds of Western Christendom 1000–1700*. Chicago, IL: University of Chicago Press.

White, David Gordon (1996) *The Alchemical Body: Siddha Traditions in Medieval India*. Chicago, IL: University of Chicago Press.

White, David Gordon (2005) *The Kiss of the Yogini: "Tantric Sex" in Its South Asian Context*. Chicago, IL: University of Chicago Press.

White, Hayden (2010) *The Fiction of Narrative: Essays on History, Literature, and Theory, 1957–2007*. Baltimore, MD: Johns Hopkins University Press.

White, James F. (1999) *The Sacraments in Protestant Practice and Faith*. Nashville, TN: Abingdon Press.

Whitehouse, Harvey (2000) *Arguments and Icons: Divergent Modes of Religiosity*. Oxford: Oxford University Press.

Widengren, Geo (1969) *Religionsphänomenologie*. Berlin: Walter de Gruyter.

Williams, Cyril (1990) "Religious Studies in the Universities: Wales." In *Turning Points in Religious Studies: Essays in Honour of Geoffrey Parrinder*. Edited by Ursula King. Edinburgh: T & T Clark, pp. 46–56.

Williams, Raymond (1963) *Culture and Society*. New York: Columbia University Press.

Wilson, Bryan (1973) *Magic and Millennium: A Sociological Study of Religious Movements of Protest among Tribal and Third-World Peoples*. London: Heinemann.

Wilson, Bryan (1982) *Religion in Sociological Perspective*. New York: Oxford University Press.

Wilson, Monica (1970) *Rituals of Kinship among the Nyakyusa*. London: Oxford University Press.

Wimbush, Vincent I. and Valantasis, Richard (1995) (eds.) *Asceticism*. New York: Oxford University Press.

Winkelman, Michael (1992) *Shamans, Priests, and Witches: A Cross-cultural Study of Magico-religious Practitioners*. Tempe, AZ: Arizona State University.

Xu, Francis L. H. (1948) *Under the Ancestors Shadow: Chinese Culture and Personality*. London: Routledge & Kegan Paul.

Yinger, J. Milton (1970) *The Scientific Study of Religion*. New York: Macmillan.

Zaehner, R. C. (1957) *Mysticism: Sacred and Profane*. Oxford: Clarendon Press.

Zucker, Wolfgang (1967) "The Clown as the Lord of Disorder." *Theology Today* 24/3: 306–317.

INDEX

spirits 240–242; guardian 233,
  241–242
Śrī Vaiasnavism sect 102
Staal, Frits 208
stability: vow of 143
Stace, W. T. 153
Stahl, Georg 26
Sthavīras 166
structural method 159–160, 199
stūpas 29, 30, 204, 263
substantive definition of religion 12
suffering 169, 242–244
Sufi 43, 65, 136, 149
Sufism 189, 218
sun 244–245
Sun Dance 170, 215
sunna 126
Sūrya 244
Susano-o-no Mikoto 245
Sutta Pitaka 223
suzerainty covenant 59
Svātantrika 200
Swahili 65
sweat lodge 216
Swing festival 89
symbolism 27
symbols 62, 245–246
Symeon of Emesa 132
synagogues 29
Synoptic Gospels 221

taboo 50, 119, 191, 246
Tambiah, Stanley 172, 199, 209, 240
Tanakh 221
Tantric 27
Tartarus 118
Taylor, Charles 21, 22, 225
Taylor, Mark C. 10, 36, 250
ta'ziya 247
Temiar 65
temples 29–30
Tertullian 46
Tewa Pueblo 206, 238–239
theatrical performances 246–247
theism 247–248
theocracy 179–180

theology 13, 248–251; fields 249;
  and politics 80; schools of 250;
  types 249
theophany 89
Theravāda Buddhism 94–95, 120,
  201
Thomas Aquinas 102, 249
thunderbirds 241–242
Tiele, Cornelis Petrus 4, 54–55
Tillich, Paul 249
time 251–252; end of 27, 28; linear
  vs. cyclical 252
tīrtha-yatra 175
Tokerau 141
Tongu 24
Torah 111, 125, 204, 220
totemic spirits 242
totemism 5, 26, 252–253
totemistic spirits 242
transiency 152
transition: rites of 69, 205–206
trans-sexuality 231
Trappists 144
trickster 50–51
truth 226, 253
Tungas 183
Turner, Victor 128–129, 172, 173,
  178, 208, 240
'twice-born' 193
Tylor, Edward B. 2–3, 26, 54, 62,
  134, 158, 199, 207

Umar ibn al-Khattab 222
umma 52
unconcious: collective 194
Underhill, Evelyn 154
understanding 116, 198
universal church 47
universities 14–15
Untouchables 48–49, 182
Upagupta 219
Upanisads 222

Vaikuntha Ekādasī 89
Vaiśālī, Council of 166
Vaiśesika 199